Discover
Greece

Contents

Throughout this book, we use these icons to highlight special recommendations:

 The Best...
Lists for everything from bars to wildlife – to make sure you don't miss out

 Don't Miss
A must-see – don't go home until you've been there

 Local experts reveal their top picks and secret highlights

 Detour
Special places a little off the beaten track

 If you like...
Lesser-known alternatives to world-famous attractions

These icons help you quickly identify reviews in the text and on the map:

Sights

Eating

Drinking

Sleeping

Information

This edition written and researched by

Korina Miller
Kate Armstrong, Alexis Averbuck, Michael Stamatios Clark,
Chris Deliso, Des Hannigan, Victoria Kyriakopoulos,
Andrea Schulte-Peevers, Richard Waters

Contents

Contents

On the Road

In Focus

Survival Guide

This Is Greece

It's easy to understand how so many myths of gods and giants originated in this varied landscape. Wide-open skies; dramatic, plunging coastlines; and mysterious ancient ruins beckon with the promise of stories yet to be discovered. Walled medieval towns and hill-top villages transport you to long-ago eras, remote beaches tell epic tales of many-oared ships, and city life overflows with creativity as vibrant as Apollo's and a passion as pure as Aphrodite's.

Let the Greece you've been imagining fill your senses. Whether it's through the pulsing nightclubs of Mykonos or the solemnity of Meteora; the grandeur of Delphi or the earthiness of Metsovo; the rugged Cretan hillsides and the lush wildflowers of spring, it's not difficult to find the Greece you were hoping for.

Greece embraces the past passionately while simultaneously welcoming the future. You'll quickly become acquainted with the melancholic throb of *rembetika* (blues songs) and the ability of the ancient sights to unleash an imagination you might not have realised you had. You'll also encounter thought-provoking modern art and a vivacious contemporary music scene, stumbling across galleries, impressively modern museums, and live-music acts in the most unexpected places.

Stretch your legs and your love of the outdoors. Greece offers endless activities and is a magnet for anyone who enjoys the great outdoors. Wander along cobbled Byzantine footpaths, hike volcanoes, watch for dolphins and sea turtles, and cycle through lush forests. Greece also offers some of the world's top kitesurfing, diving and rock-climbing locations.

Greece is essentially a laid-back place. Lounge endlessly at cafes over coffee, stroll along the seafront, park yourself on a beach, take your time over meals and you'll fit right in. Greeks know how to enjoy life and are renowned as some of the most hospitable people on the globe. Their generosity and warmth is as genuine as the soft sand between your toes and the glow of the Aegean sun.

> "
> Wide-open skies; dramatic, plunging coastlines; and mysterious ancient ruins beckon…
> "

Hillside town of Oia (p227)

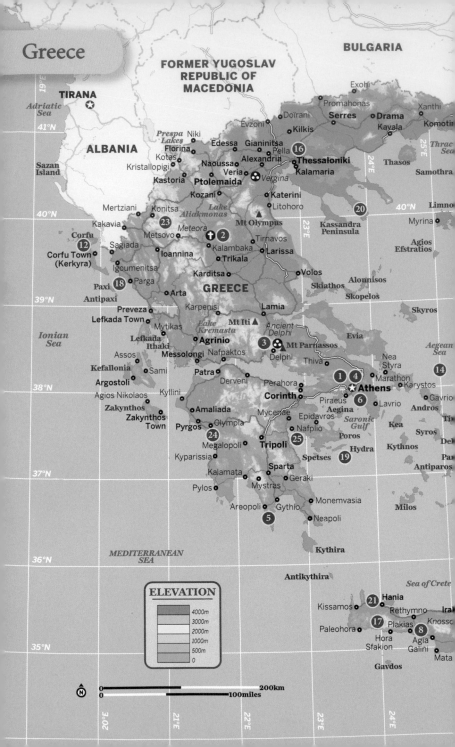

25

Top Experienc

25 Greece's Top Experiences

The Acropolis

There's a reason the Acropolis (p67) in Athens remains the quintessential landmark of Western civilisation – it is spectacular. Whether from an early morning stroll up its flanks or from a dinnertime terrace with the Parthenon all lit up and glorious, the Acropolis embodies harmony, power and beauty that speaks to all generations. Look beyond the Parthenon and you'll find more intimate spots like the exquisite, tiny Temple of Athena Nike (p70), newly restored and resplendent. The Acropolis Museum (p76) does the Acropolis' superb artefacts justice with its sleek facade and clean lines that showcase the ethereal grace of the statues and metopes

1

2

Meteora

You're not likely to forget the first moment the magnificent Meteora (p165) comes into view – soaring pillars of rock jut heavenward, and a handful of monasteries rest at the summit (some dating back to the 14th century). The rope ladders that once enabled the monks to reach the top have long been replaced by steps carved into the rock. Today, the spectacular stone towers beckon rock climbers from around the world.

Ancient Delphi

Arrive early to catch the magic of the sun's rays pouring over the Sanctuary of Athena Pronea (p161) at Delphi, the centre of the Ancient Greek world. Only three columns remain of the magnificent sanctuary, but that's enough to let your imagination soar. Nearby, the Sacred Way meanders past the Temple of Apollo (p160) where the Delphic oracle uttered prophecies that sent armies to battle and lovers to swoon. Sanctuary of Athena Pronea

The Best...
Outdoor Activities

CLIMBING MT OLYMPUS
Ascend to the realm of the gods. (p187)

KAYAKING ON KEFALLONIA
Explore the coastline of soaring cliffs, golden beaches and azure waters. (p139)

SAILING ACROSS SANTORINI'S CALDERA
Join a tour on an 18th-century schooner to cruise across the breathtaking caldera. (p224)

METSOVO SKI CENTRE
Zip downhill or cross-country across the stunning Pindos Mountains. (p189)

The Best...
Beaches

MYRTOS BEACH
Greece's most idyllic beach, nestled between limestone cliffs and unbelievably blue water. (p143)

PREVELI BEACH
Palm-fringed riverbanks, freshwater pools and a hilltop monastery. (p268)

KEFALOS BAY
A paradise of wide sandy beaches and warm turquoise water. (p316)

AGIA ANNA
A long stretch of glittering sand. (p220)

4 Odeon of Herodes Atticus

Few theatres in the world evoke the palpable sense of history and awe you'll feel sitting on the worn marble seats of this ancient amphitheatre (p72). With the floodlit Acropolis as a backdrop, you might be watching anything from the staging of an ancient drama to contemporary performances to the world's leading ballets. Originally built in AD 161, the theatre brings history alive like few other sites.

GEORGE TSAFOS/LONELY PLANET IMAGES ©

5 The Mani

Holding a magic unlike anywhere else in Greece, the footpaths and landscape of the Mani (p124) beckon hikers from around the world. With everything from rugged rocky highlands reminiscent of Scotland and hidden lush green oases, to small fishing tavernas and severe rock-solid tower houses, this pocket of the Peloponnese is well worth exploring. Vathia (p129)

IMAGE BROKER/LONELY PLANET IMAGES ©

Athens

Athens (p66) is a magnificent mash-up of the ancient and the contemporary. Beneath the facades of venerable landmarks, the city teems with life and creativity. Galleries and clubs hold exhibitions, performances and installations. Trendy restaurants and humble tavernas rustle up fine fare. Ubiquitous cafes fill with cool locals whose styles run from punk rock to haute couture. Discos and bars abound and swing deep into the night.

Santorini

There's more to Santorini (p222) than sunsets, but this remarkable island, shaped by the nuclear fire of prehistoric eruptions, has made the celebratory sunset its own. On summer evenings the clifftop towns of Fira (p223) and Oia (p227) are packed with visitors awed by the vast blood-red canvas of the western sky as the sun struts its stuff. You can catch the sunset without the crowds from almost anywhere along the cliff edge. And if you miss sundown, you can always face east at first light for some stunning sunrises too. Fira

Preveli Beach

Preveli Beach (p260) has one of Greece's most instantly recognisable stretches of sand. Bisected by a freshwater river and flanked by cliffs concealing sea caves, Preveli is lapped by the Libyan Sea, with clear pools of water along its palm-lined riverbank – perfect for cool dips. The beach lies under the sacred gaze of a magnificent monastery perched high above. Once the centre of anti-Ottoman resistance and later a shelter for Allied soldiers, this tranquil building offers magnificent views.

8

The Best...
Ancient Architecture

ACROPOLIS
Visually arresting monument of the ancient world. (p67)

METEORA
Mystical monasteries perched atop towering rock pinnacles. (p165)

ANCIENT DELPHI
The atmospheric centre of the Ancient Greek world. (p160)

MONEMVASIA
A magical medieval village resting like a giant sandcastle in the sea. (p121)

ANCIENT DELOS
Magnificent, sacred ruins set on a tiny island at the centre of the Cyclades. (p215)

Rhodes Old Town

Away from the crowds in Rhodes Old Town (p293), you'll find yourself meandering down twisting alleyways with archways above and squares opening up ahead. In these hidden corners your imagination will take off with flights of medieval fancy. Explore the ancient Knights Quarter, the old Jewish neighbourhood or the Turkish Quarter. Enjoy traditional live music in tavernas or dine on fresh seafood at outdoor restaurants. Wander along the top of the city's walls, with the sea on one side and a bird's-eye view into this living museum. Museum of Archaeology

The Best...
Cultural
Experiences

HELLENIC FESTIVAL
Greece's premier cultural festival featuring music, dance and theatre. (p91)

EASTER ON PATMOS
Celebrated with atmospheric services and grand revelry. (p314)

EPIDAVROS THEATRE
Catch a classical drama in this ancient site with near-perfect acoustics. (p119)

CAFE CHANTANT
Live, traditional folk music enjoyed until the morning hours. (p299)

10 Slowing Down

Visit some of Greece's quieter or slightly more remote shores, and island life will urge you to slow right down. Join locals as they contemplate life from coffee houses or unwind on sandy stretches of isolated beach. It's not the sights that draw you to these islands but the pace of life. Try Symi (p303), with its colourful harbour and relaxed cafes; visit tiny Paxi (p138) for its pristine beaches; or head to the lush island of Naxos (p215) for amazing food and enchanting villages. Time seems to stand still in these places – or at least moves very, very slowly. Paxi

Patmos

Visiting the atmospheric Monastery of St John the Theologian (p318) is an awe-inspiring experience. Protected by a giant heavy wall, the inside is filled with wafting incense, chanting priests and elaborate decor. Few sights capture the spirit of a place so well – on Patmos, artists and the spiritually inclined linger and a sense of peace flows free.

MARKA / ALAMY ©

Corfu Town

The story of Corfu Town (p131) is written across the handsome facades of its buildings. A stroll takes you from decaying Byzantine fortresses to neoclassical palaces, from Parisian-style arcades to Orthodox church towers, and across narrow, sun-dappled alleyways of the Venetian Old Town; all of it the legacy of the Mediterranean's tumultuous history.

Nisyros' Volcano

Descending into Nisyros' volcano (p309) feels like stepping onto the set of an old Star Trek episode. Picking your way through the scree towards the crater floor where the lava is bubbling away, is an other-worldly experience. And when you' done there, there are still fo other craters to sneak a pe at, as well as the lush slope of the caldera to explore.

Island Hopping

From islands filled with spirited nightlife to celebrity hideaways and tiny, far-flung specks with isolated sandy coasts, jumping from island to island is a Greek experience not to be missed. Peppered with ancient ruins, mystical castles, lush scenery and rare wildlife, the islands are spread like Greek jewels across the sea. Pinpoint the ones that take your fancy and join the dots by speeding over the Aegean on catamarans or swaying on old-fashioned ferry boats. You won't regret a single saltwater-splashed second of it.

Santorini (p222)

The Best...
Hiking Trails

THE MANI
Wild and rugged with steep tumbling mountains, tiny coves and Maniot villages. (p124)

MT OLYMPUS
Set out across the slopes of Greece's highest peak. (p187)

VIKOS-AOÖS NATIONAL PARK
Watch for wildlife while hiking with seminomadic shepherds. (p189)

SAMARIA GORGE
Cross wooden bridges and wade through rivers in Europe's longest gorge. (p268)

NAXOS
A lush and mountainous interior criss-crossed with ancient footpaths. (p215)

The Best...
Gastronomic Experiences

HYDRA'S SUNSET VIEWS
Local fish, marinated and served in front of stunning sunsets. (p99)

ATHENS' STREET FOOD
Fill up on traditional cheese pies and souvlaki from streetside vendors. (p84)

THESSALONIKI'S PATISSERIES
Sinfully scrumptious treats influenced by the Ottoman East. (p181)

CRETAN WINE
Tour the fertile Peza region for vineyards and tasting rooms. (p236)

SANTORINI'S CALDERA VIEW
Sample imaginative dishes like artichoke *saganaki* (skillet-fried cheese) and smoked trout. (p226)

Mykonos

Settle into a waterfront seat with a cocktail to watch the sun melt into the ocean before you head on to clubs, wine bars or drag shows. The sparkling nightlife of Mykonos (p206) is infamous and can be as laid-back or as glitzy as you want it to be. And the next day you can lose yourself in the atmospheric cobbled streets or wander to the beach to stretch out on the sand and pay homage to the sun.

LEFT: JAN VLODARCZYK/ALAMY © RIGHT: IMAGEBROKER ©

15

Thessaloniki

Stylish 'Saloniki (p170) remains northern Greece's liveliest town – thanks to its universities, cultural scene and nightlife. There's little hassle and getting about by foot is easy. Take in the city at dusk from the viewing station up by the Byzantine walls in the old quarter, known as Ano Poli (Upper Town). It's a neighbourhood full of colourful, winding little streets marked by white-plastered houses, lazy cats and Byzantine churches.

Samaria Gorg

The gaping gorge of Samaria (p268), startir at Omalos and running down through an ancie riverbed to the Libyan Sea, is the most-trod canyon in Crete – and with good reason. The magnificent gorge is home to varied wildlife, soaring birds of prey and a dazzling array of wildflowers in spring. It a full day's work (about six hours down), and you'll have to start earl but it certainly builds character.

Cuisine

You don't have to be a fan of octopus and ouzo to enjoy Greek cuisine (p348). The Greek kitchen is inspired by local produce alongside Turkish and Italian influences. Traditional Greek bakeries will leave your mouth watering with honey-drenched pastries. Village restaurants will satisfy you with home-cooked roasts, fresh fish and salads picked from the back garden. Contemporary chefs will wow you with tantalising fusion dishes; even tiny islands like Paxi (p138) have mouth-watering menus. Try locally pressed olive oil, freshly made feta and strong coffee. Bougasta (custard pie)

18

The Best...
Quiet Retreats

PELION PENINSULA
Dramatic and lush, with a plunging coastline, mountain villages and quiet sandy coves. (p164)

PAXI
Ancient olive groves, windmills and beckoning coves. (p138)

ZAGOROHORIA'S VILLAGES
Preserved mountain hamlets with strong Greek traditions and gorgeous guesthouses. (p191)

LYKAVITTOS HILL
Escape the hustle of Athens on easily accessible forest paths. (p74)

The Best...
Local Architecture

CORFU TOWN
Venetian-era pastel-coloured mansions. (p131)

CAPTAINS' HOUSES
Impressive 17th-century buildings with sea views. (p300)

TOWER HOMES
Traditional houses nestled in the mountains. (p124)

PELION VILLAGES
White-washed half-timbered homes with overhanging balconies. (p164)

Hydra

Everyone approaches Hydra (p98) by sea. There is no airport, there are no cars. As you sail in, you find, simply, a stunningly preserved stone village, white-gold houses filling a natural cove and hugging the edges of surrounding mountains. Then you join the ballet of port life. Sailboats, caïques and megayachts fill Hydra's quays, and the harbourside cafes are a people-watching potpourri. Here, a mere hour and a half from Athens, you'll find a great cappuccino, rich naval and architectural history, and the raw seacoast beckoning you for a swim.

FUNKYFOOD LONDON - PAUL WILLIAMS/ALAMY ©

20 Halkidiki

Northern Greece's 'three fingers' stretch out in the Aegean, where the Halkidiki peninsula (p182) combines great beaches, nightlife, camping spots and some serious history. The first finger, Kassandra, buzzes in summer with open air discos and crowded beaches; while the second, Sithonia has much quieter sandy distant shores. Ouranoupoli, on the third finger, offers family-friendly beaches. This is also home to the heavily forested Mt Athos, with its monastic community (p184) that has preserved its Byzantine rituals for more than 1000 years.

TZULIYAN NEDELCHEV / ALAMY ©

Hania

Explore the former Venetian port town of Hania (p260), Crete's most beautiful and historic town. The pastel-hued buildings along the harbour seem to almost shimmer in the reflection of the sea. Behind them is a web of evocative, winding stone lanes filled with restored Venetian and Turkish architecture. Shop, see the sights, dine and relax; Hania's offerings excel in all of these pursuits.

Knossos

Rub shoulders with the ghosts of the Minoans, a Bronze Age people who attained a high level of civilisation and ruled large parts of the Aegean from their capital in Knossos (p251) some 4000 years ago. Until the site's excavation in the early 20th century, an extraordinary wealth of frescoes, sculptures, jewellery, seals and other remnants lay buried under the Cretan soil. Knossos is an important archaeological site and is Crete's most visited tourist attraction.

The Zagorohoria

After passing through a seemingly endless array of tunnels, the Egnatia Odos highway brings you into rugged Epiros, home of the Pindos Mountains and the Zagorohoria (p191) – an immaculately preserved region of traditional villages spread along the ridges of Europe's deepest canyon, the Vikos Gorge (p191). Here, the air is clear, fresh and cool, and the views astounding. You can explore the region by hiking or mountain biking, or simply get cosy by the fire in one of many rustic B&Bs dotting the region. Vikos Gorge

The Best...
Colourful Harbours

SYMI
Restored homes and bright, bobbing fishing boats. (p303)

HYDRA
No cars or power lines – just traditionally stunning village architecture. (p98)

NAFPLIO
Elegant homes set beneath a romantic fortress. (p115)

MYKONOS
Sugar-cube buildings meet glamour. (p206)

AGIOS NIKOLAOS
Family-friendly destination set along a curving harbour. (p270)

Ancient Olympia

As you immerse yourself in these ruins (p128), it's not difficu
to imagine the first Olympic competitors wrestling or sprint
ing. As you emerge from the tunnel into the Olympic stadiun
it's hard to ignore the ghosts of thousands of cheering spec
tors. At Olympia, past and present merge magically. And to
spur on your imagination, you can still see the original start
and finish lines and take it all in from the judges' seats.

The Best...
Atmospheric Old Towns

RHODES
Lively medieval world contained within large stone
walls. (p293)

ATHENS
The old Turkish quarter of
Plaka nestled along the
slopes of the Acropolis.
(p66)

HANIA
Venetian and Turkish
architecture along nar-
row, criss-crossed lanes.
(p260)

IOANNINA
Evocative old quarter from
Byzantine and Ottoman
times. (p187)

25

Nafplio

Romantically set in a small harbour beneath the ruins of a fortress, Nafplio (p115) – with its elegant mansions and flower-bedecked balconies – is one of Greece's prettiest towns. With slow seaside cafes and coastal walks to sandy coves, it has all the elements of a perfect holiday destination, without the crowds. And just in case you wanted more, in the town's backyard rests the acoustically perfect, 3rd-century-BC Theatre of Epidavros. Hidden amid pine-clad hills, it's a striking setting in which to soak up classic lines beneath the stars.

Greece's
Top Itineraries

Athens to Meteora

Architectural Wonders

Greece's mainland sites are diverse and intriguing. In just five days you can sample the magnificent ruins of Athens, take in the wonder of Ancient Delphi and experience the spiritual vibe and architectural awe of Meteora.

① Athens (p66)

There is little that can prepare you for the awe-inducing spectacle of the **Acropolis**. Be sure to visit the impressive **Acropolis Museum** which brings the ruins to life. Take in the **Ancient Agora**, the heart of ancient Athens, as well as the **Temple Of Olympian Zeus**, remarkable for the sheer size of its Corinthian columns. On your second day, continue to explore the sites of Athens or take a day trip to the **Temple of Poseidon** in southern Attica. Return to Athens to dine in one of the many restaurants with views over the lit-up Acropolis.

ATHENS ⊖ DELPHI

Three hours From Athens' Terminal B. **Two hours 30 minutes** Along the E75.

② Ancient Delphi (p160)

There are few sites in the world that compare to Ancient Delphi. The Ancient Greeks believed it to be the centre of the world and there's an almost palpable atmosphere when you're here. Built in a breathtaking setting on the slopes of Mt Parnassos and overlooking the sea,

these ruins will undoubtedly inspire you. Spend a day taking in both the site and the nearby museums, particularly the **Delphi Museum** where many of the site's original artefacts are displayed. Delphi has some comfortable hotels with views and it's worth spending the night so you're not rushed for time.

DELPHI ⊖ METEORA

Five Hours 10am departure to Kalambaka via Lamia and Trikala, rather than Larisa. **Four hours 30 minutes** Along E65, E75 and then E92.

③ Meteora (p165)

Base yourself in Kastraki, within the shadow of the towering forest of rock pinnacles. Spend the afternoon soaking up the scenery, relaxing or maybe setting out along one of the many walking routes. Head off early the next morning and spend the day exploring the many monasteries perched like birds' nests atop the smooth rocks, being sure to take in **Moni Megalou Meteorou** and at least one of the smaller monasteries like **Moni Agias Triados**. If you're interested in learning more about the frescos, history or architecture of the monasteries, organise a guide the evening before.

Caryatids of the Erechtheion (p71), the Acropolis
PHOTOGRAPHER: DIMITRIOS/SHUTTERSTOCK ©

33

5 DAYS

Rhodes to Patmos

Evocative Towns & Beaches

Medieval fortress towns, Ottoman adventure and biblical mysteries make this an unforgettable journey through the Dodecanese. Even better, these sights are strung together with sandy beaches and relaxed island hopping across the bright blue Aegean.

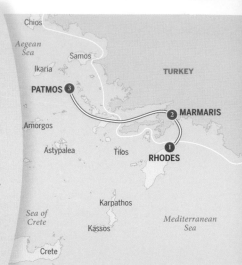

① Rhodes (p290)

Get yourself settled in Rhodes' magical **Old Town**, enclosed within medieval stone walls. Head out and get lost in the labyrinth of alleyways, visit the impressive **museums** and join in the buzzing restaurant, cafe and nightlife scenes. The next day, rent a car to visit **Lindos**, a pedestrianised village of whitewashed buildings, topped with an awe-inspiring **Acropolis**. Relax on pretty **St Paul's Bay**, a sandy cove with warm water just below Lindos, or explore the beaches along the south coast on your way back to Rhodes Town.

RHODES ⊙ MARMARIS RETURN
⚓ **50 minutes each way** From Rhodes' Commercial Harbour to Marmaris.

② Marmaris, Turkey (p307)

Turkey's influence on the Dodecanese is undeniable. Just a short hop across the sea, it's easy to visit this neighbouring country on a day trip from Rhodes, heading for the port of Marmaris. While a tourist hotspot, it's a bustling harbour with a lively bazaar, offering a window into Turkish culture. Nearby is an unspoilt azure coastline backed by pine-covered mountains that's easily reached from the city. As the yacht capital of Turkey, Marmaris has buzzing cafe and shopping scenes and fashionable nightlife that you can enjoy if you stay on into the evening.

RHODES ⊙ PATMOS
⚓ **Six hours** Via high-speed catamaran from Rhodes' Commercial Harbour to Skala.

③ Patmos (p314)

Base yourself in **Skala** but spend the day exploring the hill-top old town of **Hora**, with its sugar-cube buildings, winding alleyways and traditional squares. Follow the Byzantine stone path through the woods to the **Monastery of the Apocalypse**, where it's believed St John wrote the Book of Revelations, and visit the incense-filled **Monastery of St John the Theologian**. Spend the next day at sheltered **Kambos Beach**, with its shallow waters, kayaking and beach restaurant, or take an excursion boat to the idyllic, tree-shaded **Psili Ammos Beach**.

Monastery of St John the Theologian (p318)

Athens to Keffalonia

Exploring the Peloponnese

If you've a hankering for beautiful medieval towns, ancient sights, dramatic scenery and island life, a tour of the Peloponnesian peninsula and neighbouring Ionian Islands will more than satisfy you. This is doubly true if you're keen on outdoor activities.

1 Athens (p51)

Packed with big sights and quiet corners, Athens never fails to impress. Stroll along the pedestrianised **Apostolou Pavlou**, sandwiched between the **Acropolis** and the stunning **Acropolis Museum**. Get lost in the historic Turkish quarter of **Plaka** and take in the local scene at one of the countless sidewalk cafes. Spend the evening at the **National Theatre** or hang out at an atmospheric **rembetika club**.

ATHENS ⊙ NAFPLIO

🚌 **Two hours 30 minutes** From Athens' Terminal A. 🚗 **Two hours** Follow E75, E94 then E65.

2 Nafplio (p115)

Head west to the Peloponnesian peninsula for graceful **Nafplio**, set on a beautiful bay beneath a hill-top fortress. Explore its winding streets, museums and lively port. Just east of here is the ancient theatre of **Epidavros** where it's well worth taking in a star-lit classical performance. It's also easy to do a day trip from Nafplio to the impressive citadel of **Mycenae**.

NAFPLIO ⊙ AREOPOLI

🚌 **Four hours** Change in Gythio. 🚗 **Three hours** Follow E65.

3 Areopoli (p124)

Spend a couple of days exploring the rugged and remote **Mani** where you'll encounter villages filled with fascinating architecture and the remnants of the unique Maniot culture. This region is a haven for hikers, with the dramatic Taÿgetos Mountains and tiny, isolated coves. It's also home to one of mainland Europe's most southerly points at **Cape Tenaro**, made famous in Homer's *Iliad,* and offers dazzling views. Base yourself in **Areopoli**, capital of the Mani. From here, with your own vehicle, you can easily reach the cape along with the extraordinary **Diros Caves** and scenic towns like **Gerolimenas** or **Alika**.

AREOPOLI ⊙ OLYMPIA

🚌 **Six hours** Change in Tripoli. 🚗 **Four hours** Follow E55 then route 76.

4 Ancient Olympia (p128)

Visit the sanctuary of **Ancient Olympia** where you can stand in the stadium that hosted the first Olympic Games. Upon arrival, take in the excellent **museums** and the following day explore the site itself, immersing yourself in its history.

OLYMPIA ⊙ KEFALLONIA

🚌 **Five hours** Including ferry to Argostoli on Kefallonia. 🚗 **One hour 30 minutes** Follow E45 to Kyllini, txhen ⛴ **Three hours** From Kyllini to Argostoli.

5 Kefallonia (139)

Head to the port town of Kyllini where you can hop on a ferry to Kefallonia. Stay in the picturesque village of **Fiskardo** and spend a couple of days kayaking to isolated golden beaches and sample the island's well-reputed local wine. With rugged mountain ranges, soaring coastal cliffs and traditional villages, this is an ideal spot to experience island life. If returning to Athens, you can hop on a flight from Kefallonia (55 minutes).

Acropolis Museum (p76)
PHOTOGRAPHER: GEORGE TSAFOS/LONELY PLANET IMAGES ©

Thessaloniki to Zagorohoria

Experiencing the North

This areas has Greece's best ancient sites, unique villages, gorgeous landscape, hip cities and sandy beaches to stretch out on. You could easily extend your trip by a week or two.

❶ Thessaloniki (p170)

Begin in **Thessaloniki**, a laid-back city with a cutting-edge art scene. Spend a couple of days exploring the backstreets, taking in the diverse architecture and indulging in delicious Ottoman-inspired cuisine. It's equally enjoyable to get lost in the enchanting old town of Ano Poli or the growing number of Turkish-baths-turned-art-galleries. Take an excursion to nearby **Sithonia** on the Halkidiki Peninsula for a day surrounded by aquamarine water, pine forests and long sandy beaches.

THESSALONIKI ➤ LITOHORO

🚌 **One hour 30 minutes** From Thessaloniki's main bus terminal. 🚗 **One hour** Follow E90 then E75.

❷ Litohoro (p185)

Next, venture west to appreciate the lofty heights of **Mt Olympus**, Greece's highest mountaintop and home of the gods. Hikers can take to the slopes, or simply stay the night in a Macedonian-style house in nearby **Litohoro** to enjoy the view from a traditional wooden balcony.

LITOHORO ➤ METEORA

🚌 **Three hours** Buses from Thessaloniki for Kalambaka. 🚗 **Two hours 30 minutes** Follow E75 then E92.

❸ Meteora (p165)

Carry on to Meteora: these ancient monasteries set atop seemingly swaying pinnacles of rock are instantly recognisable and stunningly mesmerising in real life. Spend a day taking in the views and the tremendous artwork within the monasteries. Stay in the nearby otherworldly village of **Kastraki** to see the sun rise from behind the rocks.

METEORA ➤ IOANNINA

🚌 **Two hours 30 minutes** Buses from Kalambaka. 🚗 **Two hours** Follow E92 then E90.

❹ Ioannina (p187)

Liven things up by spending a couple of days in **Ioannina**, a city with an arresting lakeside location and a backdrop of sheer mountains. Wander through the evocative old quarter that's filled with Byzantine and Ottoman architecture and take in the buzzing cultural scene and nightlife that's buoyed by the city's large student population.

IOANNINA ➤ ZAGOROHORIA

🚌 **One hour 30 minutes** Buses to Dilofo. 🚗 **One hour** For Dilofo, follow E90.

❺ Zagorohoria (p191)

Head into the Pindos Mountains and a region known as **Zagorohoria**, with its endless walking opportunities and beautiful, timeless stone and slate hamlets tucked into the range. Base yourself in enchanting, tiny **Dilofo** and stay in one of the countless restored, traditional guesthouses. Explore the area's stone bridges and footpaths, taking in **Vikos Gorge**, one of the deepest in the world.

Moni Agias Varvaras Rousanou (p166)
PHOTOGRAPHER: RECHITAN SORIN/SHUTTERSTOCK ©

Athens to Thessaloniki

The Grand Tour

This island-hopping adventure allows you to combine your sightseeing with a little time for enjoying city life, relaxing at the beach or experiencing traditional island life. En route you'll take in captivating villages, long stretches of divine sand and ancient ruins that will awe and inspire you.

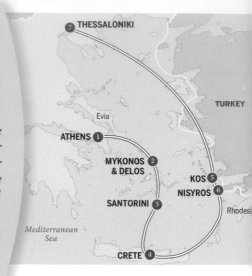

❶ Athens (p51)

Begin your tour with a day or two in Athens, home to some of the world's most important ancient sites and museums. Take in Athens' markets, contemporary art scene and brilliant nightlife.

ATHENS ➔ MYKONOS

✈ **50 minutes** 🚢 **Three hours** High-speed service from Piraeus.

❷ Mykonos & Delos (p206 & p215)

After arriving in **Mykonos**, spend the morning wandering through **Hora**, getting lost in the narrow alleyways, boutiques, galleries and museums. Spend the afternoon on the island's famous sandy beaches. Spend the next day at the dazzling site of **Delos**, one of the most important ancient sites in Greece and just a short boat ride from Mykonos. Return to Mykonos and join in the revelry of Hora's vibrant **nightlife**.

MYKONOS ➔ SANTORINI

✈ **30 minutes** 🚢 **Two hours 20 minutes** High-speed service.

❸ Santorini (p222)

Head to breathtaking **Santorini**. Perched on the edge of the caldera, **Fira** has a few worthwhile museums and spectacular views over the multicoloured cliffs. Base yourself there and spend the day wandering through the town, checking out the neoclassical mansions and ancient houses dug into volcanic rock. Join a **boat cruise** across the caldera and then sip cocktails at sunset in the view-filled bars. Spend the next day on the striking east-coast black-sand beaches such as **Kamari** and **Perissa**.

SANTORINI ➔ CRETE

✈ **30 minutes** To Iraklio. 🚢 **One hour 45 minutes** High-speed service to Iraklio.

❹ Crete (p233)

Catch a flight or high-speed ferry to **Iraklio** in Crete. You'll be there in time to visit the impressive **Archaeological Museum**, a treasure trove of Minoan pottery, jewellery, sculptures and frescoes. The next day, join a day trip or hop on a bus to **Knossos**, a marvellous, partially restored Minoan palace that will ignite your imagination. Move west

Rimondi Fountain (p255), Rethymno's Old Quarter
PHOTOGRAPHER: ANDREI NEKRASSOV/SHUTTERSTOCK ©

6 Nisyros (p305)

Hop on a day trip to Nisyros and delve into the depths of this verdant, volcanic island's caldera. Hike through lush terrain, take in a modern geological museum in a stunning hill-top village and refuel on home cooking. Then jump back on a ferry to Kos.

KOS ➲ THESSALONIKI
⚓ 21 hours

7 Thessaloniki (p170)

Book a cabin and experience life at sea on an overnight trip. Your minicruise will end at Thessaloniki in northern Greece. Check out the impressive Roman and Byzantine architecture, sample some Ottoman-inspired cuisine (particularly the pastries!) and enjoy the vivacious arts scene.

to **Rethymno** where you can settle into atmospheric accommodation and explore the impressive old town. The next day, hop on a bus or rent a car to reach gorgeous **Preveli Beach**, overlooked by a stunning monastery and boasting a long stretch of wide sand, palm-lined riverbanks and fresh-water pools. Head back to Iraklio.

CRETE ➲ KOS
✈ 35 minutes From Iraklio to Kos Town.

5 Kos (p307)

Kos Town is wrapped prettily along a palm-fringed harbour. Take in the **archaeological sites**, the cafe and restaurant scene and the nearby ruins of **Asklipiion**. The next day, hop on a bus or rent a car to reach the seven magnificent sandy beaches of **Kefalos Bay**, set between green hills and warm turquoise water, and offering tranquil patches of paradise. You'll have a hard time dragging yourself away.

KOS ➲ NISYROS
⚓ 45 minutes High-speed ferry

Greece Month by Month

Top Events

 Orthodox Easter, April

 Hellenic Festival, June–August

 Carnival, February

Thessaloniki International Film Festival, November

August Moon Festival, August

January

While most of the islands are snoozing during the winter months, the capital and the surrounding mainland are awake and welcome visitors with nontouristy festivals that offer some local insight. Expect warmth from hospitality – not the sun.

Feast of Agios Vasilios (St Basil)

The first day of January first sees a busy church ceremony followed by gifts, singing, dancing and feasting. The *vasilopita* (golden glazed cake for New Year's Eve) is cut; if you're fortunate enough to get the slice containing a coin, you'll supposedly have a lucky year.

Epiphany (Blessing of the Waters)

The day of Christ's baptism by St John is celebrated throughout Greece on 6 January. Seas, lakes and rivers are all blessed, with the largest ceremony held at Piraeus.

Gynaikokratia

The villages of the prefectures of Rodopi, Kilkis and Seres in northern Greece hold a day of role reversal on 8 January. Women spend the day in *kafeneia* (coffee houses) while the men stay at home to do the housework.

February

While February is an unlikely time to head to Greece, if you like a party and can time your visit with Carnival, it's well worth it.

Carnival

Carnival season kicks off three weeks prior to the fasting of Lent, from mid-January to late February or early March. A host of minor events leads up to a wild weekend of costume

(left) April Orthodox Easter Processsion

parades, colourful floats, feasting and traditional dancing. Celebrations see distinct regional variations; the Patra Carnival is the largest, while the most bizarre is on Skyros.

Clean Monday (Shrove Monday)

On the first day of Lent (a day which is referred to as Kathara Deftera), people take to the hills throughout Greece to enjoy picnicking and kite flying.

March

The islands are still sleepy but the weather is warming up, making March a quiet, relaxed time to visit. Although the national calendar is quiet, there are countless religious festivals that towns and entire islands celebrate with great gusto. Ask locally, and see also the destination chapters.

Independence Day

The anniversary of the hoisting of the Greek flag by independence supporters at Moni Agias Lavras is celebrated with parades and dancing on 25 March. This act of revolt marked the start of the War of Independence in 1821.

April

In Greece, the biggest day of the year is Easter, when the country, particularly the islands, shakes off its winter slumber. The holiday weekend is busy with Greeks hopping on planes and boats and booking out hotels; be sure to reserve well in advance.

Orthodox Easter

Communities joyously celebrate Jesus' resurrection beginning with candle-lit processions on Good Friday. One of the most impressive of these climbs Lykavittos Hill in Athens. The Lenten fast ends after 40 days on Easter Sunday with the cracking of red-dyed Easter eggs, lighting of fire-crackers, feasting and dancing. The Monastery of St John the Theologian on Patmos is a great place to witness it.

Festival of Agios Georgios (St George)

The feast day of St George, the country's patron saint and the patron saint of shepherds, falls on 23 April or the first Tuesday following Easter. It's celebrated with particular exuberance in Arahova, near Delphi. Expect dancing, feasting and a general party atmosphere.

May

If you're planning to head out on hiking trails, May is a great time to visit. Temperatures are still relatively mild and wildflowers create a huge splash of colour. Local greens, vegies and produce fill Greek kitchens.

May Day

The first of May is marked by a mass exodus from towns for picnics in the country. Wildflowers are gathered and made into wreaths to decorate houses.

June

For festival goers looking for contemporary acts rather than traditional village parties, June is hopping on the mainland. Top national and international performers fill atmospheric stages with dance, music and drama.

Navy Week

Celebrating their long relationship with the sea, fishing villages and ports throughout the country host historical re-enactments and parties in early June.

ancient Odeon of Herodes Atticus on the slopes of the Acropolis in Athens, and also at the world-famous Theatre of Epidavros, near Nafplio in the Peloponnese. Events run from June through August. Get details and tickets at www.greekfestival.gr.

 July

Temperatures soar and life buzzes on the islands' beaches, while outdoor cinemas and giant beach clubs continue to draw visitors to Athens' nightlife. If you're staying anywhere near the water, fill your belly with seafood that's hauled in daily.

Wine & Culture Festival
Held at Evia's coastal town of Karystos, this festival runs through July and August and includes theatre, traditional dancing, music and visual-art exhibits. It ends with a sampling of every local wine imaginable.

Speed World Cup
Kitesurfers from around the world hit Karpathos in July or August for its excellent surfing conditions and big prize money. Event dates change annually; check www.speedworldcup.com for more details.

Delphi Cultural Festival
Every July, the European Cultural Centre of Delphi hosts a 10-day cultural festival with fine arts, a sculpture park and drama performances at its own open-air theatre.

August

Respect the heat of August; expect to do just a little bit less, move a little more slowly and relax just a little more fully. If you're planning to travel mid-month, reserve well ahead as Greeks take to the roads and boats in large numbers.

Nafplion Festival
Featuring Greek and international performers, this classical music festival in the Peloponnese uses the Palamidi fortress as one of its atmospheric concert venues. Check out www.nafplionfestival.gr for dates and details.

Feast of St John the Baptist
The country is ablaze with bonfires on 24 June as Greeks light up the wreaths they made on May Day.

Rockwave Festival
International artists (past acts includes Moby, the Killers and Mötley Crüe) and massive crowds in late June on a huge parkland at the edge of Athens. See www.rockwavefestival.gr for details.

Hellenic Festival
The most prominent Greek summer festival (p91) features local and international music, dance and drama staged at the

August Moon Festival

Under the brightest moon of the year, historical venues in Athens open with free moonlit performances. Watch theatre, dance and music at venues like the Acropolis or Roman Agora. The festival is also celebrated at other towns and sites around the country; check locally for details.

 ## Feast of the Assumption

Assumption Day is celebrated with family reunions on 15 August; the whole population is seemingly on the move on either side of the big day. Thousands also make a pilgrimage to Tinos to its miracle-working icon of Panagia Evangelistria.

 # November

Autumn sees temperatures drop and the islands quieten down, although city life continue apace. Olive-picking is in full swing in places like Crete, and feta production picks up, giving you the opportunity to taste some seriously fresh cheese.

 ## Thessaloniki International Film Festival

Close to 150 films are crammed into 10 days of screenings around the city in mid-November. The focus is on independent film-makers and the festival is gaining increasing notoriety. For details, check out www.filmfestival.gr.

Far left: February Carnival parade
Below: February Carnival celebrations in Crete

PHOTOGRAPHERS: (FAR LEFT) GIOTA KORBAKI/CORBIS ©; (BELOW) ECOSTECERA2/ALAMY ©

Get Inspired

 Books

○ **Falling for Icarus: A Journey Among the Cretans** (2004) Rory MacLean journeys to Crete to live out his dream of constructing his own plane; the tale is entwined with history, myths and portrayals of village life.

○ **It's All Greek to Me!** (2004) John Mole's much-acclaimed account of an English family converting a stone ruin into a home on Evia.

○ **My Family and Other Animals** (1977) Gerald Durrell's classic, witty story of a childhood spent on Corfu, told by a now-famous naturalist and conservationist.

○ **The Island** (2006) Victoria Hislop's tale of Spinalonga, Greece's leper colony until 1973. A true story of a charismatic Athenian lawyer with leprosy, and now an incredibly popular TV series in Greece.

 Films

○ **Mediterraneo** (1991) Award-winning comedy about Italian soldiers stranded on Kastellorizo during WWII.

○ **Mamma Mia** (2008) Taking the world by storm, this ABBA-based musical was filmed on Skopelos, the Pelion Peninsula and Skiathos.

○ **Zorba the Greek** (1964) A steamy performance by Anthony Quinn as an uptight English writer who finds love in Crete, the beach dance scene was at Stavros, near Hania.

 Music

○ **Anthologio** A musical journey with Greece's most formidable female singer, Haris Alexiou, covering hits from 1975 to 2003.

○ **Itane Mia Fora** A broad range of music from Crete's favourite son, Nikos Xylouris.

○ **To Hamogelo tis Tzokontas** Manos Hatzidakis' timeless classical recording.

 Websites

○ **GNTO** (Greek National Tourist Organisation; www.gnto.gr) For concise tourist information.

○ **Greek Travel Pages** (www.gtp.gr) One-stop site with access to ferry schedules, accommodation listings and destination details.

○ **Ministry of Culture** (www.culture.gr) Details of events, sights, galleries, monuments and museums.

Short on time?

This list will give you an instant insight into the country.

Read *Eurydice Street: A Place In Athens* (Sofka Zinovieff, 2004) is an expat's tale, covering etiquette, culture and modern history.

Watch *Captain Corelli's Mandolin* (2001), based on the popular book, weaves together history, humour, romance and culture alongside scenes of Kefallonia.

Listen *Ta Rembetika* is an excellent compilation, featuring all the foremost exponents of the genre.

Log on www.visitgreece.gr for Greek culture, sights, maps, accommodation, weather and activities.

Left: Damouchari, Pelion (p164)
Above right: Kastellorizo (Megisti; Map p279)
PHOTOGRAPHER: (LEFT) RAWDON WYATT/ALAMY © (ABOVE) IMAGES & STORIES/ALAMY ©

Need to Know

Currency
Euro (€)

Language
Greek

ATMS
Widely available. Not always in service on smaller islands.

Credit Cards
Accepted in larger establishments, destinations and in resorts.

Visas
Generally not required for stays of up to 90 days; some nationalities may require a visa.

Mobile Phones
Local SIM cards can be used in dual- or tri-band phones.

Wi-Fi
Available in many cafes and common in hotels.

Internet Access
Internet cafes are common; €2 to €4 per hour.

Driving
Drive on the right; steering wheel is on the left of the car.

Tipping
Round fares up for taxis; service charge included in restaurant bills; 5% to 10% tip when service is good.

When to Go

Dry climate
Warm summer, mild winter
Mild summer, very cold winter

Thessaloniki
GO May-Nov

Corfu
GO May-Sep

Athens
GO May-Sep

Rhodes
GO Apr-Sep

Iraklio
GO May-Oct

High Season
(May–Aug)
o Accommodation often costs twice as much

o Crowds and temperatures soar

o Also applies to Easter (April)

Shoulder
(Apr & Sep)
o Accommodation prices can drop by 20%

o Temperatures are milder

o Internal flights and ferries have reduced schedules

o Lesser crowds

Low Season
(Oct–Mar)
o Many hotels, sights and restaurants shut

o Accommodation up to 50% less than during high season

o Temperatures drop significantly

o Ferry schedules skeletal

Advance Planning

o **Three months before** Book boutique accommodation in places like the Zagorohoria, Rhodes Old Town or Hania.

o **One month before** Check ferry schedules. Book any other accommodation, overnight ferries and activities. Look online for festivals and events and book tickets for the larger ones.

o **Two weeks before** Book interisland ferries and trains.

o **One week before** Make reservations at an Athens restaurant with an Acropolis view.

Your Daily Budget

Budget less than €60

o Dorm beds: €10–20; *domatia* (Greek B&B): from €25

o Eat at markets and street stalls (€2–4)

o Travel in the shoulder season

Midrange €60-100

o Double room in midrange hotel: €35–60

o Plenty of local tavernas with midrange fare (€10–20)

o Majority of sights have reasonable entrance fees (€0–8)

Top End over €150

o Double room in top hotel: from €90

o Excellent dining, some Michelin stars (€20–50)

o Activities like diving and sailing readily available (€25–50 per day)

o Nightlife and cocktail bars abound

Exchange Rates

Australia	A$1	€0.74
Canada	C$1	€0.71
Japan	Yen100	€0.97
New Zealand	NZ$1	€0.57
UK	£1	€1.3
US	US$1	€0.70

For current exchange rates see www.xe.com,

What to Bring

o **Waterproof money belt** For sudden downpours.

o **Phrasebook** Making the effort is hugely appreciated.

o **Lightweight raincoat** You never know when a cloud will burst.

o **Seasickness remedies** For island-hoppers.

o **Mosquito repellent** An unfortunate necessity.

o **Clothes pegs and laundry line** Rinse out your swimsuit.

Arriving in Greece

o **Athen's Eleftherios Venizelos International Airport**

Express buses 24 hours between the airport, city centre and Piraeus.

Metro trains Half-hourly between the city centre and airport 5.30am to 11.30pm.

Taxis €30 to the city centre (one hour).

o **Thessaloniki's Makedonia Airport**

Bus 78 Half-hourly from the airport to the city's main bus station, via the train station.

Taxis €12 to the city centre.

Getting Around

o **Boat** True Greek island-hopping experience, from slow clunkers to speedy hydrofoils.

o **Car** Affordable car rental.

o **Air** Domestic flights between major mainland cities and larger islands.

o **Bus** Major routes serviced by air-conditioned buses. Remote areas and small islands have limited services.

o **Cycling** Gaining popularity with tourists. Many regions and islands are very mountainous.

Accommodation

o **Domatia** Greek equivalent of a B&B, minus the breakfast. Many are self-catering.

o **Hotels** Categorised by amenities, with prices controlled by the tourist police. Maximum rates are displayed in each room.

o **Pensions** Indistinguishable from hotels.

o **Rental accommodation** Furnished apartments and villas offer good value; many require a minimum week's stay.

Be Forewarned

o **Ferries** Weather can play havoc with schedules.

o **Winter time** Many islands virtually shut down over winter months.

o **ATMs** Island ATMs can lose connection for days; ensure you have backup cash.

Athens & Around

Ancient and modern, with equal measures of grunge and grace, bustling Athens is a heady mix of history and edginess, lively cafes and alfresco dining, chaos and pure fun.

The magnificent Acropolis that rises majestically above the sprawling metropolis has stood witness to the city's many transformations. In over a decade of radical urban renewal, Athens has reinvented itself. Post-Olympics Athens is conspicuously wealthier, more sophisticated and more cosmopolitan. The shift is evident in the stylish new restaurants, shops and hip hotels, and in the emerging artsy-industrial neighbourhoods and entertainment precincts. The car-free historic centre is an open-air museum, yet the city's cultural and social life takes place around these ancient monuments, reconciling past and present. Just beyond this seductive city lies the plain of Attica, with awe-inspiring sites, such as the Temple of Poseidon. Nearby, across a short stretch of the Aegean, Hydra beckons, offering an island getaway from the city.

Odeon of Herodes Atticus (p72)
GEORGE TSAFOS/LONELY PLANET IMAGES ©

Athens & Around

See Omonia Map (p80)

See Gazi & Thisio Map (p75)

See Central
Athens Map (p68)

Lansis Train
Station
Filadelphias
Larisis Metro
Station

Ioulianou

Viktoria

Metaxa Neof

Aristotelous

Ipirou

Ioanninon
Petras

Delgianni

Liossion

Lenorman

Plateia
Akadimias
Platonos

Palamidiou

Andromahis

OMONIA

Plateia
Vathis

Kapodistri

Marni

Halkokondyl

Leof Athinon

Metaxourghio

Karolou

National
Theatre

Ag Konstantinou

Plateia
Omonias

Omonia

Pireos

Athinas

Plateia
Kotzia

Thermopylon

Kolokinthous

Stoa
Athanaton

Plateia
Theatrou

Varvakios
Agora (Athens
Central Market

Iera Odos

Leof Konstantinoupoleos

Iera Odos

Mylerou

Dipylou

PSYRRI

Patsi Spyrou

GAZI

Keramikos

Keramikos

Ermou

Kerameikos

Technopolis

Thisio

Plateia
Monastirakiou

Monastiraki

Thisio Park

THISIO

Thisio

Plateia
Thisiou

Plat
Mitropole

Iraklidon

Poulopoulou

Nileos

Apostolou Pavlou

Roman
Agora

Tzaferi

Venue

Areopagus
Hill

ANAFIOTIKA

Pireos

Hill
of the
Nymphs

Hill of
the Pnyx

Odeon of
Herodes
Atticus

Acropolis

Dionysiou Areopagitou

Thessalonikis

Trion Ierarhon

Dimofontos

ANO
PETROLONA

Petralona

Filopappou
Hill

Dora Stratou
Dance Theatre

Ious

Kilis

KOUKAKI

Veikou

Dimitrakopoulou N

Syngro
Fix

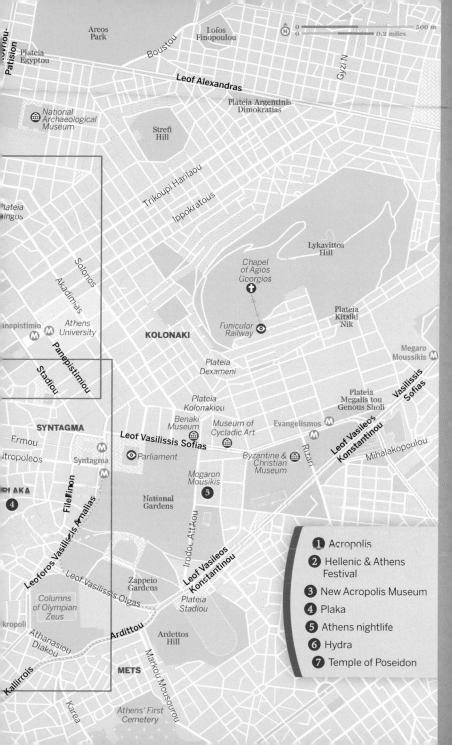

Athens' Highlights

① Acropolis

As you step through the monumental entrance way to the Acropolis, the ruins demand your respect. It doesn't matter how many people crowd around you or how many times you've visited before, the majesty of the Acropolis and its timeless significance inevitably fills you with awe. Above: Caryatids of Erechtheion; Top Right: Parthenon; Bottom Right: Ceiling painting

Need to Know

BEST TIME Early morning before it gets too busy and hot **HOW LONG?** At least two hours **NEXT STOP** The Acropolis Museum (p76) **For further coverage, see p67**

Acropolis Don't Miss List

BY CATHERINE TRIANTIS, TOUR GUIDE

1 PARTHENON

This is the crowning achievement of Greek architecture. Walk around the temple (p71) to view its geometry; stop at the northeastern corner to see its curves. Looking at the eastern steps, you can see them gradually ascend and then descend, forming a curve.

2 ERECHTHEION

Have a look at each side of this ornate and architecturally unique temple (p71), characterised by elegance, grace and elaborate decoration. The most interesting side is the porch of the Caryatids with six female Korae statues. Although the statues are copies, the artists' craftsmanship is evident in the transparency of the clothing and unique hairstyles.

3 VIEWS OF ATHENS

The Acropolis offers aerial views of the city. To the north you'll see Plaka and Ancient Agora, to the east the Temple of Olympian Zeus and the National Gardens, to the south the new Acropolis Museum and Filopappou Hill, and to the west the Athenian Observatory.

4 COLOURFUL PAST

Built to protect the Acropolis after the Persian Wars in 479 BC, the massive northern fortification walls were made from columns taken from the sites of earlier temples. Look closely to spot hints of colour on these columns – almost everything was rendered with colour in the past.

5 TEMPLE OF ATHENA NIKE

An absolute jewel, this temple (p70) was dedicated to the victory goddess Athena Nike; it contained a wingless statue of her to keep her from flying away from Athens and therefore keeping the city victorious.

The Acropolis

Cast your imagination back in time, two and a half millennia ago, and envision the majesty of the Acropolis. Its famed and hallowed monument, the Parthenon, dedicated to the goddess Athena, stood proudly over a small city, dwarfing the population with its graceful grandeur. In the Acropolis' heyday in the 5th century BC, pilgrims and priests worshipped at the temples illustrated here (most of which still stand in varying states of restoration). Many were painted brilliant colours and were abundantly adorned with sculptural masterpieces crafted from ivory, gold and semi-precious stones.

As you enter the site today, elevated on the right, perches one of the Acropolis' best-restored buildings: the diminutive **Temple of Athena Nike ❶**. Follow the Panathenaic Way through the Propylaia and up the slope toward the Parthenon – icon of the Western world. Its **majestic columns ❷** sweep up to some of what were the finest carvings of their time: wraparound **pediments, metopes and a frieze ❸**. Stroll around the temple's exterior and take in the spectacular views over Athens and Piraeus below.

As you circle back to the centre of the site, you will encounter those renowned lovely ladies, the **Caryatids ❹** of the Erechtheion. On the Erechtheion's northern face, the oft-forgotten **Temple of Poseidon ❺** sits alongside ingenious **Themistocles' Wall ❻**. Wander to the Erechtheion's western side to find Athena's gift to the city: **the olive tree ❼**.

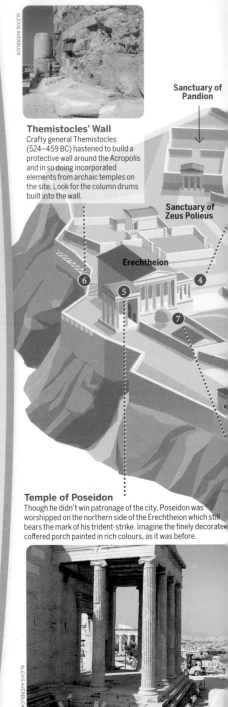

Sanctuary of Pandion

Themistocles' Wall
Crafty general Themistocles (524–459 BC) hastened to build a protective wall around the Acropolis and in so doing incorporated elements from archaic temples on the site. Look for the column drums built into the wall.

Sanctuary of Zeus Polieus

Erechtheion

Temple of Poseidon
Though he didn't win patronage of the city, Poseidon was worshipped on the northern side of the Erechtheion which still bears the mark of his trident-strike. Imagine the finely decorated coffered porch painted in rich colours, as it was before.

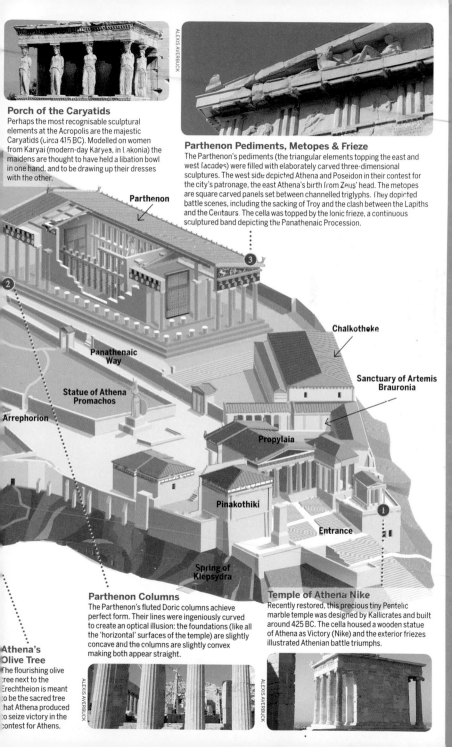

Porch of the Caryatids

Perhaps the most recognisable sculptural elements at the Acropolis are the majestic Caryatids (circa 415 BC). Modelled on women from Karyai (modern-day Karyes, in Lakonia) the maidens are thought to have held a libation bowl in one hand, and to be drawing up their dresses with the other.

Parthenon Pediments, Metopes & Frieze

The Parthenon's pediments (the triangular elements topping the east and west facades) were filled with elaborately carved three-dimensional sculptures. The west side depicted Athena and Poseidon in their contest for the city's patronage, the east Athena's birth from Zeus' head. The metopes are square carved panels set between channelled triglyphs. They depicted battle scenes, including the sacking of Troy and the clash between the Lapiths and the Centaurs. The cella was topped by the Ionic frieze, a continuous sculptured band depicting the Panathenaic Procession.

Parthenon

Chalkotheke

Panathenaic Way

Sanctuary of Artemis Brauronia

Statue of Athena Promachos

Arrephorion

Propylaia

Pinakothiki

Entrance

Spring of Klepsydra

Athena's Olive Tree

The flourishing olive tree next to the Erechtheion is meant to be the sacred tree that Athena produced to seize victory in the contest for Athens.

Parthenon Columns

The Parthenon's fluted Doric columns achieve perfect form. Their lines were ingeniously curved to create an optical illusion: the foundations (like all the 'horizontal' surfaces of the temple) are slightly concave and the columns are slightly convex making both appear straight.

Temple of Athena Nike

Recently restored, this precious tiny Pentelic marble temple was designed by Kallicrates and built around 425 BC. The cella housed a wooden statue of Athena as Victory (Nike) and the exterior friezes illustrated Athenian battle triumphs.

Hellenic & Athens Festival

With venues scattered throughout the city, the Athens Festival brings an exceptional variety of performances to the capital. The festival is partnered with theatres and festivals in France, London, Berlin and New York, bringing new and co-produced works from around the world to Athens. A performance at the Odeon of Herodes Atticus (p72; pictured below) is not to be missed.

Need to Know

TICKETS Three weeks prior **ONLINE PROGRAM** www.greekfestival.gr **AVERAGE TICKET PRICE** €25 **ETIQUETTE** Arrive on time or you have to wait until intermission **For more, see p91**

Hellenic Festival Don't Miss List

BY YORGOS LOUKOS, PRESIDENT & ARTISTIC DIRECTOR

1 ODEON OF HERODES ATTICUS

This is one of Athens' most important venues (p72). Get comfortable in one of the 4600 seats in this atmospheric Roman Odeon and take in a performance in much the same way Ancient Greeks did in the first century. See classical music from world-famous orchestras, singers from around the world and theatre performances. The location of the venue is unique – it's in the very heart of the city on the slope beneath the Acropolis.

2 PEIRAIOS 260

Once an abandoned factory, this **venue** (Pireos 260, Tavros, Athens) lies in an industrial area that's being transformed into a budding arts neighbourhood. The factory is now a wonderful place of contemporary works – mostly theatre and dance from around the world, but you'll also find installations and exhibitions. This is where young people head to every night to discover the new works from all over Europe and the US.

3 EPIDAVROS

Nothing beats seeing classic lines acted out in this traditional setting (p119; pictured left). Although not in Athens (it's a couple of hours from the capital), this is one of the most interesting venues of the Greek Festival. On Fridays and Saturdays during July and August, people travel to enjoy a performance at this 3rd-century theatre, a real jewel of ancient architecture set in the middle of the woods. The program is mainly Greek drama but not always.

4 MEGARON MOUSIKIS

One of the most prestigious multipurpose arts centres in Europe, the Megaron (Athens Concert Hall, p86; pictured above left) constitutes a major focal point for music, art and education. Open since 1991, the Megaron has received the praise of internationally acclaimed artists for its stunning environment, exceptional aesthetics and superb acoustics.

Acropolis Museum

Feast your eyes on the treasures unearthed from the Acropolis at the stunning ultramode Acropolis Museum (p76). The vast collection includes pieces held for years in storage as v as objects returned from abroad. In addition to the awe-inspiring sculptures, the museum contains the site and ruins of an ancient Athenian city discovered during the building's construction.

3

Historical Meanderings

4

Get lost in Athens' historic centre (p66) The old Turkish quarter in Plaka is virtually all that existed when Athens was declared capital of Greece. Its paved, narrow streets nestle into the northeastern slope of the Acropolis. Nearby, the former traffic-clogged thoroughfare Apostolou Pavlou has been transform into a lovely green pedestrian promen and heritage trail below the Acropolis

Evening Pursuits

Athen is pumping at night. Whether you want to be wowed by phenomenal theatre at the National Theatre (p87) and opera at Megaron Mousikis (p86), mesmerised by traditional Greek folk dancing at the starlit Dora Stratou Dance Theatre (p87) under the stars, sung to in an atmospheric *rembetika* (Greek blues) club like Stoa Athanaton (p86) or danced off your feet in a top European club like the mammoth Venue (p85) – the nightlife in Athens is electrifying.

Hydra

Easily reached from Athens as a day trip or overnight excursion, Hydra (p98) offers a taste of the best of island life. Sail into its vibrant harbour, explore its picturesque town with its winding alleyways and colourful houses, and then sit back and enjoy fresh seafood at dockside restaurants. Hydra beckons you to slow down, relax and soak up the island vibe.

Temple of Poseidon

Stand before the ruins of this magnificent temple (p97), with the sun pouring down on it and the glittering Aegean stretching endlessly beyond it. Imbued with a formidable, majestic quality, the atmosphere here is thick enough to slice.

Athens' Best...

Places to Chill

o **Keramikos** (p74) Stroll through the green, tranquil grounds of this ancient cemetery.

o **Lykavittos Hill** (p74) Stretch your legs on forest paths.

o **National Gardens** (p75) Relax in a shady retreat.

o **Temple of Poseidon** (p97) Be spellbound by a seaside sunset behind glimmering ruins.

Gastronomic Delights

o **Diporto Agoras** (p83) Experience an eccentric eatery serving traditional cuisine and wine by the giant barrel.

o **Street Food** (p84) Fill up on scrumptious meals from streetside vendors.

o **Mani Mani** (p84) Sample regional cuisine from the Peloponnese.

o **Palia Taverna tou Psara** (p82) Dine on some of the best seafood in Plaka.

Acropolis Views

o **Filopappou Hill** (p74) Take your camera for prime vantage points.

o **Café Avyssinia** (p82) Eat bohemian-style while your eyes feast on the vista.

o **Magna Grecia** (p80) Wake up to your own view at this boutique hotel.

o **Vitrine** (p85) Sip a cocktail with a view to the spotlit ruins.

Need to Know

Windows to the Past

Ancient Agora (p72) Walk in Socrates' footsteps.

National Archaeological Museum (p78) Get up close to the precious treasures.

Changing of the Guard (p77) See the traditional presidential guards in full ceremonial dress.

Byzantine & Christian Museum (p74) Be awed by icons, frescoes, textiles and manuscripts.

ADVANCE PLANNING

○ **Two months before** Sort out your hotel and tickets for the theatre or festivals.

○ **One month before** Book tours, activities and onward travel.

○ **Two weeks before** Prebook top-end restaurants.

RESOURCES

○ **Athens Tourism** (www. breathtakingathens.gr) Handy what's-on listings.

○ **Ministry of Culture** (www.culture.gr) Guide to museums, sites and events.

○ **www.elculture.gr** (in Greek) Arts and culture, including theatre, music and cinema listings.

○ **Kathimerini** (www. ekathimerini.com) English-language daily with listings and ferry schedules.

○ **Odyssey** (www.odyssey. gr) Includes an annual summer guide to Athens.

GETTING AROUND

○ **Walk** Most big sights are within easy walking distance.

○ **Bus** For anywhere off the metro or train lines; 24-hour airport service.

○ **Metro** The most efficient way to get around.

○ **Suburban rail** Fast and comfortable service to the airport and beyond.

○ **Trams** Scenic but slow.

BE FOREWARNED

○ **Pickpockets** Guard your belongings on the metro and around Omonia and Monastiraki.

○ **Public transport** Ensure you have a valid ticket. Fines are steep.

: Changing of the guard at Parliament (p77)
Above: Bust inside the Stoa of Attalos (p73)

(LEFT) HEMIS/ALAMY ©; (ABOVE) GEORGE TSAFOS /LONELY PLANET IMAGES ©

Athens Walking Tour

With ancient ruins, Turkish baths, presidential guards and a look into island life, this tour will give you a taste of the diverse mix that makes Athens one of Europe's most dynamic cities.

WALK FACTS
- **Start** Syntagma
- **Finish** Monastiraki
- **Distance** 5.5km
- **Duration** One to three hours

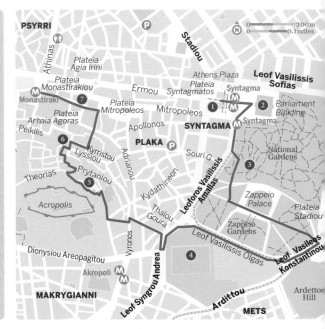

① Plateia Syntagmatos

This square has been a favourite place for protests ever since the rally that led to the granting of a constitution in 1843. The historic **Hotel Grande Bretagne** (built in 1862) was a Nazi headquarters during WWII, and in 1944 the hotel was the scene of an attempt to assassinate Winston Churchill.

In the northeastern corner of the square, next to the northern metro entrance, you can see a section of the ancient cemetery and the **Peisistratos aqueduct**, which was unearthed during metro excavations. Take the metro underpass toward the Parliament, checking out the archaeological dig displays en route.

② Parliament

The underpass emerges on the west side of the former royal palace, now the Parliament. In front of the Parliament, you will see the much-photographed *evzones* (presidential guards) and the Tomb of the Unknown Soldier. Time your visit to catch the changing of the guard, every hour on the hour.

③ National Gardens

Walk through these lush gardens and exit at **Zappeio Palace**, used as the Olympic village in the 2004 Olympics. Follow the path east until you see the crossing to **Panathenaic Stadium**, where the first Olympic Games were held in 1896.

④ Temple of Olympian Zeus

Crossing back towards the gardens, walk along their periphery until you approach the entrance to this striking temple, the largest ever built. Heading towards Plaka, on the corner ahead of you and teetering on the edge of the traffic, **Hadrian's Arch** is the ornate gateway erected to mark the boundary of Hadrian's Athens.

⑤ Anafiotika Quarter

Head west past the 12th-century **Church of Agia Ekaterini** and continue, climbing the steps up to Stratonos and turning right. Just ahead you will see the **Church of St George of the Rock**, which marks the entry to the Anafiotika quarter. This picturesque maze of little whitewashed houses is the legacy of stonemasons from the small Cycladic island of Anafi, who were brought in to build the king's palace after Independence.

⑥ Roman Agora

Following the narrow path winding around the houses, hand-painted signs point the way to the Acropolis and Acropolis road. Turn right and then left into Prytaniou, veering right after 50m into Tholou and then right on Klepsidras. Narrow steps lead to little **Klepsidra Café** (Thrasyvoulou 9), perfect for a rest before continuing down to the ruins of the 1st-century Roman Agora. From here, head east down Kyrristou to the beautifully refurbished 17th-century **Turkish Baths**.

⑦ Pandrosou

Take the first left after the baths and head north to Pandrosou. This relic of the old Turkish bazaar is full of souvenir shops. The street is named after King Cecrops' daughter, Pandrosos, who was the first priestess of Athens. Head left for the colourful, chaotic square at **Monastiraki** and the metro.

Athens in...

TWO DAYS

Start by climbing to the glorious **Acropolis** then winding back down through **Plaka** and exploring the **Monastiraki Flea Market**. Head to the **Acropolis Museum** for the Parthenon masterpieces. Amble around the **grand promenade** before dinner at a restaurant with Acropolis views.

On day two, spend the morning taking our walking tour. In the afternoon, take a trolleybus to the **National Archaeological Museum** then catch an evening show at the historic **Odeon of Herodes Atticus**, or head to **Gazi** for dinner and nightlife.

FOUR DAYS

On day three, visit the **Benaki Museum** and **Museum of Cycladic Art** before lunch and shopping in **Kolonaki**. Take the *teleferik* (funicular railway) or climb **Lykavittos Hill** for panoramic views. Enjoy live music at a **rembetika club**.

On day four explore the **Keramikos site**. Trip along the coast to Cape Sounion's **Temple of Poseidon** or save your energy for summer nightlife at Glyfada's **beach bars**.

Shop selling textiles, Plaka (p60)
GREECE/ALAMY ©

Discover Athens & Around

At a Glance

- **Syntagma** The Heart of modern Athens.

- **Plaka** The old Turkish quarter and home to ancient sites.

- **Monastiraki** Market district.

- **Psyrri** Entertainment district.

- **Thisio** Pedestrian promenade beneath the Acropolis.

- **Kolonaki** Chic and trendy shops and galleries.

Cafes in pedestrianised Thisio (p82)
GEORGE TSAFOS/LONELY PLANET IMAGES ©

Sights

Plateia Syntagmatos (Syntagma Sq; translated as Constitution Sq) is the heart of modern Athens (Αθήνα), dominated by the Parliament, and most major sites are located within walking distance. South of Syntagma, the old Turkish quarter in Plaka is virtually all that existed when Athens was declared capital of Greece. Its paved, narrow streets nestle into the northeastern slope of the Acropolis and pass by many of the city's ancient sites. Plaka is touristy in the extreme, but it is still the most character-filled part of Athens.

Centred on busy Plateia Monastirakiou (Monastiraki Sq), the area just west of Syntagma is the city's grungier but nonetheless atmospheric market district. Psyrri (pseeree), just north of Monastiraki, has morphed into a busy entertainment precinct, with bars, restaurants and theatres. The Thisio neighbourhood's Apostolou Pavlou is a lovely green pedestrian promenade under the Acropolis, with a host of cafes and youth-filled bars. Kolonaki, tucked beneath Lykavittos Hill east of Syntagma, is undeniably chic. Its streets are full of classy boutiques and private art galleries as well as dozens of cafes and trendy restaurants. To the east of the Acropolis, Pangrati is an unpretentious residential neighbourhood with interesting music clubs, cafes and restaurants.

The quiet residential neighbourhoods Makrygianni and Koukaki, south of the Acropolis, around the new Acropolis Museum, are refreshingly untouristy. The commercial district around Omonia was once one of the city's smarter areas, but

espite ongoing efforts to clean it up, it
s still super-seedy, especially at night –
xercise caution. Exarhia, the bohemian
raffiti-covered neighbourhood squashed
etween the Polytechnio and Strefi Hill, is
lively spot popular with students, artists
nd left-wing intellectuals.

The revival of Gazi started with the
ansformation of the historic gasworks
ito a cultural centre. The red neon-lit
himney stacks illuminate the surrounding
treets, packed with bars and restaurants
nd it is one of the burgeoning gay-friendly
eighbourhoods of Athens.

The swank suburbs of Kifisia (inland)
nd Glyfada (seaside) have their own
hopping, cafe and nightlife scenes.

Ancient Ruins

CROPOLIS   Ancient Site
Map p68; 📞 210 321 0219; http://odysseus.
ulture.gr; adult/child €12/6; ⏱ 8am-8pm Apr-Oct,
30am-3pm Nov-Mar; Ⓜ Akropoli) The Acropo-
s is the most important ancient site in the
Vestern world. Crowned by the Parthenon,
stands sentinel over Athens, visible from
most everywhere within the city. Its mon-
ments of Pentelic marble gleam white in
ne midday sun and gradually take on a
oney hue as the sun sinks, while at night
ey stand brilliantly illuminated above the
ty. A glimpse of this magnificent sight
annot fail to exalt your spirit.

Inspiring as these monuments are, they
re but faded remnants of Pericles' city.
ericles spared no expense – only the best
naterials, architects, sculptors and artists
ere good enough for a city dedicated
 the cult of Athena. The city was a
howcase of lavishly coloured colossal
uildings and of gargantuan statues, some
f bronze, others of marble plated with
old and encrusted with precious stones.

There are several approaches to the
te. The main approach from Plaka is
ong the path that is a continuation of
ioskouron. From the south, you can walk
ong Dionysiou Areopagitou to the path
ist beyond the Odeon of Herodes Atticus
 get to the main entrance, or you can go
rough the Theatre of Dionysos entrance
ear the Akropoli metro station, and wind

your way up from there. Anyone carrying a
backpack or large bag (including camera
bags) must enter from the main entrance
and leave bags at the cloakroom.

Arrive as early as possible, or go late
in the afternoon, as it gets incredibly
crowded. Wear shoes with rubber soles –
the paths around the site are uneven
and slippery. People in wheelchairs
can access the site via a cage lift rising
vertically up the rock face on the northern
side. Those needing this service should
present at the main entrance.

HISTORY

The Acropolis was first inhabited in neolithic times (4000–3000 BC). The first
temples were built during the Mycenaean
era in homage to the goddess Athena.
People lived on the Acropolis until the late
6th century BC, but in 510 BC the Delphic
oracle declared that it should be the
province of the gods.

After all the buildings on the Acropolis
were reduced to ashes by the Persians
on the eve of the Battle of Salamis (480
BC), Pericles set about his ambitious
rebuilding program. He transformed the
Acropolis into a city of temples, which
has come to be regarded as the zenith of
classical Greek achievement.

Ravages inflicted upon them during the
years of foreign occupation, pilfering by
foreign archaeologists, inept renovations
following Independence, visitors'
footsteps, earthquakes and, more recently,
acid rain and pollution have all taken their
toll on the surviving monuments. The
worst blow was in 1687 when the Venetians
attacked the Turks, opening fire on the
Acropolis and causing an explosion in the
Parthenon, where the Turks were storing
gunpowder, damaging all the buildings.

Major restoration programs are
continuing and many of the original
sculptures have been moved to the
Acropolis Museum and replaced with
casts. The Acropolis became a World
Heritage–listed site in 1987.

PROPYLAIA

The Propylaia formed the monumental entrance to the Acropolis. Built by

Central Athens

200 m
0.1 miles

PSYRRI

MONASTIRAKI

Monastiraki Flea Market

Ancient Agora

Areopagus Hill

Panepistimiou

Stadiou

Plateia Klafthmonos

SYNTAGMA

PLAKA

Old Athens University

Ancient Agora

Vasileos Georgiou I

Plateia Syntagmatos

Stadiou

Buses to Glyfada

Buses to Cape Sounion

Plateia Rallou Manou

National Gardens

Leoforos Vasilissis Amalias

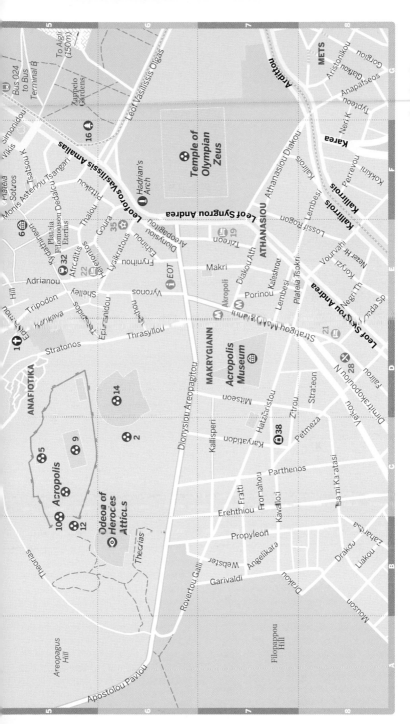

To Aiglí (150m)

Bus 024 to Bus Terminal B

Zappeio Gardens

16

METS

Aristonikou

Giakou

Gorgiou

Anapafseos

Typldou

Neri K

Karea

Temple of Olympian Zeus

Hadrian's Arch

Kallirrois

Kallirrois

Athanasiou Diakou

Kallíou

Lembesi

Lossif Rogon

Perrevou

Kokkini

Leof Syngrou Andrea

ATHANASIOU

Diakou Ath

Vourvahi

Neter Hi

Korýzi

Sp

Efron

Makri

Kaleshtou

Porinou

Lembesi

Platela Tsokri

Negri H

Tzíreon

19

Platela

Monis Sotros

Monis Asterfou Tsatsou K

Sydathineon

6

32

Afroditis

Heforstou

Lysikratous

Goura

35

Dionysiou

Ershinou

Thalou

Frynihou

Pittakou

Leoforos Vasilissis Amalias

Leoforos Vasilissis Olgas

Areopagitou

Eterias

Filomouson Dedalou

Platela

Eratzias

Adrianou

Shelley

Tripodon

Epicharidou

Vyronos

Vyronos

EOT

21

Akropoli

Stratlou Makrlgiann

Akropoli

Stratlou Makrlgiann

28

Falírou

Dimitrakopoulou N

Vellou

Leof Sk,tou Andrea

Flitou Chi

Sodicleous

Kavalava

Stratonos

Thrasyllou

MAKRYGIANN

Acropolis Museum

Mitseon

Stratsen

Zítrou

Petmeza

ANAFIOTIKA

EB

14

Dionysiou Areopagitou

Kallisperi

Hatzihristou

38

Karyatidon

Thecrias

5

9

2

Acropolis

Parthenos

Fratti

Erehthiou

Fromahou

Kavaloi

Sami Karatasi

Zaharitsa

Odeon of Heroes Atticus

10

12

Theorias

Propyleon

Angelikara

Webster

Drakou

Liakou

Areopagus Hill

Apostolou Pavlou

Rovertou Galli

Garivaldi

Drakon

Mouson

Filopappou Hill

69

Central Athens

Mnesicles between 437 BC and 432 BC, its architectural brilliance ranks with that of the Parthenon. It consists of a central hall with two wings on either side. Each section had a gate, and in ancient times these five gates were the only entrances to the 'upper city'. The middle gate (which was the largest) opened onto the Panathenaic Way. The ceiling of the central hall was painted with gold stars on a dark-blue background.

The Propylaia is aligned with the Parthenon – the earliest example of a building designed in relation to another.

TEMPLE OF ATHENA NIKE
The exquisitely proportioned small Temple of Athena Nike stands on a platform perched atop the steep southwest edge of the Acropolis, to the right of the Propylaia. The temple was dismantled piece by piece in 2003 in a controversial move to restore it offsite and is now resplendent after its painstaking reassembly.

Designed by Kallicrates, the temple was built of Pentelic marble between 427 BC and 424 BC. The building is almost square, with four graceful Ionic columns at either end. Only fragments remain of the frieze, which had scenes from mythology, the Battle of Plataea (479 BC) and Athenians fighting Boeotians and Persians. Parts of the frieze are in the Acropolis Museum, as are some relief sculptures, including the beautiful depiction of Athena Nike fastening her sandal. The temple housed a wooden statue of Athena.

PARTHENON

The Parthenon is the monument that more than any other epitomises the glory of Ancient Greece. *Parthenon* means 'virgin's apartment' and it is dedicated to Athena Parthenos, the goddess embodying the power and prestige of the city. The largest Doric temple ever completed in Greece, and the only one built completely of Pentelic marble (apart from the wood in its roof), it took 15 years to complete.

Built on the highest part of the Acropolis, the Parthenon had a dual purpose – to house the great statue of Athena commissioned by Pericles, and to serve as the new treasury. It was built on the site of at least four earlier temples dedicated to Athena. It was designed by Iktinos and Kallicrates to be the pre-eminent monument of the Acropolis and was completed in time for the Great Panathenaic Festival of 438 BC.

The temple consisted of eight fluted Doric columns at either end and 17 on each side. To achieve perfect form, its lines were ingeniously curved to create an optical illusion – the foundations are slightly concave and the columns are slightly convex to make both look straight.

At the eastern end was the holy cella (inner room of a temple), into which only a few privileged initiates could enter. Here stood the statue for which the temple was built – the Athena Polias (Athena of the City), considered one of the wonders of the ancient world. Designed by Pheidias and completed in 432 BC, it was gold plated over an inner wooden frame and stood almost 12m high on its pedestal. In AD 426 the statue was taken to Constantinople, where it disappeared. There is a Roman copy (the Athena Varvakeion) in the National Archaeological Museum.

ERECHTHEION

Although the Parthenon was the most impressive monument of the Acropolis, it was more of a showpiece than a sanctuary. That role fell to the Erechtheion, built on the part of the Acropolis held most sacred, where Poseidon struck the ground with his trident, and where Athena produced the olive tree. Named after Erechtheus, a mythical king of Athens, the temple housed the cults of Athena, Poseidon and Erechtheus.

The Erechtheion is immediately recognisable by the six larger-than-life maiden columns that support its southern portico, the **Caryatids** (so called because they were modelled on women from Karyai, modern-day Karyes, in Lakonia). Those you see are plaster casts. The originals (except for one removed by Lord Elgin, and now in the British Museum) are in the Acropolis Museum.

Architecturally, it is the most unusual monument of the Acropolis, a supreme example of Ionic architecture ingeniously built on several levels to counteract the uneven bedrock.

Six for the Price of One

The €12 Acropolis admission includes entry to Athens' main ancient sites: Ancient Agora, Roman Agora, Keramikos, Temple of Olympian Zeus and Theatre of Dionysos. The ticket is valid for four days; otherwise individual site fees apply (though this is not strictly enforced). The same opening hours (8am to 8pm April to October, 8.30am to 3pm November to March) apply for all of these sites, but it pays to double-check as hours fluctuate from year to year. Enter the sites free on the first Sunday of the month (except for July, August and September) and on certain holidays.

The **northern porch** consists of six Ionic columns; on the floor are the fissures supposedly left by the thunderbolt sent by Zeus to kill King Erechtheus. To the south of here was the Cecropion – King Cecrops' burial place.

SOUTH SLOPE OF THE ACROPOLIS

THEATRE OF DIONYSOS Ancient Site
(Map p68; ☎ 210 322 4625; Dionysiou Areopagitou; admission €2, free with Acropolis Pass; ⏰ 8am-8pm Apr-Oct, 8.30am-3pm Nov-Mar; Ⓜ Akropoli) The importance of theatre in the Athenian city-state can be gauged from the dimensions of the enormous Theatre of Dionysos on the southeastern slope of the Acropolis.

The first theatre on this site was a timber structure erected sometime during the 6th century BC, after the tyrant Peisistratos introduced the Festival of the Great Dionysia. The theatre was reconstructed in stone and marble by Lycurgus between 342 BC and 326 BC, with a seating capacity of 17,000 spread over 64 tiers, of which about 20 survive. Apart from the front row, the seats were built of Piraeus limestone and were occupied by ordinary citizens, although women were confined to the back rows. The front row's 67 **thrones**, built of Pentelic marble, were reserved for festival officials and important priests. The grandest was reserved for the Priest of Dionysos, who sat shaded from the sun under a canopy. His seat can be identified by well-preserved lion-claw feet at either side.

ODEON OF HERODES ATTICUS Ancient Site
West from the Asclepion is the Odeon of Herodes Atticus, built in AD 161 by wealthy Roman Herodes Atticus in memory of his wife Regilla. It was excavated in 1857–58 and completely restored between 1950 and 1961. Performances of drama, music and dance are held here during the Athens Festival (p91).

ANCIENT AGORA Ancient Site
(Market; Map p68; ☎ 210 321 0185; Adrianou; adult/child €4/2, free with Acropolis pass;

🕐 8am-8pm Apr-Oct, 8.30am-
8pm Nov-Mar, museum closed
8-11am Mon; M Monastiraki) The heart
of ancient Athens was the Agora, the
lively, crowded focal point of administrative, commercial, political and social activity. Socrates expounded his philosophy
here, and in AD 49 St Paul came here to
win converts to Christianity.

First developed as a public site in the
5th century BC, the Agora was devastated
by the Persians in 480 BC, but a new one
was built in its place almost immediately.
It was flourishing by Pericles' time and
continued to do so until AD 267, when it
was destroyed by the Herulians, a Gothic
tribe from Scandinavia. The Turks built
a residential quarter on the site, but this
was demolished by archaeologists after
independence and later excavated to
classical and, in parts, neolithic levels.

The site today is a refreshing break
from congested city streets, and is dotted
with beautiful monuments. The most
convenient entrance is the northern one
from Adrianou.

STOA OF ATTALOS

The Stoa of Attalos was the first-ever
shopping arcade. Built by its namesake
King Attalos II of Pergamum (159–138
BC), this majestic two-storey stoa has 45
Doric columns on the ground floor and
Ionic columns on the upper gallery.

The excellent **Agora Museum**, inside
the stoa, is a good place to start to make
sense of the site. The museum has a
model of the Agora as well as a collection
of finds from the site.

TEMPLE OF HEPHAESTUS

The best-preserved Doric temple in
Greece, this gem on the western edge of
the Agora was dedicated to Hephaestus,
god of the forge, and was surrounded by
foundries and metalwork shops. Built in
449 BC by Iktinos, one of the architects
of the Parthenon, it has 34 columns and
a frieze on the eastern side depicting nine
of the Twelve Labours of Heracles.

73

CHURCH OF THE HOLY APOSTLES
This charming little church, near the southern entrance, was built in the early 10th century to commemorate St Paul's teaching in the Agora. It contains some fine Byzantine frescoes.

KERAMIKOS Ancient Site
(Map p75; ☏ 210 346 3552; Ermou 148, Keramikos; adult/child incl museum €2/free, free with Acropolis pass; ⊗8am-8pm Apr-Oct, 8.30am-3pm Nov-Mar; Ⓜ Thisio) The city's cemetery from the 12th century BC to Roman times, Keramikos was originally a settlement for potters who were attracted by the clay on the banks of the River Iridanos. Because of frequent flooding, the area was ultimately converted to a cemetery. Rediscovered in 1861 during the construction of Pireos St, Keramikos is now a lush, tranquil site with a fine museum. Head for the small knoll, where you'll find a plan of the site.

TEMPLE OF OLYMPIAN ZEUS Landmark, Ruins
(Map p68; ☏ 210 922 6330; adult/child €2/free, free with Acropolis pass; ⊗8am-8pm Apr-Oct, 8.30am-3pm Nov-Mar; Ⓜ Syntagma) You can't miss this striking marvel, smack in the centre of Athens. It is the largest temple in Greece and was begun in the 6th century BC by Peisistratos, but was abandoned for lack of funds. Various other leaders had stabs at completing it, but it was left to Hadrian to complete the work in AD 131. In total, it took more than 700 years to build.

The temple is impressive for the sheer size of its 104 Corinthian columns (17m high with a base diameter of 1.7m), of which 15 remain – the fallen column was blown down in a gale in 1852. Hadrian put a colossal statue of Zeus in the cella and, in typically immodest fashion, placed an equally large one of himself next to it.

Museums & Galleries

BYZANTINE & CHRISTIAN MUSEUM Religious Museum
(Map pp52-3; ☏ 210 721 1027; www.byzantinemuseum.gr; Leoforos Vasilissis Sofias 22, Kolonaki; adult/child €4/free; ⊗8am-8pm Tue-Sun May-Oct, 8.30am-3pm Tue-Sun Nov-Apr; Ⓜ Evangelismos) This outstanding museum presents a priceless collection of Christian art, dating from the 3rd to the 20th centuries. Thematic snapshots of the Byzantine and post-Byzantine world – a part of Greek history that is often ignored in favour of its ancient past – are exceptionally presented in the expansive multilevel underground galleries. The collection includes icons, frescoes, sculptures, textiles, manuscripts, vestments and mosaics.

NATIONAL ART GALLERY Art Museum
(☏ 210 723 5857; www.nationalgallery.gr; Leoforos Vasileos Konstantinou 50, Kolonaki; adult/child €6.50/free; ⊗9am-3pm Mon & Wed-Sat, 10am-2pm Sun; Ⓜ Evangelismos) Greece's national art museum presents a rich collection of Greek art spanning four centuries from the post-Byzantine period. The newer wing houses its permanent collection and traces the key art movements chronologically. The 1st floor includes the post-Byzantine period, the gallery's prized El Greco paintings, including *The Crucifixion* and *Symphony of the Angels,* and works from the Ionian period until 1900. The 2nd floor holds leading 20th-century artists, including Parthenis, Moralis, Maleas and Lytras. The gallery also has works by European masters, including paintings by Picasso, and hosts major international exhibitions.

Hills of Athens

LYKAVITTOS HILL Landmark, Park
(Map pp52-3; Ⓜ Evangelismos) Lykavittos means 'Hill of Wolves' and derives from ancient times when the hill was surrounded by countryside and its pine-covered slopes were inhabited by wolves. Today the hill rises out of a sea of concrete to offer the finest panoramas of the city. A path leads to the summit from the top of Loukianou. Alternatively, take the **funicular railway** (☏ 210 721 0701; return €6; ⊗9am-3am, half-hourly), referred to as the *teleferik,* from the top of Ploutarhou in Kolonaki. Perched on the summit is the little **Chapel of Agios Georgios**, floodlit like a beacon over the city at night.

FILOPAPPOU HILL Landmark, Park
(Map pp52-3; Ⓜ Akropoli) Also called the Hill of the Muses, Filopappou is identifiable

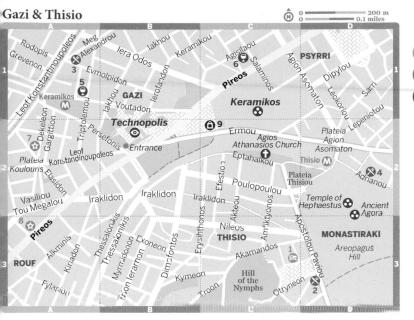

Gazi & Thisio

to the southwest of the Acropolis by the **Monument of Filopappos** at its summit. The monument was built between AD 114 and AD 116 in honour of Julius Antiochus Filopappos, who was a prominent Roman consul and administrator.

The pine-clad slopes are a pleasant place for a stroll, and offer good views of the plain and mountains of Attica and of the Saronic Gulf, and some of the best vantage points for photographing the Acropolis. Small paths weave all over the hill, but the paved path to the top starts near the *periptero* (kiosk) on Dionysiou Areopagitou. After

250m, the path passes the **Church of Agios Dimitrios Loumbardiaris** which contains fine frescoes.

Parks & Gardens

NATIONAL GARDENS   Park, Garden
(Map p68; entrances on Leoforos Vasilissis Sofias & Leoforos Vasilissis Amalias, Syntagma; ◷7am-dusk; ⓜSyntagma) A delightful refuge, the National Gardens were formerly the royal gardens designed by Queen Amalia. There's also a large children's **playground**, a duck pond and a shady **cafe**.

BILL BACHMANN/ALAMY

Don't Miss **Acropolis Museum**

The long-awaited Acropolis Museum opened with much fanfare in 2009 in the southern foothills of the Acropolis. Ten times larger than the former on-site museum, the imposing modernist building brings together the surviving treasures of the Acropolis, including items formerly held in other museums or storage, as well as pieces returned from foreign museums. While the collection covers the Archaic and Roman periods, the emphasis is on the Acropolis of the 5th century BC, considered the apotheosis of Greece's artistic achievement.

Beneath the entrance you can see the ruins of an ancient Athenian neighbourhood, which have been cleverly incorporated into the museum design after being uncovered during excavations.

Finds from the slopes of the Acropolis are on display in the first gallery, which has an ascending glass floor that emulates the climb up to the sacred hill, while allowing glimpses of the ruins below. Exhibits include painted vases and votive offerings from the sanctuaries where gods were worshipped, and more recent objects found in excavations of the settlement, including two clay statues of Nike at the entrance.

Bathed in natural light, the 1st-floor **Archaic Gallery** is a veritable forest of statues, mostly votive offerings to Athena. The museum's crowning glory is the top-floor **Parthenon Gallery**, a glass atrium built in alignment with the temple, and a virtual replica of the cella of the Parthenon, which can be seen from the gallery. It showcases the temple's sculptures, metopes and 160m frieze, which for the first time in more than 200 years is shown in sequence as one narrative about the Panathenaic Procession.

THINGS YOU NEED TO KNOW

Map p68; 210 900 0901; www.theacropolismuseum.gr; Dionysiou Areopagitou 15, Akropoli; 8am-8pm Tue-Sun, to 10pm Fri; admission €5; M Akropoli

ZAPPEIO GARDENS   Garden

Map p68; www.zappeion.gr; entrances on
Leoforos Vasilissis Amalias & Leoforos Vasilissis
Olgas, Syntagma; M Syntagma) These gardens
sit between the National Gardens and the
Panathenaic Stadium and are laid out in
a network of wide walkways around the
grand **Zappeio Palace**. The palace was
built in the 1870s for the forerunner of the
modern Olympics, with money donated by
the wealthy Greek-Romanian benefactor
Konstantinos Zappas. The Zappeio hosts
conferences, events and exhibitions, and
there's a pleasant cafe, restaurant and
open-air **Aigli cinema** next door.

Other Attractions

PARLIAMENT   Notable Building

Map pp52-3; Plateia Syntagmatos, Syntagma;
M Syntagma) Designed by the Bavarian
architect Von Gartner and built between
1836 and 1842, Greece's Parliament was
originally the royal palace. The **Tomb of
the Unknown Soldier**, a war memorial
in the forecourt of Parliament building, is
guarded by the city's famous statuesque
evzones, the presidential guards whose
uniform of short kilts and pom-pom
shoes is based on the attire worn by the
klephts (the mountain fighters of the War
of Independence). The **changing of the
guard** takes place every hour, while every
Sunday at 11am the *evzones* perform an
extended ceremony in full dress, accompanied by a military band.

TURKISH BATHS   Bathhouse

Map p68, ☎ 210 324 4340; Kyrristou 8,
Plaka; admission €2; �
9am-2.30pm Wed-Mon;
M Monastiraki) This beautifully refurbished
17th-century bathhouse is the only surviving public bathhouse in Athens and one
of the few remnants of Ottoman times. A
helpful free audio tour takes you back to
the bathhouse days.

PLANETARIUM   Planetarium

☎ 210 946 9600; www.eugenfound.edu.gr; Leoforos Syngrou 387, Palio Faliro; adult €6-8, child
€4-5; �
5.30-8.30pm Wed-Fri, 10.30am-8.30pm
Sat & Sun, closed mid-Jul–late Aug) Athens
boasts the world's largest and most technologically advanced digital planetarium.

Detour:
Hellenic Cosmos

To put ruins and museums into
perspective, take a virtual-reality
trip to Ancient Greece at the
futuristic **Foundation for the
Hellenic World** (☎ 212 254 0000;
www.hellenic-cosmos.gr; Pireos 254,
Tavros; per show adult €5-10, child €3-8,
day-pass adult/child €15/12; �
9am-4pm
Mon-Fri, 10am-3pm Sun, closed 2 weeks
mid-Aug; M Kalithea), about 2km
southwest of the city centre. The
Tholos virtual-reality theatre takes
you on an interactive tour of the
Ancient Agora or allows you to get
a feel for life in ancient Athens.
The **Kivotos time machine** has 3D
floor-to-ceiling screens with a live
guide taking you through ancient
Olympia and Miletus. Take bus 049
or 914 from Omonia, or the metro
to Kalithea.

The 280-seat planetarium, with a 950-sq-
m hemispherical dome, offers 3D virtual
trips to the galaxy, as well as IMAX movies
and other high-tech shows. There is simul-
taneous narration in English (€1).

Beaches

Athens is the only European capital with
beaches within easy distance of the city
centre. **Glyfada**, about 17km southeast of
Athens, marks the beginning of a stretch of
coastline known as the Apollo Coast, which
has a string of fine beaches and upmarket
resorts running south to Cape Sounion.
This is where Athenians cool off and where
much of the summer nightlife takes place.

The better beaches are privately run
and charge admission (€4 to €15 per
adult). They're usually open between
8am and dusk, May to October (later
during heatwaves), and have sun beds

AEGEANPHOTO/ALAM

Don't Miss National Archaeological Museum

One of the world's most important museums, the National Archaeological Museum houses the finest collection of Greek antiquities. With 10,000 sq m of exhibition space, it could take several visits to appreciate the museum's vast holdings, but it is possible to see the highlights in a half-day.

The fabulous collection of **Mycenaean antiquities** (Gallery 4) is the museum's tour de force. The first cabinet holds the celebrated **Mask of Agamemnon**, unearthed at Mycenae by Heinrich Schliemann, along with key finds from Grave Circle A, including bronze daggers with intricate representations of the hunt. The exquisite **Vaphio gold cups**, with scenes of men taming wild bulls, are regarded as among the finest surviving examples of Mycenaean art.

The **Cycladic collection** (Gallery 6) includes the superb figurines of the 3rd and 2nd centuries BC that inspired artists such as Picasso.

Backtrack and enter the galleries to the left of the entrance, which house the oldest and most significant pieces of the **sculpture collection**. Head upstairs to the museum's other big crowd-puller, the spectacular **Minoan frescoes** from Santorini (Thira).

THINGS YOU NEED TO KNOW

off Map p80; ☎ 210 821 7717; www.namuseum.gr; 28 Oktovriou-Patision 44, Exarhia; adult/child €7/free; ⏱ 1.30-8pm Mon, 8am-8pm Tue-Sun Apr-Oct, 8.30am-3pm Nov-Mar; Ⓜ Viktoria

and umbrellas (additional charge in some places), changing rooms, children's playgrounds and cafes.

The flashiest and most exclusive summer playground is **Astir Beach** (☎ 210 890 1621; www.astir-beach.com; adult/child €15/8 Mon-Fri, €25/13 Sat & Sun), with water

sports, shops and restaurants. You can even book online.

The following can be reached by tram and then buses from Glyfada or Voula:

Akti Tou Iliou (☎ 210 985 5169; Alimo; adult/child €6/3 Mon-Fri, €8/4 Sat & Sun)

Asteras Beach (210 894 1620; www.asterascomplex.com; Glyfada; adult/child €6/3 Mon-Fri, €7/3 Sat & Sun)

Yabanaki (210 897 2414; www.yabanaki.gr; Varkiza; adult/child €7/4.50 Mon-Fri, €8/4.50 Sat & Sun)

There are free beaches at Palio Faliro (Edem), Kavouri and Glyfada. You can swim year-round at **Limni Vouliagmenis** (Map p96; 210 896 2239; Leoforos Vouliagmenis; adult/child €8/5; 7am-8pm), a part-saltwater/part-springwater lake whose temperature usually doesn't fall below 20°C, and which is known for its therapeutic mineral qualities.

Tours

CITYSIGHTSEEING ATHENS Bus Tours
(Map p68; 210 922 0604; www.city-sightseeing.com; Plateia Syntagmatos, Syntagma; adult/child €18/8; every 30min 9am-8pm; Syntagma) Open-top double-decker buses cruise around town on a 90-minute circuit starting at Syntagma. You can get on and off at 15 stops on a 24-hour ticket.

ATHENS HAPPY TRAIN Mini-Train Tours
(Map p68; 210 725 5400; www.athenshappytrain.com; Plateia Syntagmatos, Syntagma; adult/child €6/4; 9am-midnight; Syntagma) Mini-train tours, with stops including the Acropolis, Monastiraki and the Panathenaic Stadium. Tours take one hour if you don't get off, or you can get on and off over five hours. Trains leave from the top of Ermou every 30 minutes.

TREKKING HELLAS Excursions
(210 331 0323; www.trekking.gr; Rethymnou 2, Exarhia; Viktoria) Activities range from Athens walking tours (€22) to two-hour hike tours (€35) and bungee jumping in the Corinth Canal (€60).

Sleeping

Plaka & Syntagma

NEW Boutique Hotel €€€
(Map p68; 210 628 4565; www.yeshotels.gr; Filellinon 16, Plaka; s/d from 150/160, ste 240;

(; Syntagma) The swanky and chic NEW just opened smack in the middle of Athens. Whether you dig the groovy, top-designer Campana Brothers furniture or the pillow menu (tell 'em how you like it!), you'll find some sort of decadent treat here to tickle your fancy. Part of a renowned local design hotel group, NEW is the latest entry on the high-end Athens scene.

ELECTRA PALACE Luxury Hotel €€€
(Map p68; 210 337 0000; www.electrahotels.gr; Navarhou Nikodimou 18, Plaka; s/d/ste incl breakfast from €160/180/295; (@ ; Syntagma) Plaka's smartest hotel is one for the romantics. You can have breakfast under the Acropolis on your balcony (higher-end rooms), and dinner in the chic rooftop restaurant. Completely refurbished with classic elegance, the well-appointed rooms are buffered from the sounds of the city streets. There is a gym, an indoor swimming pool as well as a rooftop pool with Acropolis views.

HOTEL PHAEDRA Hotel €
(Map p68; 210 323 8461; www.hotelphaedra.com; Herefontos 16, Plaka; s/d/tr €80/80/95; @ ; Akropoli) Many of the rooms at this small, family-run hotel have balconies overlooking a church or the Acropolis. The hotel is tastefully furnished, though room sizes vary from small to snug. Some

---

What's on in Athens

For comprehensive events listings in English, with links to online ticket-sales points, try the following:

○ **www.breathtakingathens.gr** Athens tourism site.

○ **www.elculture.gr** Arts and culture listings, in Greek.

○ **www.tickethour.com** Also has sports matches.

○ **www.tickethouse.gr** Rockwave and other festivals.

○ **www.ticketservices.gr** Range of events.

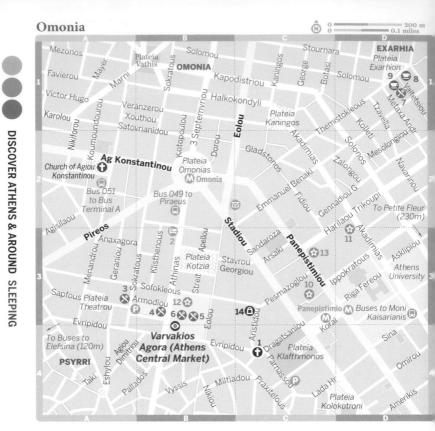

rooms have private bathrooms across the hall. A great rooftop terrace, friendly staff and a good location make this one of the better deals in Plaka.

Monastiraki & Thisio

MAGNA GRECIA Boutique Hotel €€
(Map p68; ☎ 210 324 0314; www.magnagrecia hotel.com; Mitropoleos 54, Monastiraki; s €110 d €135-180, all incl breakfast; ❄ ☎; M Monastiraki) This intimate boutique hotel, in a restored historic building opposite the cathedral, has magnificent Acropolis views from the front rooms and rooftop terrace. Each of the 12 individually decorated rooms with murals are named after Greek islands, and offer excellent amenities, including comfortable mattresses, DVD players and minibars. Staff are friendly and the hotel is dripping with character.

HOTEL ERECHTHION Hotel €
(Map p75; ☎ 210 345 9606; www.hotelerech thion.gr; Flammarion 8, cnr Agias Marinas, Thisio; s/d/tr incl breakfast €40/70/100; ❄ ☎; M Thisio) Simple, clean rooms with TVs, refrigerators, veneer furniture and basic bathrooms are not the highlights here. Much more impressive are the fantastic Acropolis views from the balconies, the low price and the great neighbourhood.

Omonia & Exarhia

BABY GRAND HOTEL Boutique Hotel €€
(Map p80; ☎ 210 325 0900; www.classicalhotels. com; Athinas 65, Omonia; s/d incl breakfast from €92/100; ❄ @ ☎; M Omonia) A reception desk created out of two Mini Coopers sets the tone for this fun hotel with original murals throughout. Individually decked-out rooms have iPod docking stations and

Omonia

designer furniture, plus anything from chandeliers to faux animal skins.

Makrygianni & Koukaki

ATHENS GATE Business Hotel €€
(Map p68; 210 923 8302; www.athensgate.gr; Leoforos Syngrou 10, Makrygianni; r incl breakfast €110-185; ✳ @ 🛜; M Akropoli) With stunning views over the Temple of Olympian Zeus from the spacious front rooms, and a central (if busy) location, this totally refurbished hotel is a great find. The chic, stylish rooms are immaculate and have all the mod cons, staff are friendly and breakfast is served on the superb rooftop terrace with 360-degree Athens views.

HERA HOTEL Boutique Hotel €€
(Map p68; 210 923 6682; www.herahotel.gr; Falirou 9, Makrygianni; s/d from €110/130, ste incl breakfast from €250; ✳ @ 🛜; M Akropoli) This elegant boutique hotel, a short walk from the Acropolis and Plaka, was totally rebuilt but the formal interior design is in keeping with the lovely neoclassical

facade. There's lots of brass and timber, and stylish classic furnishings. The rooftop garden, restaurant and bar have spectacular views.

MARBLE HOUSE PENSION Pension €
(210 923 4058; www.marblehouse.gr; Zini 35a, Koukaki; s/d/tr €39/49/59, d/tr without bathroom €45/55; ✳ 🛜; M Syngrou-Fix) Tucked into a quiet cul-de-sac is one of Athens' best-value budget hotels. Rooms have been artfully updated, with wrought-iron beds, and bathrooms have just had a sleek marble makeover. All rooms have a fridge and ceiling fans and some have air-con (€9 extra). It is a fair walk from the tourist drag, but close to the metro.

Kolonaki & Pangrati

PERISCOPE Boutique Hotel €€
(210 729 7200; www.periscope.gr; Haritos 22, Kolonaki; s/d/ste incl breakfast from €126/140/210; ✳ 🛜; M Evangelismos) Right in chic Kolonaki overlooking Lykavittos, Periscope is a chic hotel with industrial decor. Clever gadgets are sprinkled throughout including the lobby slide show, the sea-level measure on the stairs, and aerial shots of the city on the ceilings. Korres organic toiletries and the hip new restaurant, **Pbox**, add to the vibe. The penthouse's private rooftop spa has sensational views.

 Eating

Plaka & Syntagma

TZITZIKAS & MERMINGAS Taverna, Mezedhes €
(Map p68; 210 324 7607; Mitropoleos 12-14, Syntagma; mezedhes €6-11; M Syntagma) Greek merchandise lines the walls of this cheery, modern mezedhopoleio that sits smack in the middle of downtown. It serves up a tasty range of delicious and creative mezedhes (like the honey-drizzled, bacon-wrapped cheese) to a bustling crowd of locals.

MONO Fine Dining €
(off Map p68; 210 322 6711; Paleologou Venizelou 4, Plaka; mains €8-15; ⊙ Mon-Sat; M Monastiraki) This swishy taverna, on the

If You Like...
Byzantine Bling

If you like the frescoes and glittering collection at the Byzantine & Christian Museum, we think you'll like these amazing Byzantine churches:

1 **CHURCH OF AGII THEODORI**
(Map p80; cnr Dragatsaniou & Agion Theodoron, Syntagma; M Panepistimio) This 11th-century church behind Plateia Klafthmonos has a tiled dome and walls decorated with a pretty terracotta frieze of animals and plants.

2 **AGIOS NIKOLAOS RANGAVAS**
(Map p68; cnr Prytaniou & Epiharmou, Plaka; M Akropoli) This lovely 11th-century church was part of the palace of the Rangavas family, who counted among them Michael I, emperor of Byzantium. The church bell was the first installed in Athens after liberation from the Turks (who banned them), and was the first to ring in 1833 to announce the freedom of Athens.

3 **CHURCH OF SOTIRA LYKODIMOU**
(Map p68; Plateia Rallou Manou, Plaka; M Syntagma) Now the Russian Orthodox Cathedral, this unique 11th-century church is the only octagonal Byzantine church and has an imposing dome.

outskirts of Plaka near the cathedral, is one of the new breed of restaurants serving refined contemporary Greek cuisine. Decor is subtle Greek chic with splashes of orange and fresh-cut flowers, there's a lovely courtyard, and the presentation and ambience are top-rate.

PURE BLISS Cafe €
(Map p68; 210 325 0360; www.purebliss.gr; Romvis 24a, Syntagma; items €3-9; 10am-1am Mon-Sat, 5-9pm Sun; ; M Syntagma) Enjoy the laid-back vibe at one of the few places in Athens where you can get organic fair-trade coffee, exotic teas and soy products. There's a range of healthy salads, sandwiches, smoothies and mostly organic food, wine and cocktails.

PALIA TAVERNA TOU PSARA Taverna, Seafood €€
(Map p68; 210 321 8734; Erehtheos 16, Plaka; mains €12-24; M Akropoli) Away from the main hustle and bustle of Plaka, this taverna is a cut above the rest, which is why they fill the tables on the street, the terrace and the place next door. There is a choice of mezedhes but it is known as the best seafood taverna in Plaka (top fresh fish €65 per kilogram).

Monastiraki & Thisio

CAFÉ AVYSSINIA Fine Dining €€
(Map p68; 210 321 7047; www.avissinia .gr; Kynetou 7, Monastiraki; mains €10-16; 11am-1am Tue-Sat, 11am-7pm Sun; M Monastiraki) Hidden away on colourful Plateia Avyssinias, in the middle of the flea market, this bohemian mezedhopoleio gets top marks for atmosphere, food and friendly service. It specialises in regional Greek cuisine, from warm fava to eggplants baked with tomato and cheese, and has a great selection of ouzo, raki (Cretan firewater) and tsipouro (distilled spirit similar to ouzo but usually stronger). There is often acoustic live music, from Manos Hatzidakis to rembetika (blues). Snag fantastic Acropolis views from the bistro seats upstairs.

KUZINA Taverna €€
(Map p75; 210 324 0133; www.kuzina.gr; Adrianou 9, Monastiraki; mains €12-25; Tue-Sun; M Thisio) Light streams through the plate-glass windows here, warming the crowded tables in winter. Or, eat outside on pedestrianised people-watching Adrianou in summer. The modern mood and music set the tone for inventive Greek fusion, like Cretan pappardelle or chicken with figs and sesame.

FILISTRON Mezedhes €€
(Map p75; 210 346 7554; Apostolou Pavlou 23, Thisio; mezedhes €8-14; Tue-Sun; M Thisio) It's wise to book a prized table on the rooftop terrace of this excellent mezedhopoleio, which enjoys breathtaking Acropolis and Lykavittos views. Specialising in regional cuisine, it has a great range of tasty mezedhes – try the grilled

vegetables with haloumi (€11) or the Mytiline onions stuffed with rice and mince. There's also an extensive Greek wine list worth working your work through.

Gazi & Rouf

KANELLA Taverna €

(Map p75; ☏ 210 347 6320; Leoforos Konstantinoupoleos 70, Gazi; dishes €7-10; ⏱1.30pm-late; Ⓜ Keramikos) Homemade village-style bread, mismatched retro crockery and brown-paper tablecloths set the tone for this trendy, modern taverna serving regional Greek cuisine. Friendly staff serve daily specials such as lemon lamb with potatoes, and an excellent zucchini and avocado salad.

Omonia & Exarhia

VARVAKIOS AGORA Market €

(Athens Central Market; Map p80; Athinas, Omonia; ⏱ Mon-Sat; Ⓜ Monastiraki)The streets around the colourful and bustling Varvakios Agora are a sensory delight. The meat and fish market fills the historic building on the eastern side, and the fruit and vegetable market is across the road. The meat and fish market might sound like a strange place to go for a meal, but the tavernas here, such as **Papandreou**

(Map p80; ☏ 213 008 2297; Aristogitonos 1; mains €7-8; ⏱24hr), are an Athenian institution, turning out huge quantities of tasty, traditional fare.

DIPORTO AGORAS Taverna €

(Map p80; ☏ 210 321 1463; cnr Theatrou & Sokratous, Omonia; plates €5-6; ⏱8am-6pm Mon-Sat, closed first 3 weeks Aug; Ⓜ Monastiraki) This quirky old taverna is one of the dining gems of Athens. There's no signage, only two doors leading to a rustic cellar where there's no menu, just a few dishes that haven't changed in years. The house speciality is *revythia* (chickpeas), usually followed by grilled fish and washed down with wine from one of the giant barrels lining the wall. The often-erratic service is part of the appeal.

ROZALIA Taverna €

(Map p80; ☏ 210 330 2933; Valtetsiou 58, Exarhia; mains €5-11; Ⓜ Omonia) An old-style Exarhia favourite on a lively pedestrian strip, this family-run taverna serves grills and home-style fare such as *pastitsio* (layers of buttery macaroni and seasoned minced lamb). Large courtyard/garden fans spray water to keep you cool.

Market stall in Omonia

Makrygianni & Koukaki

MANI MANI Taverna €€

(Map p68; ☎210 921 8180; www.manimani.
com.gr; Falirou 10, Makrygianni; mains €9.50-16;
⏱3pm-12.30am Tue-Thu, from 1pm Fri & Sat,
1-5.30pm Sun, closed Jul & Aug; MAkropoli)
Forgo a view and head upstairs to the
relaxing dining rooms of this delightful
modern restaurant, which specialises in
regional cuisine from Mani in the Peloponnese. The ravioli with Swiss chard, chervil
and cheese, and the tangy Mani sausage
with orange are standouts. It's great value
and almost all starters and mains can be
ordered as half-serves (at half-price), allowing you to try a range of dishes.

Kolonaki & Pangrati

SPONDI Fine Dining €€€

(☎210 752 0658; Pironos 5, Pangrati; mains
€35-50; ⏱8pm-late) Two Michelin–starred
Spondi is consistently voted Athens' best
restaurant, and the accolades are totally
deserved. It offers Mediterranean haute
cuisine, with heavy French influences, in
a relaxed, chic setting in a charming old
house. Choose from the menu or a range
of set dinner and wine *prix fixes*. The restaurant has a lovely bougainvillea-draped
garden.

ALATSI Cretan €€

(☎210 721 0501; Vrasida 13, Ilissia; mains €12-
16.50; MEvangelismos) Cretan food is in.

Alatsi represents the new breed of trendy
upscale restaurants, serving traditional
Cretan cuisine, such as *gamopilafo* (wedding pilaf) with lamb or rare *stamnagathi*
(wild greens), to fashionable Athenians.
The food and service are excellent. Find it
near the Hilton.

Drinking

Expect bars to begin filling after 11pm and
stay open till late. Right now, Gazi has the
most action, while Kolonaki steadfastly
attracts the trendier set.

HOXTON Bar

(Map p75; Voutadon 42; MKeramikos) Join the
hip, artsy crowd for shoulder-to-shoulder
hobnobbing amidst original art, iron
beams and leather sofas.

NIXON BAR Bar

(Map p75; Agisilaou 61b; MThisio) More chic
than most, Nixon Bar serves up food and
cocktails and sits next door to swinging
Belafonte.

CITY Bar

(Haritos 43; MEvangelismos) One of the best
bars on hopping Haritos, City makes an
excellent *mastiha* (liquor seasoned with
mastic resin) cocktail.

Street Food

From vendors selling *koulouria* (fresh pretzel-style bread) and grilled corn or
chestnuts, to the raft of fast-food offerings, there's no shortage of snacks on the
run in Athens.

You can't go wrong with local *tiropites* (cheese pies) and their various
permutations. **Ariston** (Map p68; ☎210 322 7626; Voulis 10, Syntagma; pies €1.40-2;
⏱10am-4pm Mon-Fri; MSyntagma) has been around since 1910, serving a great
range of tasty, freshly baked pies with all manner of fillings.

Greece's favourite savoury snack is **souvlaki**, packing more punch for €2.50
than anything else. You can't miss the aroma wafting from the souvlaki hub at
Monastiraki, but you'll find one of the best souvlaki joints in Athens nearby at
tiny **Kostas** (Map p68; ☎210 323 2971; Plateia Agia Irini 2, Monastiraki; souvlaki €2; ⏱5am-
5pm; MMonastiraki). In a pleasant square opposite Agia Irini church, Kostas churns
out tasty pork souvlakia and kebabs, with their signature spicy tomato sauce.

BRETTOS
Bar

(Map p68; Kydathineon 41, Plaka; M Akropoli)
You won't find any happening bars in
Plaka, but Brettos is a delightful old bar
and distillery, with a stunning wall of
colourful bottles and huge barrels. Sample shots of their home brands of wine,
ouzo, brandy and other spirits.

 # Entertainment

English-language entertainment information appears daily in the *Kathimerini*
supplement in the *International Herald
Tribune; Athens News* and *Athens Plus*
also have listings. Check out entertainment websites (see boxed text, p79)
for events and concerts around town.

Nightclubs

Athens' famous nightlife heats up
after midnight. Admission usually
ranges from €10 to €15 and includes
one drink. Most top clubs close in
summer or move to outdoor venues
by the beach.

VENUE
Club

(Map p75; ☎ 210 341 1410; www.venue
club.com; Pireos 130, Rouf; ☺ Sep-May;
M Keramikos) Arguably the city's biggest dance club with the biggest dance
parties by the world's biggest DJs. The
three-stage dance floor jumps.

ETOM
Club

(Map p75; ☎ 699 224 0000; Dekeloon 26, Gazi;
M Keramikos) Late-night clubbers flock
to dance parties at this trendy club, with
its giant mirrorball elephant, top line-up
of international and local DJs, and gay-friendly, hip young crowd.

VITRINE
Club

(☎ 210 924 2444; www.vitrine.gr; Markou Mou-
rourou 1, Mets; ☺ Oct-Jun; M Akropoli) A firm
favourite among downtown nightspots
with Acropolis and city views from the top.

SUMMER CLUBS

Athens has some excellent open-air
venues, but in summer much of the city's

If You Like...
Art & Artefacts

If you like the impressive sculptures
and artefacts housed in the National
Archaeological Museum, we think you'll like
what you find in these museums, too:

1 **BENAKI MUSEUM**
(Map pp52-3; www.benaki.gr; Koumbari 1, cnr
Leoforos Vasilissis Sofias, Kolonaki; adult/child €6/
free, free Thu; ☺ 9am-5pm Mon, Wed, Fri & Sat, 9am-
midnight Thu, 9am-3pm Sun; M Syntagma) Greece's
finest private museum contains the vast collection
of Antonis Benakis, including Bronze Age finds from
Mycenae and Thessaly, works by El Greco and a
stunning collection of Greek regional costumes.

2 **MUSEUM OF CYCLADIC ART**
(Map pp52-3; www.cycladic.gr; Neofytou Douka 4,
cnr Leoforos Vasilissis Sofias, Kolonaki; adult/child €7/
free; ☺ 10am-5pm Mon, Wed, Fri & Sat, 10am-8pm Thu,
11am-5pm Sun; M Evangelismos) This private museum
houses an outstanding collection of Cycladic art. The
1st-floor collection, dating from 3000 BC to 2000 BC,
includes the marble figurines that inspired many 20th-
century artists, like Picasso and Modigliani, with their
simplicity and purity of form. The rest of the museum
features Greek and Cypriot art dating from 2000 BC
to the 4th century AD.

3 **PIRAEUS ARCHAEOLOGICAL MUSEUM**
(Map p94; Harilaou Trikoupi 31, Piraeus;
admission €3; ☺ 8.30am-3pm Tue-Sun) This
museum's star attraction is the magnificent statue
of Apollo, the *Piraeus Kouros*, the larger-than-life,
oldest hollow bronze statue yet found. It dates
from about 520 BC and was discovered in Piraeus,
buried in rubble, in 1959.

serious nightlife moves to glamorous,
massive seafront clubs. Many are on the
tram route, which runs to 2.30am on Friday and Saturday. If you book for dinner
you don't pay cover; otherwise admission
usually ranges from €10 to €20, and
includes one drink. Glam-up to ensure
you get in.

AKROTIRI
Club

(210 985 9147; www.akrotirilounge.gr; Vasileos Georgiou B 5, Agios Kosmas) This top beach club holds 3000, in bars, a restaurant and lounges over different levels. Jamming party nights bring top resident and visiting DJs. Pool parties rock during the day.

BALUX
Club

(210 894 1620; www.baluxcafe.com; Leoforos Poseidonos 58, Glyfada) This glamorous club/restaurant/lounge right on the beach has poolside chaises, four-poster beds with flowing nets, and a night-time line-up of top DJs next door at **Akanthus** (210 968 0800; www.akanthus.gr).

ISLAND
Club

(210 965 3563; www.islandclubrestaurant.gr; Varkiza, 27th km, Athens-Sounion road) Dreamy classic summer club/restaurant on the seaside with superb island decor.

Live Music

GAGARIN 205 CLUB
Rock

(www.gagarin205.gr; Liosion 205, Thymarakia; M Agios Nikolaos) Friday and Saturday night gigs feature leading rock and underground bands. Advance tickets at **Ticket House** (Map p80; 210 360 8366; www.tickethouse.gr; Panepistimiou 42, Syntagma; M Panepistimio).

HALF NOTE JAZZ CLUB
Jazz

(210 921 3310; www.halfnote.gr; Trivonianou 17, Mets; M Akropoli) Athens' stylish, principal and most serious jazz venue hosts an array of international musicians. Near Athens' cemetery.

ALAVASTRO CAFÉ
Live Music

(210 756 0102; Damareos 78, Pangrati) A mix of modern jazz, ethnic and quality Greek music in a casual, intimate setting.

STOA ATHANATON
Rembetika Club

(Map p80; 210 321 4362; Sofokleous 19, Omonia; 3-6pm & midnight-6am Mon-Sat, closed Jun-Sep; M Omonia) This legendary club occupies a hall above the central meat market. Popular for classic *rembetika* and *laïka* (urban popular music) from a respected band of musicians, it often starts from mid afternoon. Access is by a lift in the arcade.

PERIVOLI TOU OURANOU
Rembetika Club

(Map p68; 210 323 5517; Lysikratous 19, Plaka; 9pm-late Thu-Sun, closed Jul-Sep; M Akropol A favourite rustic, old-style Plaka music haunt with dinner (mains €18 to €29) an *laïka* and *rembetika*.

Classical Music & Opera

MEGARON MOUSIKIS
Performing Art

(Athens Concert Hall; 210 728 2333; www.megaron.gr; Kokkali 1, cnr Leoforos Vasilissis Sofias Ilissia; box office 10am-6pm Mon-Fri, 10am-2pm Sat; M Megaro Mousikis) The city's state-of-the-art concert hall presents a rich winte program of operas and concerts featuring world-class international and Greek performers.

Making cookies at the Hellenic Children Museum
ANDERS BLOMQVIST/LONELY PLANET IMAGES ©

Athens for Children

Athens is short on playgrounds but there is plenty to keep kids amused. The shady **National Gardens** (p75) has a playground, duck pond and mini-zoo. There is also a fully enclosed shady playground in the **Zappeio Gardens** (p77).

The **Hellenic Children's Museum** (Map p68; ☎ 210 331 2995; www.hcm.gr; Kydathineon 14, Plaka; admission free; ⏱10am-2pm Tue-Fri, 10am-3pm Sat & Sun; Ⓜ Syntagma) is more of a play centre, with a games room and a number of 'exhibits', such as a mock-up of a metro tunnel, for children to explore. Workshops range from baking to bubble-making. Parents must be on hand to supervise their children at all times.

The **Museum of Greek Children's Art** (Map p68; ☎ 210 331 2621; www.childrensartmuseum.gr; Kodrou 9, Plaka; admission free; ⏱10am-2pm Tue-Sat, 11am-2pm Sun, closed Aug; Ⓜ Syntagma) has a room set aside where children can let loose their creative energy, or learn about Ancient Greece.

Further afield, the enormous **Allou Fun Park & Kidom** (☎ 210 425 6999; www.allou.gr; cnr Leoforos Kifisou & Petrou Rali, Renti; admission free, rides €2-4; ⏱5pm-1am Mon-Fri, 10am-1am Sat & Sun) is Athens' biggest amusement park complex. Kidom is aimed at younger children. Saturday and Sunday they run a bus from Syntagma and the metro station at Faliro.

Attica Zoological Park (☎ 210 663 4724; www.atticapark.gr; Yalou, Spata; adult/child €15/11; ⏱9am-sunset) has an expanding collection of big cats, birds, reptiles and other animals, including a monkey forest and Cheetahland. The 19-hectare site is near the airport east of the city. Take bus 319 from Doukissis Plakentias metro station or the shuttle (€5) from Plateia Syntagmatos (see the zoo's website).

You can always escape the heat and amuse the kids with a virtual-reality tour of Ancient Greece at the **Hellenic Cosmos** (p87), or explore the universe at the impressive **Planetarium** (p77).

GREEK NATIONAL OPERA   Opera
(Ethniki Lyriki Skini; ☎ 210 360 0180; www.nationopera.gr) The season runs from November to June. Performances are usually held at the **Olympia Theatre** (Map p80; ☎ 210 361 1461; Akadimias 59, Exarhia; Ⓜ Panepistimio) or the Odeon of Herodes Atticus in summer,

Theatre & Dance

Athens has more theatres than any city in Europe but, as you'd expect, most performances are in Greek. Theatre buffs may enjoy a performance of an old favourite if they know the play well enough.

NATIONAL THEATRE   Theatre
(☎ 210 522 3243; www.n-t.gr; Agiou Konstantinou 22-24, Omonia; Ⓜ Omonia) Performances of contemporary plays and ancient theatre happen in one of the city's finest

neoclassical buildings. Also held in venues around town, and in summer in ancient theatres across Greece, such as Epidavros.

DORA STRATOU
DANCE THEATRE   Traditional Dance
(☎ 210 921 4650; www.grdance.org; Filopappou Hill; adult/child €15/5; ⏱performances 9.30pm Wed-Fri, 8.15pm Sat & Sun, late May–mid-Sep; Ⓜ Petralona) Every summer this company performs its repertoire of folk dances from all over Greece at its open-air theatre on the western side of Filopappou Hill.

Cinema

One of the delights of hot summer nights in Athens is the enduring tradition of open-air cinema, where you can watch the latest Hollywood or

art-house flick under moonlight. Many refurbished original outdoor cinemas are still operating in gardens and on rooftops, with modern sound systems.

AIGLI
Cinema

(off Map p68; ☎ 210 336 9369; Zappeio Gardens, Syntagma; M Syntagma) The most historic outdoor cinema is Aigli, in the verdant Zappeio Gardens, where you can watch a movie in style with a glass of wine.

Sport

Greece's top teams are Athens-based Panathinaikos and AEK, and Piraeus-based Olympiakos, all three of which are in the European Champions League. Big games take place at the **Olympic Stadium** in Marousi or the **Karaiskaki Stadium** in Piraeus, the country's best soccer stadium.

Generally, tickets can be bought on the day at the venue; some are available at www.tickethour.gr. Check club websites or www.greeksoccer.com.

Shopping

Downtown Athens is one big bustling shopping hub, with an eclectic mix of stores and specialist shopping strips. The central shopping street is Ermou, the pedestrian mall lined with mainstream fashion stores running from Syntagma to Monastiraki.

MONASTIRAKI FLEA MARKET
Market

(Map p68; Adrianou, Monastiraki; ⏱ daily; M Monastiraki) This traditional market has a festive atmosphere; permanent antiques and collectables shops are open all week while the streets around the station and Adrianou fill with vendors selling jewellery, handicrafts and bric-a-brac.

SUNDAY FLEA MARKET
Market

(Map p75; Ermou, Thisio; ⏱ dawn-2pm Sun; M Thisio). Peddlers fill the end of Ermou, towards Gazi; you can find some bargains collectables and kitsch delights among the junk. Test your haggling skills.

Left: Glassware on display at the Monastiraki Flea Market
Below: National Archaeological Museum (p78)

'O PANTOPOLEION
Food & Drink

Map p80; ☎ 210 323 4612; Sofokleous Omonia; Ⓜ Syntagma) Expansive store selling traditional food products from all over Greece: from Santorini capers to boutique olive oils, Cretan rusks, jars of foodies for edible souvenirs, and Greek wines and spirits.

MORGOS
Handicrafts

Map p68; ☎ 210 324 3836; www.amorgosart.gr; odrou 3, Plaka; Ⓜ Syntagma) Charming store rammed with Greek folk art, trinkets, eramics, embroidery and woodcarved urniture made by the owner.

MELISSINOS ART
Clothing, Accessories

Map p68; ☎ 210 321 9247; www.melissinos-art. om; Agias Theklas 2, Psyrri; Ⓜ Monastiraki) antelis Melissinos continues the sandal-naking tradition of his famous poet/andal-maker father Stavros, whose ustomers included the Beatles, Sophia oren and Jackie Onassis. Pantelis' aughter runs excellent **Olgianna Melis-**

sinos (Map p68; ☎ 210 331 1925; Normanou 7, Monastiraki; Ⓜ Monastiraki) with a wide range of leather goods. Can be made to order.

GREECE IS FOR LOVERS
Souvenirs

(Map p68; ☎ 210 924 5064; www.greeceis forlovers.com; Karyatidon 13a, Makrygianni; Ⓜ Akropoli) Browse the cheeky designer plays on Greek kitsch: from Corinthian column dumb-bells to crocheted iPod covers.

COMPENDIUM
Books

(Map p68; ☎ 210 322 1248; Navarhou Nikodimou 5, cnr Nikis, Plaka; Ⓜ Syntagma) Athens' main English-language bookstore also has a popular secondhand section.

ⓘ Information

Dangers & Annoyances

Crime has heightened in Athens with the onset of the financial crisis. Streets surrounding Omonia have become markedly seedier, with an

If You Like…
Cafe Culture

If you enjoy people-watching in Athens' bustling squares or wandering along the pedestrianised Apostolou Pavlou, we think you'll like taking in the local scene from one of Athens' cafes. These ubiquitous and inevitably packed places have Europe's most expensive coffee (between €3 and €5); you're essentially hiring the chair, but you can linger for hours.

1 **PETITE FLEUR**
(Map p80; Omirou 44; M Panepistimio) Petite Fleur serves up large mugs of hot chocolate and speciality cappuccinos in a quiet, almost-Parisian ambience.

2 **MELINA**
(Map p68; Lysiou 22, Plaka; M Akropoli) An ode to the pop icon Merkouri, Melina offers charm and intimacy out of the hectic centre.

3 **ZONAR'S**
(Map p68; Voukourestiou 9, cnr Panepistimiou, Syntagma; M Syntagma) Pricey Zonar's dates from the 1920s and creates excellent pastries.

4 **GINGER ALE**
(Map p80; Themistokleous 80, M Omonia) Dip back in time to a '50s veneered coffee shop cum rocking nightspot. Sip espresso by day and catch a rotating lineup of live acts by night.

5 **FLORAL**
(Map p80; Themistokleous 80, M Omonia) Floral is sleekly modern with grey-toned images of retro life and – you guessed it – flowers on the walls. Locals come to buy books, chat and people-watch.

increase in prostitutes and junkies; avoid the area, especially at night.

PICKPOCKETS Favourite hunting grounds are the metro, particularly the Piraeus-Kifisia line, and crowded streets around Omonia, Athinas and the Monastiraki Flea Market.

TAXI DRIVERS Most (but not all) rip-offs involve taxis picked up from ranks at the airport, train stations, bus terminals and particularly the port of Piraeus. Some drivers don't turn on the meter and demand whatever they think they can get away with. Only negotiate a set fare if you have some idea of the cost. Otherwise, find another taxi. At Piraeus, avoid the drivers at the port exit asking if you need a taxi; hail one off the street.

In extreme cases, drivers have accelerated meters or switch them to night rate (tariff 2 lights up) during the day. Check the extra charges for airport pick-ups and tolls, which are set and must be displayed in every taxi.

TRAVEL-AGENT SCAMS Some travel agents in the Plaka/Syntagma area employ touts to promote 'cheap' packages to the islands. Touts hang out at the bus and metro stops, hoping to find naive new arrivals, take them back to the agency and pressure them into buying outrageously overpriced packages.

BAR SCAMS Bar scams target tourists in central Athens, particularly around Syntagma. One scam goes like this: friendly Greek approaches solo male traveller; friendly Greek reveals that he, too, is from out of town or does the old 'I have a cousin in Australia' routine and suggests they go to a bar for a drink. Before they know it women appear, more drinks are ordered and the conman disappears, leaving the traveller to pay an exorbitant bill. Smiles disappear and the atmosphere turns threatening.

ADULTERATED DRINKS Some bars and clubs in Athens serve what are locally known as *bombes,* adulterated drinks diluted with cheap illegal imports or methanol-based spirit substitutes. They leave you feeling decidedly low the next day.

Internet Resources

Arts and culture (www.elculture.gr) Bilingual including theatre, music and cinema listings.

Ministry of Culture (www.culture.gr) Museum, archaeological sites and cultural events.

Official visitor site (www.breathtakingathens.gr) Athens Tourism and Economic Development Agency site with what's-on listings.

Tourist Information

EOT (Greek National Tourist Organisation; ☎ 210 331 0347/0716; www.visitgreece.gr; Dionysiou Areopagitou 18-20, Makrygianni; ⊕ 9am-7pm; M Akropoli) Free Athens map, public-transport information and *Athens & Attica* booklet.

ROGER CRACKNELL 01/ALAMY ©

Don't Miss **Hellenic Festival**

Greece's premier cultural festivals, held annually under the auspices of the Hellenic Festival, feature a top line-up of local and international music, dance and theatre.

Major shows in the **Athens Festival** take place at the Odeon of Herodes Atticus (p72; pictured above), one of the world's most historic venues, with the floodlit Acropolis as a backdrop. Patrons sit on cushions on the centuries-old marble seats. The festival, which has been running for more than 50 years, presents a diverse program of international standing, ranging from ancient theatre and classical music to contemporary dance. Events are also held in various modern theatres and venues around town.

The festival also incorporates the **Epidavros Festival**, which presents Ancient Greek drama at the famous Theatre of Epidavros (p119) in the town of Epidavros in the Peloponnese, two hours west of Athens. Performances are held every Friday and Saturday night during July and August. Special **KTEL buses** (☎210 513 4588; return €20) to Epidavros depart from Kifissos Terminal A on Friday and Saturday, returning after the show.

The festival program should be available in April on the festival website and at the **Hellenic Festival Box Office**. Book tickets online or by phone or purchase them on the day of the performance at the theatre box offices – but queues can be very long.

THINGS YOU NEED TO KNOW

Hellenic Festival (www.greekfestival.gr; ⊙late-May–Oct); **Box Office** (Map p80; ☎210 327 2000; arcade, Panepistimiou 39, Syntagma; ⊙8.30am-4pm Mon-Fri, 9am-2pm Sat Jul & Aug; Ⓜ Panepistimio)

---

❶ Getting There & Away

Air

Modern **Eleftherios Venizelos International Airport** (ATH; ☎210 353 0000; www.aia.gr) at

Spata, is 27km east of Athens. Olympic Air has flights to all islands with airports, and the more popular are also serviced by Aegean Airlines and Athens Airways.

Travel Pass

For short-stay visitors, the 24-hour travel pass (€4) and one-week ticket (€14) allow unlimited travel on all public transport inside Athens, excluding the airport services.

Aegean Airlines (☎801 112 0000, 210 626 1000; www.aegeanair.com; Othonos 10, Syntagma; ⓂSyntagma)

Athens Airways (☎801 801 4000, 210 669 6600; www.athensairways.com)

Olympic Air (☎801 801 0101, 210 926 4444; www.olympicair.com; Filellinon 15, Syntagma; ⓂSyntagma)

Sky Express (☎281 022 3500; www.skyexpress.gr)

Boat

Most ferry, hydrofoil and high-speed catamaran services to the islands leave from Athens' massive port at Piraeus. Piraeus is the busiest port in Greece, with a bewildering array of departures, including daily service to all island groups, except the Ionians.

All ferry companies have online timetables and booths on the quays. Ferry schedules are reduced in April, May and October, and are radically cut in winter, especially to smaller islands. Buy tickets online (www.openseas.gr or companies' websites) or phone agents directly. See the Getting There & Away sections for each island's agents. Or contact the Piraeus Port Authority (☎1441; www.olp.gr) for information.

Some services for the Cyclades also depart from the smaller ports at Rafina and Lavrio. Rafina, on Attica's east coast, is Athens' main fishing port and the second-most important port for passenger ferries. The port is far smaller than Piraeus and less confusing – and fares are about 20% cheaper – but it does take an hour on the bus to get here. Frequent buses run from Athens to Rafina (€3, one hour) between 5.45am and 10.30pm, departing Athens' Mavromateon bus terminal (p92). Rafina Port Authority (☎229 402 8888) can provide information on ferries.

Lavrio, an industrial town on the coast 60km southeast of Athens, is the port for high-season catamarans to the western Cyclades. Buses to Lavrio (€5.20, 1½ hours, every 30 minutes) run from the Mavromateon terminal in Athens (p92). Lavrio Port Authority (☎229 202 5249) has ferry information.

Bus

Athens has two main intercity (IC) KTEL (☎14505; www.ktel.org) bus stations, one 5km and one 7km to the north of Omonia. Pick up timetables at the tourist office.

Kifissos Terminal A (☎210 512 4910; Kifissou 100, Peristeri; ⓂAgios Antonios) Buses to Thessaloniki, the Peloponnese, Ionian Islands, and western Greece (like Ioannina).

Liossion Terminal B (☎210 831 7153; Liossion 260, Thymarakia; ⓂAgios Nikolaos) Buses to central and northern Greece, like Trikala (for Meteora) and Delphi.

Mavromateon Terminal (☎210 880 8000, 210 822 5148; cnr Leoforos Alexandras & 28 Oktovriou-Patision, Pedion Areos; ⓂViktoria) Buses for destinations in southern Attica leave from here, about 250m north of the National Archaeological Museum. Buses to Rafina and Marathon leave from the northern section of the Mavromateon terminal (just 150m to the north).

Train

Intercity trains to central and northern Greece depart from the central Larisis train station (Map pp52-3), about 1km northwest of Plateia Omonias. For the Peloponnese, take the suburban rail to Kiato and change for other OSE services there, or check for available lines at the Larisis station.

Note: at the time of research, Athens' train system was in a state of flux due to the financial crisis. Schedules/fares should be confirmed at one of the OSE offices (☎1110; www.ose.gr; ⏱24hr) Syntagma (☎210 362 4402/5; Sina 6, Syntagma; ⏱8am-3pm Mon-Sat; ⓂPanepistimio); Omonia (☎210 529 7005; Karolou 1, Omonia; ⏱8am-3pm Mon-Fri; ⓂMetaxourghio).

ℹ Getting Around

To/From the Airport

For taxis, check that the meter is set to the correct tariff and add airport surcharge (€3.77), toll

€2.70) and €0.38 for each bag over 10kg. Total fares vary depending on traffic; expect from €30 to €50 from the airport to the city centre, and €30 to Piraeus. Both trips should take about an hour, longer with heavy traffic.

Express buses operate 24 hours between the airport and the city centre, Piraeus and KTEL bus terminals. At the airport, buy tickets (€5; not valid or other forms of public transport) at the booth near the stops.

Metro line 3 goes to the airport. Trains run every 30 minutes, leaving Monastiraki between 5.50am and midnight, and the airport between 5.30am and 11.30pm. Airport tickets cost €8 per adult or €14 return (return valid 48 hours). The fare for two or more passengers is €7 each, so purchase tickets together (same with suburban rail). Tickets are valid for all forms of public transport for 90 minutes (revalidate your ticket on final mode of transport to show it's the same journey).

. . . .

Public Transport

Athens has an extensive and inexpensive integrated public transport network of buses, metro, trolleybuses and trams. Pick up maps and timetables at the EOT tourist office, the airport and train stations or check the website of the Athens Urban Transport Organisation (OASA; 185; www.oasa.gr; Metsovou 15, Exarhia/ Mouseio; 6.30am-11.30pm Mon-Fri, 7.30am-10.30pm Sat & Sun).

Tickets good for 90 minutes (€1.40), a 24-hour travel pass (€4) and a weekly ticket (€14) are valid for all forms of public transport except for airport services. Bus-/trolleybus-only tickets (€1.20) cannot be used on the metro. Children under six travel free; people under 18 and over 65 pay half-fare. Buy tickets in metro stations or transport kiosks or most *periptera* (kiosks). Validate the ticket in the machine as you board your transport of choice.

EXCURSIONS FROM ATHENS

Piraeus Πειραιάς

Piraeus is Greece's main port and the biggest in the Mediterranean. It's not a place where many visitors choose to linger. If you're catching an early ferry you can stay in Piraeus instead of central Athens, but many hotels around Megas Limin (the Great Harbour) are shabby and aimed at sailors and clandestine liaisons.

Temple of Poseidon (p97), Capo Sounion

ADINA TOVY AMSEL/LONELY PLANET IMAGES ©

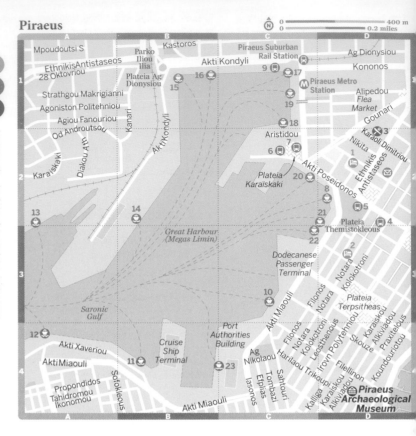

Piraeus

◎ Top Sights
Piraeus Archaeological Museum.......... D4

🛏 Sleeping
1 Hotel Triton..................................... D2
2 Piraeus Dream Hotel......................... D3

✕ Eating
3 Rakadiko.. D2

ℹ Transport
4 Bus 040 to Syntagma......................... D2
5 Bus 049 to Omonia........................... D2
6 Bus Station...................................... C2
7 Bus X96 to Airport........................... C2
8 Catamarans & Hydrofoils to the
   Peloponnese & Saronic Gulf D2
9 Free Shuttle Bus to Gates E1 to
   E3...C1
10 Gate E10... C3

11 Gate E11...B4
12 Gate E12...A4
13 Gate E1–Ferries to the
   Dodecanese A2
14 Gate E2–Ferries to Crete &
   Northeastern Aegean Islands.........B2
15 Gate E3...B1
16 Gate E4–Ferries to Crete B1
17 Gate E5...C1
18 Gate E7–Catamarans to the
   Cyclades....................................... C1
19 Gate E7–Ferries to the Western &
   Central Cyclades.......................... C1
20 Gate E8–Ferries to the Saronic
   Gulf Islands..................................C2
21 Gate E9–Ferries to the Cyclades..........D2
22 Gate E9-Ferries to the Cyclades,
   Samos, Ikaria...............................C3
23 International Ferries C4

The fastest and most convenient link between Athens and Piraeus is the metro (€1.40, 30 minutes, every 10 minutes, 6am–midnight). Take extra care as the section between Piraeus and Monastiraki is notorious for pickpockets.

Sleeping & Eating

HOTEL TRITON   Hotel €€
(210 417 3457; www.htriton.gr; Tsamadou 8; s/d/tr incl breakfast €55/70/80; ❄ @) This refurbished hotel with sleek executive-style rooms is a treat compared to the usual run-down joints in Piraeus. Some rooms overlook the bustling market square.

PIREAUS DREAM
HOTEL   Business Hotel €€
(210 411 0555; www.piraeusdream.gr; Filonos 79-81; s/d/tr incl breakfast €55/65/85; ❄ @) With quiet rooms starting on the 4th floor, this renovated hotel about 500m from the station has good facilities, including laptop and PlayStation rental, and serves a big American breakfast.

RAKADIKO   Taverna €
(210 417 8470; Stoa Kouvelou, Karaoli Dimi-triou 5; mains €12-20; lunch & dinner Tue-Sat) Dine quietly under grapevines on mezed-es from all over Greece. Live *rembetika* on weekends.

PLOUS PODILATOU   Seafood €€
(210 413 7010; www.plous-podilatou.gr; Akti Koumoundourou 42, Mikrolimano; mains €12-20)

This modern restaurant in Mikrolimano has a Mediterranean menu, with an emphasis on well-prepared fresh fish and seafood.

MARGARO   Seafood €€
(210 451 4226; Hatzikiriakou 126; mains €25-28; lunch daily, dinner Mon-Sat) This long-time local favourite is known for its fresh crayfish, eaten in a giant pile.

Getting There & Away

The metro and suburban rail lines from Athens terminate at the northeastern corner of the Great Harbour on Akti Kalimassioti. Most ferry departure points are a short walk over the footbridge from here. A left turn out of the metro station leads 250m to Plateia Karaïskaki, the terminus for airport buses.

Boat

Piraeus is the busiest port in Greece, with a bewildering array of departures, including daily service to all island groups, except the Ionians (see Patra and Igoumenitsa) and the Sporades (see Rafina and Lavrio). Departure docks are indicated on Map p94, but always double-check with the ticketing agent. Note that there are two departure points for Crete at Piraeus port: ferries for Iraklio leave from the western end of Akti Kondyli, but ferries for other Cretan ports occasionally dock there as well, or in other places.

Tickets All ferry companies have online timetables and booths on the quays. Ferry schedules are reduced in April, May and October, and are radically cut in winter,

Marathon Μαραθώνας

The plain surrounding the unremarkable, small town of Marathon, 42km northeast of Athens, is the site of one of the most celebrated battles in world history. In 490 BC an army of 9000 Greeks and 1000 Plataeans defeated the 25,000-strong Persian army, proving that the Persians were not invincible. At the end of the day, 6000 Persians and only 192 Greeks lay dead. The story goes that after the battle a runner was sent to Athens to announce the victory. After shouting, *'Enikesame!'* ('We won!') he collapsed and died. This is the origin of today's marathon race.

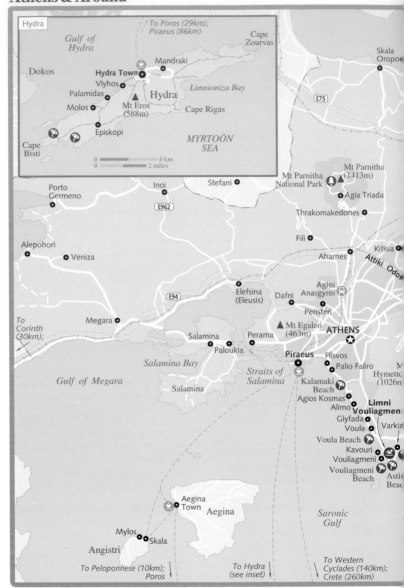

especially to smaller islands. Buy tickets online (www.openseas.gr or companies' websites) or phone agents directly. contact the **Piraeus Port Authority** (📞1441; www.olp.gr) for information.

Bus

The X96 Piraeus–Athens Airport Express (€5) leaves from the southwestern corner of Plateia Karaïskaki and also stops on Kalimassioti.

Akti Kalimassioti. Take extra care as the section between Piraeus and Monastiraki is notorious for pickpockets.

Suburban Rail

Piraeus is also connected to the suburban rail whose terminus is located opposite the metro station. To get to the airport or the Peloponnese, change trains at Nerantziotissa.

❶ Getting Around

The port is massive and a **free shuttle bus** runs regularly along the quay from the metro station (see signposted maps).

The city of Piraeus has its own network of buses. The services likely to interest travellers are buses 904 and 905 between Zea Marina and the metro station.

Temple of Poseidon

The Ancient Greeks knew how to choose a site for a temple. Nowhere is this more evident than at Cape Sounion, 70km south of Athens, where the **Temple of Poseidon** (☎ 229 203 9363; adult/child €4/free; ⏰ 9.30am-8pm) stands on a craggy spur that plunges 65m down to the sea. Built in 444 BC at the same time as the Parthenon, it is constructed of local marble from Agrilesa, and its slender columns, of which 16 remain, are Doric.

The temple looks gleaming white when viewed from the sea and is perceptible from a long distance: it gave great comfort to sailors in ancient times who knew they were nearly home when they saw it. The views from the temple are equally impressive: on a clear day you can see Kea, Kythnos and Serifos to the southeast, and Aegina and the Peloponnese to the west.

Visit early in the morning before the tourist buses arrive, or head there for the sunset if you wish to indulge the sentiments of Byron's lines from *Don Juan:* 'Place me on Sunium's marbled steep, Where nothing save the waves and I, May hear our mutual murmurs sweep.'

There are a couple of tavernas just below the site if you want to combine a visit with lunch and a swim.

Metro

e fastest and most convenient link between e Great Harbour and Athens is via the metro 1.40, 30 minutes, every 10 minutes, 5am-dnight), near the ferries at the northern end of

FELIX ZASKA/ALAM

Coastal buses (€6.50, 1½ hours) leave Athens half-hourly (fewer in the evening) from the Mavromateon bus terminal (p92).

Peania & Around Παιανία

Perhaps Peania's biggest claim to fame was as the birthplace of Greek states-man Demosthenes (384–322 BC). Today the area is known primarily for **Vorres Museum** (🕽 210 664 2520; www.culture.gr; Parodos Diadohou Konstantinou 4, Peania; adult/ child €4.40/free; ⊙10am-2pm Sat & Sun). This impressive 20th-century Greek art and folk museum is on the lovely 32-hectare estate that was the home of Ion Vorres. Vorres migrated to Canada as a young man but built his home here in 1963 and began collecting contemporary art, furniture, artefacts, textiles and historic objects from around Greece to preserve the national heritage.

Take bus 308 to Koropi-Peania from Athens' Nomismatikopio metro station

Also visit the **Koutouki Cave** (🕽210 664 2910; www.culture.gr; adult/child €5/free; ⊙9am-3pm Mon-Fri, 9.30am-2.30pm Sat & Sun) This two-million-year-old cave is one of the finest in Greece, covering 3300 sq

metres and containing stalagmites and stalactites. The cave is best visited by ca

Hydra ΥΔΡΑ
POP 2913

Hydra (*ee-dhr-ah*) is truly the gem of the Saronic Gulf and stands alone among Greek islands as the one free of wheeled vehicles. No cars. No scooters. Just tiny marble-cobbled lanes, donkeys, rocks and sea. Artists (Brice Marden, Nikos Chatzikyriakos-Ghikas, Panayiotis Tetsis musicians (Leonard Cohen), celebrities (Melina Mercouri, Sophia Loren) and tra ellers (you) have all been drawn to Hydra over the years.

Hydra Town is the centre of island life and more than a standard harbour. Its historic feel, mansions and cafe scene give the island an amphitheatre-like focal point. But if you're an outdoors person, don't be lulled by the hubbub of port life into forgetting the mountainous interior, the coastal paths and the hidde swimming bays.

The mules and donkeys are the main means of heavy transport and they, alon with the rustic aspects of life on the islar give Hydra its two faces: chic and earthy

Sights

LAZAROS KOUNDOURIOTIS HISTORICAL MANSION Museum

(22980 52421; www.nhmuseum.gr; adult/child €4/free; 10am-2pm & 6-9pm Apr-Oct, by appointment Nov-Mar) Hydra's star cultural attraction is this handsome ochre-coloured *archontiko* (stone mansion) sitting high above the harbour. It was the home of one of the major players in the Greek Independence struggle and is an exquisite example of late-18th-century traditional architecture. It is filled with original furnishings, folk costumes and handicrafts, and a painting exhibition. Find it a steep hike up from the southwest corner of the harbour.

Around Hydra

An unbeatable Hydra experience is the long haul up to **Moni Profiti Ilia**, but you need to be fit and willing. The wonderful **monastery complex** in a walled compound contains beautiful icons and serenity. Starting up **Miaouli** street from the harbour, it's a solid hour or more through relentless zigzags and pine trees to panoramic bliss on the top.

The coastal road turns into a simple, beautiful trail about a 1.5km walk west from the port, after **Kamini**. Kamini has a tiny **fishing port**, several good tavernas, **swimming rocks** and a small pebble beach.

Sleeping

HYDRA HOTEL Boutique Studios €€

(22980 53420, 6972860161; www hydra-hotel, Petrou Voulgari 8; studio incl breakfast €100-?, apt €160-230, maisonette €230; ❄ 🛜) Climb high on the south side of the port to swishy, top-of-the-line apartments in an impeccably renovated ancient mansion with kitchenettes and sweeping views. Get room 202 for a tiny balcony with panoramas to die for.

NEREIDS Pension €€

(22980 52875; www.nereids-hydra.com; Kouloura; d €65-80; ❄ 🛜) This carefully restored stone house contains lovely rooms of exceptional value and quality. Spacious, peaceful and with beautiful decor, rooms have open views to Hydra's rocky heights and top-floor rooms have sea views. Find it a few minutes' walk up Tombazi from the harbour.

PITEOUSSA Pension €€

(22980 52810; www.piteoussa.com; Kouloura; d €65-75; ❄ 🛜) Jolly owners maintain beautiful rooms in two buildings on a quiet, pine tree–lined street. Rooms in the restored corner mansion drip with period character and modern amenities, while the smaller rooms in the second building were renovated in 2010 and have a chic feel. This is one of the best deals on the island.

Eating

SUNSET Mediterranean €€

(22980 52067; mains €9-22; lunch & dinner Easter-Oct) Famed for its splendid, panoramic spot near the cannons to the west of the harbour, Sunset also has fine, fresh cuisine. Tasty salads, inventive pastas and local fish are prepared with flair.

BARBA DIMAS Italian €€

(22980 52967; Tombazi; mains €11-20; dinner) Authentic Italian food like their Neapolitan grandmother used to make. Menus change daily. Reserve a table.

VERANDA Mediterranean €€

(22980 52259; Lignou; mains €7-15; dinner Apr-Oct) Cheerful brothers run this terrace restaurant with views looking out across the port and mountains. Tasty salads.

Getting There & Around

High-speed ferries link Hydra with Piraeus (One to two hours, €25.50, seven to eight daily); service is greatly reduced in winter.

In summer, caïques from Hydra Town go to the island's beaches. Water taxi (22980 53690) fares are posted on the quay (Kamini costs €10, Vlyhos €14).

Donkey owners clustered around the port charge €10 to €15 to transport your bags to your hotel. Quick donkey rides around the port cost about €10 per person.

Peloponnese, Corfu & Kefallonia

The Peloponnese is the stuff that legends are made of. This is where gods and heroes strutted. Its treasure trove of historical sites includes Classical temples, Mycenaean palaces, Byzantine cities, and Frankish and Venetian fortresses. Flex your muscles at Ancient Olympia, recite from *Oedipus Rex* in the theatre of Epidavros or hike in the rugged Mani. And when you want to kick back and relax, the Ionian Islands are strung like jewels along the peninsula's western coast. Greece's first capital, Nafplio, is today a cosmopolitan and romantic city, and it's surrounded by a natural playground of lofty, snow-capped mountains, lush gorges, valleys of citrus groves and vineyards, and sun-speckled beaches.

Just off the coast, the Ionian Islands offer a fast track to the Greek island experience. Corfu and Kefallonia seduce visitors with their heat, intense colour and dazzling light. In Corfu Town you can admire British neoclassical palaces, drink beneath Parisian-style arcades and wander through Venetian alleyways. And on both islands it's still possible to find isolated swimming coves and laid-back villages.

Venetian Fortress, Methoni (p118)
IMAGE BROKER/LONELY PLANET IMAGES ©

Cheese maturing in a cool room
ALAN BENSON/LONELY PLANET IMAGES ©

Peloponnese, Corfu & Kefallonia

ALBANIA

Lake Aliakmonas

Gerakini

Sidhari

Corfu

Corfu Town

lekas

6

Issos

Kavos

Igoumenitsa

Metsovo

Ioannina

Meteora

Kalambaka

Larisa

AEGEAN SEA

EPIROS

Arachthos

THESSALY

Volos

Parga

Paxi **7**

Antipaxi

Arta

Karditsa

Pelion Peninsula

Skiathos

IONIAN ISLANDS

Preveza

Lefkada Town

Mytikas

Lefkada

Agrinio

Karpenisi

Lamia

Loutra Edipsou

Mt Iti (2125m)

STEREA ELLADA

Evia

Ancient Delphi

Mt Parnassos (2457m)

Fiskardo

Ithaki

Kefallonia **2**

Sami

Argostoli

Pesada

Poros

Skala

Messolongi

Lake Kremasta

Aheloös

E65

Delphi

Livadia

Thiva (Thebes)

Agios Nikolaos

Kyllini

Elis

Gulf of Patra

Patra

Diakofto

Gulf of Corinth

Derveni

Xylokastro

Corinth

Zakynthos

Zakynthos Town

Pyrgos

Amaliada

Olympia

1

Ancient Olympia

Kalavryta

PELOPONNESE

Ancient Corinth

Mycenae

Argos

Aegina

Epidavros

Adami

4

Nafplio

Andritsena

Tripoli

Megalopoli

Kyparissia

Ancient Tegea

Kosta

Spetses

Hydra

Ancient Messini

Messini

Messinian Mani

Mystras

Sparta

Leonidio

Pylos

Methoni

Kardamyli

5

Geraki

MYRTOÖN SEA

Koroni

Areopoli

Gythio

Monemvasia **3**

Lakonian Mani

Gerolimenas

Lakonian Gulf

Elafonisi

Neapoli

Kythira

1 Ancient Olympia

2 Kefallonia

3 Monemvasia

4 Nafplio

5 The Mani

6 Corfu Town

7 Paxi

0 — 50 km
0 — 30 miles

MEDITERRANEAN SEA

Antikythira

Peloponnese, Corfu & Kefallonia's Highlights

1

Exploring Ancient Olympia

The atmosphere at this ancient site is almost magical. Feel the watchful eye of Zeus as you tour the ruins, imagining the thousands of men that gathered to compete with hands full of offerings. The historical significance of this site is both humbling and inspiring. You may even be motivated to run a lap or two. Above: Palaestra; Top Right: Temple of Zeus; Bottom Right: Archaeological Museum of Olympia

Need to Know
BEST TIME OF YEAR Spring & autumn **BEST TIME OF DAY** Late afternoon for fewer vistors & dusk light **ESSENTIALS** Walking shoes, sunhat, water **For more, see p127**

Olympia Don't Miss List

BY NIKI VLACHOU, TOUR GUIDE & CLASSICAL SCHOLAR

1 PALAESTRA & STADIUM

Use your imagination as you follow in the footsteps of the competitors from the partially restored palaestra, where they trained their body and mind, to the ruins of the stadium where they competed in front of 45,000 spectators. Enter the stadium through an archway and watch for the start and finish lines of the 120m spring track that still survives, along with the judges' seats.

2 TEMPLE OF ZEUS

This immense 5th-century BC Doric temple lies at the heart of the Sacred Precinct of Zeus. Its size reflects its original role as a home to the gold-and-ivory statue of Athena by Pheidias, one of the seven wonders of the ancient world. A single column has been restored and re-erected. Looking up at it gives you an idea of just how massive the temple must have been.

3 TEMPLE OF HERA

Built in the 6th century BC, this beautiful Doric temple is the most intact structure at the site. It's here that the modern Olympic torch is lit.

4 OLIVE TREE

Myth is inextricably entwined with the history of Olympia. According to mythology, Hercules was the protector of athletes and honoured his father Zeus by starting the Games at Olympia. He is also believed to have planted the site's first olive tree, from which wreaths were made for winners. This tree can still be found in the Sacred Precinct of Zeus.

5 ARCHAEOLOGICAL MUSEUM OF OLYMPIA

This excellent museum (p128) will round out your knowledge and is a fascinating place to begin your exploration of Olympia.

Kayaking on Kefallonia

With endless sunshine and calm, amazingly clear water, Kefallonia is an ideal spot for kayaking. Paddle alongside a coastline of impressive white limestone cliffs and secluded forested coves. Remote and dramatic, it's an outdoor lovers haven. Below: Myrtos; Top Right: Kefallonia cafes at night; Bottom Right: Fiskardo

Need to Know

BEST FOR KAYAKING Jun &Sep **BEST TIMES** Morning and late afternoon **SKILL LEVEL** From complete novices upwards **PRICES** Day trips from around €60 **For more, see p139**

Kayaking Kefallonia Don't Miss List

BY PAVLOS GEORGILAS & YVONNE WALSER, SEA KAYAK TOUR OPERATORS

1 MYRTOS TO ASSOS

Paddle down the dramatic west coast of Kefallonia towards gorgeous Myrtos (p143). From there, head for Assos (p143), a spectacular whitewashed fishing village on the isthmus of the Assos peninsula. The cypress trees and pines that cover the surrounding hills, the impressive limestone cliffs and the fortress standing guard on the peninsula create breathtaking scenery.

2 GULF OF MYRTOS

Head out from the fishing port of Agia Kyriaki for an easy trip along a coastline of pristine beauty. This is one of the most remote parts of Kefallonia. Stop at the white limestone cliffs, wide beaches and turquoise waters of Fteri for a swim, and then paddle back to Agia Kyriaki.

3 FISKARDO

Paddle out from the secluded cove of Emplyssi and south along the coast to Fiskardo (p144). This picturesque village was left untouched by the 1953 earthquake and has traditional houses and abundant signs of an aristocratic past that make it simply unique. Continue kayaking to Phoki, a colourful little bay with crystal-clear waters and a forest of cypress trees covering the surrounding slopes. From there head for Evreti Bay, paddling over three wrecked caïques.

4 PADDLING CALM WATER

There are a lot of great experiences that you can enjoy while kayaking, such as complete remoteness, encounters with dolphins and breathtaking sunsets. But for us, the greatest experience of all is the unsurpassed feeling of paddling in a mirror-calm sea with warm, turquoise and superbly transparent waters...as close as you can get to your soul.

Magical Monemvasia

Resting like a giant sandcastle in the sea, Monemvasia (p121) was part of the mainland until it was cut off by an earthquake in 375. To reach it, you must travel through a narrow tunnel in a massive fortifying wall that conceals the enchanting town until you emerge, blinking, on the other side. Enclosed within massive walls, the island's medieval village is wonderful place to get lost in.

Enchanting Nafplio

You may arrive here simply looking for a base from which to explore the nearby ruins, but Nafplio (p115) will quickly charm with its picturesque harbour setting, winding streets and romantic architecture. Relax in seaside cafes beneath the hilltop Palamidi fortress, check out worthwhile local museums and pamper yourself in boutique hotels.

The Mani

With its strong, independent people; unique architecture; and wild, rough terrain the Mani (p124) is a region well worth exploring. Whether you're following the countless trails on foot or taking in the winding roads on a driving tour, the crashing waves, crumbling mountains, deep ravines and phenomenal caves will leave you breathless.

5

6

Corfu Town

With a majestic seafront, beautiful pastel architecture and a bustle that draws you in, Corfu Town (p131) is like no other Greek town. Wander the marble-paved streets, join in the lively cafe scene or take in the museums and famous Palaio Frourio. You may wonder at times if you're in Greece, Italy or France, but wherever it is, it's enchanting.

7

Serene Paxi

The kind of island we all daydream about, tiny Paxi (p138) seems too pretty to be true. Ancient olive groves and windmills dot the interior while tranquil coves beckon from the coastline. With colourful Venetian-style harbour towns and restaurants and hotels that beg you to stay, it's a wonder we all don't move to Paxi.

Peloponnese, Corfu & Kefallonia's Best.

Encounters with Nature

○ **Corfu's West Coast** (p138) Explore pretty countryside or hop on excursion boats to hidden grottoes.

○ **Diros Caves** (p126) Explore deep caverns inhabited in neolithic times.

○ **Myrtos** (p143) Towering limestone cliffs, white sand and shimmering water.

○ **Cape Tenaro** (p129) Stand on Greece's most southerly point.

Architectural Gems

○ **Epidavros Theatre** (p119) Drop a coin to check ancient acoustics.

○ **Tower homes** (p124) Count traditional houses nestled in the mountains.

○ **Mystras** (p119) Captivating ruins of churches, libraries and palaces.

○ **Palamidi fortress** (p115) Enjoy classical music in a magical setting.

○ **Mon Repos Estate** (p135) Elegant neoclassical villa set in wooded parkland.

Maniot Villages

○ **Vathia** (p129) The most dramatic traditional Mani hamlet.

○ **Kardamyli** (p127) Nestled between the sea and the mountains.

○ **Gerolimenas** (p126) Secluded fishing village.

Mouth-Watering Meals

○ **Omorfi Poli** (p117) Tasty Italian and Greek cuisine with non-Greek twists.

○ **La Cucina** (p135) Hand-rolled pasta and Cajun shrimp.

○ **Hotel Kirimai** (p126) Sample the creations of one of Greece's top chefs.

○ **Ladokolla** (p142) Piping-hot souvlaki served right onto the tabletop.

○ **Elies** (p127) Idyllic setting and top nosh like lemon lamb casserole.

○ **Arhontiko** (p142) Kefallonian meat pie. Enough said.

ADVANCE PLANNING

○ **Two months before** Book your accommodation and tickets for plays at the Epidavros theatre.

○ **One month before** Make ferry or bus reservations for trips between the peninsula and the islands. Book tickets for the Diakofto–Kalavryta rack-and-pinion train.

RESOURCES

○ **www.mani.org.gr/en/** Provides information on history, sights and customs in the Mani.

○ **www.greeka.com/ionian** The low-down on the Ionians, including accommodation bookings, maps and nightlife.

○ **www.olympia-greece.org** Sights, accommodation and history of Olympia and Ancient Olympia.

GETTING AROUND

○ **Bus** Comprehensive routes throughout the Peloponnese and from Athens to the Ionian Islands.

○ **Flights** Short hops from Athens to Corfu.

○ **Ferry** Boats to the Ionian Islands from Patra and Kyllini on the Peloponnese.

○ **Car** The best way to explore the Peloponnese is with your own wheels.

BE FOREWARNED

○ **Sights** Many have reduced hours in the winter or are totally shut.

○ **Islands** The Saronic Gulf Islands are popular with Athenians and can get very busy; be sure to book ahead!

Mosaic floor at a town on Capte Tenaro (p129)
ove: A hotel pool on Corfu's west coast (p138)

Peloponnese, Corfu & Kefallonia Itineraries

With ancient ruins, rugged landscape, unique villages, sun-soaked resorts and island coves, this region makes it easy to squeeze a lot of adventure in.

GYTHIO TO MONEMVASIA
Architectural Goodie Bag

5 DAYS

The southern coast of the Peloponnese is home to architectural treats. Base yourself in the engaging seaside town of **(1) Gythio**, a bustling fishing village with excellent restaurants and swimming beaches. Offshore is the tiny Marathonisi Islet with the 18th-century Tzanetakis Grigorakis tower. From Gythio, spend a few days delving into **(2) the Mani**. Join a hiking group or rent a car to explore the rugged setting – Diros Caves, Cape Tenaro and the Vyros Gorge. En route you'll see tower settlements built in the 17th century as defences against clan wars. Stop at one of these villages for lunch in the lively squares, where you'll get great

local food and soak up a bit of the Maniot culture. Next, head north of Gythio for the day to visit the fascinating Byzantine ruins of **(3) Mystras**, a fortress town set against the mountains; the ruins date back to 1249. On the last day, head east to spectacular **(4) Monemvasia**, a medieval walled town suspended like an iceberg in the sea. Wander through the winding pedestrian alleys and take in the impressive churches before escaping the crowds and heading back to relaxed Gythio.

KEFALLONIA TO EPIDAVROS

Sun, Sea & Sights

7 DAYS

Begin your adventure with a few days on the island of **(1) Kefallonia**. The rugged mountains, fruitful vineyards, stunning coastline and golden beaches make it an excellent place to hike, kayak and unwind. Hop on a ferry to Kyllini on the Peloponnese and spend a day at the nearby site of **(2) Ancient Olympia**. From here, head to **(3) Diakofto** for a trip on the unique rack-and-pinion train, an extraordinary journey through unforgettable, lush scenery to Kalavryta and back. From Diakofto, drive or hop on a train to stunning **(4) Nafplio**, one of the Peloponnese's most romantic seaside towns with worthwhile museums,

Venetian architecture and an impressive fortress. You'll also find hopping nightlife and snug hotels. Take in the ruins of **(5) Epidavros** and, if you're visiting in summer, try to get tickets for a classical play at the site's amazing ancient theatre. From Nafplio, it's an easy trip back to Athens.

Gythio (p122)
HERCULES MILAS/ALAMY ©

113

Discover Peloponnese, Corfu & Kefallonia

At a Glance

- **Nafplio** (p115) Scenic seaside town and impressive nearby ruins.

- **Mystras** (p119) Ancient ruins.

- **Monemvasia** (p121) Fairytale fortress in the sea.

- **The Mani** (p124) Wild, rugged and gorgeous.

- **Olympia** (p127) Ancient site of the original Games.

- **Corfu** (p130) Greenest and most popular Ionian island with lots of sand and a lively capital.

- **Kefallonia** (p139) Vineyards and rugged coastline.

PELOPONNESE
Ancient Mycenae Μυκήνες

In the barren foothills of Mt Agios Ilias (750m) and Mt Zara (600m) stand the sombre and mighty ruins of Ancient Mycenae (☎27510 76585; citadel, Treasury of Atreus & museum €8; ☺site 8am-8pm summer, 8.30am-3pm winter). For 400 years (1600-1200 BC) this vestige of a kingdom was the most powerful in Greece, holding sway over the Argolid (the modern-day prefecture of Argolis) and influencing the other Mycenaean kingdoms.

Due to the sheer size of the citadel walls (13m high and 7m thick), formed by stone blocks weighing 6 tonnes in places, the Ancient Greeks believed they must have been built by a Cyclops, one of the giants described in the 'Odyssey'. Archaeological evidence indicates that the palaces of the Mycenaean kingdoms declined some time around 1200 BC and the palace itself was set ablaze around 1100 BC.

EXPLORING THE SITE
Before exploring the site, head to the impressive **museum** (admission incl site fee €8; ☺noon-8pm Mon, 8am-7.30pm Tue-Sun). Inside the citadel, you will find **Grave Circle A** on the right as you enter. This was the royal cemetery and contained six grave shafts. Five shafts were excavated by archeologist Henrich Schliemann between 1874 and 1876, uncovering the famous and magnificent gold treasures, including a well-preserved gold death mask. To the south of Grave Circle A are the remains of a group of houses. In one was discovered the famous Warrior Vase, regarded by Schliemann as one of his greatest discoveries because it offered

Mystras (p119)

IMAGE BROKER/LONELY PLANET IMAGES ©

a glimpse of what Mycenae's legendary warriors looked like.

The main path leads up to **Agamemnon's Palace**, centred on the **Great Court**. The rooms to the north were the private royal apartments. One of these rooms is believed to be the chamber in which Agamemnon was murdered.

 Getting There & Away

Three daily buses head to Mycenae from Nafplio (€2.60, one hour).

Nafplio Ναύπλιο

POP 13,822

For better or worse, the secret is out about Nafplio, one of Greece's prettiest and most romantic towns. It occupies a knockout location – on a small port beneath the towering Palamidi fortress – and is graced with attractive narrow streets, elegant Venetian houses, neoclassical mansions and interesting museums. With good bus connections and services, the town is an ideal base from which to explore many nearby ancient sites.

Sights

PALAMIDI FORTRESS Fortress
(adult/concession €4/2; ⊙8am-7.30pm summer, 8am-4.30pm winter) This vast and spectacular citadel stands on a 216m-high outcrop of rock with excellent views down onto the sea and surrounding land. It was built by the Venetians between 1711 and 1714, and is regarded as a masterpiece of military architecture.

There are two main approaches to the fortress. You can go via the road (taxis cost about €8 one way) or the energetic can tackle the seemingly endless steps that begin southeast of the bus station.

AKRONAFPLIA FORTRESS Fortress
Rising above the old part of town, the Akronafplia fortress is the oldest of Nafplio's three castles, although there's much less to see here than at the other two forts. The lower sections of the walls date back to the Bronze Age.

There's a lift up to the fortress from Plateia Poliko Nosokomiou at the western edge of town – look for the flags at the entrance of the tunnel leading to the lift.

BOURTZI Fortress
The island fortress of Bourtzi lies about 600m west of the town's port. Most of the existing structure was built by the Venetians. Boats (€4 return) to the island leave from the northeastern end of Akti Miaouli.

PELOPONNESE FOLKLORE FOUNDATION MUSEUM Museum
(Vasileos Alexandrou 1; admission €2; ⊙9am-3pm & 6-9pm Mon & Wed-Sat, 9.30am-3pm Sun, closed Tue mornings) Nafplio's award-winning musuem is a beautifully arranged collection of folk costumes and household items from Nafplio's former times. Established by the philanthropic owner, it's not to be missed.

ARCHAEOLOGICAL MUSEUM Museum
(Plateia Syntagmatos; ⊙8.30am-3pm Tue-Sun; adult/concession €2/1) Overlooking Plateia Syntagmatos, this museum reopened in 2009 following seven years of renovations. It features fine exhibits over two light and airy floors. The oldest exhibits, fire middens, date from 32,000 BC. Another highlight is the only bronze armour in existence from near Mycenae, dating from the 12th to 13th centuries BC.

NATIONAL GALLERY – ALEXANDROS SOUTZOS MUSEUM Art Gallery
(Sidiras Merarhias 23; adult/concession €3/2, admission free Mon; ⊙10am-3pm Mon, Thu & Sat, 10am-3pm & 6-9pm Wed & Fri; 10am-2pm Sun) This arm of the Athens National Gallery, is housed in a stunningly restored neoclassical building. It features works on the 1821 Greek War of Independence, including paintings of Greek painters Vryzakis and Tsokos, considered the most important painters of the postwar years.

 Sleeping

PENSION MARIANNA Hotel €€
(☎27520 24256; www.pensionmarianna.gr; Potamianou 9; s/d/tr incl breakfast €70/85/100;

Nafplio

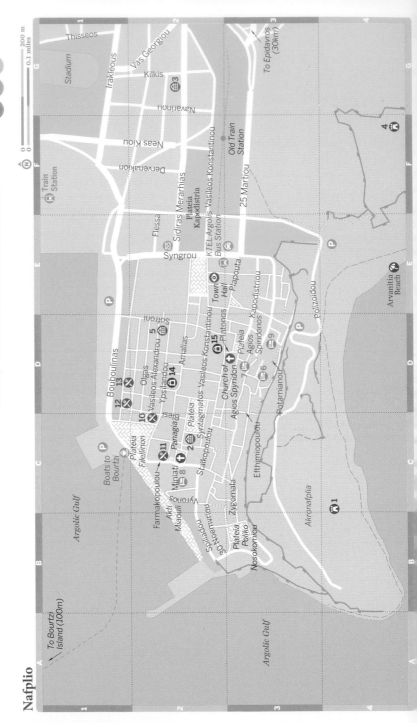

⊃ ❄ 🛜) This delightful abode is the best
value and most hospitable in Nafplio, if
not Greece. The wonderful owner-hosts,
the warm and welcoming Zotos brothers,
epitomise Greek *filoxenia* (hospitality) and
serve up more than delicious breakfasts
(don't miss their homemade organic lem-
nade), including conviviality and travel
advice. Clean and comfortable rooms (all
different, and some smaller than others)
open onto terraces where you can feast on
the killer view from your hill-top position.
Heights come at a small cost – several
flights of stairs.

IPOLITI Boutique Hotel €€
(📞 27520 96088; www.ippoliti.gr; Miniati 9;
€120-180; ❄) The 19 rooms in this
discretely luxurious place are decked
out in tasteful muted Tuscan furnishings
with neoclassical touches. There are even
glass-screened fireplaces in some of the
rooms. It has the feel of a boutique pension with hotel services, including a gym.

HOTEL BYRON Hotel €€
(📞 27520 22351; www.byronhotel.gr; Platonos
d €50-70, tr €80; ❄) Occupying a fine
Venetian building, the Byron is a reliable
favourite, with friendly management,
neat rooms, iron bedsteads and period
furniture. Breakfast costs €5.

EKAS DIMITRIS Pension €
(📞 27520 24594; Efthimiopoulou 26; s/d/tr
24/32/42) A good, friendly and central
budget option. The clean, homey rooms
have a top-value location on the slopes of
the Akronafplia.

 Eating

**ANTICA GELATERIA
DI ROMA** Confectioner €
(📞 27520 23520; www.anticagelateria.gr; cnr
Farmakopoulou & Komninou) Our favourite ge-
lato shop in Nafplio is here, where Italian
gelati maestro and maestra Marcello and
Claudia Raffo greet you with: '*Bongiorno* –
this is an Italian gelati shop!'

OMORFI POLI Taverna €
(📞 2752029452; Bouboulinas 75; mains €9-17.50;
🕐 dinner) This friendly restaurant's chef
whips up Greek and Italian dishes. The
mezedhes (from €5) have a slight non-
Greek twist – there's mushroom risotto
plus Greek favourites including *saganaki*
(fried cheese) and sausages in ouzo (€6).

ARAPAKOS Seafood €
(📞 27520 27675; Bouboulinas 81; mains €8-15,
fish per kilogram €35-85; 🕐 lunch & dinner)
Fish lovers should hook onto this smart,
efficient place for quality seafood.

ALALOUM Regional €
(📞 27520 29883; Papanikolaou 10; mains €8-17;
🕐 lunch & dinner Wed-Mon) Situated in a lovely
spot looking out on to the leafy square,
serving up Greek Mediterranean fare.

 Drinking

Despite being simply jammed with cafes
and bars, there still doesn't seem to
be enough of them in town to hold the

Nafplio

If You Like...
Coastal Towns

If you like the colourful, picturesque town of **Nafplio** (p115), we think you'd also like to linger in these scenic coastal towns:

1 **KORONI**
Head for this lovely Venetian port town, situated on Messinia Bay. Medieval mansions and churches line the town's quaint, winding streets. These lead to a promontory, on which perches an extensive castle. Koroni's main attraction is **Zaga Beach**, a long sweep of golden sand just south of the town. Koroni also sees loggerhead turtles.

2 **METHONI**
South of Pylos, this is another pretty seaside town with a popular sandy beach, next to which crouches the vast and romantic 15th-century **Venetian fortress** (admission free; ⊙8am-7pm May-Sep, to 3pm Oct-Apr).

3 **PYLOS**
Presiding over the southern end of an immense bay which is punctuated by a castle at each end, Pylos is one of the most picturesque towns in the Peloponnese. Hang out in the delightful tree-shaded central square, walk in the surrounding pine-covered hills or hop on a boat tour to see silt-covered wrecks of sunken Turkish ships, still discernible in the clear waters.

4 **GIALOVA**
On the northeastern edge of Navarino Bay, this town boasts a fine sandy beach and safe swimming. The nearby Gialova Lagoon is a prime birdwatching site; between September and March the lagoon is home to up to 20,000 assorted waterbirds, while many others pause here on their spring migration between Africa and Eastern Europe.

throngs of trendy party animals who flock to Nafplio in summer. Most options are on Bouboulinas – just cruise along until you find an image (and the latest decor) to your taste and a volume level you can handle.

Shopping

KARONIS Food & Drink
(☑27520 24446; www.karoniswineshop.gr; Amalias 5) Wine enthusiasts can find a fine selection of wines from all over the country, especially Nemean reds and spirits. Wine tastings offered.

MUSEUM OF THE KOMBOLOI Souven
(☑27520 21618; www.komboloi.gr; Staïkopoulou 25; adult/concession €3/free; ⊙9.30am-8pm, hours change seasonally) This shop – with a private museum above – sells komboloï (worry beads) evil-eye charms and amulets.

PELOPONNESE FOLKLORE FOUNDATION MUSEUM Souveni
The attractive ground-floor gift shop has a range of items, including books, from Greece and around the world.

Information

Staikos Travel (☑27520 27950; www. staikostravel.gr; Bouboulinas 50; ⊙8.30am 2pm & 5.30-9pm, closed Sun winter) A travel agent that is also happy to help with genera tourist enquiries.

To Kentrikou (Main plaza) Nafplio is strangely short of internet opportunities. Your best bet is here, a bar where, for the price of a drink or two you can happily browse away.

Getting There & Away

KTEL Argolis bus station (☑27520 27323; Syngrou 8) has buses to Athens (€13.10, 2½ hours, hourly), Epidavros (€2.60, 45 minutes, three daily, one Sunday) and Mycenae (€2.60, one hour, two daily). Note: weekend schedules ar often reduced.

Getting Around

For taxis call ☑27520 24120 or head to the rank on Syngrou.
Avis (☑27520 24160/1; www.carrental-greece. gr; Bouboulinas 51)

ounos Rent a car (📞 27520 24390; www
ounos-carrental.com; Dervenakion 7)

Iermes Car Rental (📞 27520 25308; www
ermestravel.gr; Amalias 1)

Epidavros Επίδαυρος

Its day, **Epidavros** (sometimes referred
o on signs as Sanctuary of Asklepios)
📞 27530 22009; adult/concession €6/3;
🕐8am-7.30pm summer, 8am-5pm winter), 30km
ast of Nafplio, was famed and revered as
ar away as Rome as a place of miraculous
ealing. Visitors came great distances to
his Sanctuary of Asclepius (god of medi-
ine) to seek a cure for their ailments.

Today visitors are more likely to flock to
ne site for its amazingly well-preserved
heatre, which remains a venue during
ne Hellenic Festival (p44)for classical
reek theatre (along with other more
nodern plays, opera and music), first
erformed here up to 2000 years ago.
he site occupies a glorious setting amid
ne-clad hills. Not surprisingly, Epidavros
 protected under the World Heritage
stings. It is one of the best-preserved
assical Greek structures, renowned for
s amazing acoustics; a coin dropped in
ne centre can be heard from the highest

ystras

seat. Built of limestone, the theatre seats
up to 14,000 people.

🛈 Getting There & Away

There are buses from Nafplio to Epidavros (€3, 45
minutes, three to five daily) and two to three buses
daily to Athens from nearby Ligourio (around €13,
2½ hours). Taxis (📞 27530 23322) from Ligourio
cost around €6; we don't recommended walking
to Epidavros from here, it's along a main road.

Mystras Μυστράς

The captivating ruins of churches,
libraries, strongholds and palaces in the
fortress town of **Mystras** (miss-*trahss*)
(📞 27310 83377; adult/concession €5/3;
🕐8am-7.30pm summer, 8.30am-3pm winter, a
World Heritage–listed site, spill from a
spur of the Taÿgetos Mountains 7km west
of Sparta. The site is among the most
important, historically speaking, in the
Peloponnese. This is where the Byzantine
Empire's richly artistic and intellectual
culture made its last stand before an invading Ottoman army, almost 1000 years
after its foundation.

At least half a day is needed to do
justice to the ruins of Mystras. Wear
sensible shoes and bring plenty of water.

DISCOVER PELOPONNESE, CORFU & KEFALLONIA EPIDAVROS

KASTRO & UPPER TOWN

From opposite the upper entrance ticket office, a path (signposted 'kastro') leads up to the fortress. The fortress was built by the Franks and extended by the Turks. The path descends from the ticket office leading to **Agia Sofia**, which served as the palace church, and where some frescoes survive.

From the palace, a winding, cobbled path leads down to the **Monemvasia Gate**, the entrance to the lower town.

LOWER TOWN

Through the Monemvasia Gate, turn right for the well-preserved, 14th-century **Convent of Pantanassa**. This features a beautifully ornate stone-carved facade and is still maintained by nuns, Mystras' only inhabitants. The exquisite, richly coloured, 15th-century frescoes here are among the finest examples of late-Byzantine art. The nuns ask that, before entering, you cover bare legs with the cloths provided.

The path continues down to the **Monastery of Perivleptos** (☼summer),

built into a rock. Inside, the 14th-century frescoes, preserved virtually intact, equal those of Pantanassa.

The **Mitropolis** (Cathedral of Agios Dimitrios) is a complex of buildings enclosed by a high wall. The original church was built in the 1200s, but was greatly altered in the 15th century. The church also has some fine frescoes. The adjoining small but modern **museum** houses some quirky pieces, including female hair, buttons and embrodiery, and other everyday items of Mystras' inhabitants.

Beyond the Mitropolis is the **Vrontokhion Monastery**. This was once the wealthiest monastery of Mystras, the focus of cultural activities and the burial place of the despots.

. . . .

🛈 Getting There & Away

Frequent buses go to Mystras from Sparta (€1.6, 30 minutes, 11 daily). A radio taxi from Sparta to Mystras' lower entrance (Xenia Restaurant) costs around €12, or slightly more to the upper

Left: Methoni's Venetian fortress (p118)
Below: Monemvasia
(LEFT) NAGELESTOCK.COM/ALAMY ©; (BELOW) IMAGEBROKER/ALAMY ©

ntrance. A cheaper option is to
ake a taxi (📞 27310 25300) from
lystras but these can be elusive.

Monemvasia & Gefyra
Μονεμβάσια & Γέφυρα

ast, imposing, spectacular Monemva-
ia (mo-nem-vah-*see*-ah or mo-nem-
ah-see-ah) is the Greek equivalent to
rance's Mont St-Michel. This perfect
ortress is an iceberg-like slab of rock
noored off the coast, with sheer cliffs
ising hundreds of feet from the sea, and
single, highly defendable causeway.

These days Monemvasia incorporates
oth the rock, whose medieval village is
nclosed within the walls of the rock's
astro, plus the modern mainland village
f Gefyra just across the causeway.
n summer, both places brim with
isitors. Fortunately, the extraordinary
isual impact of the medieval village in
articular – and the delights of exploring
– override the effects of mass tourism.

 Sights

FREE **MONEMVASIA**
ARCHAEOLOGICAL MUSEUM   Museum
(📞 27320 61403; ⊙ 8am-8pm Tue-Sun summer, 8.30am-3pm Tue-Sun winter) This small
museum displays a useful detailed map
of Monemvasia. It also houses finds unearthed in the course of excavations and
building around the old town.

 Sleeping

A pocket torch and sensible shoes are a
good idea for those staying on the cobbled, dimly lit *kastro.*

MONOPATI ROOMS &
APARTMENTS   B&B €€
(📞 27320 61772; www.byzantine-escapade.com;
Monemvasia; apt €70-85, 'little house' €110-140)

121

These two delightful stone options ooze personality, as do the hospitable owners. Stylish decor fills the apartments' quirky spaces, and both include kitchenettes. Breakfast – which can be served where you like it, when you like it – costs €6.

HOTEL BYZANTINO   Hotel €€
(27320 61254/351; Monemvasia; s/d/tr €60/100/120;) Helpful, English-speaking management oversees a range of great-value, atmospheric rooms all decked out in antiques and occupying various historic buildings. Some have sea-facing balconies, others don't, but these are delightfully cool in summer. Breakfast costs €6.

 Eating

Three tavernas sit cheek to cheek in Monemvasia's old town: **Matoula** (27320 61660), **Marianthi** (2732 61371) and **To Kanoni** (27320 61387). You can't really go wrong with any (unless you don't like the village cats) – choose between them for dish type (all traditional Greek) or ambience. Mains are around €8 to €14.

TAVERNA TRATA   Seafood €€
(Gefyra; mains €5-10, fish per kilogram €45-60) On the right immediately after you cross the causeway back to Gefyra. The hanging gulls and model yachts point to a nautical theme – seafood and grills are the go here.

🔵 Getting There & Away

Buses leave from outside Malvasia Travel (27320 61752; malvtrv@otenet.gr), just over the causeway in Geyfra; Malvasia also sells tickets. There are buses to Athens (€30, six hours, four to five daily) via Corinth Isthmus (€22.90, 4½ hours).

🔵 Getting Around

The medieval *kastro* of Monemvasia is inaccessible to cars and motorcycles, but these can cross the causeway. A shuttle bus (8am-midnight Jun-Sep, Christmas & Easter) ferries visitors between Geyfra and the *kastro*.

Car hire is available from Kypros Rent a Car (6934 609700; www.kypros-rentacar.gr, houtris@otenet.gr).

Gythio Γύθειο
POP 4489

Once the port of ancient Sparta, Gythio (*yee*-thih-o) is the gateway to the Lakonian Mani. This attractive fishing town's bustling waterfront has pastel-coloured, 19th-century buildings, behind which crumbling old Turkish houses and scruffy streets cling to a steep, wooded hill.

 Sights & Activities

There's safe swimming along the 6km of sandy beaches that extend from the village of Mavrovouni, 2km south of Gythio.

MARATHONISI ISLET   Historic Area
According to mythology, tranquil pine-shaded Marathonisi is ancient Cranae, where Paris and Helen consummated the affair that sparked the Trojan Wars. The 18th-century **Tzanetakis Grigorakis tower** houses a small **Museum of Mani History** (adult/concession €2/1; 8am-2.30pm), which relates Maniot history through the eyes of Europeans who visited the region between the 15th and 19th centuries.

 Sleeping & Eating

SAGA PENSION   Hotel €
(27330 23220; www.sagapension.gr; Kranais; d €50;) This is a good-value, saga-free, comfortable place with balconies. It's 150m from the port, overlooking Marathonisi Islet. The upmarket Saga Restaurant is below (mains €9 to €15, fish per kilogram €40 to €60). Breakfast €5.

PALAI (O) POLIS   Taverna €
(27330 23322; Irakeous 10; mains €6-14; lunch & dinner) Gythio's newest addition is popular for its attractive decor – the traditional objects and chandeliers are a stylish take on traditional Greek. Choose from the daily specials on show. Ask the owner to explain the pun in the title.

MICHAEL WEBER/IMAGEBROKER ©

Don't Miss **Kastro – Medieval Town**

The narrow main street of Monemvasia's *Kastro* is lined with souvenir shops and tavernas, flanked by winding stairways that weave between a network of stone houses with walled gardens. The main street leads to the central square and the **Cathedral of Christ in Chains**, dating from the 13th century. Opposite is the **Church of Agios Pavlos** (pictured above), built in 956. Further along the main street is the **Church of Myrtidiotissa**, virtually in ruins, but still with a small altar and a defiantly flickering candle. Overlooking the sea is the whitewashed 16th-century **Church of Panagia Hrysafitissa**.

🚍 Getting There & Away

Boat

ANE Lines (www.lane.gr, in Greek) has one weekly summertime ferry to Crete via Kythira and Antikythira. Check the ever-changing schedule with Rozakis Travel (☏27330 22207; rozakis_agency@hol.gr), on the waterfront at Pavlou 5.

Bus

TEL Lakonia bus station (☏27330 22228; vrikleos) is found northwest along the waterfront near Jande Café. Services run north to Athens (€23.80, 4½ hours, six daily) and south to Areopoli (€2.60, 30 minutes, four daily), the Diros Caves (€3.70, one hour, one daily) and Vathia (€6.80, 1½ hours, one weekly).

Helpful staff will explain the best way to see the Mani from Gythio (return) in one day. Getting to Kalamata can be fiddly; it involves taking onward connections from either Itilo (€3.80, 45 minutes) or Sparta. There are only two buses daily (5am and 1pm) except Sunday to Itilo (the 1pm bus may require a change at Areopoli). For Monemvasia, change at Sparta.

🛈 Getting Around

Moto Makis (☏27330 25111; Kranais) Hires out mopeds and scooters.

Rozakis Travel (☏27330 22207; rozakis_agency@hol.gr) Has cars for hire.

Taxis (☏27330 23400) Found opposite the bus station.

The Mani Η Μάνη

The Mani, the region covering the central peninsula in the south of the Peloponnese, is a wild, rugged place, and Greeks from elsewhere will tell you, so are its people. For centuries the Maniots were a law unto themselves, renowned for their fierce independence, resentment of attempts to govern them and for their bitter, spectacularly murderous internal feuds. Dotted around the territory – particularly in the inner Mani – you'll find bizarre tower settlements that were built as refuges during clan wars from the 17th century onwards.

Thankfully these feuds, some of which took entire armies to halt, are long forgotten and the Maniots are as friendly and hospitable as Greeks elsewhere.

It's worth including this region in your itinerary. The steep tumbling skirts of the Taÿgetos Mountains (threaded with wonderful walking trails) and the tiny coves and ports nestling beside them make for some memorably dramatic scenery. As well as the towers, there are magnificent churches, and caves.

Keen explorers should ask at local shops for *Inside The Mani: A Walking Guide* by Mat Dean, and *The Mani* by Bob Barrow and Mat Dean. The books are full of walking and information gems about the region's villages, towers and churches.

Areopoli Αρεοπολη
POP 774

Areopoli (ah-reh-o-po lih), capital of the Mani, is aptly named after Ares, the god of war. The town retains many other reminders of its rumbustious past. There are some fine examples of Maniot architecture to be found in the narrow alleyways surrounding Plateia 17 Martiou.

In the southern end of town (ask for directions), the **Pikoulakis Tower House Museum** (www.culture.gr; admission free; Tue-Sun 8.30am-2.30pm) is a must-see. Housed in a restored tower, the museum houses exquisite Byzantine pieces from Mani churches, including superb manuscripts and jewellery.

There is some fabulous walking in the area – look for the signs in the main square; hikers should be experienced in using compasses and equipment as the routes may not be maintained.

The Arcadian Gate at Ancient Messini (p126)

PETER EASTLAND/ALAMY

Detour:
Langada Pass Ορεινή Διάβαση Λαγκάδα

The 59km Sparta–Kalamata road is one of the most stunning routes in Greece, crossing the Taÿgetos Mountains by way of the Langada Pass.

The climb begins in earnest at the village of **Trypi**, 9km west of Sparta, where the road enters the dramatic **Langada Gorge**. To the north of this gorge is the site where the ancient Spartans left babies too weak or deformed to become good soldiers to die.

From Trypi, the road follows the course of the Langada River before climbing sharply through a series of hairpin bends to emerge in a sheltered valley. This is a good spot to stop for a stroll among the plane trees along the riverbank. The road then climbs steeply once more, to the high point of 1524m – crossing the boundary from Lakonia into Messinia on the way. The descent to Kalamata is equally dramatic.

If you need a bed and a feed, stop at the friendly **Hotel Taÿgetos** (27210 99236; fax 27210 98198; s/d/tr €30/40/50). It has a superb location at the very top of the Langada Pass. It also boasts a good restaurant with specialities such as roasted goat, rooster with red wine and rabbit *stifadho*. It's 24km from Sparta.

Sleeping

LONDAS PENSION   B&B €€
(27330 51360; www.londas.com; d/tr incl breakfast €80/110) This 200-year-old tower is the undisputed king of the castle: stylish whitewashed rooms tastefully decorated in an antique and modern fusion. The small rusty sign is hard to spot near the Church of Taxiarhes.

HOTEL TRAPELA   Hotel €€
(27330 52690; www.trapela.gr; s/d/tr €60/80/90; ❄) This small 12-room place is promoted as a 'new traditional' hotel, as indeed it is. The comfortable wood-and-stone rooms have tasteful muted colours and the design is along Maniot lines.

Eating

NICOLA'S CORNER TAVERNA Taverna €
(27330 51366; Plateia Athanaton; mains €8-10; ☉ lunch & dinner) Ignore the menu – this popular spot on the central square displays a good choice of tasty taverna staples that change daily. Don't miss the handmade maccaroni with fried local (read salty) cheese.

TO KATOI   Taverna €€
(27330 51201; mains €7-10) This cosy place is recommended for its daily specials (not on the menu). It's in a lovely location near the Church of Taxiarhes.

Shopping

Invincible Mani (27330 53670; Plateia Athanaton) Has an excellent selection of maps and books on the region.

Information

The town is split into two parts: the new upper town, around Plateia Athanaton, and the old lower town, around Plateia 17 Martiou. The two squares are linked by a 'main' lane (formerly Kapetan Matapan but no longer officially referred to).

Getting There & Away

At the time of writing, the bus station (27330 51229; Plateia Athanaton) was about to relocate to near the high school at the town's northern end. There are buses to Gythio (€2.60, 30 minutes, four daily), which proceed to Athens (€27). There are bus services to Itilo (€1.60, 20 minutes, two daily Monday to Saturday, no service Sunday) via Limeni, to Gerolimenas (€3.40, 45 minutes, three daily), the Diros Caves (€1.60, 15 minutes, one daily;

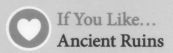

If You Like…
Ancient Ruins

If you like wandering through the absorbing ruins of **Mystras** (p119), we think you'd like stepping back in time at these other ruins:

1 ANCIENT MESSINI
These fascinating ruins lie scattered across a small valley, 25km northwest of Kalamata. Built on the site of an earlier stronghold, this Messinian capital was one of a string of defensive positions designed to keep watch over Sparta. Apart from its defensive potential, Ancient Messini was also favoured by the gods. According to local myth, Zeus was born here – not in Crete.

2 NESTOR'S PALACE
(site only adult/concession €3/2, site & museum €4/2; ⊙8.30am-3pm, museum closed Mon) Believed to have been the court of the mythical hero Nestor, who took part in the voyage of the Argonauts and fought in the Trojan War, this is the best preserved of all Mycenaean palaces. Some of the fine frescoes discovered here are housed in the museum in the nearby village of Hora.

3 TEMPLE OF EPICUREAN APOLLO AT VASSES
(adult/concession €3/2; ⊙8am-8pm) Situated on a wild, isolated spot overlooking rugged mountains and hills, this is one of Greece's most romantic and atmospheric archaeological sites. The striking and well-preserved temple stands at an altitude of 1200m. Built in 420 BC, it combines Doric and Ionic columns and a single Corinthian column – the earliest example of this order.

returns at 12.45pm), Lagia (€3.70, 40 minutes, one daily) and Vathia (€4.20, one hour, two weekly).

Diros Caves Σπηλαιο Διρου

These extraordinary **caves** (☎27330 52222; adult/concession incl tour €12/7; ⊙8.30am-5.30pm Jun-Sep, 8.30am-3pm Oct-May) are 11km south of Areopoli, and signposted near the village of **Pyrgos Dirou**.

The natural entrance to the caves is on the beach and locals like to believe the legend that they extend as far north as Sparta (speleologists have so far estimated the caves to be 14km; tourists enter to 1.5km). They were inhabited in neolithic times, but were abandoned after an earthquake in 4 BC and weren't rediscovered until 1895. Systematic exploration began in 1949. The caves are famous for their stalactites and stalagmites, which have fittingly poetic names such as the Palm Forest, Crystal Lily and the Three Wise Men.

Unfortunately, the half-hour guided tour through the caves is disappointingly brief – it covers only the lake section, and bypasses the most spectacular formations of the dry area.

The nearby **Neolithic Museum of Diros** (☎27330 52233; adult/concession €2/1; hours unreliable) houses items found in an adjoining neolithic cave, the **Alepotrypa Cave**.

Gerolimenas Γερολιμενας
POP 55

Gerolimenas (yeh-ro-lih-*meh*-nahss) is a tranquil fishing village built around a small, sheltered bay at the south-western tip of the peninsula. It's the perfect place for scenic seclusion.

🛏 Sleeping & Eating

HOTEL KIRIMAI　Luxury Hotel **€€€**
(☎27330 54288; www.kyrimai.gr; d €110-210, ste €240-340; P ✳ ☒) The luxurious Kirimai is one of the fanciest hotels in the region. It sits in an idyllic setting at the far southern end of the harbour. The stone-floored, timber-beamed rooms are individually finished with decor-magazine flair. Its restaurant is open to nonguests (mains €15 to €25).

HOTEL AKROGIALI　Hotel **€€**
(☎27330 54204; www.gerolimenas-hotels.com; s €25-30, d €50-80, tr €70-120, 2-/3-/4-person apt €80/100/120; ✳) The Akrogiali has a great setting overlooking the bay on the western edge of town. It offers various sleeping options, from OK doubles in the traditional hotel building to squishier

ooms in a newer stone wing, and apartments nearby. Breakfast costs €6.

Getting There & Away

here are three buses daily from Gerolimenas Areopoli (€5, 45 minutes) – and on to Athens €30), Gythio (€10, 1¼ hours) and Sparta 2¼ hours). The bus stop is outside Hotel krotenaritis; tickets are bought on board.

Kardamyli ΚαρδαμΥλη
POP 400

t's easy to see why Kardamyli (kahr-dah-nee-lih) was one of the seven cities offered to Achilles by Agamemnon. This tiny illage has one of the prettiest settings n the Peloponnese, nestled between the lue waters of the Messinian Gulf and the aÿgetos Mountains. The **Vyros Gorge**, vhich emerges just north of town, runs to he foot of **Mt Profitis Ilias** (2407m), the ighest peak of the Taÿgetos.

Today the gorge and surrounding areas re very popular with hikers. The hills ehind the village are criss-crossed with n extensive network of colour-coded valking trails. Many guesthouses in the illage can supply you with route maps of varying detail and quality). Most of he hikes around here are strenuous, so trong footwear is essential to support our ankles on the often relentlessly rough ground, particularly if you venture into the oulder-strewn gorge itself. You will also eed to carry plenty of drinking water.

For those who don't want to go it lone, the cool Action Jacksons at **2407 Mountain Activities** (☐ 27210 73752; vww.2407m.com) offer a range of activities ncluding hiking (€20 to €30 per person, ninimum four people) and mountain-ike trips (€20 to €30) in and around he Taÿgetos Mountains, venturing into secret' forested and rocky regions. The ffice is half-way along the main street.

Sleeping

KALAMITSI HOTEL   Hotel €€
☐ 27210 73131; www.kalamitsi-hotel.gr; d/ste 110/160) 1km south of town, the Kalamitsi s a modern, stone-built hotel with serene, well-appointed rooms (family bungalows also available for €220). Within its shady grounds are paths leading to a secluded pebbly beach. Home-cooked dinners (set menu €20, guests only) and fresh buffet breakfasts (€10) are also available.

Eating

ELIES   Taverna €
(☐ 27210 73140; mains €6-12; ⊙ lunch) Location, location. Right by the beach, 1km north of town, and nestled in olive groves. It's got the atmosphere of a provincial Mediterranean private garden with top-quality nosh to boot. Think lemon lamb casserole (€7).

Information

Kardamyli is on the main Areopoli–Kalamata road. The central square, Plateia 25 Martiou 1821, lies at the northern end of the main thoroughfare.

Kardamyli's main pebble-and-stone beach is off the road to Kalamata; turn left beyond the bridge on the northern edge of town. The road up to Old (or Upper) Kardamyli is on the right before the bridge.

The useful website at www.kardamili-greece.com can also provide some information.

Getting There & Around

Kardamyli is on the main bus route from Itilo to Kalamata (around €4, one hour, two to five daily). The bus stops at the central square at the northern end of the main thoroughfare, and at the bookshop at the southern end.

Two daily buses head to Exohorio (€1.60; runs to changing times); most travellers prefer to take a taxi (around €18).

Olympia Ολυμπία
POP 1000

With countless overpriced souvenir shops and eateries, the modern village of Olympia (o-lim-bee-*ah*) panders unashamedly to the hundreds of thousands of tourists who continually pour through here on their way to Ancient Olympia. Despite this, the town is far from kitsch.

Only 500m south of the well-kept leafy streets over the Kladeos River is Ancient Olympia. Although the site's surrounds were tragically burnt in the 2007 bushfires, rendering it devoid of trees, Ancient Olympia survived, thanks to efforts of locals and firefighters. It remains one of the most luxuriantly green, beautiful and historically important sites.

Sights

Four museums focus on Ancient Olympia (and Olympics) mania. The Archaeological Museum of Olympia and Museum of the History of the Olympic Games in Antiquity are not to be missed; the other two are only worth it if you have time to kill or interest to satisfy. And this is before you even hit the Olympic site itself.

FREE **MUSEUM OF THE HISTORY OF THE OLYMPIC GAMES IN ANTIQUITY** Museum
(⊙12.30-7.30pm Mon, 8am-7.30pm Tue-Sun May-Oct, 10.30am-5pm Mon, 8.30am-3pm Tue-Sun Nov-April) This museum, opened in 2004 (after the Athens Olympics), is a beautifully presented space depicting the history of all things athletic, as well as the Nemean, Panathenaic and, of course, Olympic Games. The sculptures, mosaics and other displays all pay tribute to athletes and athleticism. Women – and their involvement (or lack of) – are also acknowledged.

ARCHAEOLOGICAL MUSEUM OF OLYMPIA Museum
(⌨/fax 26240 22742; adult/concession €6/3, inc site visit €9/5; ⊙1.30-8pm Mon, 8am-8pm Tue-Sun Apr-Oct, 10.30am-5pm Mon, 8.30am-3pm Tue-Sun Nov-Mar) This superb museum – Ancient Olympia's archaeological site museum – about 200m north of the sanctuary's ticket kiosk, is a great place to start or end your visit to the site of Ancient Olympia.

The museum includes a scale model of the site, and spectacular (if not complete) reassembled pediments and metopes from the Temple of Zeus. The **eastern pediment** depicts the chariot race between Pelops and Oinomaos, the **western pediment** shows the fight between the Centaurs and Lapiths, and the **metopes** depict the Twelve Labours of Hercules.

SITE OF ANCIENT OLYMPIA Ancient Site
(⌨26240 22517; adult/concession €6/3, site & archaeological museum €9/5; ⊙8am-8pm Apr-Oct, 8.30am-3pm Nov-Mar) The Olympics were undoubtedly the Ancient World's biggest sporting event. During the games warring states briefly halted their squabbles, corporate sponsors vied to outdo each other, and victorious competitors won great fame and considerable fortune. You could say much the same about the modern-day equivalent, the main difference being that back then only men could compete and they did most of it sans underpants. Held every four

Gerolimenas (p126)
CHRISTOS MARKOU/ALAMY ©

Detour:
Gerolimenas to Porto Kagio
ΓερολιμΕνας προς ΠΟρτο ΚΑγιο

South of Gerolimenas, the road continues 4km to the small village of Alika, where it divides. One road leads across the mountains to the east coast, and the other goes south to Vathia and Porto Kagio. The southern road follows the coast, passing pebbly beaches. It then climbs steeply inland to **Vathia**, the most dramatic of the traditional Mani villages, comprising a cluster of closely packed tower houses perched on a rocky spur.

A turn-off to the right 9km south of Alika leads to **Marmari**, with its two sandy beaches, while the main road cuts across the peninsula to the tiny east-coast fishing village of **Porto Kagio**, set on a perfect horseshoe bay.

A 10-minute walk will take you to a peninsula, on which perches the tiny church **St Nicholas**. Hardier walkers should head to one of Europe's southernmost points, **Cape Tenaro** (or Cape Matapan), whose beautiful lighthouse has been recently restored. The cape has been an important location for millenia and was first mentioned by Homer in his 'Iliad'. Follow the signs from Porto Kagio; from the car park it's a 45-minute walk.

ears until their abolition by killjoy Emperor Theodosius I in AD 394, the games lasted at least 1000 years. The World Heritage–listed site of Ancient Olympia is still a recognisable complex of temples, priests' dwellings and public buildings. The site contains excellent explanatory boards, with depictions of what the buildings would have looked like, along with a plan and description in English.

Ancient Olympia is signposted from the modern village. The entrance is beyond the bridge over the Kladeos River. Allow a minimum of half a day.

Sleeping

OTEL PELOPS   Hotel €
(/fax 26240 22543; www.hotelpelops.gr; Vare-2; s/d/tr/ste incl breakfast €40/55/75/105;) Opposite the church, this is among the town's best contenders, with comfortable rooms. The delightful Greek-Australian owners, the Spiliopoulos family, provide friendly, knowledgable service and a buffet breakfast fit for an athlete. On request is the Pelops Platter, a massive dish of gourmet mezedhes.

HOTEL KRONIO   Hotel €
(26240 22188; www.hotelkronio.gr; Tsoureka 1, s €45, d/tr incl breakfast €50/66;) In 2008 this place had a makeover. Its contemporary look and bright and airy rooms make it excellent value. The helpful multilingual owner adds to the package.

 Eating

TAKIS TYROPITAS   Greek €
(Praxitelis Kondilis, 36; snacks €1.50; 7am-3pm) This nondescript blink-and-you'll-miss-it takeaway joint has been here for 20 years, and with good reason. Owner Takis makes the best tyropita (cheese pie) and other homemade treats in the Pelops – some would say, Greece.

O THEA   Taverna €
(26240 23264; Floka; mains €6-11; dinner all year, lunch May-Oct) It's worth the effort to venture the winding route to the small village of Floka, 1.5km north of Olympia, for this hearty traditional taverna fare. Enjoy the grills, zucchini balls and views of Floka from the large terrace. That is, if the locals

don't beat you to it. It's open irregularly outside high season.

ℹ Information

EOT Olympia (☏ 26240-22262; www.eot.gr; Praxitelous Kondyli; ⏱ 8.30am-7.30pm Mon-Fri May-Oct) Only open on weekdays. Public transport schedules (including ferries from Kyllini and Patra) are posted on the window.

ℹ Getting There & Away

There is no direct service from Olympia to Athens. Eight or so of the 16 buses (reduced schedule on Sunday) go via Pyrgos (€1.90, 30 minutes) and allow time to connect for services to Athens. From Olympia, there are also buses east to Tripoli (€11.10, three hours, at least two daily). Note: For tickets to Tripoli, you must reserve your seat with **KTEL Pyrgos** (☏ 26210 20600) one day prior to travel; hotels will call on your behalf.

CORFU KEPKYPA

POP 122,670

The greenest Ionian island Corfu, or Kerkyra (*ker*-kih-rah) in Greek, was Homer's 'beautiful and rich land'. Mountains dominate the northern half where the east and west coastlines can be steep and dramatic and where the island's interior is a rolling expanse of peaceful countryside.

Corfu was a seat of European learning in the early days of modern Greece. While the rest of the nation struggled simply to get by, the Corfiots established cultural institutions such as libraries and centres of learning. To this day, Corfu remains proud of its intellectual and artistic roots. This legacy is visible from its fine museums to its high-calibre, Italian-influenced cuisine.

ℹ Getting There & Away

AIR

Corfu's Airport is about 2km southwest of the town centre.

DOMESTIC

Aegean Air (www.aegeanair.com) Direct flights to Thessaloniki.

Olympic Air (☏ 26610 22962; www.olympicair.com) At the airport.

Sky Express (☏ 28102 23500; www.skyexpress.gr) Operates a route to Preveza, Kefallonia and to Iraklio, Crete.

INTERNATIONAL

EasyJet (www.easyjet.com) has daily direct flights between London and Corfu (May to October). From May to September, many charter flights come from northern Europe and the UK.

BOAT

Petrakis Lines (☏ 26610 31649; Ethnikis Antistasis 4) and **Bouas** (☏ 26610 49800; Eleftheriou Venizelou 32) operate two different passenger-only hydrofoil lines between Corfu and Paxi from May until mid-October. Book ahead; places fill quickly.

US

TEL (📞26610 28898) services go to Athens (€43, 8½ hours, three daily Monday, Wednesday and Friday via Lefkimmi) and Thessaloniki (€38, eight hours, daily). For both, budget another €7.50 for the ferry to the mainland. Purchase tickets from Corfu Town's long-distance bus station.

🚍 Getting Around

O/FROM THE AIRPORT

There is no bus between the airport and Corfu Town. Taxis between the airport and Corfu Town cost around €12.

US

LONG-DISTANCE BUSES Long-distance KTEL buses (known as green buses) travel from Corfu Town's long-distance bus station (📞26610 3927/30627; Ioannou Theotoki), between Plateia San Rocco and the new port.

Fares cost €1.60 to €4.40. Printed timetables are at the ticket kiosk. Sunday and holiday services are reduced considerably, or don't run at all.

orfu Town

LOCAL BUSES Local buses (blue buses) depart from the local bus station (📞26610 31595; Plateia San Rocco) in Corfu Old Town.

Tickets are €1.10 or €1.50 depending on journey length; purchase at the booth on Plateia San Rocco (although tickets for Ahillion, Benitses and Kouramades are bought on the bus). All trips are under 30 minutes.

CAR & MOTORCYCLE

Budget (📞26610 22062; Ioannou Theotoki 132)

Easy Rider (📞26610 43026) Opposite the new port; has scooters and motorbikes.

International Rent-a-Car (📞26610 33411/37710; 20a Kapodistriou)

Sunrise (📞26610 26511/44325; www.corfusunrise.com; Ethnikis Antistasis 6)

Top Cars (📞26610 35237; www.carrentalcorfu.com; Donzelot 25)

Corfu Town
POP 28,692

Charming, cosmopolitan Corfu Town (also known as Kerkyra) takes hold of you and never lets go. Pedestrians stroll between pastel-hued Venetian-era mansions. Museums, cultural offerings and some of the region's finest restaurants dot the Old

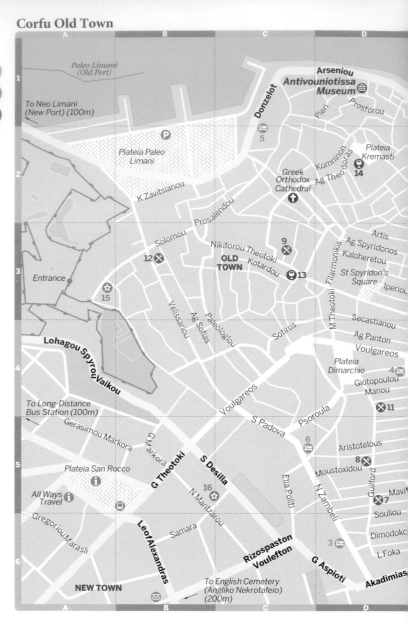

Town. The grand seaside esplanade, known as the Spianada, is lined with handsome buildings and an arcaded promenade, the Liston. Built by the French as a precursor to Paris' Rue de Rivoli, today the Liston, with its swath of packed cafes, is the town's social hub.

◉ Sights & Activities

PALACE OF ST MICHAEL & ST GEORGE   Palace, Art Museu
(☏26610 30443; adult/child incl audio-guide €4/2; ⊗8.30am-8pm Tue-Sun Jun-Oct,

0 ——— 200m
0 ——— 0.1miles

Apolodorou

Elenis

Vouthirotou

Kapodistriou

Epidamnou

Eleftherias

1 ⛪

2 🏛️ 🎨 **Palace of St Michael & St George**

🅿️

10
🍴 Liston

Old Cricket Ground

🅿️

Palaio Frourio (Old Fortress) 🏰

The Spianada

Agoniston Polytehniou

Neo Limani (New Port)

Kapodistriou

Dimokratias

Bay of Garitsa

To Archaeological Museum (300m); Airport (2km)

Corfu Old Town

informative English-language placards, the collection's approximately 10,000 artefacts collected from China, Japan, India, Tibet, Nepal, Korea and Thailand include priceless prehistoric bronzes, ceramics, jade figurines, coins and magnificent works of art in onyx, ivory and enamel. Behind the eastern side of the palace, the **Municipal Art Gallery** (admission €2; ⊙9am-5pm Tue-Sun) houses a fine collection featuring the work of leading Corfiot painters, a highlight being *The Assassination of Capodistrias* by Charalambos Pachis.

PALAIO FROURIO   Fortress
(Old Fortress; ☎26610 48310; adult/child €4/free; ⊙8am-8pm May-Oct, 8.30am-3pm Nov-Mar) Constructed by the Venetians in the 15th century on the remains of a Byzantine castle and further altered by the British, this spectacular landmark offers respite from the crowds and superb

3.30am-2.30pm Tue-Sun Nov-May) Originally the residence of a succession of British high commissioners, this palace now houses the world-class **Museum of Asian Art**, which was founded in 1929. Expertly curated with extensive,

N. REED OF QEDIMAGES/ALAMY

Don't Miss Diakofto–Kalavryta Railway

One of the unmissable journeys to make in the Peloponnese is aboard the tiny, unique **train** running along the railway from Diakofto to Kalavryta. It takes travellers on an unforgettable ride through the dramatic **Vouraïkos Gorge**. The train climbs over 700m in 22.5km, using a rack-and-pinion (cog) system for traction on the steep sections, effectively clamping itself to the notched girder you can see running between the rails. Built by an Italian company between 1885 and 1895, the railway was a remarkable feat of engineering for its time, with only a handful of equivalents around the world (most notably in the Swiss Alps). Between 2007 and 2009 the trains were off the tracks as the entire rails and cog sections were completely replaced, and four new modern trains were constructed to replace the former carriages.

As you head through the gorge, the line switches back and forth under a leafy canopy of plane trees and clings to a narrow ledge overhanging the river, passing through seven curving tunnels along the way.

The original steam engines that first plied the route were replaced in the early 1960s by diesel cars, but the old engines can still be seen outside Diakofto and Kalavryta stations. Hourly KTEL buses between Patras and Athens stop at Diakofto (one hour).

The journey takes just over an hour, stopping en route at Zahlorou.

THINGS YOU NEED TO KNOW

📞 in Diakofto 26910 43228; www.odontotos.com; one way/return €10/20

views of the region. Climb to the summit of the inner outcrop which is crowned by a lighthouse for a 360-degree panorama. The gatehouse contains a Byzantine museum.

ANTIVOUNIOTISSA MUSEUM Museum
(📞 26610 38313; adult/child €2/free; ⊗ 8am-2.30pm Tue-Sun) The exquisite aisle-less and timber-roofed 15th-century Church

of Our Lady of Antivouniotissa holds an outstanding collection of Byzantine and post-Byzantine icons and artefacts dating from the 13th to the 17th centuries.

FREE **MON REPOS ESTATE** Park, Ruins
(☉8am-7pm May-Oct, 8am-5pm Nov-Apr) On the southern outskirts of Corfu on the Kanoni Peninsula, an extensive lushly wooded parkland estate surrounds an elegant neoclassical villa. They were created in the 1830s by the second British commissioner of the Ionians, Sir Frederick Adam, as a tribute to his Corfiot wife. The British gave Mon Repos to King George I of Greece in 1864 and it was the birthplace, in 1921, of King George's grandson, the UK's current Duke of Edinburgh (Queen Elizabeth II's husband, Philip). Tracks and paths lead through the wooded grounds to the ruins of two Doric temples; the first is vestigial, but the southerly one, the **Temple of Artemis**, is serenely impressive.

The villa houses the excellent **Museum of Palaeopolis** (☎26610 41369; adult/concession €3/2; ☉8am-7pm Tue-Sun May-Oct), with entertaining archaeological displays and exhibits on the history of Corfu Town. Buses run south to Kanoni from the Spianada (every 20 minutes).

ARCHAEOLOGICAL MUSEUM Museum
(☎26610 30680; P Vraïla 5; adult/child €3/free; ☉8.30am-3pm Tue-Sun) Among the museum's fine collection, the massive **Gorgon pediment** (590–580 BC) is one of the best-preserved pieces of Archaic sculpture found in Greece. It was part of the west pediment of the 6th century BC Temple of Artemis, a Doric temple on nearby Kanoni Peninsula.

Sleeping

SIORRA VITTORIA Boutique Hotel €€
(☎26610 36300; www.siorravittoria.com; Stefanou Padova 36; r incl breakfast €135-150, ste €165-190; P ❄ 🛜) Expect luxury and style at this 19th-century mansion where painstakingly restored traditional architecture and modern amenities meet. Marble bathrooms, crisp linens and

genteel service make for relaxation in this quiet mansion. Breakfast is in the peaceful garden beneath an ancient magnolia tree. The Vittoria suite (€190) has views to the sea.

BELLA VENEZIA Boutique Hotel €€
(☎26610 46500; www.bellaveneziahotel.com; N Zambeli 4; s/d incl breakfast €102/123; ❄ 🛜) In a neoclassical former girls' school, the Venezia has comfy rooms and an elegant ambience. Conscientious staff welcome you and the gazebo breakfast room in the garden is delightful.

HOTEL ASTRON Hotel €€
(☎26610 39505; www.citymarina.gr; Donzelot 15; s/d/tr incl breakfast €75/80/95; ❄ 🛜) Centrally located and overlooking Plateia Palaio Limani (Old Port Sq), the new fortress and the seaside, the Astron is steadily updating its airy, comfortable rooms and installing a gym. Some rooms have balconies. No credit cards.

HOTEL ARCADION Hotel €€
(☎26610 37670; www.arcadionhotel.com; Vlasopoulou 2; s/d/tr €75/95/110; ❄ 🛜) Straightforward clean rooms are not the enticement here; it's the location. Right on the Liston's busiest corner, balconies overlook the hubbub and the old fort.

Eating

LA CUCINA Italian €€
(mains €10 25) Guilford (☎26610 45029; Guilford 17; ☉dinner); Moustoxidou (☎26610 45799; cnr Guilford & Moustoxidou; ☉lunch & dinner) A long-established favourite, La Cucina shines for

Domestic Flights from Corfu

DESTINATION	DURATION	FARE	FREQUENCY
Athens	1hr	€75	2-4 daily
Kefallonia	1hr 5min	€46	3 weekly
Thessaloniki	55min	€69	3 weekly

its well-run ethos and its creative cuisine, with hand-rolled pasta dishes at the fore. Cajun shrimp with cherry tomatoes, spring onions and mascarpone sauce is delicious or try the range of innovative mezedhes, salads and pizzas. Excellent wines accompany it all. The original Guilford location is cosy warm tones and murals, while the Moustoxidou annexe (with identical menu) is chic in glass and grey.

LA FAMIGLIA
Italian €

(26610 30270; Maniarizi-Arlioti 26; mains €8-12; lunch & dinner) Tucked away in a back street, this homey spot highlights creative salads and pastas. Cool tunes and low-key chatter set the mood. Flavours are both light and rich – how do they manage that?

REX
Mediterranean €

(26610 39649; Kapodistriou 66; mains €8-21; lunch & dinner) Set back from the Liston, this elegant restaurant elevates Greek home cooking to fine dining, and serves a full array of seafood and Continental dishes. Attentive staff inform you of the specials of the day. Pair them with a fine wine or the local Corfu Beer ales.

TO TAVERNAKI TIS MARINAS
Taverna €

(6981656001; 4th Parados, Agias Sofias 1; mains €6-16; lunch & dinner) Restored stone walls, smooth hardwood floors and cheerful staff lift the ambience of this traditional taverna (traditional restaurant) a cut above the rest. Check the daily specials or choose anything from *mousakas* (baked layers of eggplant or zucchini, minced meat and potatoes topped with cheese sauce) to bolognese or steak.

STARENIO
Bakery €

(Guilford 59; snacks under €3) Huge selection of gourmet pies, breads and the *best* cakes.

 **Drinking**

MIKRO CAFÉ
Cafe, Bar

(26610 31009; cnr N Theotoki 42 & Kotardhou) Laid-back locals gather at this little cafe-bar with occasional live entertainment in

Left: Palace of St Michael & St George (p132)
Below: Palaio Frourio (p133)
(LEFT) KEN GILLHAM/ALAMY ©; (BELOW) PAUL WILLIAMS/ALAMY ©

DISCOVER PELOPONNESE, CORFU & KEFALLONIA CORFU TOWN

the heart of the Old Town. Mikro has a leafy raised terrace and seating that clambers up a narrow lane.

VENETIAN WELL Lounge
(☎ 26610 44761; Plateia Kremasti) Though technically a restaurant, forego the food and come for a pre-dinner drink in this tiny ambience-rich square centred around a beautiful Venetian well.

 Entertainment

Check www.corfuland.gr for current listings.

JAZZ ROCK Club
(Solomou 29) The artsy set gathers for eclectic DJs and live music near the centre of town.

MUNICIPAL THEATRE Performing Arts
(☎ 26610 33598; Mantzarou) Corfu's cultural powerhouse stages classical music,

opera, dance and drama here and at the theatre next to Mon Repos.

For bigger dance venues after 11pm head to Corfu's disco strip, 2km northwest of the new port, along Ethnikis Antistasis (take a taxi; it's a busy unlit road without walkways).

 Information

Tourist Information

Get *Corfiot* (€2), an English-language monthly newspaper with listings, at kiosks.

All Ways Travel (☎ 26610 33955; www.corfuallwaystravel.com; Plateia San Rocco) Helpful English-speaking staff.

Municipal tourist kiosk (Plateia San Rocco; ☺ 9am-4pm Mon-Sat Jun-Sep) Similar kiosk may operate at the ferry arrival terminal in high season.

137

South of Corfu Town

The coast road south from Corfu Town leads to a turn-off to well-signposted **Ahillion Palace** (26610 56245; adult/child €7/2, audioguide €3; 8am-7pm Apr-Oct, 8.45am-3.30pm Nov-Mar) near the village of Gastouri. The Ahillion was built in the 1890s by the Empress Elisabeth of Austria, known as Sisi, as a retreat from the world and in tribute to her hero, Achilles. Arrive early when there are less crowds for a fascinating journey through neoclassicism, fabulous furnishings and bold statuary, along a very thin line between style and kitsch (think cherubs).

West Coast

Some of Corfu's prettiest countryside, villages and beaches line the west coast. The scenic and very popular resort of **Paleokastritsa**, 26km from Corfu Town, rambles for nearly 3km down a valley to a series of small, picturesque coves hidden between tall cliffs. Craggy mountains swathed in cypresses and olive trees tower above. Venture to nearby grottoes or one of the dozen or so local beaches by small **excursion boat** (per person €8.50, 30 minutes); water taxis can drop you at your beach of choice. Or partake in a range of water sports.

Perched on the rocky promontory at the end of Paleokastritsa is the icon-filled **Moni Theotokou** (9am-1pm & 3-8pm), a monastery founded in the 13th century (although the present building dates from the 18th century). Just off the monastery's lovely garden, a small **museum** (Apr-Oct) and olive-mill exhibition have a shop selling oils and herbs.

Paxi ΠΑΞΟΙ

POP 2440

Paxi (population 2440) lives up to its reputation as one of the Ionians' most idyllic and picturesque islands. At only 10km by 4km it's the smallest of the main holiday islands and makes a fine escape from Corfu's quicker-paced pleasures. Three colourful harbour towns, Gaïos, Loggos and Lakka, have charming waterfronts with pink-and-cream buildings set against lush green hills. Gemlike coves can be reached by motorboat, if not by car or on foot. The dispersed inland villages sit within centuries-old olive groves, accented by winding stone walls, ancient windmills

Lakkos beach, Paxi

and olive presses. On the less accessible west coast, sheer limestone cliffs plunge hundreds of metres into the azure sea and are punctuated by caves and grottoes. Old mule trails are a walker's delight. Find *Bleasdale Walking Map of Paxos* (€12) at travel agencies.

 Sleeping

SAN GIORGIO APARTMENTS Pension €
(☎26620 32223; Galios; s/d €40/55; ❄) Pink, blue and white are the colours of these peaceful, airy and clean studios with basic cooking facilities (no stove). Rooms 1 and 2 have fantastic balconies over the channel, others share a terrace. One apartment with a full kitchen sleeps three (€90). Head towards town from the port by the lower (pedestrian) harbour road, and follow the signposted steps.

PAXOS BEACH HOTEL Hotel €€€
(☎26620 32211; www.paxosbeachhotel.gr; Galios; d incl breakfast €120-170, ste €170-230; ❄ ⊞) On a tiny cove with private beach, jetty, swimming pool, tennis court and restaurant, 1.5km south of Gaïos; bungalow-style rooms step down to the sea. Port transfers available.

TORRI E MERLI Boutique Hotel €€€
(☎26212 34123, 6932201116; Lakka; www.torriemerli.com; ste €290; ⊙May-Oct; P ❄ ⊕ ⊞) The island's premier lodging; a tiny, perfect boutique hotel in a renovated stone house tucked into the hills 800m south of Lakka.

 Eating

VASILIS Mediterranean €
(☎26620 31587; Laggos; mains €9-16; ⊙lunch & dinner) You may have your best meal in the Ionians here. The waterside ambience is distinctly low-key, but the food is excellent. Lighter-than-air zucchini balls are to die for; salads are perfectly balanced; and everything is fresh, fresh, fresh. Specialities include octopus in red wine

sauce, lamb casserole, pasta and risotto. Reserve ahead in summer.

ERIMITIS BAR Bar, Mediterranean €
(☎6977753499; www.erimitis.com; Magazia; mains €9-14; ⊙noon-10pm May-Oct) Rumble down dirt roads under olive trees to find this spectacular spot overlooking majestic cliffs plunging straight into the bluest of seas. Whether for sunset or an afternoon drink, it's well worth the journey if you have your own wheels.

ℹ **Getting There & Away**

Boat
Ferries dock at Gaïos' new port, 1km east of the central square. Excursion boats dock along the waterfront.

Two different busy passenger-only hydrofoils link Corfu and Paxi from May until mid-October. Petrakis Lines in Corfu handle Ionian Cruises and Bouas Tours in Corfu handle *Ilida*. Two car ferries operate daily services between Paxi and Igoumenitsa and Corfu. There's also a ferry information office (☎26650 26280) in Igoumenitsa

Bus
Twice-weekly direct buses go between Athens and Paxi (€55, plus €7.50 for ferry between Paxi and Igoumenitsa, seven hours) in high season. On Paxi, get tickets from Bouas Tours.

KEFALLONIA
ΚΕΦΑΛΛΟΝΙΑ
POP 37,296

Kefallonia, the largest of the Ionian Islands, stands simultaneously proud and welcoming. Its exquisite bounty includes friendly people, bucolic villages, rugged mountains, rich vineyards, soaring coastal cliffs and golden beaches. The 1953 earthquake devastated many of the island's settlements and much of the architecture is relatively modern. Surviving villages like Assos and Fiskardo, and the ebullient quality of life as in rebuilt Argostoli, the capital, enliven everything.

If You Like...
Village Beauty

If you like exploring the picturesque villages on Corfu's **west coast** (p138), we think you'd like to while away a little time in Corfu's other enchanting villages:

1 BENITSES
In Corfu's south, this resort has a pleasant old village, from where tracks and paths lead into the steep, wooded slopes above. Fill up at the well-known taverna **O Paxinos** (☎26610 72339) on mezedhes and fish dishes (by the kilo).

2 BOUKARI
A winding coastal road leads to this tranquil village, also in the south of Corfu, with a little harbour and waterside tavernas, including the good *psarotaverna* (fish restaurant) **Spiros Karidis** (☎26620 51205).

3 KALAMI
This bayside village is famous for the picturesque **White House**, perched above the water. For a time it was home to the Durrell family, who lived on the island for many years prior to WWII. Lawrence Durrell became an outstanding writer, penning *Prospero's Cell,* while his brother Gerald wrote the equally splendid *My Family and Other Animals*. Both books are based on their life on Corfu.

🛈 Getting There & Away

AIR
May to September, many charter flights come from northern Europe and the UK.

Olympic Air (☎26710 41511; airport) Serves Athens.

Sky Express (☎28102 23500; www.skyexpress.gr) Serves Corfu.

BOAT
Frequent Ionian Ferries (www.ionianferries.gr) connect Poros and Argostoli to Kyllini in the Peloponnese. Strintzis Lines (www.strintzisferries.gr) has two ferries daily connecting Sami with Patra in the Peloponnese. Port Authority (☎26710 22224)

BUS
Three daily buses connect Argostoli with Athens (€45, seven hours), via Patra (€25, four hours); also buses go to Athens from Sami (two daily), Poros (one daily) and Lixouri (one daily).

KTEL bus station (☎26710 22276/81; kefaloniakteltours@yahoo.gr; A Tritsi 5) is on Argostoli's southern waterfront.

🛈 Getting Around

TO/FROM THE AIRPORT
The airport is 9km south of Argostoli. There's no airport bus; taxis cost around €17.

BOAT
Car ferries connect Argostoli and Lixouri, on the island's western Paliki Peninsula (per person/car €3.50/4.50, 30 minutes, hourly from 7.30am to 10.30pm, half-hourly and to midnight July and August).

BUS
Argostoli's KTEL bus station (☎26710 22276/81; kefaloniakteltours@yahoo.gr; A Tritsi 5) sits on the southern waterfront. No buses run on Sunday. Services go to Lassi Peninsula (€1.60, seven daily), Sami (€4.50, four daily), Poros (€5, two daily), Skala (€5, two daily) and Fiskardo (€6, one daily). Once-daily east-coast service links Katelios with Skala, Poros, Sami, Agia Evfymia and Fiskardo.

CAR & MOTORCYCLE
Europcar (☎26710 42020) At the airport.

Greekstones Rent a Car (☎26710 42201; www.greekstones-rentacar.com) Delivers to the airport and within 15km of their base at Svoronata (7km from Argostoli, near the airport).

Hertz (☎26710 42142) At the airport.

Karavomilos (☎26740 22779) In Sami; does deliveries.

Argostoli ΑΡΓΟΣΤΟΛΙ
POP 8932

Animated and appealing Argostoli bubbles with activity in its pastel-bright streets. It was laid flat during the 1953 earthquake

nd is now a town of broad boulevards
nd pedestrianised shopping streets,
ke Lithostroto, centring on lively inland
lateia Valianou. In summer, *kantadoroi*
mble the streets singing *kantades,* tradi-
onal songs accompanied by guitar and
1andolin.

 ## Sights & Activities

ick up the events booklet from the EOT
> see what's on.

ORGIALENIO HISTORY &
OLKLORE MUSEUM   Museum
☎ 26710 28835; www.corgialenios.gr; Ilia
ervou 12; admission €4; ⊙9am-2pm Mon-Sat)
 'edicated to preserving Kefallonian art
nd culture, this fine museum houses a
ollection of icons and pre-earthquake
urniture, clothes and artwork from the
omes of both gentry and farm workers.

OCAS-KOSMETATUS
OUNDATION   Museum, Garden
☎ 26710 26595; Valianou; admission €3;
⊙9.30am-12.30pm Mon-Sat & 7-9.30pm Tue-Sat,
osed mid-May–mid-Oct) The Valianou loca-

tion is another hot spot for displays on
Kefallonia's cultural and political history
in a pre-earthquake building. Admission
includes entrance to the **Cephalonia
Botanica** (☎26710 26595; ⊙8.30am-2.30pm
Tue-Sat), a lovely botanical garden abound-
ing in native flora and shrubs, about 2km
from the centre of town. The museum has
directions.

BEACHES   Beaches
The town's closest, largest sandy beaches are **Makrys Gialos** and **Platys Gialos**,
5km south on Lassi Peninsula, and are
therefore crowded. **Lourdata**, 16km
from Argostoli on the Argostoli-Poros
road, also has an attractive expansive
beach set against a mountainous green
backdrop.

 ## Tours

KTEL TOURS   Bus Tour
(☎26710 23364; www.kefaloniakteltours.gr)
Excellent-value tours of Kefallonia (€18,
twice-weekly) visit villages around the
island. Once-weekly tours go to Ithaki
(€38). Book at the KTEL bus station.

rgostoli

Sleeping

VIVIAN VILLA   Pension €€
(26710 23396; www.kefalonia-vivianvilla.gr;
Deladetsima 11; d/tr/apt €60/65/100; ❄ 🛜 🛗)
Friendly owners operate big, bright, tidy
rooms, some with kitchens. The top-floor
two-bedroom apartment is excellent;
there's a lift. Located in a residential
neighbourhood near the centre.

HOTEL IONIAN PLAZA   Hotel €€
(26710 25581; www.ionianplaza.gr;
Plateia Valianou; s/d/tr/q incl breakfast from
€65/79/99/140; P ❄ @ 🛜 🛗) Argostoli's
smartest hotel, smack on the square, has
a stylish marble-decorated lobby and
small well-appointed rooms with balconies. Top-floor rooms have the best views.

Eating

CASA GREC   Mediterranean €€
(26710 24091; Metaxa 12; mains €12-22;
🕐dinner nightly, closed Sun & Mon Nov-Apr)
Prepare yourself for perhaps one of
the best meals in the Ionians. Elegant,
magical lighting; textiles and murals; and
a candle-lit courtyard set the stage for
refined dishes, each made from scratch
by the chef-owner, Costas. Pastas are
dressed with nuanced sauces, steaks are
succulent, desserts a dream. The chef's
Greek-Canadian wife assists tableside
with charm and humour, and the wine list
is excellent.

ARHONTIKO   Kefallonian €
(26710 27213; 5 Risospaston; mains €7-17;
🕐breakfast, lunch & dinner) Tuck into top
Kefallonian cuisine with starters such as
a soufflé of spinach, and excellent mains
like the whopping Kefallonian meat pie
or *exohiko,* pork stuffed with tomatoes,
onions, peppers and feta. Good house
wines; relaxed, helpful service; and a cosy
atmosphere round out the experience.

LADOKOLLA   Souvlaki €
(26710 25522; Xarokopou 13; dishes €2-8;
🕐1pm-1am) Piping-hot chicken, pork, lamb
kebabs and pittas are delivered without
plates onto table-top covers. They'll bring
a plate for anything saucy, but this is
down-to-earth noshing, popular locally
and with lively service.

Argostoli (p140)

JEFF MORGAN 01/ALAMY ©

Don't Miss Assos ΑΣΟΣ

Tiny, gorgeous Assos is an upmarket gem of whitewashed and pastel houses, many of them pre-earthquake. Baby Italian cypresses dot the steep mountain descending to the town which straddles the isthmus of a peninsula topped by a Venetian fortress. The fortress makes a great hike, with superlative views and old-world ambience, and the tiny green bay is imminently swimmable.

One of Greece's most breathtaking and picture-perfect beaches is **Myrtos**, 8km south of Assos along an exciting stretch of the west coast road. Think clichéd turquoise and aqua water. And crowds in summer.

Despite being a tiny village, Assos won't leave you wanting for comfort. **Cosi's Inn** has the marks of the young and hip interior designer owner: iron beds and sofas, frosted lights and white decor. For dinner, head to **Platanos**, admired island-wide for its locally sourced, fresh ingredients and top-notch cooking. Located in a shady plaza near the waterfront, it's strong on meat dishes but also offers fish and vegetarian options such as vegetable mousaka.

THINGS YOU NEED TO KNOW

Cosi's Inn (☎26740 51420; www.cosisinn.gr; 2-/3-person studio €65/80; ۝May-Sep; ❄@)
Platanos(☎6944671804; mains €6-15; ۝breakfast, lunch & dinner Easter-Oct)

🍷 Drinking & Entertainment

Cafes line Plateia Valianou and Lithostro-to. Plateia Valianou's breezy music bars like Le Sapin Noir and Platanos bounce by late evening. Bass Club draws a younger set, **Sin City** (Lavraga 8), the over 18s. The popular club-restaurant **Katavothres** (☎26710 22221; waterfront) contains unusual geological formations, top-name DJs and a mixed crowd. Stavento, in Makrys Gialos, hops in summer.

ⓘ Getting There & Away

The main ferry quay is at the northern end of the waterfront and the bus station is at its southern end. See p140 for more information.

Around Argostoli

◉ Sights

FREE **AGIOS GIORGOS KASTRO** Ruins
(Castle of St George; ⊙8.30am-3pm Tue-Sun)
This Venetian *kastro* from the 1500s sits atop a hill southeast of Argostoli and was the capital of Kefallonia for about two hundred years. Well worth a visit for its smooth stones and stellar views, the castle is also surrounded by a small village with Byzantine churches and restaurants also with stunning vistas.

Palatino (☎ 26710 68490; mains €7-10; ⊙lunch & dinner May-Oct) creates home-cooked Kefallonian specialities, while **Astraios** (☎ 26710 69152) is a live Greek music bar owned by venerated musician Dionysos Frangopoulos.

MONI AGIOU GERASIMOU Monastery
(⊙9am-1pm & 3.30-8pm) Dedicated to Kefallonia's patron saint, this monastery, 16km west of Argostoli, is cared for by nuns. Inside the chapel lies the famous cave where Gerasimos escaped from the rigours of monastic life to even greater self-abnegation. Descend with great care via a steep metal ladder into a small chamber 6m below. From this chamber a narrow squeeze leads to another tiny chamber. There are lights, but it's not for the claustrophobic. Use the pile of wraps outside the chapel to cover bare arms and shoulders, at least, before entering.

Fiskardo ΦΙΣΚΑΡΔΟ
POP 230

Tiny, precious Fiskardo, 50km north of Argostoli, was the only Kefallonian village left intact after the 1953 earthquake. Its fine Venetian buildings, framed by cypress-mantled hills, have an authentic picturesque appeal and it's popular with well-heeled yachting fans. The outstanding restaurants and chilled-out feel might entice you to stay a while.

🛏 Sleeping

EMELISSE HOTEL Resort €€€
(☎ 26740 41200; www.arthotel.gr; Emblissi Bay; d €480-630, ste €510-7100, 4-person apt €950-1800; ⊙mid-Apr–mid-Oct; P ✳ @ 🛜 ≋) Situated in a superb position overlooking the unspoiled Emblissi Bay, 1km to the west of Fiskardo, this stylish, luxurious hotel has every facility for the pampered holiday. Beautifully appointed rooms (think sleek comfort) tuck into immaculately cultivated terraces

Fiskardo

Ionian on the Vine

The Ionian Islands would not be the same without wine, and Kefallonia especially has outstanding vintages, most notably from the unique *robola* grape (VQRPD). Other varieties like mavrodaphne (AOC) and muscat (AOC) enhance the viniculture.

High in the mountains southeast of Argostoli, at the heart of verdant Omala Valley, lies the fascinating winery of the **Cooperative of Robola Producers of Kefallonia** (26710 86301; www.robola.gr; Omala; admission free; 9am-8.30pm May-Oct, 9am-3pm Mon-Fri Nov-Apr). Here, grapes from about 300 independent growers are transformed into the yellow-green *robola*, a dry white wine of subtle yet lively flavours. *Robola* is said to have been introduced by the Venetians and its wine was a favourite of the Doge. It grows exuberantly on high ground, and the light soils, wet winters and arid summers of Kefallonia are ideal for its cultivation. A tasting will help you understand the grape's excellent qualities.

leading down to the crowning glory: a lavish swimming pool and restaurant with open sea views to Lefkada, Ithaki and beyond.

ARCHONTIKO   Boutique Hotel €€
(26740 41342; www.archontiko-fiskardo. gr; r €70-80;) Overlooking the harbour, people-watch from the balconies of these luxurious rooms in a restored stone mansion.

 ## Eating & Drinking

TASSIA   Mediterranean €€
(26740 41205; mains €7-25; lunch & dinner) Tassia Dendrinou, celebrated chef and writer on Greek cuisine, runs this portside Fiskardo institution. Everything is a refined delight, but specialities include baby marrow croquettes and a fisherman's pasta incorporating finely chopped squid, octopus, mussels and prawns in a magic combination that even includes a dash of cognac. Meat dishes are equally splendid and Tassia's desserts are rightfully famous.

CAFÉ TSELENTI   Italian €€
(26740 41344; mains €10-23; lunch & dinner) Housed in a lovely 19th-century building owned by the Tselenti family since 1893, this noted restaurant has a romantic outdoor terrace at the heart of the village. The outstanding cuisine includes starters like cheese and mushroom patties or aubergine rolls, and terrific mains like linguine with prawns, mussels and crawfish in a tomato sauce or pork fillet with sun-dried apricots and fresh pineapple.

Information

Nautilus Travel (26740 41440) and Pama Travel (26740 41033; www.pamatravel.com) arrange everything.

Delphi, Meteora & Thessaloniki

Greece's vast and varied north is unmatched for geographical, cultural and even gustatory diversity. Here, great stretches of mountains, lakes, forest and coastline await discovery. The tangible reminders of a history both triumphant and traumatic are scattered throughout the region. You'll find a myriad of monuments, fortresses, churches and mosques to explore.

The ruins at Delphi remain one of Greece's most inspiring archaeological sites, while the sheer cliffs of monastery-topped Meteora are breathtaking. The Pelion Peninsula is criss-crossed with historic cobblestone paths that link lush mountain hamlets with beaches that rival those on the best islands, only without the crowds.

Thessaloniki, Greece's second city, offers outstanding eateries, nightlife and culture, while Epirot university town Ioannina is a lively spot close to the magnificent Pindos Mountains. Head to Halkidiki's Sithonian Peninsula to watch the sun sink into the shimmering horizon from a lengthy patch of soft sand.

Moni Varlaam (p166)

The Rotunda of Galerius (p171)

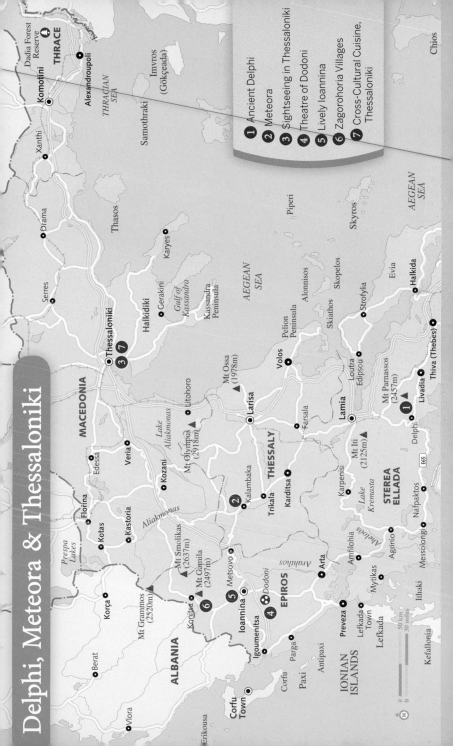

Delphi, Meteora & Thessaloniki

1 Ancient Delphi
2 Meteora
3 Sightseeing in Thessaloniki
4 Theatre of Dodoni
5 Lively Ioannina
6 Zagorohoria Villages
7 Cross-Cultural Cuisine, Thessaloniki

Delphi, Meteora & Thessaloniki's Highlights

1

Ancient Delphi

The atmosphere at Ancient Delphi is imposing. This is a place where myth and history meet, where nature and art are intertwined. Delphi has a unique quality of light, something best witnessed at dusk. Not surprisingly, this was a site dedicated to Apollo, the god of light.

Above: Tholos; Top Right: Theatre; Bottom Right:Temple of Apollo

Need to Know
BEST TIME TO VISIT
Late spring or early autumn
EQUIPMENT Walking shoes
sunhat, umbrella, water **TOP**
EXPERIENCE The ruins
bathed by full-moon light
For more, see p160

Ancient Delphi Don't Miss List

BY RANIA VASSILIADOU, LICENSED TOUR GUIDE

1 TEMPLE OF APOLLO

This 4th-century temple was the star of the sanctuary. Inside an eternal light burned in a hearth while the oracle inhaled fumes, awaiting visitors to enlighten with prophesies. The temple also housed a statue of Apollo and the vestibule was inscribed with the words of Greek philosophers, such as 'Know Thyself' and 'Nothing in Excess'.

2 THEATRE

Also built in the 4th century and restored by the Pergamenon kings in the 1st century BC, this theatre yields magnificent views from the top row. Plays were performed here every four years during the Pythian Festival.

3 STADIUM

This is the best preserved ancient stadium in Greece. Look for the sprinters' etched-stone starting blocks at the eastern end.

4 BRONZE CHARIOTEER

Housed in the Delphi Museum, this celebrated life-sized sculpture commemorates a victory in the Pythian Games of around 478 BC. The beauty and lifelike quality of the face is breathtaking.

5 THOLOS

The rotunda is Delphi's most striking and quickly recognised monument. Located in the Sanctuary of Athena, this graceful circular structure was once made of 20 columns on a three-stepped podium. Three of the columns were re-erected in the 1940s and continue to tower gracefully. The white portions of the columns are the original marble while the darker areas are new material. The *tholos* has been heavily damaged by rock slides and an earthquake.

1

Meteora

This forest of rocks with monasteries balanced on top of them is breathtaking. It's mysterious in winter as the lofty heights disappear into heavy clouds and beautiful in spring when nature is in full bloom. The atmosphere is heavily spiritual and it's a popular pilgrimage destination for Eastern and Orthodox Christians. Meteora also draws rock-climbers, architects and those with wanderlust.

Need to Know

BEST TIME OF YEAR
Spring, early summer & early autumn **ETIQUETTE**
Dress respectfully (no shorts or short skirts), no photos inside the monasteries
For more, see p165

2

Meteora Don't Miss List

BY ANTONIS BEKIARIS, ARCHAEOLOGIST

1 METAMORPHOSIS MONASTERY

The dawn of monasticism in the region goes back to the late 11th century, when the first monks climbed the rocks of Meteora. At least 20 monasteries, including this one, were founded during the 14th century. Also known as Moni Megalo Meteoro, it's the area's most significant monastery and a must-see. As one of the best-preserved monasteries, it offers a general view of the monastic communities.

2 MONI AGIOU NIKOLAOU

The most important wall paintings in Meteora are found in this monastery (pictured above left) from 1527 as they are the first signed examples of one of the greatest painters in the 16th century, Theophanes Strelizas. Originally from Crete, his frescoes and icons here and at Mt Athos represent the Cretan School of Byzantine art.

3 VARLAAM MONASTERY

The frescoes at this monastery are excellently executed and very original. They are believed to have been painted by Frangos Kastellanos, the second great monumental painter of the time. As my professor used to say, 'If Theophanis is considered the great master of the 16th century, Katelanos was an artistic genius.'

4 ROUSANOU MONASTERY

I've always preferred small monasteries. They are unique and historically significant in their own right. Their size and tranquillity creates a special atmosphere that's well worth experiencing. Access to the Moni Agias Varvaras Rousanou (pictured below left) is via a small wooden bridge. Other than the awe-inducing architecture, the main draw to this monastery is the stunning illuminated coloured glass found in the central church.

5 GUIDED TOUR

Meteora is an outstanding centre of artistic activity and preserves some of the most notable frescoes of the 15th, 16th and 17th centuries. Having a guide gives you the opportunity to gain a deeper understanding of the historical and cultural significance of these paintings and also of the monasteries.

15

Sightseeing in Thessaloniki

Deservedly applauded for its buzzing nightlife, shopping and packed cultural calendar, T...saloniki (p170) is also brimming with sights. See the cool interactive museum at the Whit...Tower, the phenomenal mosaics at the Church of Agios Dimitrios or Greece's oldest surviv...papyrus piece at the Archaeological Museum.

3

4 ## Theatre of Dodoni

A place of worship since 2000 BC, this valley site beneath majestic peaks is, according to legend, where an earth g...dess spoke through an oracle, and Ze...was heard through a sacred oak tree...now home to a colossal 3rd-century-theatre (p190) that's best enjoyed fr...one of the ancient stone seats durin...July's Festival of Ancient Drama.

Lively Ioannina

Idyllically positioned on the edge of Lake Pamvotis and looking out to the towering mountains, Ioannina (p187) has atmospheric sights such as the captivating old town, and a hip vibe that's nurtured by 20,000 university students. Get lost in the narrow alleyways, be dazzled by the Ottoman architecture and then live it up with top nosh, hanging at lively cafes and energetic bars.

Zagorohoria Villages

Tucked in the Pindos Mountains are the preserved hamlets of the Zagorohoria (p191). Tiny cottages and grand mansions are nestled into the scenery, while footpaths and stone bridges link microcommunities. The villages retain a feeling of remoteness, having safeguarded Greek traditions and culture through numerous invasions. These days, many of the stunning homes are guesthouses where you can soak up the atmosphere in style.

Cross-Cultural Cuisine

Thessaloniki's kitchens are at the crossroads between the East and West. Food here is influenced by Eastern flavours introduced by Asia Minor refugees, and involves spices and peppers. Thankfully, the Ottoman-style sweets (p181) are not a well-kept secret and you'll find plenty of bakeries overflowing with wild cherry sweet bread, Eastern-style crème brûlée, and pastries flavoured with honey, citrus, cinnamon and cloves.

Delphi, Meteora & Thessaloniki's Best.

Walking Trails

o **Parnassos National Park** (p163) Soaring peaks, wild animals and profusion of flowers.

o **Pelion Peninsula** (p164) Follow cobbled mule paths from village to village.

o **Meteora** (p165) Step along the once-secret *monopatia* (monk paths).

o **Mt Olympus** (p186) Climb to the top of Greece's highest mountain.

o **Ioannina** (p187) Serious hikers can tackle the sheer mountains facing the city.

o **Vikos Gorge** (p191) Descend into the world's deepest gorge.

Spectacular Views

o **Sithonia's Southern Tip** (p182) Rugged and dramatic with views of Mt Athos.

o **Litohoro** (p185) Admire Mt Olympus from the wooden balconies of Macedonian-style homes.

o **Lake Pamvotis** (p187) Cruise on this lake for fabulous views of Ioannina and towering peaks.

o **Kastraki** (p169) Dramatic views of nearby Meteora.

Atmospheric Sleeps

o **Hotel Apollonia** (p162) Luxuriate in swish rooms with views over Delphi.

o **Dafni Traditional Hotel** (p187) Unique rooms in Ioannina, built into the old town's outer walls.

o **Arhontiko Dilofo** (p192) Get cosy in a 450-year-old restored mansion in the Zagorohoria.

o **Daios** (p156) Sophisticated and sleek, with wrap-around balconies over the water.

Creative Cuisine

Paparouna (p177) Serves dishes such as chicken with peppermint and honey, washed down with organic Greek beer.

Gastrodromio (p185) Traditional decor with scrumptious sauces and marinades for meat and seafood – think wine, almonds, cinnamon and nutmeg.

Es Aei (p188) Ottoman flair and organic ingredients add to Ioannina specials such as grilled pork sausage.

Taverna Vakhos (p157) Home cooking – local cheese, lemon lamb-and-rabbit stew – washed down with regional wine.

Need to Know

ADVANCE PLANNING

○ **Two months before** Sort out your accommodation, especially in Delphi. Book any activity tours.

○ **One month before** Check online for events in Thessaloniki and Ioannina, and make advance bookings.

RESOURCES

○ **Ministry of Culture & Tourism** (www.culture.gr) Details on Delphi, including history, descriptions of the ruins and visiting info.

○ **Routes** (www.routes.gr) Hiking guide with detailed information on routes in central Greece.

○ **Matt Barrett's Travel Guides** (www.greecetravel.com/macedonia) Matt Barrett's guide to the sights and cities of the region.

○ **Ioannina Tourist Guide** (www.about-ioannina.gr) A guide to Epiros, including Ioannina, Dodoni and the Zagorohoria, with background info, links to accommodation and sights.

GETTING AROUND

○ **Bus** Comprehensive routes with direct bus links from Athens to Delphi and Thessaloniki.

○ **Train** Fast trains between Thessaloniki and Athens.

○ **Car** A great way to explore the Zagorohoria and other remote regions.

BE FOREWARNED

○ **Sights** Many are closed Mondays, particularly in Thessaloniki and Ioannina.

○ **Weather** Can be very unpredictable, especially on Mt Olympus. If you're setting out on a trek, always check with local hiking organisations before setting out.

○ **Accommodation** Conferences and the Thessaloniki International Film Festival in November can make it next to impossible to find a place. Book early!

Left: Litohoro (p185) village square
Above: View from the summit of Mytikas, Mt Olympus (p186)
(LEFT) GREECE/ALAMY ©; (ABOVE) BANANA PANCAKE/ALAMY ©

157

Delphi, Meteora & Thessaloniki Itineraries

See the ruins at Ancient Delphi and mystifying Meteora. Also take in soaring Mt Olympus, suave Thessaloniki and the gorgeous villages of Zagorohoria.

3 DAYS

ANCIENT DELPHI TO KASTRAKI
Architectural wonders

There are few ancient sites in the world that compare to **(1) Ancient Delphi**. The Ancient Greeks believed it to be the centre of the world and there's an almost palpable atmosphere when you're here. Built in a breathtaking setting on the slopes of Mt Parnassos and overlooking the sea, these ruins will undoubtedly inspire you. Spend a day taking in both the site and the nearby museums, particularly the Delphi Museum where many of the site's original artefacts are displayed. Delphi has some comfortable hotels with views, and it's worth spending the night so you're not rushed for time. From Delphi, drive or take a bus to the incredible site of **(2) Meteora**. Here you can spend a couple of days exploring the numerous monasteries perched like birds' nests atop ancient pinnacles of smooth rock. Base yourself in **(3) Kastraki**; with its impressive location beneath the towering rocks, it's a great spot to soak up the scenery and relax.

Top Left: Kastraki (p169); **Top Right:** Fetiye Cami (Victory Mosque; p187), Ioannina

5
DAYS

Northern High Points

Start with a day in **(1) Thessaloniki**, an increasingly fashionable destination with a dynamic arts and culture scene. Take in theatre, festivals and galleries before delving into the excellent shopping and nightlife. Visit Kastra, the atmospheric Turkish quarter. Be sure to stop in at a few *zaharoplasteia* (patisseries) where you can sample some unique and mouth-watering local sweets. When you've gotten your fill of city life, head by bus or car to **(2) Litohoro**, a stunning village with traditional Macedonian architecture and cobbled streets. Litohoro is the base for visiting **(3) Mt Olympus**, Greece's highest peak. Cloaked in thick forest and home to countless rare and endemic plants, it's the land of legends and ancient gods. The energetic can venture up the many paths on foot or you can simply admire the views from town. From Litohoro, head for **(4) the Zagorohoria** and check yourself into a boutique hotel set in a traditional stone house. Explore the villages and footpaths tucked in the Pindos Mountains as one day melts into two. From here, travel to the buzzing city of **(5) Ioannina** where you can wander through the narrow lanes of the old town, between buildings from the Byzantine and Ottoman eras.

Discover Delphi, Meteora & Thessaloniki

Sanctuary of Athena Pronea
ANDREW BAIN/LONELY PLANET IMAGES ©

Delphi   Δελφοί
POP 1500

If the Ancient Greeks hadn't chosen Delphi (from *Delphis,* or womb) as their navel of the earth and built the Sanctuary of Apollo here, someone else would have thought of a good reason to make this eagle's nest village a tourist attraction. Its location on a precipitous cliff edge is spectacular and, despite its overt commercialism and the constant passage of tour buses through the modern village, it still has a special feel. Delphi is 178km northwest of Athens and is the base for exploring one of Greece's major tourist sites.

◉ Sights

ANCIENT DELPHI   Ruins
(Map p161;www.culture.gr, www.delphi
gr; ◷8am-8pm summer, 8am-3pm
winter) Of all the archaeological sites in Greece, Ancient Delphi is the one with the most potent 'spirit of place'. Built on the slopes of Mt Parnassos, overlooking the Gulf of Corinth and extending into a valley of cypress and olive trees, this World Heritage site's allure lies both in its stunning setting and its inspiring ruins. The Ancient Greeks regarded Delphi as the centre of the world; according to mythology, Zeus released two eagles at opposite ends of the world and they met here. Ancient Delphi is 500m along the pine-shaded main road towards Arahova.

SANCTUARY OF APOLLO
The Sanctuary of Apollo, considered the heart of the oracle, is on the left of the main road as you walk towards Arahova.

om the main entrance, the steps on our right lead to the **Sacred Way** (Map p161), which winds gradually up to the foundations of the Doric Temple of Apollo. In ancient times the Sacred Way was lined with treasuries and statues given by grateful city-states – Athens, Sikyon, Siphnos, Knidos and Thiva (Thebes) etc – all in thanks to Apollo.

The 4th-century-BC **Temple of Apollo** (Map p161) dominated the entire sanctuary. Above the temple is the well-preserved 4th-century-BC **theatre** (Map p161), which was restored by the Pergamenon kings in the 1st century BC, yielding magnificent views from the top row. From the theatre the path continues to the **stadium** (Map p161), the best-reserved in all of Greece.

From the Sanctuary of Apollo, the paved path towards Arahova runs parallel to the main road and leads to the **Castalian Spring** (Map p161) on the left, where pilgrims cleansed themselves before consulting the oracle.

SANCTUARY OF ATHENA PRONEA
The Sanctuary of Athena Pronea is the site of the 4th-century-BC **tholos** (rotunda), the most striking of Delphi's monuments. This graceful circular structure comprised 20 columns on a three-stepped podium – three of its columns were re-erected in the 1940s. The white portions of each column are the original marble; the darker portions are new material. To its west, the foundations of the **Temple of Athena Pronea** are all that remain of a rectangular structure which was heavily damaged by the same rockslides and earthquake that levelled much of the *tholos*.

DELPHI MUSEUM
(Map p161; ☎ 22650 82312; www.culture.gr/war/index_en.jsp; adult site or museum €6, adult/student site & museum €9/5, free Sun winter; ⏰8.30am-3pm Sun-Tue, 8am-8pm Wed-Sat summer, 8am-2.45pm winter) From around the 8th century BC, Ancient Delphi managed to amass a considerable treasure trove, much of it reflected in its magnificent museum.

Upon entering the museum, in room 5 you'll first notice the Sphinx of the Naxians, dating from 560 BC. Also residing here are well-preserved parts of the frieze from the Siphnian treasury,

Ancient Delphi

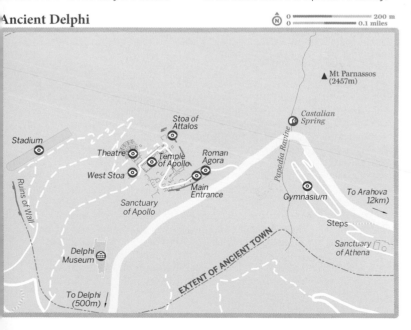

which depicts not only the battle between the gods and the giants, but also the Judgment of Paris (far left corner as you enter), who was called upon to decide which goddess was most beautiful (he chose Aphrodite).

Tours

English-language tours of Delphi are offered by **Georgia Hasioti** (6944943511; hasioti1@otenet.gr) who also speaks Japanese, French and Italian; **Penny Kolomvotsos** (6944644427; kpagona@hotmail. com) who also speaks German; **Electra Togia** (6937813215) who also speaks Italian and Spanish; and **Vicki Tsonis** (6945494583) who also speaks French.

Sleeping

HOTEL APOLLONIA Hotel €€
(22650 82919; www.hotelapollonia .gr; Syngrou; s/d/tr/ste incl breakfast €80/100/120/150; ❄ 🛜) The swank Apollonia has an intimate feel to it, tucked away on Delphi's upper Syngrou street.

Rooms are quite modern with elegant dark-wood furnishings, carpet, large basin-sink bathrooms and balcony views over all Delphi.

HOTEL LETO Hotel €€
(22650 82302; www.leto-delphi.gr; Apollonos 15; s/d/tr incl breakfast €50/65/90; ❄ 🛜) If the traditional Greek motif is getting you down, head to these smartly decorated digs whose slick lighting and cream and orange trim makes it one of the town's most contemporary choices.

HOTEL HERMES Hotel €
(22650 82318; www.hermeshotel.gr; Vasileon Pavlou & Friderikis 27; s/d/tr/f incl breakfast €40/50/65/80; ❄ @ 🛜) The family-run Hermes is in the heart of Delphi. Most of the large wood-shuttered rooms have balconies facing the gulf. Views from the breakfast lounge are splendid.

HOTEL SIBYLLA Hotel €
(22650 82335; www.sibylla-hotel.gr; Vasileon Pavlou & Friderikis 9; s €25-30, d from €35, tr €42-48; ❄ 🛜) An excellent budget choice, cosy Sibylla has helpful staff along with seven light and spotless rooms, all with fans and several with views across to the gulf.

The Delphic Oracle

The Delphic oracle, the most powerful in Greece, sat on a tripod at the entrance to a chasm that emitted intoxicating vapours. A popular story proposes that the earliest oracles were young women who regularly ran off with their advice-seeking pilgrims, leaving the post temporarily vacant. Hence it became customary for the appointed seer (Pythia) to be at least 50 years of age.

When she was consulted for divine advice, the priestess inhaled the fumes and entered a trance. Her inspired, if somewhat vague, answers were translated into verse by a priest. In fact, the oracle's reputation for infallibility may have rested with the often ambiguous or cryptic answers. Wars were fought, marriages sealed and journeys begun on the strength of the oracle's visions.

Legend holds that one oracle suffered for her vagueness, whether vapour-induced or not. When Alexander the Great visited, hoping to hear a prophecy that he would soon conquer the ancient world, the oracle refused direct comment, instead asking that he return later. Enraged, he dragged her by the hair out of the chamber until she screamed, 'Let go of me; you're unbeatable'. He quickly dropped her, saying 'I have my answer'.

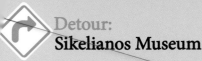

Detour:
Sikelianos Museum

Fans of Greek drama should head to the intimate **Sikelianos Museum** (Delphic Festivals Museum; 22650 82353/4; admission by appointment €1) in a classic mansion overlooking Delphi, dedicated to Greek poet Angelos Sikelianos and his American-born wife Eva Palmer, who together in the late 1920s established Delphi as a European centre for drama and the arts, with masks, costumes and photos on display. Every July, the European Cultural Centre of Delphi hosts a 10-day cultural festival.

Eating

TAVERNA VAKHOS Taverna €
(22650 83186; www.vakchos.com; Apollonos 1; mains €6-17) Take the steps above the National Bank to this excellent family taverna featuring traditional local fare. You could make a meal of appetisers alone, like *formaela,* the local cheese (€6), followed by *kouneli stifadho* (rabbit stew) or lamb in lemon sauce (both €9). Choose from an all-Greek wine list to wash it down.

TAVERNA GARGADUAS Taverna €
(Vasileon Pavlou & Friderikis; mains €6-10) Easily the local favourite for grilled meats and good value as well. The house summer speciality is *provatina* (slow-roasted lamb). You can also tuck into a combo of pasta, souvlaki, salad and seasonal fruit for a modest €13.

TAVERNA TO PATRIKO MAS Taverna €
(22650 82150; Vasileon Pavlou & Friderikis; mains €7.50-13) Set in a 19th-century stone building, this swank taverna is decidedly upscale, and the food keeps its end of the bargain. You'll find generous mezedes and salads, great grills including a vegie souvlaki, along with a fine all-Greek wine list.

SOUVLAKI PITA GYROS Kebab €
(Apollonos; mains €2-6) The budget option: cheap, fast, fresh, go. Opposite Hotel Leto.

Information

Almost everything you'll need in Delphi is on Vasileon Pavlou & Friderikis. The small bus station (22650 82317; Vasileon Pavlou & Friderikis) is next to Taverna Gargaduas on the Itea side of town.

At the time of research, the future of the municipal tourist office was uncertain due to the recent change to municipal boundaries. It's worth checking on its status.

Getting There & Away

Buses depart from the bus station (22650 82317; Vasileon Pavlou & Friderikis) at the Itea end of town. Travellers to Kalambaka/Meteora should find better connections via Lamia rather than Larisa, especially with the 10am Delphi departure.

Mt Parnassos
Παρνασσός Ορος

Established in 1938, **Parnassos National Park** (www.routes.gr), to the north of Delphi and Arahova, has three peaks over 2300m: Liakoura (2457m, the highest), Gerondovrachos (2396m) and Tsarkos (2416m). Kouvelos (1882m) is a popular rock-climbing face. Mt Parnassos is part of the elaborate E4 European long-distance path *(orivatiko monopati)* from Gibraltar to Cyprus, also known as the European Ramblers Path, or E4 European Path. See the **European Ramblers Association** (www.era-ewv-ferp.org) website for more information.

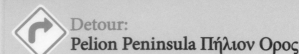

Detour:
Pelion Peninsula Πήλιον Όρος

The Pelion Peninsula, a dramatic mountain range whose highest peak is Pourianos Stavros (1624m), lies to the east and south of Volos. The largely inaccessible eastern flank consists of high cliffs that plunge into the sea. The gentler western flank coils round the Pagasitikos Gulf. The interior is a green wonderland where trees heavy with fruit vie with wild olive groves and forests of horse chestnut, oak, walnut, eucalyptus and beech trees to reach the light of day. The villages tucked away in this profuse foliage are characterised by whitewashed, half-timbered houses with overhanging balconies, grey slate roofs and old winding footpaths.

Many lodgings in the Pelion are traditional *arhontika* (stone mansions), tastefully converted into pensions and reasonably priced. The peninsula has an enduring tradition of regional cooking, often flavoured with mountain herbs. Local specialities include *fasoladha* (bean soup), *kouneli stifadho* (rabbit stew), *spetsofaï* (stewed pork sausages and peppers) and *tyropsomo* (cheese bread).

A wonderful place to stay is **Old Silk Store** (☎24260 49086, 6937156780; www.pelionet.gr; Mouressi; d from €65). This 19th-century neoclassical gem, with personality to spare, is a Mouressi landmark and features traditional-style rooms in a garden setting, with an available breakfast of homemade goodies. British transplant Jill Sleeman runs the show, and can handle travel details, arrange cooking lessons and organise guided walks in the Pelion, often accompanied by the resident donkey, Boy George.

Between 800m and 1800m, the slopes of Parnassos support Kefallonian fir, spruce and juniper, interspersed with yellow-flowered shrubs, plum trees and the rare purple-flowered Daphne jasminea. Above the tree line are meadows of fescue grass. Spring flowers including crocuses, squills, tulips, orchids and irises sprout from the limestone rocks. Greece's most common mammals, foxes, hares, squirrels and jackals, may be seen, as well as vultures, passerines and hawks.

 Activities

PARNASSOS SKI CENTRE   Skiing
(☎22340 22694; www.parnassos-ski.gr/en; ☉Nov-May) Handles ski and snowboard operations for the most popular slope on the mountain, **Kelaria** (1950m). At last count, there were 13 lifts covering more than 20 ski runs and alpine trails. The centre is 24km from Arahova and 17km from Amfiklia. It has hip cafes and restaurants, a safety network and a medi-cal centre, along with ski and snowboarding schools. Adjacent to Kelaria are the steeper slopes of **Fterolakkas** (six lifts), popular with extreme skiers. For more information, see www.snowreport.gr. There is no public transport between Arahova and the ski centre. A taxi from Delphi costs around €45.

 **Sleeping**

For accommodation it's best to stay in nearby Arahova; most of the lodges on the plateau before the centre are private.

HOTEL LIKORIA   Hotel €€
(☎22670 31180; www.likoria.gr; r/tr incl breakfast from €95/120; P ❄ @ ☎) Off the main road, 250m northwest of Plateia Xenias, the low-key Likoria feels more like a country inn. Rooms are quite traditional, with carpeting, huge soft beds and shuttered doors opening to large balconies. The friendly English-speaking staff is a plus.

ENSION NOSTOS   Hotel €
📞22670 31385; d/tr incl breakfast €50/65)
his handsome chalet-style lodging over-
oking Delphi and Mt Parnassos sports
wank bathrooms, a worthy breakfast and
bby photos of some famous visitors: the
eatles slept here in 1967.

ⓘ Getting There & Away
he six daily buses that run between Athens
nd Delphi (€15.10, 2½ hours) stop at Arahova's
ateia Xenias. Regular local buses head to Delphi
.60, 20 minutes).

Meteora Μετέωρα
he World Heritage–listed Meteora (meh-
eh-o-rah) is an extraordinary place, and
ne of the most visited in all of Greece.
he massive pinnacles of smooth rock
re ancient and yet could be the setting
or a futuristic science-fiction tale. The
nonasteries atop them add to this
trange and beautiful landscape.

From the 11th century, hermit monks
ved in the scattered caverns of Meteora.
y the 14th century, the Byzantine power
f the Roman Empire was on the wane
nd Turkish incursions into Greece were
n the rise, so monks began to seek safe
avens away from the bloodshed. The
naccessibility of the rocks of Meteora
nade them an ideal retreat.

The earliest monasteries were reached
y climbing removable ladders. Later,
indlasses were used so monks could be
auled up in nets. A story goes that when
urious visitors asked how frequently the
opes were replaced, the monks' stock
eply was 'when the Lord lets them break'.

These days, access to the monasteries
by steps that were hewn into the rocks
n the 1920s, and by a convenient back
ad.

◉ Sights

Monasteries

efore setting out, decide on a route. If
ou start early, you can see several, if
ot all, mones (monasteries) in one day.

The main asphalt road surrounding the
entire Meteora complex of rocks and
monasteries is about 15km; with your
own transport, you can easily visit them
all. Alternatively, take the bus (€1.20, 20
minutes) that departs from Kalambaka
and Kastraki at 9am, and returns at 1pm.
That's enough time to explore three
monasteries – Moni Megalou Meteorou,
Moni Varlaam and Moni Agias Varvaras
Rousanou. Perhaps the best route is to
take the bus one way to the top and then
work your way down and around on foot,
finishing at either Moni Agiou Nikolaou on
the Kastraki side, or at Moni Agios Triados
on the Kalambaka side.

Keen walkers should definitely explore
the area on foot on the old and once-
secret monopatia (monk paths). Walking
and climbing around the rocks cans be
thirsty work. In summer mobile canteens
sell drinks and snacks at some monastery
car parks.

Entry to each monastery is €2, and
dress codes apply: no bare shoulders
are allowed, men must wear trousers
and women must wear skirts below the
knee (wrap-around skirts are generally
provided at the entrances).

MONI AGIOU NIKOLAOU   Monastery
(Monastery of St Nikolaou Anapafsa; 📞24320
22375; 🕘9am-3.30pm Sat-Thu) Moni Agiou
Nikolaou is the nearest moni to Kastraki,
just 2km from the village square to the
steep steps leading to the moni. The monastery was built in the 15th century, and
the exceptional frescoes in its katholikon

Bus Services from Delphi

DESTINATION	DURATION	FARE	FREQUENCY
Athens	3hr	€15.10	5-6 daily
Lamia	2hr	€9.10	1 daily
Larisa	3½hr	€20	1 daily
Thessaloniki	5hr	€35	1 daily

(principal church) were painted by the monk Theophanes Strelizas from Crete. Especially beautiful is the 1527 fresco *The Naming of Animals by Adam in Paradise*.

MONI VARLAAM   Monastery
(📞 24320 22277; 🕙 9am-4pm Sat-Thu) About 700m down from Moni Megalou, Moni Varlaam has a small museum, an original rope-basket (until the 1930s the method for hauling up provisions and monks) and fine late-Byzantine frescoes by Frangos Kastellanos. For a panoramic break, visit the rambling **Psaropetra lookout**, 300m east of the signposted fork northeast of Moni Varlaam.

MONI AGIAS VARVARAS ROUSANOU   Monastery
(📞 24320 22649; 🕙 9am-6pm Thu-Tue Apr-Oct, 9am-2pm Nov-Mar) Access to Moni Agias Varvaras Rousanou is via a small wooden bridge. The beautiful coloured glass–illuminated *katholikon* is the highlight here, with superb frescoes of the *Resurrection* (on your left entering)

and *Transfiguration* (on your right). The imposing steep structure of Rousanou is itself a stunning accomplishment, and is today home to an order of 15 nuns.

MONI AGIAS TRIADOS   Monastery
(Holy Trinity Monastery; 📞 24320 22220; 🕙 9am-5pm Fri-Wed Apr-Oct, 10am-3pm Fri-Tue Nov-Mar) Of all the monasteries, Moni Agias Triados has the most remote feel about it, plus the longest approach. It was featured in the 1981 James Bond film *For Your Eyes Only*. The views here are extraordinary, and the small 17th-century *katholikon* is beautiful, in particular the *Judgement of Pilate* and the *Hospitality of Abraham*. A well-marked 1km *monopati* leads back to Kalambaka.

MONI AGIOU STEFANOU   Monastery
(📞 24320 22279; 🕙 9am-1.30pm & 3.30-5.30pm Tue-Sun Apr-Oct, 9.30am-1pm & 3-5pm Nov-Mar) After the austere Moni Agias Triados, Moni Agiou Stefanou resembles a return to civilisation, with efficient nuns selling religious souvenirs and DVDs of Meteora.

Left: Fresco in Moni Agias Triados
Below: Moni Agias Varvaras Rousanou
(LEFT) CRAIG PERSHOUSE/LONELY PLANET IMAGES ©; (BELOW) GREECE/ALAMY ©

Among the exhibits in the museum is an exquisite embroidered picture of Christ on his *pitafios* (bier). The monastery is at the very end of the road, 1.5km beyond Agias Triados.

Kalambaka Καλαμπακά
POP 7550

Kalambaka, the gateway to Meteora, is almost entirely modern, having been burned to the ground by the Nazis in WWII. It takes at least a day to see all of the monasteries of Meteora, so you'll need to spend the night either in Kalambaka or the village of Kastraki.

 **Sleeping**

ALSOS HOUSE   Pension, Apartments €
(Map p168; ☎ 24320 24097; www.alsoshouse.gr; Kanari 5; s/d incl breakfast €35/50, f incl breakfast €75-80, 5-person apt €100; P ✳ @ 🛜) The well-managed Alsos House has a well-stocked communal kitchen, a laundry, and wide views of the rocks. It's 500m from the centre and near a *monopati*. Welcoming English-speaking owner Yiannis Karakantas knows as much about the area as the monks do their prayers.

MONASTIRI GUEST HOUSE   Boutique Hotel €€
(Map p168; ☎ 24320 23952; www.monastiri-guesthouse.gr; s/d/tr/ste incl breakfast €50/60/70/100; P ✳ 🛜) Opposite the railway station, this converted stone mansion has colourful decorations, long poster beds, and light and airy bathrooms. The handsome wood-and-stone lobby sports a fireplace and a bar.

GUEST HOUSE ELENA   Boutique Hotel €
(Map p168; ☎ 24320 77789; www.elenaguesthouse.gr; Kanari 3; s/d/tr incl breakfast from €45/55/75, ste €100; P ✳ @ 🛜) Period furnishings in intimate atmosphere; multilingual owner.

167

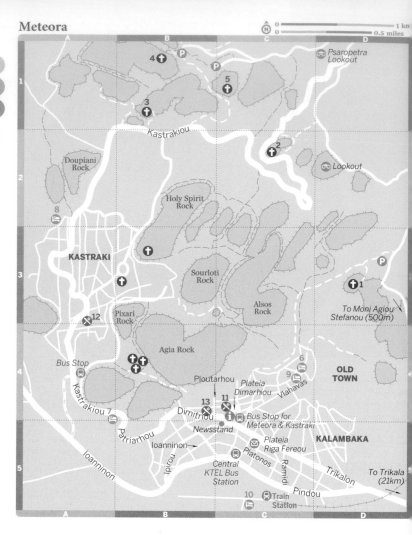

0   1 km
0   0.5 miles

Psaropetra Lookout

4

P

5

P

3

Kastrakiou

Doupiani Rock

2

8

Lookout

Holy Spirit Rock

KASTRAKI

Sourloti Rock

P

1

Alsos Rock

To Moni Agiou Stefanou (500m)

12

Pixari Rock

Agia Rock

6

OLD TOWN

Bus Stop

9

Vlahavas

Ploutarhou

Plateia Dimarhiou

Kastrakiou 7

13

11

Dimitriou

Bus Stop for Meteora & Kastraki

KALAMBAKA

Patriarhou

Ioanninon→

Newsstand

Plateia Riga Fereou

Ipirou

Ramidi

Ioanninon

Central KTEL Bus Station

Platonos

Trikalon

To Trikala (21km)

Pindou

10

Train Station

Eating

TAVERNA TO PARAMITHI Taverna €
(Map p168; ☏24320 24441; Patriarhou Dimitriou
14; mains €6-9) Along with very good grills
and fresh pasta served in a convivial
environment, owner-cooks Makis and
Eleni bring in fresh seafood daily. Other
specialities include lamb ribs (€8.50) and
roka (rocket lettuce) salad (€3.50). Local
musicians often end the night here, with
guitar or bouzouki in hand (and possibly a

glass of the tasty house wine or homemade tsipouru (ouzo-like spirit).

TAVERNA PANELLINION Taverna €
(Map p168; ☏24320 24735; Plateia Dimarhiou;
mains €6.50-12) Opposite the fountain and
filled with antique bric-a-brac, the popula
Panellinion serves first-rate mezedhes,
such as roasted feta, and fine versions
of traditional dishes such as pastitsio
(spaghetti and meat bake) and chicken in
lemon sauce. Local ingredients are all the
go here.

Meteora

Getting There & Away

Bus

Kalambaka's KTEL bus station (Map p168; ☑24320 22432; Ikonomou) is 50m down from the main square and fountain, and the arrival/departure point for regular Trikala bus connections. Travellers to Delphi should go via Trikala and Lamia (not Larisa), taking the 9am bus, changing in Lamia to the 12.45pm Amfissa/Delphi bus, arriving by 3.30pm.

Train

Trains depart from the Kalambaka train station (☑24320 22451). Trains to Thessaloniki and Volos change at Paleofarsalos

Getting Around

Three daily buses for Kastraki (€1.40) leave from the Plateia Dimarhiou fountain, and on weekends two of these (8.20am and 12.30pm Saturday and Sunday) continue on to Meteora. Note that three daily Meteora-bound buses depart from the KTEL station (also picking tourists up at the town hall) between May and September (€1.60). Check with the tourist office for the schedule.

Taxis (opposite the fountain) go to Kastraki (€5) and all the monasteries (for example, Moni Megalou Meteorou for €10). Some drivers speak English, German or French, and you can arrange a taxi tour from about €20 per hour.

Bikes (€10) and motorcycles (€20) can be hired for the day from **Hobby Shop** (☑/fax 24320 25262; Patriarhou Dimitriou 28).

Kastraki Καστράκι
POP 1200

The village of Kastraki is less than 2km from Kalambaka, but its impressive location right under the rocks gives it an otherworldly feel. If you want a base for exploring the Meteora monasteries, or for climbing the rocks themselves, Kastraki is a good choice.

🛏 Sleeping

DOUPIANI HOUSE　　Boutique Hotel €€
(Map p168; ☑24320 75326; www.doupiani house.com; r €50-70, tr €60-80, incl breakfast; P ❄ @ 🛜) The delightful Doupiani House has the lot: spotless, tastefully decorated rooms, with balconies or garden access. Its location – just outside the village – provides a window to Meteora; it boasts one of the region's best panoramic views. There's breakfast on the terrace, birdsong and the attentive hosts, Toula and Thanasis.

DELLAS BOUTIQUE HOTEL　　Boutique Hotel €€
(Map p168; ☑24320 78260; www.dellasboutique hotel.com; s €60-75, d €70-85) While it doesn't boast a wide-angled panoramic view, this handsome place – between Kastraki and Kalambaka – receives accolades for its elegant, tidy rooms and high service standards. Prices vary according to the views; breakfast is included.

🍴 Eating

TAVERNA PARADISOS　　Taverna €
(Map p168; ☑24320 22723; mains €6.50-8.50) The traditional meals at the roomy Paradisos will have you 'nostimo-ing!' (exclaiming 'delicious'!) all the way through your dishes, thanks to local and high-quality ingredients and owner-chef Koula's magic touch. Leave space for spit roast on Sunday.

Thessaloniki Θεσσαλονίκη

POP 363,987

Thessaloniki (thess-ah-lo-*nee*-kih) is at once the hippest, most cultured and most expensive place to sleep and eat in northern Greece – though budget options are thankfully starting to emerge. As Greece's second city, Thessaloniki (also called Salonica) offers the best nightlife, shopping, fine-dining and cultural events outside of Athens, but with a friendlier, less hectic vibe.

As with Athens, the enduring symbols of a glorious history are visible here. These include the White Tower, watching over the cafe-lined waterfront, erstwhile Ottoman *hammams* (Turkish baths), many turned into art galleries, and lengthy Byzantine walls culminating at the Ano Poli (Upper Town), an enchanting neighbourhood of colourful old houses, where little Byzantine churches peek from winding alleyways.

Thessaloniki is also a major college town, fleshed out by some 80,000 university students who enliven the city's innumerable cafes, restaurants and bars. Thessaloniki thus remains lively during the long months when the more touristy parts of Greece hibernate. And, though one could easily spend weeks here, Thessaloniki and its sites are compact enough for travellers with only a few days to spare.

 Sights

FREE **WHITE TOWER** Historic Building
(2310 267 832; Lefkos Pyrgos; ⏲8.30am-3pm Tue-Sun) The history of Thessaloniki's most famous landmark, the pacific White Tower, is actually bathed in blood. In 1826 Ottoman Sultan Mahmud II ordered the massacre of janissaries (elite troops made up of forcibly Islamicised Christian boys) deemed disloyal. After the Greek reconquest in 1913, the 'bloody tower' was whitewashed to expunge this grisly past. Although the tower's whitewash has long been removed, the name stuck. The tower's new interactive **museum** presents the city's history through several levels of cool multimedia displays (designed by Apple).

The Meteora: Geology of a Rock Forest

The jutting pinnacles and cliffs of the Meteora were once sediments of an inland sea. About 10 million years ago vertical tectonic movements pushed the entire region out of the sea at a sloping angle. The same tectonic movements caused the flanking mountains to move closer, exerting extreme pressure on the hardened sedimentary deposits. The Meteora developed netlike fissures and cracks. The weathering and erosion that followed formed the towering outcrops of rock that now vault heavenwards. The rocks were conglomerates of many types: limestone, marble, serpentinite and metamorphic, interspersed with layers of sand and shale.

By the dawn of human civilisation, the rocks had weathered and eroded into fantastic shapes; the sandstone and shale washed away, isolating blocks of rock and cliffs. Where erosion was less extreme, caves and overhangs appeared in the rock face.

As early as the 11th century AD, these awesome natural caves had become the solitary abodes of hermit monks. Eventually, 24 monasteries were built on these pinnacles. Today, six are active religious sites, occupied by monks or nuns and visited by the faithful and curious alike.

JOHN ELK III/LONELY PLANET IMAGES ©

Don't Miss **Moni Megalou Meteorou**

The best known of the monasteries, Moni Megalou Meteorou is an imposing form built on the highest rock in the valley, 613m above sea level. Founded by St Athanasios in the 14th century, it became the richest and most powerful monastery thanks to the Serbian emperor Symeon Uros, who turned all his wealth over to the monastery and became a monk. Its *katholikon* (principal church) has a magnificent 12-sided central dome. Its striking series of frescoes entitled *Martyrdom of Saints* depicts the graphic persecution of Christians by the Romans.

THINGS YOU NEED TO KNOW

Grand Meteora Monastery, Metamorphosis; ☎24320 22278; ⊗9am-5pm Wed-Mon Apr-Oct, 9am-4pm Thu-Mon Nov-Mar

---

FREE **PALACE, ARCH & ROTUNDA OF GALERIUS** Historic Area
Three major Roman monuments associated with the early-4th century Emperor Galerius spill across Egnatia at Plateia Navarinou. The ruined **Palace of Galerius** (Plateia Navarinou; ⊗8.30am-3pm Tue-Sun), sprawling east–west across the square, contains floor mosaics, columns and some walls. North of Egnatia at Kamara, the **Arch of Galerius** features sculpted soldiers in combat; it was erected in AD 303 to celebrate a victory over the Persians.

Just above the arch is the unmistakable **Rotunda of Galerius** (Mausoleum; ☎2310 218 720; Plateia Agiou Georgiou; ⊗8am-5pm Tue-Sun), a hulking brick structure built by Galerius as his future mausoleum (he never used it, dying in retirement in today's Serbia instead). Constantine the Great made the rotunda Thessaloniki's first church (Agiou Georgiou), and later the Ottomans transformed it into a mosque; the minaret they added has now been restored. Some interior frescoes survive.

171

Thessaloniki

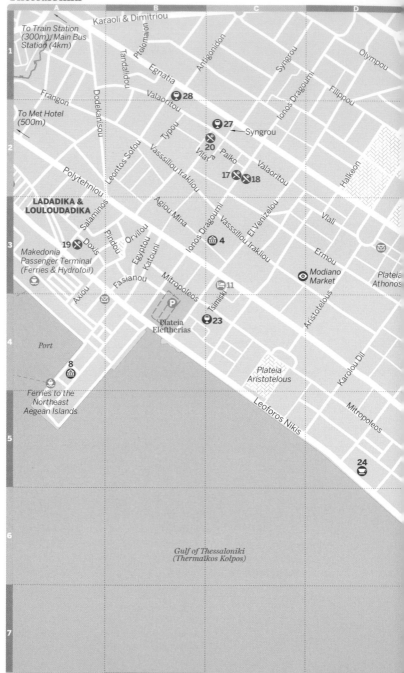

KASTRA
(ANO POLI)

Theotokopoulou

Moreas

Agiou Nikolaou

Sofokleous

Agias Sofias

Olympiados

Irodotou

Plateia
Dikastirion

Kassandrou

3

6

Agnostou Stratiotou

Amynda

Agiou Dimitriou

Apostolou Pavlou

Filippou

Olympou

Manolaki Kyriakou

2

Iasonidou

Dragoumi

Dimitriou Gounari

Kastritsiou

Egnatia

Armenopoulou

16

Agias Sofias

Plateia
Agias
Sofias

Irinou

7

30

Plateia Agiou
Georgiou

Ethnikis Argyris

Dimitriou Gounari

Konstantinou Melenidou

13

12

Aristotle
University
Campus

15 1

Palion Patron Germanou

Kamara

Svolou

Dimitriou Gounari

5

Egnatia

Plateia
Navarinou

26

Nikiforos Fokas

Proxenou
Koromila

Smyrnis

Tsimiski

To Rihardos (1km);
Halkidiki Bus Terminal
(2.5km)

10

22

Ethnikis Argyris

Leoforos Nikis

Angelaki

14 21

Pavlou Mela

Tsirogianni

25

29

Plateia
Lefkos Pyrgos

Nikolaou
Germanou

To Halkidiki
(45km)

9

To Archaeological
Museum (200m)

173

FREE ROMAN AGORA Ruins
(Plateia Dikastirion; ⊙8am-3pm Tue-Sun) The
Roman Agora lies north of Plateia Aristotelous, across Egnatia on Plateia Dikastirion. Ancient Macedonian commercial activity, starting in the 3rd century BC, peaked
under the Romans, when the area was
buzzing with public affairs, services and
shops. A helpful, English-language placard
explains the site, which contains clustered
shop walls and mosaic floor remnants.

CHURCH OF AGIOS DIMITRIOS Church
(☎2310 270 008; Agiou Dimitriou 97; ⊙8am-
10pm, crypt 1.30-7.30pm Mon, 8am-7.30pm
Tue-Thu & Sun, 9-11pm Fri) Perhaps the grandest church in Greece, the enormous,
5th-century Church of Agios Dimitrios
honours Thessaloniki's patron saint. A Roman soldier, Dimitrios was killed around
AD 303 on the site (then a Roman bath),
on orders of Emperor Galerius, infamous
for persecuting Christians. The martyrdom site is now an eerie underground
crypt, open during the day and for the
special Friday-night service, which can be
attended. In 1980, the saint's relics were
returned from Italy, and now occupy a
silver reliquary inside.

The Ottomans made Agios Dimitrios a
mosque, plastering over the wall frescoes.
After the 1913 Greek reconquest,
the plaster was removed, revealing
Thessaloniki's finest church mosaics.
While the 1917 fire was very damaging,
five 8th-century mosaics have survived,
spanning the altar.

ARCHAEOLOGICAL MUSEUM Museum
(☎2310 830 538; www.amth.gr; Manoli
Andronikou 6; adult/student & child €6/free;
⊙8.30am-8pm) Thessaloniki's Archaeological Museum showcases prehistoric,
ancient Macedonian and Hellenistic
finds. You can see the **Derveni Crater**
(330–320 BC), a huge, ornate Hellenistic
vase of bronze and tin. Used for mixing
wine and water, and later as a funerary
urn, it's marked by intricate relief carvings illustrating the life of Dionysos, with
mythical figures, animals, vines and ivy
branches. The **Derveni Treasure** contains
Greece's oldest surviving papyrus piece
(250–320 BC). The ground-floor exhibit,
Pre-Historic Thessaloniki, boasts the
Petralona Hoard – axes and chisels in
an urn, abandoned by the artisan, in the
Petralona Cave north of Halkidiki, plus
daggers, pottery and tools from mound

KUTTIG - TRAVEL/ALAMY ©

Don't Miss Ano Poli (Kastra) & the Byzantine Walls

Homes in **Ano Poli** (Upper Town), also called Kastra (Castle), largely survived the 1917 fire – although the fire had originated there, the wind swept the flames down towards the sea. It had been the Turkish Quarter during Ottoman times, and contains Thessaloniki's most atmospheric urban architecture.

Here, timber-framed, pastel-painted houses with overhanging upper storeys are clustered on small winding streets. Ambling through Ano Poli's steep, wiggly lanes, marked by steps and tiny rivulets, is a great pleasure. Panoptic views of the city and the Thermaic Gulf can be had from the **Byzantine walls** above. Several important Byzantine churches are found here.

Kastra's walls were built by Emperor Theodosius (AD 379–475), who modelled them on his own great Constantinopolitan wall system. Rebuilt in the 14th century, the walls were strengthened with marble stones from the Jewish cemetery in 1821. It's possible to walk up almost to the top of them from opposite the university (Panepistimio Aristotelion).

Today this old quarter has also become a refuge for Thessaloniki's leftists. Slumbering cafes and expletive-rich displays of anarchist graffiti, spray-painted in several languages and colours on the walls, are a part of what lend it its character.

tombs dating from the neolithic period to the late Bronze Age.

THESSALONIKI MUSEUM OF PHOTOGRAPHY Museum
(☏ 2310 566 716; www.thmphoto.gr; Warehouse A, Thessaloniki Port; adult/child €2/free; ☾11am-7pm Tue-Fri, 11am-9pm Sat & Sun) In a former portside warehouse,

this hip museum displays historic and contemporary Greek photography, plus dynamic temporary exhibitions, and has a waterfront cafe.

FREE **ATATÜRK'S HOUSE** Historic Building
(☏ 2310 248 452; Apostolou Pavlou 75; ☾9am-5pm) Located within the Turkish consu-

175

late grounds, this was the birthplace of modern Turkey's illustrious founder, the dashing Mustafa Kemal, in 1881. Have your identity card or passport ready. The helpful staff will lead you through this faithfully restored house. Along with numerous original furnishings and memorabilia, you'll see other Atatürk paraphernalia like dapper suits, white gloves and a cane. Sporting!

FREE **JEWISH MUSEUM OF THESSALONIKI** Museum
(☎ 2310 250 406; www.jmth.gr; Agiou Mina 13; ⏰ 11am-2pm Tue, Fri & Sun, 11am-2pm & 5-8pm Wed & Thu) Traces Thessaloniki Judaism from 140 BC to the Sephardic immigrations following 1492, ending with the Holocaust. The museum also houses remains from Thessaloniki's large **Jewish cemetery**, vandalised in 1942 by the Nazis.

Tours

BUS TOUR Bus Tours
(€3; ⏰ hourly 8am-9pm Jun-Sep, 9am-4pm Oct-May) A new city-sponsored bus tour leaves from the White Tower, heading in zigzag fashion uphill past various sites, and finishing in the Ano Poli (Upper Town). Jump on, jump off, or continue alone between sites. The tourism office has leaflets detailing the route and sights covered.

Sleeping

RENT ROOMS THESSALONIKI Hostel €
(☎ 2310 204 080; www.rentrooms-thessaloniki.gr; Konstantinou Melenikou 9 near Kamara; dm/s/d/tr/q incl breakfast €19/35/48/65/78; ❄ 🛜) Cheery, clean and modern, this new hostel is very well situated near Kamara, and has a back-garden cafe with views of the rotunda. A full bookshelf, free wi-fi, communal breakfast/cafe nook, locked safeboxes and cheap bike hire add to the appeal. Some dorms and rooms have mini-kitchens, and all have bathrooms. The friendly staff can provide local info. It's very popular – book ahead online or by phone.

DAIOS Boutique Hotel €€€
(☎ 2310 250 200; www.daioshotels.com; Leoforos Nikis 59; s/d/ste with sea view €170/225/260;

Palace of Galerius (p171)

Monastery Opening Hours

Before planning your route, double-check days and opening hours; the monks are an independent lot, and no two monasteries keep exactly the same hours. The following is a list of closures as at the time of research:

- **Moni Agiou Stefanou** Closed Monday
- **Moni Megalou Meteorou** Closed Tuesday (and Wednesday November to March)
- **Moni Agias Varvaras Rousanou** Closed Wednesday
- **Moni Agias Triados** Closed Thursday (and Wednesday November to March)
- **Moni Agiou Nikolaou** Closed Friday
- **Moni Varlaam** Closed Friday

🌊 🛜 🏊) This boutique hotel near the White Tower has become a favourite among Greece's upper stratum. A keen sensitivity to light and shadow pervades the whole hotel, which has contemporary, minimalist design. Suites have enormous, sound-proofed windows and wrap-around balconies (from some you only see water, not streets). The hotel's waterfront cafe is equally sophisticated and colour-rich. Staff are friendly and professional. Enter on the side street (2 Smyrnis).

MET HOTEL Luxury Hotel €€
📞 2310 017 000; www.themethotel.gr; 26 Oktovriou 48; s/d incl breakfast from € 70/100; 🌊 🛜 🏊) Not that central (though close to both bus and train stations), this spiffy new spa hotel down near the commercial port is notable for its minimalist decor, sleek modern baths and a revitalising spa centre. Amenities include designer soaps, flat-screen TVs and some seriously comfortable mattresses. There's a nice bar in similar style, and a rooftop outdoor swimming pool too.

LE PALACE HOTEL Hotel €€
📞 2310 257 400; www.lepalace.gr; Tsimiski 3; s/d/tr incl breakfast €72/88/95; 🌊 🛜) At night gaze down from your little balcony at twinkling Tsimiski roaring by below (there's soundproofing). Le Palace

has spacious, modern rooms with all mod cons. Valet parking costs €11 per 24 hours. The buffet breakfast is good quality and the restaurant therein works all day.

 Eating

PAPAROUNA Fine Dining €
(📞 2310 510 852; www.paparouna.com; cnr Syngrou 7 & Vilara 2; mains €8-16; ⏱1pm-1am; 🛜) Built a century ago as a bank, this lively restaurant is marked by lofty ceilings, great bursts of red (like the name, which means 'poppy') and checkerboard floor. The creative cuisine includes chicken with peppermint and honey, linguini with aromatic lemongrass and cherry tomatoes, and even organic Greek beer. It makes phenomenal desserts, too.

TO ETSI Street Food €
(📞 2310 222 469; Nikoforos Fokas 2; grills €2.80-4) This bawdily decorated, iconic eatery near the White Tower is a local institution offering refreshingly light souvlaki and *soutzoukakia* (meat rissoles in tomato sauce) with vegetable dips, in Cypriot-style pita bread. Look for the neon sign.

MOLYVOS
Fine Dining €

(☎2310 555 952; cnr Ionos Dragoumi & Kapodistriou; mains €8-15) Molyvos' refined setting elevates Greek cuisine to fine dining; nearby **Molyvos Ethnik** (☎2310 555 952; cnr Ionos Dragoumi & Papadopoulou; mains €6-10) is its freewheeling companion eatery, with high ceilings and polished mirrors, imaginative almost-fusion cuisine and Latin music.

DORE ZYTHOS
Taverna €

(☎2310 279 010; Tsirogianni 7; mains €8-12) Grab a table outside when the weather's warm and watch the White Tower across the way while savouring imaginative Mediterranean cuisine. Sister establishment **Zythos** (☎2310 540 284; Katouni 5; mains €8-12) in Ladadika has great architecture and equally fine food.

PANELLINION
Taverna €

(☎2310 567 220; Salaminos 1; mains €6-10) This friendly taverna has traditional Ladadika decor, with its wooden floors and walls lined with olive-oil bottles and tins of produce. Panellinion's varied choices include a world of ouzos and cheeses to delicious seafood mezedhes; only organic vegetables are used.

 Drinking

SPITI MOU
Bar

(cnr Egnatia & Leontos Sofou 26; ☉1pm-late; 🛜) A new bar upstairs in a lofty old building in the Syngrou/Valaoritou district, 'My House' (as the name means in Greek) was opened after its young owners realised their parties were becoming too big to fail. The ambient music, well-worn decor and big couches spread across a chequered floor all add character. There's live music on Sundays, occasional costume parties, and yes, even wi-fi. The entrance is unmarked, but is the doorway closest to Egnatia on Leontos Sofou.

BEERSTORE
Bar

(☎2310 233 438; www.beer.gr; Kalapothaki 6; ☉noon-2am) A spiffy corner shop that doubles as a well-lit, stand-up bar for beer connoisseurs, the Beerstore sells brews from everywhere from Crete to California (with Belgium and Central Europe especially well represented). Prices are about €2 higher for consumption on premises.

PARTIZAN BAR
Bar

(☎2310 543 461; Valaoritou 29; ☉8am-3am Mon-Thu, 8am-5am Fri & Sat, noon-3am Sun) Another Syngrou/Valaoritou hotspot, this popular place has bohemian flair and gets packed with late-night revellers, from students to older folks.

LOXIAS
Cafe

(☎2310 233 925; Isavron 7; ☉4pm-2am) Educated Greeks have gravitated for years to this whimsical *steki* (hang-out), where they might discuss philosophy, politics or literature over ouzo and snacks. Loxias is decorated with wine casks and bursting bookshelves, and photos of Greek writers, Montenegrin princesses and the dervishes of old Hania. Romantics can duck the commotion on the back balcony's table for two, overlooking Roman ruins.

KAFENAI
Cafe

(☎2310 220 310; cnr Ethnikis Amynis & Tsopela; ☉9am-2am) This new *kafeneio* (coffee house), beside the Cretan restaurant Myrsini, impressively revives the spirit of old Salonica. With 1950s-style Greek decor, high ceilings supported by columns and low-key jazz, it's no wonder

Train Services from Kalambaka

DESTINATION	DURATION	FARE	FREQUENCY
Athens (normal/IC)	5½hr/ 4½	€14.60/ 24.30	2/2 daily
Thessaloniki (normal)	4hr	€12.10	3 daily
Volos	1½hr	€6	2 daily

the place attracts local artists and musicians.

KAFE NIKIS 35 — Cafe
(2310 230 449; Leoforos Nikis 35) More stylish than the adjacent waterfront places, this snug, friendly cafe just under street level is perfect for a Sunday-morning espresso. Get a window table and feel the dappled sunlight dancing through the blinds.

Entertainment

Clubs & Live Music

LIDO — Club
(2310 539 055; www.lidoparadise.gr; Frixou 5, Sfageia) Thessaloniki's big, mean disco machine, Lido pumps out R&B, house and more. Like most nightclubs, in summer it operates out on the airport road.

VOGUE — Club
(2310 502 081; admission €5) Just opposite Pyli Axiou, this is a trendy new nightclub playing the usual DJ-driven pop, R&B and house music.

BOAT BARS — Cruise
(6pm-1am) For partiers preferring an aqueous environment, take a booze cruise on one of several boat bars moored on the waterfront south of the White Tower, by Alexander the Great's statue. Each boat has slightly different decorations and themes, with music ranging from pop to reggae to R&B. These cruisers leave every 20 minutes or so for a half-hour chug around the Thermaikos Kolpos; there's no admission charge and you can stay on board whether docked or adrift, for the whole evening if you wish – just keep drinking!

Theatre & Cinema

National Theatre of Northern Greece — Theatre
(2310 288 000; www.ntng.gr; Ethnikis Amynis 2) Offers classical Greek drama and modern theatrical works, as well as operas.

 ## Shopping

GEORGIADIS — Handicrafts
(Egnatia 107; 9am-2pm, 5pm-9pm) This crammed little place has been purveying handcrafted Orthodox icons (from €15) in various shapes and sizes since 1902. It's near the Mt Athos Pilgrims Bureau.

RIHARDOS — Music
(www.rihardos.gr; Konstantinopoleos 27) Who knew there were so many different kinds of bouzouki? Rihardos, one of Greece's biggest purveyors of traditional instruments, has a huge array of Greek instruments. Friendly owner Rihardos and his English-speaking son, Joseph,

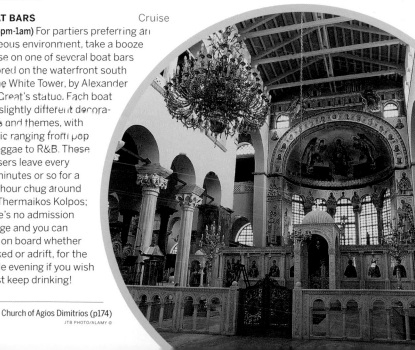

Church of Agios Dimitrios (p174)
JTB PHOTO/ALAMY ©

explain everything about these unusual instruments. Take bus 31 from Egnatia east to the Faliro stop (five to 10 minutes); continue across the intersection with Paraskeopoulos, turn left and Rihardos is facing you.

 Information

Tourist Information

Office of Tourism Directorate (☏2310 221 100; tour-the@otenet.gr; Tsimiski 136; ⏰8am-8pm Mon-Fri, 8am-2pm Sat) The new city tourism office occupies a grand building near the White Tower, replacing the former portside one. Friendly and well-informed staff provide assistance in English and German.

 Getting There & Away

Air

Makedonia Airport (☏2310 473 212; www.thessalonikiairport.gr) About 16km southeast of town, served by local bus 78. Internationally, Makedonia Airport serves a number of European destinations, and attracts frequent budget flights.

Aegean Airlines (☏2310 280 050; www.aegeanair.com; Venizelou 2) On Plateia Eleftherias. Offers flights to Athens (€60 to €93, 55 minutes, 12 daily).

Aspect Travel (☏2310 240 567; mail@aspect.ondsl.gr; Vasillis Olgas 283) A good all-purpose travel agency.

Olympic Air (☏2310 368 666; www.olympicair.com; Navarhou Koundourioti 1-3) Near the port. Operates more than 15 domestic routes; the most services go to Athens (€65 to €115, 55 minutes, seven daily).

Remember Travel (☏2310 246 026; remembertravel@mail.gr; Egnatia 119) Just off Kamara. Sells tickets and has good post-sale customer service.

Bus

Thessaloniki's **main bus station** (☏2310 595 408; www.ktel-thes.gr; Monastiriou 319), 3km west of centre, features different windows selling tickets to specific destinations, meaning the worker at one window cannot sell you a ticket for, or give information about, anything other than their specified destination. There's no general information booth and this enhances the station's unpleasant, stressful nature.

Halkidiki-bound buses leave from the totally different **Halkidiki bus terminal** (☏2310 316 555; www.ktel-chalkidikis.gr), on Thessaloniki's eastern outskirts. To get here, take bus 2 or 31 to the Botsari stop from the train station, or from anywhere along Egnatia; at Botsari bus 36 continues the final 10 minutes. With traffic, it's about one hour from the train station to the Halkidiki bus station.

Train

Buy tickets at the **train station** (☏2310 599 421; www.trainose.gr; Monastiriou), or from **OSE** (☏2310 598 120; Aristotelous 18). Book in advance for Athens (especially

White Tower (p170)
PETER PHIPP/TRAVELSHOTS.COM/ALAMY ©

Sweet Indulgences

For a quick breakfast or sinful dessert, Thessaloniki's *zaharoplasteia* (patisseries) are hard to beat. Although classics like baklava or chocolate profiterole are available throughout Greece, Thessaloniki's historic ties with the mores and populations of the Ottoman East have bequeathed it with an especially rich tradition of sweets – and a discerning local population to enjoy them. While tasty places are found everywhere, the following well-polished *zaharoplasteia* are particularly famous. Most prices are by the kilo (usually around €2 to €4 per piece).

Just above the rotunda, the classic **Kokkinos Fournos** (Apostolou Pavlou 1, Rotunda) bakery does Thessaloniki's best *koulourakia vanilias* – crunchy, slightly sweet golden cookies perfect for dipping in Greek coffee.

Since 1908, when Thessaloniki was still Ottoman, local legend **Hatzis** (☏2310 968 400; Egnatia 119) has been replicating the tastes of old Constantinople. After Hatzis, you'll never ask for a simple 'baklava' again. The veritable symphony of sweets served here includes *vezir parmak* (*politika* syrup cake with cream filling), *hanoum bourek* (handmade pastry with raisins, peanuts and cream) and *malempi mastiha* (cream from milk and rice porridge, flavoured with *mastiha*, a sweet liquor from Chios, and served with rose syrup).

The posh **Agapitos** (☏2310 268 368; Egnatia 134) offers a taste of the Continent. Its cakes, fruit concoctions and profiteroles (chocolate pudding with a crunchy base and white cream) are excellent. Try the superlative *efrosini* chocolate cake, or smudge your fingers on the delicious mini-éclairs.

A veritable institution since 1960, **Trigona Elenidis** (☏2310 257 510; cnr Dimitriou Gounari & Tsimiski) is a very rare thing in today's world: a shop specialising in only one product. Its sweet, flaky triangular cones filled with cool and unbelievably tasty cream are legendary; locals come out with 2kg boxes, but one large triangle will certainly fill you up.

---

or the cheapest train). Trains serve Athens (€36, 7¾ hours, 10 daily), travelling via Larisa (€10, two hours). Intercity trains to Athens (€48, 5½ hours) are more expensive, but not significantly faster.

ⓘ Getting Around

To/From the Airport

Bus 78 runs every 30 minutes from the airport west to the main bus station via the train station (€0.80). From the centre to the airport by taxi costs €8 to €12, except during the night (midnight until 5am), during which time more expensive rates apply.

Bus

Orange articulated buses operate within Thessaloniki, and blue-and-orange buses operate both within the centre and the suburbs. City buses have electronic rolling signs listing the next destination, accompanied by a recording repeating the same in Greek and English. Bus 1 connects the bus station and the train station every 10 minutes, bus 31 goes every six minutes to Voulgari, bus 36 continues from Voulgari to the Halkidiki bus station. Major points on Egnatia such as Aristotelous, Agias Sofias and Kamara are served by many buses, such as the 10 and 14, from the train station.

Tickets are sold at *periptera* (street kiosks) for €0.80, or from on-board ticket machines (€0.90). If you buy the former, validate it on board. However, if you'll use the bus frequently, buy a 24-hour unlimited-usage ticket (€3). Note the machine will not give change and doesn't accept bills. It's thus wiser to buy in a kiosk, but if you don't, have change when boarding the bus,

and buy a ticket immediately. Thessaloniki's ticket police combine the finesse of the amateur boxer with the efficiency of the Gestapo, and pounce at any sign of confusion – foreigners are especially easy targets. If they nab you, you'll pay €30 on the spot, or you can go with one of these specimens to plead your case to the police.

Car

Budget Rent a Car (☎ 2310 229 519; Angelaki 15) and **Euro Rent** (☎ 2310 826 333; Georgiou Papandreou 5) are two biggies.

Taxi

Thessaloniki's blue-and-white taxis carry multiple passengers, and won't take you if you're not going in the same direction as pre-existing passengers. The minimum fare is €2.80, and the more expensive 'night rate' is in effect until 5am.

Halkidiki   Χαλκιδική

Immediately recognisable on maps for its three 'fingers' stretching into the north Aegean, the **Halkidiki Peninsula** has become all too famous for its tourist sprawl

in summertime, when Thessaloniki locals descend for holidays. The first finger, **Kassandra**, has fared worst, filled with unimaginative villas, concrete and trinket shops. The second, **Sithonia**, remains somewhat less abused, and contains some truly magical beaches. Halkidiki's third finger, **Athos**, has largely escaped the clutches of modern development – most of it comprises the monastic community of Mt Athos (Agion Oros), open only to male pilgrims and accessible only by boat.

Sithonian Peninsula Χερσονησος Σιθωνιας

The coast road loops around Sithonia, skirting wide bays, climbing into pine-forested hills and dipping down to resort. The west coast has long sandy beaches between **Nikiti** and **Paradisos**, notably **Kalogria Beach** and **Lagomandra Beach**. Beyond, **Neos Marmaras** is Sithonia's largest resort, with a crowded beach but many domatia and good seafood tavernas.

Left: A beach on Kassandra
Below: Petralona Cave (p185)
(LEFT) IAN DAGNALL/ALAMY ©; (BELOW) TERRY HARRIS/ALAMY ©

From Neos Marmaras
the road climbs into the hills,
from which roads (some dirt)
descend to more beaches. **Toroni** and
Porto Koufos, two small southwestern
resorts, offer relaxing beaches and a
yacht harbour sheltered in a deep bay,
with domatia and fish tavernas. Sithonia's
relatively undeveloped southern tip
is rocky, rugged and dramatic, with
spectacular views of Mt Athos appearing
as you rounding the southeastern tip.

Sarti, further up the coast, is a quiet
resort with some nightlife, rooms and
eating options. Its long, sandy beach used
to make it a place for escapists, though
its since been 'discovered'. There are
great views of Mt Athos from here, also
visible by boat excursions run by Sarti
travel agents. **Sarti Vista Bed & Breakfast
Resort** (☎ 23750 94651; www.sartivista.
com; apt from €70; P ❄ 🛜 ☲), with a great
view over the sea across to Mt Athos, is
essentially a collection of modern self-
catering apartments with balconies, set
above the town. The outdoor barbeque

area, infinity pool and gardens add to the
friendly, relaxed vibe. The helpful owners
can advise on local activities.

Just 6km north of Sarti is a turn-off
leading to **Kavourotrypes** (Crab Holes)
– several small rocky coves great for
swimming.

Buses leave from Thessaloniki's east-
side Halkidiki bus terminal for Neos
Marmaras (€13, 2½ hours, seven daily),
Sarti (€17, 3¼ hours, five daily) and
Vourvourou (€12.20, 1¾ hours, four daily).
Most Sarti buses loop around the Sithonian
Peninsula, enjoying coastal views.

Athos Peninsula (Secular Athos) Χερσονησος του Αθω

The third finger of Halkidiki is visited by
both beachgoers, in the northerly stretches, and by religious pilgrims going to the
isolated monastic community that takes
up the mountainous southeastern part.
There's no land entry allowed between

183

the two sections. For those who can't visit Mt Athos or simply don't have time, a day trip is ideal. The boats trace the southern peninsula, passing Athos' most spectacular clifftop monasteries and wild nature.

Most day cruises run from Ouranoupoli. Try a three-hour cruise (adult/child under six €18/free) on the 300-seat *Kapetan Fotis* (leaving at 10.30am and 1.45pm daily, from Easter through October). The cruise is run by **Athos Sea Cruises** (☏ 23770 71071; www.athos-cruises.gr; Ouranoupoli) and passes nine major southcoast monasteries, some perilously perched on the remote southern cliffs. The boat gets as close as legally possible to shore (500m), meaning the monasteries are clearly visible for good photos. Running commentary on the sights is given in English, German and Greek. There's a cold buffet and on-board

shopping for icons and videos about Athos.

While the tour guide informs you of the sights, look out for the splendid Russian Monastery of Agios Panteleimon (the first, down on the beachfront), and the cliffside monasteries of Dionysiou and Simonas Petras, elevated high above the water after Dafni. The boat turns back towards Ouranoupoli at the clifftop monastery, Agiou Pavlou; behind it, the craggy peak of Mt Athos looms.

Alternatively, those based on Halkidiki's Sithonian Peninsula can get roughly the same tour, done in the opposite direction, on the large **Spirit of Athos** (☏ 23750 94066 www.athoscruises.gr; Ormos Panagias). The tour (€30) includes an afternoon lunch and sightseeing stop in Ouranoupoli. The cruise departs from Ormos Panagias daily at 9.30am and returns by 5pm.

Mt Athos (Agion Oros) Αγιον Ορος

For over a millennium, unbroken spiritual activity has survived on the isolated southeast of Halkidiki's third finger, at the monasteries of Agion Oros (the Holy Mountain). This semi-autonomous monastic republic still follows the Julian calendar, along with many other Byzantine edicts and mores, and comprises 20 working monasteries and *skites* (dependencies), plus *kelli* (cells) for ascetics. The monastic community's northern part is thickly forested, while the south is dominated by the stark, soaring peak of Mt Athos (2033m). Since there's neither industry nor hunting, it's practically a nature reserve. An enormous World Heritage site, Mt Athos is formally under the Greek state, though ecclesiastically remains under the Orthodox Patriarchate of Constantinople (İstanbul).

Apocryphal legends say that the Virgin Mary visited Athos and blessed it; the Holy Mountain is considered the Garden of the Virgin, and is dedicated exclusively to her – there's no room for other women. Although frustrated Eurocrats in Brussels have contested this prohibition, they've proven no match for 1000 years of tradition and the gold-sealed *chrysobulls* (decrees) of Byzantine emperors, whose names are still invoked in prayers and whose edicts continue to be respected.

For men, visiting monastic Athos requires advance planning. Visits are restricted to four days, though they can be extended. Experiencing the monasteries is wonderfully peaceful – and tiring. In many, you follow the monks' lifestyle, eating and attending services, which on feast days may last up to 10 hours. When you traipse the quiet Athonite forest paths and marvel at the monastic architecture and art treasures, the feeling really hits home that this is a special place; whether or not you're religious, the kind monks and pilgrims will leave a strong impression.

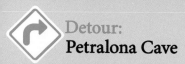

Detour:
Petralona Cave

Some 50km southeast of Thessaloniki on the main road is the stalagmite-rich **Petralona Cave** (☎23730 71671; admission €7; ☼9am to 1 hr before sunset). Discovered by Petralona village locals in 1959, it became famous when a prehistoric man's skull (dubbed *Arhanthropos*; in Greek, the 'first' or 'original man') was found; scientists have dated it as 700,000 years old, making *Arhanthropos* Europe's oldest known man. Fossils of extinct species, including lions, panthers, bears, rhinoceroses, elephants, bison, deer, numerous birds and bats have been found here. The most intriguing objects discovered, the so-called 'Petralonas Hoard', are kept at Thessaloniki's Archaeological Museum (p174). The ticket price includes a cave tour and visit to the adjacent **anthropological museum**. Photos aren't allowed..

Litohoro ΛΙΤΟΧΩΡΟ

POP 7011 / ELEV 305M

Relaxing Litohoro (lih-*to*-ho-ro) is the base for climbing or just admiring Olympus, though its winding, cobbled upper streets and lovely Macedonian-style wood-balconied houses make it appealing in its own right. The arrival here is dramatic: on the final eastern approach, the Enipeas River gorge parts, revealing the towering double peaks of Olympus. Booking ahead in summer is recommended.

 ## Sleeping & Eating

XENONAS PAPANIKOLAOU Hotel €
(☎23520 81236; www.xenonas-papanikolaou.gr; Nikolaou Episkopou Kitrous 1; s/d incl breakfast €44/54; P ✳ 🛜) Solitude-seekers, head here first. This romantic guesthouse, set in a flowery garden up in the backstreets, is far from the tourist crowds on Litohoro's main street. The self-catering rooms feel more spacious than they actually are, and the tasteful decoration is enhanced by nice views of Litohoro's traditional terracotta rooftops. The cosy downstairs lounge has a fireplace and couches, and management is friendly. To get here from the square, take 28 Oktovriou uphill and turn left on Nikolaou Episkopou Kitrous.

HOTEL OLYMPUS MEDITERRANEAN Hotel €€
(☎23520 81831; www.olympusmed.gr; Dionysou 5; d/tr incl breakfast €70/90, luxury ste €100; ✳ @ 🛜) A four-star hotel up in the backstreets, the Olympus Mediterranean occupies an imposing neoclassical building with ornate balconies, and has 20 luxurious rooms and three suites, plus an indoor pool, a mosaic-tiled jacuzzi pool and a sauna. Some rooms also have a fireplace and a jacuzzi.

GASTRODROMIO Fine Dining €
(☎23520 21300; Plateia Eleftherias; mains €7-13) If Gastrodromio was around in Olympian times, Zeus and Co would surely have eaten here. Litohoro's most delightfully inventive restaurant, the spacious, traditionally decorated Gastrodromio serves eager diners flavourful dishes such as octopus with peppercorn, cumin, garlic, hot pepper and wine; or rabbit cooked in wine and glazed with almonds, cinnamon and nutmeg. The wine list itself is 21 pages long.

❶ Information

EOS (Greek Alpine Club; ☎23520 84544; ☼9.30am-12.30pm & 6-8pm Mon-Sat Jun-Sep) Located below the public parking lot; this office distributes pamphlets with general and hiking information on Olympus. Take Ithakisiou down from the square and turn left

MARK DAF

Don't Miss **Mt Olympus ΟΛΥΜΠΟΣ ΟΡΟΣ**

Just as it did for the ancients, the cloud-covered lair of the Ancient Greek pantheon – awe inspiring Mt Olympus – fires the visitor's imagination today. Greece's highest mountain, Olympus also hosts around 1700 plant species, some rare and endemic. Its slopes are covered with thick forests of numerous different deciduous trees, conifers and pines. Bird life is equally varied. Olympus became Greece's first national park in 1937. Excepting the exertions of ancient deities, the first known mortals to reach Mytikas (2918m), Olympus' highest peak, were Litohoro local Christos Kakalos and Swiss climbers Frederic Boissonas and Daniel Baud-Bovy, in August 1913. Although it's possible to drive up Olympus, most people come for the hike.

THINGS YOU NEED TO KNOW

Consult the Litohoro-based hiking association **EOS** (Greek Alpine Club; ☎ 23520 84544; ⏱ 9.30am-12.30pm & 6-8pm Mon-Sat Jun-Sep) for maps and current conditions.

after 100m. The EOS also runs three mountain refuges.

SEO (Association of Greek Climbers; ☎ 23520 84200; ⏱ 6-10pm) This place is informative and runs an Olympus refuge; however, the EOS has more English speakers. Walk down Ithakiou, turn left and then left again.

Tourist information booth (Agiou Nikolaou; ⏱ 9am-6pm) In a white building with wooden eaves, just before Ithakiou.

www.litohoro.gr Municipal website.

❶ Getting There & Away

From the **bus station** (☎ 23520 81271; Agiou Nikolaou), buses serve Katerini (€2.30, 25 minutes, 13 daily), Thessaloniki (€8.50, 1¼ hours 13 daily) and Athens (€33, 5½ hours, three daily via Katerini). Buses from Thessaloniki to Volos/Athens leave you on the highway, where you catch a Katerini–Litohoro bus.

Litohoro's train station, 9km away, is on the Athens–Volos–Thessaloniki line.

Ioannina ΙΩΑΝΝΙΝΑ

POP 61,629

Hip Ioannina (ih-o-*ah*-nih-nah or *yah*-nih-nah) is a bustling commercial and cultural centre, and home to 20,000 university students who energise the local nightlife. Ioannina is set on the placid (though polluted) **Lake Pamvotis** and faces sheer mountains. This idyllic setting is further enhanced by an evocative old quarter (the Kastro), interspersed with narrow lanes and architectural wonders from Byzantine and Ottoman times. The city also has excellent restaurants, bars and cafes.

Sights

ITS KALE   Castle
(Inner Citadel; ⏰8am-5pm & 8-10pm Tue-Sun) The Kastro's sublime citadel rises from a long bluff overlooking lake and mountain. Also here are the **Tomb of Ali Pasha** and the restored **Fetiye Cami** (Victory Mosque), originally built in 1611 to reassert Ottoman dominance, following a failed Greek uprising that caused Christians to be expelled from the citadel.

BYZANTINE MUSEUM   Museum
(☎26510 25989; Its Kale; admission €3; ⏰8am-8pm Tue-Sun) The priceless treasures here include early printed Greek books from Venice and ornate silver jewellery boxes with cloisonné enamel. Textual accompaniments give a fascinating overview of Ioannina's history from the 4th to the 17th century.

MUNICIPAL ETHNOGRAPHIC MUSEUM   Museum
(☎26510 26356; adult/student €3/1.50; ⏰8am-8pm) At the Kastro's northern end the Aslan Pasha Mosque (1619), local costumes and period photographs are displayed, as are tapestries and prayer shawls from the **synagogue** (Ioustinianou) of Ioannina's once significant Jewish community.

ARCHAEOLOGICAL MUSEUM   Museum
(☎26510 33357; www.amio.gr; Plateia 25 Martiou 6; admission €2, free Sun; ⏰8.30am-

3pm Tue-Sun) Finally reopened after years of renovation, this top-notch museum contains over 3000 finds from all over Epiros, starting with the neolithic period. The most famous finds are from the sites of Dodoni, Vitsa and Efira. There are also temporary, monthly exhibits.

Activities

The relaxing, one-hour **lake cruise** (☎69444 70280; tickets €5; ⏰10am-midnight daily summer, Sat & Sun winter) departs from near the island ferry quay. Since swimming is not advisable, this is the best lake experience.

Sleeping

DAFNI TRADITIONAL HOTEL   Boutique Hotel €€
(☎26510 83560; www.hotelfilyra.gr; Ioustinianou 12; s/d €45/65; P ❄) This remarkable, new, traditional guesthouse is actually built into the inside of the Kastro's enormous outer walls. Rooms combine traditional and modern amenities, and there's one grand, well-decorated family room (€90). Reception is at the Filyra.

FILYRA   Boutique Hotel €
(☎26510 83567; www.hotelfilyra.gr; Andronikou Paleologou 18; s/d €45/55; P ❄) This flower-bedecked boutique hotel inside the Kastro has five spacious self-catering

Buses from Thessaloniki's Main Bus Station (KTEL)

DESTINATION	DURATION	FARE	FREQUENCY
Athens	6¼hr	€42	11 daily
Igoumenitsa	4hr	€40.80	2 daily
Ioannina	3½hr	€30	6 daily

suites on a quiet side street, and friendly and helpful owners.

HOTEL KASTRO Hotel €€
(📞26510 22866; Andronikou Paleologou 57; s/d €75/90; P) This restored Kastro mansion overlooking Its Kale has great atmosphere: antique brass beds, stained-glass windows and a tranquil courtyard create a feeling of romantic seclusion. Service is friendly and prompt. Check ahead, as it was closed for renovation at the time of writing.

Eating

SIRIOS Fine Dining €
(📞26510 77070; www.seirioskouzina.gr; Patriarhou Evangelidi 1; mains €8-12; ⏱noon-11pm) Where Greek food can oft be derided for predictability, the fare at Sirios exceeds expectations. An imaginative menu of decidedly delicious dishes whets palates. Grilled mushrooms in an oil-and-lemon sauce will titillate; as will the *yiaourtlou*

konstaninoupolitiko (sausage in a spicy Greek yoghurt sauce on pitta)! Yum!

ES AEI Fine Dining €
(📞26510 34571; Koundouriotou 50; mains €8-12) This favourite haunt of local and foreign gastronomes combines an Ottoman flair with a unique, glass-roofed courtyard dining room. Its inventive dishes include mezedhes made from organic ingredients and Ioannina specials including grilled pork sausages.

MYSTAGOGIA Taverna €
(📞26510 34571; Koundouriotou 44; mains €6; ⏱dinner) A popular late-night *tsipoura-dhiko* (place serving *tsipoura* – an ouzo-like spirit – and light snacks), the studenty Mystagogia has nourishing mezedhes and good beef *keftedhes* (meatballs).

Drinking & Entertainment

DENOUAR Bar
(📞69847 66894; Anexertasias 40-42; ⏱7pm-4am) For a cosy summer scene with chilled ambience and non-Greek music in a hidden-away, stone-panelled pedestrian street, drop your hat at Denouar. Another selling point is the price of drinks – lower than elsewhere in Ioannina.

XYTHOURKEIO Bar
(📞26510 35550; Anexertasias 144; ⏱8.30pm-3am) This newcomer to the Ioannina nightlife scene is big – from the expansive, two-floor interior with period decor and wood trimmings, to the large selection of beers, and the big, mouthwatering cheeseburgers (other international cuisine is good here too). All in all,

Litohoro (p185) village square

good place to kick back and enjoy a
ight out in Ioannina.

NANTA Bar
(26510 26261; cnr Anexartisias & Stoa Labei)
With its shadows and long bar set under
n upward-curving, bare stone ceiling,
e Ananta smacks of a Franciscan
onastery – albeit one powered by
ck music and alcohol.

Shopping

**ENTRE OF TRADITIONAL
ANDCRAFT OF
OANNINA** Handicrafts, Jewellery
ww.kepavi.gr; Arhiepiskopou Makariou 1;
9.30am-2.30pm & 5.30-8.30pm) Ioan-
na's silverwork has been famous
nce the 17th century. While shops
bound, the best bet for quality and
rices is this big place near the lake.
side are artisan's work areas and
large shop selling everything from
expensive earrings and necklaces
15) to elaborate and expensive
lver dining sets (€2000). Even if
ou don't like silver jewellery, you
robably know someone who does,
nd this is the place to buy it.

Information

ourist Information

OS (Greek Alpine Club; ☎26510 22138;
espotatou Ipirou 2; ☺7-9pm Mon-Fri)

OT (☎26510 41142; fax 26510 49139;
donis 39; ☺7.30am-2.30pm Mon-Fri)
ovides general information and hiking
dates for the Zagorohoria and Vikos Gorge.

Getting There & Away

ir

e airport is 5km northwest of town. **Olympic**
r (☎26510 26518; www.olympicair.com;
ndriki Plateia) has two daily Athens flights
80), as does **Aegean Airlines** (☎26510 6444;
rsinella 11).

If You Like...
The Outdoors

If you like stretching your legs in the
gorgeous **Vikos Gorge** (p191), we think
you'll like these awe-inspiring outdoor
experiences too:

1 METSOVO
East of the Zagorohoria region, this idyllic
town clings to a mountainside at 1156m. The fresh
mountain air and majestic setting are undeniably
appealing, and the range of all-season outdoor
activities is sure to keep the blood flowing. Metsovo's
ski centre (☎26560 41211; ☺9.30am-3.45pm) has
two downhill runs and a 5km cross-country run.

2 PERAMA CAVE
(☎26510 81521; www.spilaio-perama.gr; adult/
student €6/3; ☺8am-8pm) Just beyond Ioannina, this
is one of Greece's largest and most impressive caves,
loaded with white stalactites. Locals hiding from the
Nazis discovered it in 1940. The enormous 1100m-long
cave has three storeys of chambers and passageways.
There's an hour-long tour.

3 VIKOS-AOÖS NATIONAL PARK
The Zagorohoria's centrepiece bursts with
pristine rivers and forests, flowering meadows, and
shimmering lakes reflecting jagged mountains and
endless blue sky. Watch for foxes, chamois, rare hawks,
river otters and brown bears. You'll also see the ear-
popping Pindos Mountains and possibly seminomadic
Vlach and Sarakatsani shepherds.

4 KLISOVA LAGOON
The largest natural wetland in Greece is a
favourite winter stopover for thousands of migrating
birds, and an important breeding ground for the
endangered Dalmatian pelican. The nearby town of
Messolongi makes a decent base.

5 DELPHI
Two popular day hikes, both part of the Trans-
European E4 trail, start and end at Delphi. The first
connects the Temple of Apollo and Korikio Antro, a
sacred mountain cave-shrine for Pan and Dionysos.
En route, there are awesome views of Delphi
and the Amfissa plain. A second hike meanders
through the shady olives groves to Ancient Kirra
on the Gulf of Corinth.

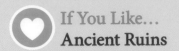

If You Like…
Ancient Ruins

If you like exploring the ruins of **Dodoni** (p190), we think you'd like delving into these ancient ruins too:

1 ANCIENT DION
(Dion Archaeological Park; adult/student €6/2; ⊘8am-8pm) Just north of Mt Olympus, this was where ancient Macedonians worshiped the Olympian gods. Watch for the Sanctuary to Isis where votive statues were found virtually intact and are now housed in the Dion's museum.

2 VERGINA
(☎23310 92347; adult €8; ⊘noon-7.30pm Mon, 8am-7.30pm Tue-Sun summer, 8.30am-3pm winter) The legendary burial site of the Macedonian kings (and their first capital), this World Heritage–listed site is also called the Royal Tombs. In 336 BC, at the wedding of his daughter Cleopatra, Philip II was assassinated here and it's believed that one of the tombs is his. There are also ruins of an extensive palatial complex.

3 NEKROMANTEIO OF AFYRA
(☎26840 41206; adult €2; ⊘8.30am-3pm) Feared by the ancients as the gate of Hades, god of the underworld, these labyrinthine ruins lay at the end of a beautiful boat ride down the coast and up the Aherondas River. The ruins were only discovered in 1958, along with the ruined monastery of Agios Ioannis Prodromos and a graveyard. The eerie underground vault is probably the place into which confused ancient visitors were lowered by windlass, thinking that they were entering the realm of Hades itself.

4 PELLA
(☎23820 31160; admission €6; ⊘8am-7.30pm Tue-Sun, noon-7.30pm Mon) The birthplace of Alexander the Great, these ruins feature spectacular mosaics. Created with naturally coloured, subtly contrasting stones, the mosaics depict mythological scenes. They were created for ancient houses and public buildings now destroyed. Check out the museum for more mosaics.

Bus

From Ioannina's **bus station** (☎26510 26286; Georgiou Papandreou) buses serve Athens (€39, 6½ hours, nine daily), Thessaloniki (€30, 3½ hours, six daily) and Metsovo (€5.80, one hour, four daily). There is also a bus in summer to Parga (€12, 1½ hours, one daily).

🛈 Getting Around

Ioannina airport is 5km northwest on the Perama road; take Bus 7 from the clock tower (every 20 minutes).

Budget Rent a Car (☎/fax 26510 43901; Dodonis 109) is at the airport, as is Auto Union Car Rental (☎/fax 25610 67751; Dodonis 66), which offers good deals.

Taxis (☎26510 46777) wait near Plateia Pyrrou and the lake.

Dodoni Δωδώνη

The colossal, 3rd-century-BC **Theatre of Dodoni** (☎26510 82287; adult €2; ⊘8am-5pm), 21km southwest of Ioannina, is Epiros' most important ancient site. An earth goddess had been worshipped here from around 2000 BC. The oracle she spoke through was reputedly Greece's oldest, and the most venerated (before the Delphic oracle took precedence in the 6th century BC). By the 13th century BC, Zeus was speaking through the rustling of leaves from a sacred oak tree to worshippers at the site. Around 500 BC a temple to Zeus was built, though today only its foundations and a few columns remain.

Under King Pyrrhus, a theatre was famously erected. Now restored, it hosts Ioannina's **Festival of Ancient Drama** in July. On its north side is the **acropolis**, where remnants of its once-substantial walls remain. Nearby are the scant remains of the **Sanctuary of Zeus**, where his sacred oak and oracle stood.

🛈 Getting There & Away

Buses from Ioannina leave at 6.30am and 4.30pm daily, except for Thursday and Sunday, returning at 7.30am and 5.30pm. One other bus, on Sunday, leaves at 6pm and returns at 6.45pm.

A taxi from Ioannina costs around €35 return
us €3 per hour for waiting.

The Zagorohoria
ΤΑ ΖΑΓΟΡΟΧΩΡΙΑ

cluster of 46 providentially preserved
ountain hamlets, the Zagorohoria takes
s name from an old Slavonic term, za
ora (behind the mountain), and horia,
he Greek word for villages. Tucked into
he Pindos range, these villages con-
eal inexhaustible local legends and
oast marvellous houses, ranging from
umble cottages of stone and slate to
rand, fortified mansions made of the
ame hardy materials. These remote
llages were once connected by paths
nd old stone bridges. Today, you'll see
he bridges arching over riverbeds and
alleys, though paved roads now connect
he villages. The Zagorohoria's literal and
gurative centrepiece, the Vikos-Aoös Na-
onal Park bursts with pristine rivers and
rests, flowering meadows and shimmer-
g lakes reflecting jagged mountains and
ndless blue sky.

ikos Gorge
αράδρα του Βίκου

secting the Zagorohoria is the 12km-
ng, 900m-deep Vikos Gorge; accord-
g to the Guinness Book of World
ecords, it is the world's deepest,
ough gorge lobbyists elsewhere
ontest the claim. In either
se, Vikos is a truly awe-
spiring work of nature.
The gorge begins near
onodendri in the south
nd runs north until the
apingo villages. You can
art from either end,
ut if you want to return
where you started,
u'll have to arrange
ansport back via the
ng road route.
The Ioannina EOT or
OS (Greek Alpine Club;
23520 84544; 9.30am-

12.30pm & 6-8pm Mon-Sat Jun-Sep) advise on
current weather conditions and provide
maps and other information. You'll need
water, stout walking boots and some
endurance – the hike takes around 6½
hours.

Starting from Monodendri, walk to the
15th-century **Moni Agia Paraskevi** for a
spectacular view over the gorge. You can
descend here, on a steep, marked path.
From there, it's a four-hour walk to the
end, from where a right-hand trail leads
to Mikro Papingo (2½ hours). The larger
Megalo Papingo is a further 2km west, but
the track splits into two at the base of the
climb. The **Klima Spring**, about halfway
along the gorge, is the only water source.

 Activities

Compass Adventures   Outdoors
(26530 71770; 69788 45232; info@compass-
sadventures.gr; Kato Pedina) In Kato Pedina,
the new, full-service organises hiking,
skiing and mountain-biking forays into

Theatre of Dodoni

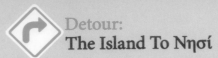

Detour:
The Island To Νησί

Ioannina's closest getaway, the Island (To Νησί) lies just opposite the town, in the middle of Lake Pamvotis. The Island's whitewashed village, built in the 17th century by refugees from Peloponnesian Mani, has around 300 permanent residents.

The Island was most notably the place where the last act unfolded in the long saga of Ali Pasha, the Albanian warlord who ruled Ioannina in the late 18th and early 19th centuries. Ali's fickle allegiances and brazen challenge to Ottoman authority caused the Sultan to take out the 'Lion of Ioannina' in 1822. The elderly Ali Pasha withdrew to **Moni Pandeleïmonos** on the Island – only to be trapped and killed by Ottoman troops. The hole in the floorboard where the fatal bullet passed through is still visible in the **Ali Pasha Museum** (adult €1; 8am-10pm summer, 9am-9pm winter), in a building inside the monastery. To get here, walk up the hill from the dock into town and take the main street left.

Moni Filanthropinon, on the Island's western side, was built in the 13th century. It boasts unusual 16th-century frescoes of pagan Greek philosophers Plato, Aristotle and Plutarch, alongside more suitably Christian personalities.

Restaurant Kyra Vasiliki (26510 81681; mains €6-8), under a giant plane tree by the ferry dock, offers a great selection of grills and some fish.

Ioannina's ferry dock is below the Kastro in Ioannina. Boats to the Island (€1.30, 10 minutes) go between 7am and 11.30pm in summer, and between 7am and 10pm in winter. In summer, the boat goes every 15 minutes in winter, only hourly.

the Pindos Mountains. In winter, Compass operates a ski school and trips for off-piste skiing on virgin terrain.

Sleeping

ARHONTIKO DILOFO
B&B €€

(26530 22455, 69784 17715; www.dilofo.com; Dilofo; d incl breakfast from €65; P) One of the most wonderful guesthouses in all of the Zagorohoria, this 475-year-old restored mansion in placid Dilofo is ideal for anyone seeking total peace and natural harmony. Rooms feature traditional carpets, furnishings and ornate painted window shutters that, when closed, give you a feeling of being inside the warm hold of a grand seafaring vessel. The Arhontiko has a lovely enclosed garden and scenic views over the village's cluttered slate rooftops. The friendly and immensely knowledgeable owner, Giorgos Kontaxis,

happily speaks of the gold pipes, secret letters and other centuries-old memento he discovered while renovating the mansion, inhabited since 1633. Greek, Englis German and Italian are spoken here.

PAPAEVANGELOU
B&B €

(George's Place; 26530 41135; www.hotelpa paevangelou.gr; Megalo Papingo; s/d/tr/studio €60/75/90/110; P) Nice stone rooms and spectacular views, along with hearty homemade breakfasts served in the rustic traditional tavern/bar, are availab here. At the central square, turn left on the unpaved road – the hotel is situated on the right.

TO ARHONTIKO TIS ARISTIS
B&B €€

(26530 42210, 69456 76261; www.arhontiko -aristis.gr; Aristi; s/d/tr €100/120/140; P) Up in Aristi, this guesthouse offers spectacu lar views and is built of solid stone, with lovely wooden floors. The bathrooms are

ery modern and there are other unexpected modern touches like billiards.

 Eating

RESTAURANT H TSOUMANIS Taverna €
(☎ 26530 42170; www.tsoumanisnikos.gr; Vikos;
mains €6-9) Gorge yourself near the gorge
at this iconic taverna in Vikos; wild boar,
goat and other mountain creatures are
recommended. It also has a nice guesthouse above.

SPIROS TSOUMANIS Taverna €
(☎ 26530 12108; Megalo Papingo; mains €8-13)
This hearty country grill at the end of
Megalo Papingo specialises in local *pites*
(pies) and roast lamb *sti gastra* (chickpea
stew), with fresh-from-the-garden *horta*
(wild greens) salads.

TA SOUDENA Taverna €
(☎ 26530 71209; Ano Pedina; mains €5-8) A
popular taverna at the entrance to Ano
Pedina, Ta Soudena offers Greek vegetable mezedhes, *pites* and grilled meats.

 Getting There & Away

From Ioannina, buses leave for Dilofo (€3.80,
40 minutes) at 5.30am and 3.15pm on Monday,
Wednesday and Friday, continuing to Tsepelovo
(€4.40, 1½ hours). Other buses leave for Megalo
Papingo and Mikro Papingo (€5.10, two hours) at
5am and 3pm on Monday, Wednesday and Friday,
with the Wednesday bus hitting Vikos (€4.80, 1¾
hours) in summer. Buses to Monodendri (€3.60,
one hour) leave at 6am and 3pm on Monday,
Wednesday and Friday. All buses return to
Ioannina immediately. On weekends, take a taxi:
Ioannina–Monodendri fares are approximately
€30 to €45, though you can negotiate.

Santorini, Mykonos & the Cyclades

The Cyclades (kih-*klah*-dhez) lie at the deep blue heart of the Aegean and are so named because they form a *kyklos* (circle) around the island of Delos, the most compelling ancient site in the Aegean. The Cyclades are where Greek life is at its most intense and seductive, where countless islands rise from the glittering Aegean, their ochre hills sparkling with bone-white cubist settlements and limestone outcrops.

This is where you find tourism on a human scale, yet with more than a dash of sun-kissed hedonism. You'll find a compelling cultural menu with major archaeological sites and small but sophisticated museums and galleries. Sample the sun-lounger beaches and raunchy nightlife of Mykonos; the glitz and glamour of Santorini; and the subtler pace of island life on Naxos. Enjoy, above all, the timeless spirit of these ancient milestones of Aegean history and the exhilaration of adventurous island hopping.

Oia (p227)
MATTHEW BIRD/SHUTTERSTOCK ©

Petros the Pelican, mascot of Mykonos (p206)

Santorini, Mykonos & the Cyclades

1 Santorini Boat Trips
2 Ancient Delos
3 Mykonos After Dark
4 Oia
5 Naxos
6 Beaches

TURKEY

Chios

AEGEAN
SEA

Ikaria

Ag os Kirykos

IKARIAN SEA

Patmos

Donousa

Amorgos

Katapola

Astypalea

Kos Town

Pserimos

Kalymnos

Mastihari

Kos

Nisyros

Tilos

To Rhodes

DODECANESE

Halki

EVIA

Evia

Petalia
Gulf

Karystos

Andros

Hora (Andros)

Gavrio

Tinos

Hora
(Tinos)

6

Mykonos

3 Hora (Mykonos)

2 Delos

Hora

Naxos

5 6

Schinousa

Little
Cyclades

Iraklia

Donousa

Anafi

Agios
Nikolaos

ATHENS

Refina

ATTICA

Avrio

Cape
Sounion

Kea (Tzia)

Ioulida

Hora

Kythnos

Gyaros

Ermoupo i

Syros

Parikia

Paros

Hora

Ios

Fira

Thirasia

Santorini
(Thira)

1 4

6

Piraeus

PELOPONNESE

Aegina

Poros

Galatas

Hydra

Angistri

Ermioni

Neapoli

Kythira

MYRTOÖN
SEA

Serifos

Hora

Sifnos

Apo lonia

Kimolos

Adamas

Milos

Artimiies

Policgos

Hora/Kastro

Sikinos

Hora

Fole garidros

To Crete

To Crete

N

0   20 km
0   12 miles

Santorini, Mykonos & the Cyclades' Highlights

1

Santorini Boat Trips

Setting sail from Santorini on an 18th-century-style schooner offers the opportunity to experience the island's most adventurous era. Santorini draws you in with its spectacular architecture, interesting grey-black beaches, white-blue houses on the cliff side, the volcano itself and the energy you get from it all.

Need to Know
BEST MONTHS TO SAIL May, June & September **BEST TIME OF DAY** Sunset & moonrise **DON'T FORGET** Swimsuit and binoculars **For more, see p222**

Santorini's Don't Miss List

BY ANTONIS KONDYLIS, SCHOONER OPERATOR

1 NEA KAMENI

This unpopulated islet in the centre of Santorini's caldera is still volcanically active and surrounded by deep green, sulphurous water. From the quaint port you can walk up to the volcano's crater. Standing atop hot, rugged rocks, you'll be surrounded by the volcano's smoke and gorgeous views.

2 ASPRONISI

This tiny speck of an island is a fabulous place for swimming in the warm water. People are always amazed by how blue the Aegean is out here and feel compelled to dive in.

3 HOT SPRINGS

On the islet of Palia Kameni, these natural hot springs (p224) are pleasingly casual. Water reaching temperatures of around 33°C bubbles to the surface and then pours into the sea. Relax among the copper-coloured rocks, soak in the warm volcanic waters or join the regulars in slathering yourself with sulphurous mud. Your skin will thank you!

4 THIRASIA

Once part of the main island, Thirasia separated from Santorini following the earthquake in 236 BC. Its relaxed, cliff-top old town is unspoilt and offers wonderful views back to Santorini. See 224 for information on tours here.

5 SUNSET

The Santorini sunset is a breathtaking spectacle and a must-see during a visit to the island. Experiencing a sunset from the centre of the caldera is even more special. Surrounded by the deep blue sea, the light illuminates the volcano and the small volcanic islets. The colours are vivid and magical.

Ancient Delos

Set foot on this small island at the centre of the Cyclades and you know you're somewhere special. Ancient Delos (p215) has had sacred status since it was chosen as the mythical birthplace of the twins of Apollo and Artemis. Inhabited since the 3rd millennium BC, with ruins dating back to the 8th century BC, its sanctuaries, shrines and theatres never fail to impress.

IMAGEBROKER ©

Mykonos After Dark

Glamorous Mykonos (p206) has a spark nightlife. Dubbed 'Little Venice', its bars and clubs are clustered along the wate and in the old town's maze of alleyway Sipping cocktails with a view of the su sinking into the Aegean Sea is blissful – as is dancing the night away among a lively crowd of tourists, celebrities, cruise-ship crowds and locals.

Oia

4

Built on a steep slope of the caldera, the tiny village of Oia (p227) has houses and hotels hewn and nestled right into the volcanic rock. Restored and well-cared for, Oia is an understandably popular place to put up your feet, pick up a cocktail and soak up some island atmosphere. Its beauty is only eclipsed by Santorini's sunset, of which Oia gets the longest and best views on the island.

5

Naxos

It was on Naxos (p215) that an ungrateful Theseus is said to have abandoned Ariadne after she helped him escape the Cretan labyrinth. But there are certainly worse places to be left behind. Naxos is the Cyclades' land of plenty – lush and fertile, fruit, veg, olives and wine are produced here in abundance. It's also crisscrossed with walking trails and ringed with sand. What more could Ariadne have wished for?

6

Beaches

Dig your toes into the black-sand beaches on Santorini (p231). Stretch out amongst fellow sun-worshippers on stylish Mykonos (p231; pictured above). Wander along footpaths to quiet stretches of sand on Naxos (p220). Wherever you choose to lay your towel, you'll not be disappointed with the Cyclades' beaches.

Santorini, Mykonos & the Cyclades' Best.

Beaches

○ **Agios Stefanos** (p231) A popular Mykonos stretch of sand.

○ **Agios Georgios** (p220) Naxos' sandy beach with shallow water; ideal for families.

○ **Perivolos & Agios Georgios** (p231) Santorini's most relaxed black-sand beaches.

○ **Agia Anna** (p220) A stretch of glistening white sand in Naxos.

Plush Sleeps

○ **Aroma Suites** (p225) Charming boutique hotel on the caldera's edge.

○ **Chelidonia Traditional Villas** (p228) Traditional cliffside dwelling turned lavish.

○ **Hotel Grotta** (p218) Enjoy sea views over the old town from the jacuzzi.

○ **Carbonaki Hotel** (p210) Family-run, ecofriendly boutique hotel.

Drinking Venues

○ **La Scarpa** (p211) Enjoy great cocktails with sunset views.

○ **Vallindras Distillery** (p221) Try local *kitron* (liqueur made from the leaves of the citron tree) and tour an atmospheric, traditional distillery.

○ **Tropical** (p226) Sip wine to trendy tunes and unbeatable caldera vistas.

○ **La Vigne** (p220) French-run wine bar with tasty nibbles.

Local Cuisine

Piccolo (p210) Sandwiches loaded with Mykonian prosciutto and manouri (soft cheese).

Selene (p227) Internationally acclaimed creative meals using unique local ingredients.

Meze 2 (p219) Dine on fresh seafood with local fishermen.

Katerina's (p211) Fresh seafood *saganaki* (fried cheese) and homemade baklava.

Need to Know

ADVANCE PLANNING

○ **Two months before** Book accommodation, especially for Mykonos and Santorini.

○ **One month before** For local events, check online and prebook tickets. Check ferry schedules.

RESOURCES

○ **Mykonos Accommodation Center** (www.mykonos -accommodation.com) Accommodation listings, bookings plus details on beaches.

○ **Santorini Guide** (www. santorini.com) History, listings, flights and ferries.

GETTING AROUND

○ **Bus** Routes across Mykonos, with less-frequent runs on Santorini and Naxos.

○ **Ferry** Frequent services to hop from the mainland and between the islands.

○ **Flights** From Athens to Santorini, Mykonos and Naxos.

○ **Car** A great way to explore.

BE FOREWARNED

○ **Transport** The Cyclades often experience fierce winds that can play havoc with ferry schedules.

○ **Ancient Delos** The site (and therefore the island) is closed on Mondays.

Left: Perivolos beach (p231)
Above: Agia Anna beach (p220)

Santorini, Mykonos & the Cyclades Itineraries

Island life at its best. With magical scenery, fabulous nightlife, peaceful retreats, great local cuisine and atmospheric sites, it's easy to fill a week or two here.

3 DAYS

FIRA TO VOLCANIC ISLETS

Scenic Wonders

Revered for its surreal landscape, Santorini will mesmerise and enchant you. Stay in a guesthouse in **(1) Fira** with a breathtaking view over the multicoloured cliffs, and take your meals and cocktails perched on the edge of the caldera. Then sail out on a boat trip. Spend a day on the black-sand beach of **(2) Perivolos**, located on the eastern side of the island. Stop in at **(3) Ancient Thira**, the site of 9th-century-BC ruins with stunning views, then head for the pretty village of **(4) Oia** for views of the spectacular sunset. On your final day, take a day trip to the uninhabited **(5) volcanic islets** of Palia Kameni and Nea Kameni for hot springs and a close encounter with an active volcano.

Top Left: Oia (p227); **Top Right:** Hora (p216)

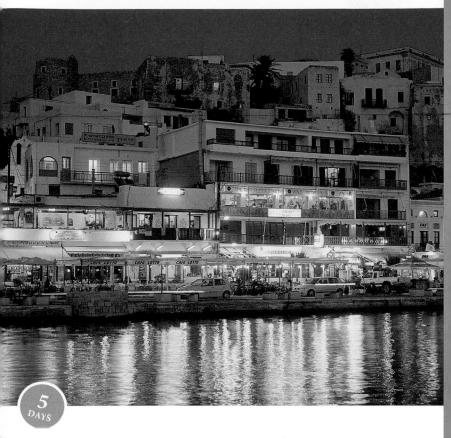

5 DAYS

Island Hopping

You come to Naxos for lots of reasons – the beaches, the mountains and the sights – but you also come for the fresh olives, figs and grapes. Fill your belly with the island's bounty as you explore **(1) Hora**, with its atmospheric Venetian Kastro. Dine on the freshest of seafood and then take in an evening concert at the Della Rocca-Barozzi Venetian Museum, a 13th-century tower. Spend the next day on the sandy beaches that trim much of the island's coast. Try **(2) Agia Anna** for a quiet stretch of white sand. The fit can spend the next day heading up **(3) Mt Zeus** or else visit **(4) Halki**, a historic village at the heart of the island's mountainous interior where a distillery cranks out traditional *kitron*. From Naxos, catch a fast ferry to Mykonos, the glamour puss of the Cyclades. Explore **(5) Hora**, the island's charming capital, letting yourself get lost in the boutiques and cafes of Little Venice and joining in the revelry of the island's infamous nightlife. On the last day, hop on a day trip to fascinating **(6) Delos**, one of Greece's most important archaeological sights, before returning to Mykonos for one last sunset cocktail.

Discover Santorini, Mykonos & the Cyclades

ΜΥΚΟΝΟΣ ΜΥΚΟΝΟΣ

POP 7929

Mykonos is the great glamour island of the Cyclades and happily flaunts its camp and fashionable reputation with style. Beneath the gloss and glitter, however, this is a charming and hugely entertaining place where the sometimes frantic mix of good-time holidaymakers, cruise-ship crowds, posturing fashionistas and preening celebrities is magically subdued by the cubist charms of Mykonos town, a traditional Cycladic maze. Local people have had 40 years to get a grip on tourism and have not lost their Greek identity in doing so.

Be prepared, however, for the oiled-up lounger lifestyle of the island's packed main beaches, the jostling street scenes and the relentless, yet sometimes forlorn, partying. That said, there's still a handful of off-track beaches worth fighting for. Plus, the stylish bars, restaurants and shops have great appeal, and you can still find a quieter pulse amid the labyrinthine old town. Add to all this the archaeological splendour of the nearby island of Delos, and Mykonos really does live up to its reputation as a fabulous destination.

ⓘ Getting There & Away

Mykonos is well served by air connections to Athens (€63 to €136, 50 minutes, three to five daily) and Thessaloniki (€196, one hour, three weekly). There are also direct easyJet flights to London from about May to mid-September.

With Mykonos being such a major tourist destination, ferry connections to the mainland ports of Piraeus and Rafina are very good, as are connections to neighbouring islands. Links south

Santorini (p222)
TPOPOVAVIEW PORTFOLIO/ISTOCKPHOTO ©

Boat Services from Mykonos

DESTINATION	PORT	DURATION	FARE	FREQUENCY
Iraklio*	Mykonos	6hr 35min	€77	1-2 daily
Naxos	Mykonos	2hr 25min	€12	1 weekly
Naxos*	Mykonos	45min	€26.50	2 daily
Piraeus	Mykonos	4¾hr	€32-39.50	1 daily
Piraeus*	Mykonos	3hr	€50-54.50	3 daily
Santorini (Thira)*	Mykonos	2½hr	€50	2-3 daily

*high-speed services

to that other popular destination, Santorini, and to points between are also excellent.

Mykonos has two ferry quays: the Old Port, 400m north of town, where some conventional ferries and smaller fast ferries dock, and the New Port, 2km north of town, where the bigger fast ferries and some conventional ferries dock. There is no hard-and-fast rule, and when buying outgoing tickets you should always double-check which quay your ferry leaves from.

ⓘ Getting Around

TO/FROM THE AIRPORT

Buses from the southern bus station serve Mykonos' airport (€1.60), which is 3km southeast of the town centre. Make sure you arrange an airport transfer with your accommodation (expect to pay around €6) or take a taxi (☏22890 22400, airport 22890 23700).

BOAT

Caïque (little boat) services leave from Platys Gialos to Paradise (€5), Super Paradise (€6), Agrari (€7) and Elia (€7) Beaches. Boats also leave from Hora (Mykonos) for Super Paradise, Agrari and Elia Beaches (June to September only)

BUS

The Mykonos bus network (☏22890 26797; www.ktelmykonos.gr) has two main bus stations and a pick-up point at the New Port. The northern bus station (Remezzo) is behind the OTE office and has frequent departures to Agios Stefanos via Tourlos (€1.60), and services to Kalafatis Beach (€2.10). Buses for the New Port, Tourlos and Agios

Stefanos stop at the Old Port. The southern bus station (Fabrika Sq [Plateia Yialos]) serves Agios Ioannis Beach, Ornos, Platys Gialos, Paraga and Paradise Beach (all trips €1.60).

Bus tickets are sold at machines, street kiosks, minimarkets and tourist shops. You must buy a ticket before boarding (buy return tickets if required), validate the ticket on the bus and hang on to it. From 12.15am to 6am all trips are €2.

CAR & MOTORCYCLE

Reliable hire agencies are the Mykonos Accommodation Centre (p213) and OK Rent A Car (☏22890 23761; Agio Stefanos).

TAXI

If you're after a taxi (☏22400 23700/22400), you'll find them at Hora's Taxi Sq (Plateia Manto Mavrogenous) and by the bus stations and ports. All taxis must have meters installed.

Hora (Mykonos) ΧΩΡΑ (ΜΥΚΟΝΟΣ)
POP 6467

Hora (also known as Mykonos), the island's port and capital, is a warren of narrow alleyways that wriggle between white-walled buildings, their stone surfaces webbed with white paint. In the heart of the Little Venice area (Venetia), tiny flower-bedecked churches jostle with trendy boutiques, and there's a deluge of bougainvillea around every corner. Without question, you will soon pass the same junction twice. It's entertaining at first,

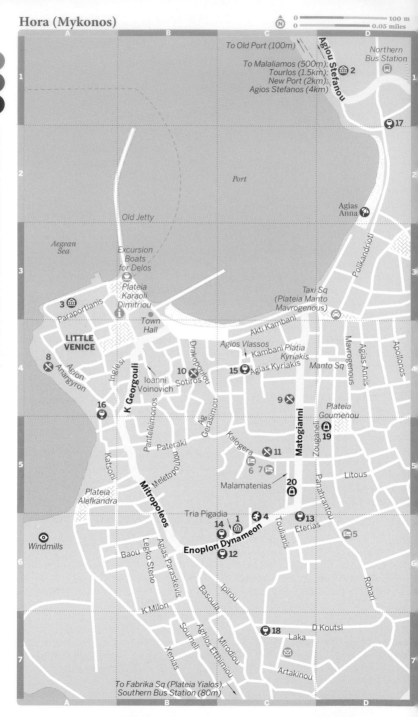

DISCOVER SANTORINI, MYKONOS & THE CYCLADES   HORA (MYKONOS)

0 ___ 100 m
0 ___ 0.05 miles

To Old Port (100m)

Agiou Stefanou

Northern Bus Station

To Malaliamos (500m);
Tourlos (1.5km);
New Port (2km);
Agios Stefanos (4km)

Port

Old Jetty

Aegean Sea

Excursion Boats for Delos

Plateia Karaoli Dimitriou

Town Hall

Paraportianis

LITTLE VENICE

Agion Anargyron

Inglesi

K Georgouli

Ioanni Voinovich

Sotiros

Drakopoulou

Panteleimonos

Pateraki

Meletopoulou

Katsoni

Mitropoleos

Plateia Alefkandra

Windmills

Baou

Legko Steno

Agias Paraskevis

K Milon

Xenias

Soumeli

Aghios Efthimiou

Mirodiou

Basoula

Ipirou

Tria Pigadia

Enoplon Dynameon

Ag Gerasimou

Kalogera

Malamatenias

Agios Vlassos

Akti Kambani

Agias Kyriakis

Kambani

Platia Kyriakis

Manto Sq

Matogianni

Plateia Goumenou

Litous

Panahrantou

Toulianis

Eterias

Rohari

D Koutsi

Laka

Artakinou

Taxi Sq
(Plateia Manto Mavrogenous)

Agias Annis

Mavrogenous

Apollonos

Polikandrioti

Agias Anna

To Fabrika Sq (Plateia Yialos),
Southern Bus Station (80m)

...ut can become frustrating as throngs of equally lost people, fast-moving locals and disdainful Mykonos veterans add to the stress. For quick-fix navigation, familiarise yourself with main junctions and the three main streets of Matogianni, Enoplon Dynameon and Mitropoleos, which form a horseshoe behind the waterfront. The streets are crowded with chic fashion salons, cool galleries, jangling jewellers, languid and loud music bars, brightly painted houses and torrents of crimson flowers – plus a catwalk cast of thousands.

Sights

ARCHAEOLOGICAL MUSEUM Museum
(☎22890 22325; Agiou Stefanou; adult/concession €2/1; ☯8.30am-3pm Tue-Sun) This museum houses pottery from Delos and some grave *stelae* (pillars) and jewellery from the island of Renia (Delos' necropolis). Chief exhibits include a statue of Hercules in Parian marble.

AEGEAN MARITIME MUSEUM Museum
(☎22890 22700; Tria Pigadia; adult/concession €4/1.50; ☯10.30am-1pm & 6.30-9pm Apr-Oct) The maritime museum has a fascinating collection of nautical paraphernalia, including ships' models.

LENA'S HOUSE Museum
(☎22890 22390; Tria Pigadia; admission €2; ☯6.30-9.30pm Mon-Sat, 7-9pm Sun Apr-Oct) Next door to the maritime museum, Lena's house is a charming late-19th-century, middle-class Mykonian house (with furnishings intact). It takes its name from its last owner, Lena Skrivanou.

FREE **MYKONOS FOLKLORE MUSEUM** Museum
(☎6932178330; Paraportianis; ☯5.30-8.30pm Mon-Sat, 6.30-8.30pm Sun Apr-Oct) This folklore museum, housed in an 18th-century sea captain's house, features a large collection of furnishings and other artefacts, including old musical instruments.

Tours

MYKONOS ACCOMMODATION CENTRE Sightseeing Tours
(MAC; ☎22890 23408; www.mykonos-accommodation.com; 1st fl, Enoplon Dynameon 10) Organises guided tours to Delos including entrance fee and authorised guide (adult/child €38/30). The MAC also runs a Mykonos bus tour (adult/child €33/22), island cruise (adult/child €43/21.50) and a wine and culture tour (adult/child €29/21).

Hora (Mykonos)

A Bent For Cycladic Travel

Long before the hip lotus eaters of the 1960s discovered their dream world in the Greek islands, a redoubtable pair of travellers had been thoroughly 'doing' the Cyclades during the late 19th century. James Theodore Bent and his wife, Mabel, travelled extensively throughout the Aegean, 'researching' the cultural life of the islands as much as their archaeology. J Theodore's 1885 book, *The Cyclades: Or Life Among the Insular Greeks*, is a quirky masterpiece and is essential reading if you want to appreciate the realities of the late-19th-century Greek islands – and the Bent's often eccentric reflections. A full edition is published by **Archaeopress** (www.archaeopress.com). An abridged edition, published by **Anagnosis** (www.anagnosis.gr) may sometimes be found in bookshops on bigger islands such as Santorini.

 Sleeping

If you plan to stay in Hora and want somewhere quiet, think carefully before settling for domatia on the main streets – bar noise until dawn is inevitable.

CARBONAKI HOTEL
Boutique Hotel €€€
(22890 24124/22461; www.carbonaki.gr; 23 Panahrantou; s/d/tr/q €140/175/220/240;) This family-run boutique hotel, right on the edge of central Mykonos, has a delightful ambience and has developed admirable eco policies regarding recycling. It also has disabled access and facilities on the ground floor. Rooms are comfortable and bright and there are relaxing public balconies dotted round the sunny central courtyards. A jacuzzi and small sauna were recently added. Breakfast is €10.

RANIA APARTMENTS　Apartments €€
(22890 28272/3; www.rania-mykonos.gr; Leondiou Boni 2; s/d/tr/apt €95/120/190/320;) A quite location high above the harbour means a bit of an uphill walk from town, but the apartments are easily accessed from Agiou Ioannou, the 'ring road'. In a lovely garden setting that imparts a sense of exclusiveness, the accommodation is charming and

well-appointed and each apartment has self-catering facilities.

FRESH HOTEL　Hotel €€€
(22890 24670; www.hotelfreshmykonos.com; Kalogera 31; d incl breakfast €195;) The gay-friendly Fresh is located right in the heart of town and is handy for all the action. There's a leafy central garden, an attractive breakfast room and bar, and a jacuzzi. Rooms have wooden floors and furnishings and are a stylish and comfortable mix of old and new. The garden is the location of the Kalita restaurant.

HOTEL PHILIPPI　Hotel €€
(22890 22294; www.phillipihotel.com; Kalogera 25; s/d €90/125;) A garden full of trees, flowers and shrubs makes this a welcome choice in the heart of Hora. There's an appealing ambience in the bright, clean rooms that open onto a railed verandah overlooking the garden.

 Eating

PICCOLO　Sandwiches €
(Drakopoulou 18; snacks €4-7.80) There are no linen-draped tables at this immaculate wayside outlet, but the food is first class and ranges from Mykonian pies to a mouth-watering selection of sandwich fillings that include local prosciutto, *manou* (soft cheese), smoked local ham, smoke

ll and crab. There's a delicious chicken-salad version with parmesan, sundried tomatoes and cucumber.

KATERINA'S   Modern Greek €€
(Agion Anargyron; mains €11-25) The famous Katerina's Bar has now branched out with its own small restaurant. There's a creative menu of crisp salads and starters such as prawn *saganaki* (skillet-fried) or wild porcini mushrooms. Mains include fresh sea bass or mixed seafood plate for two (€50) or vegetarian options. For dessert try the homemade baklava.

O MAEREIO   Modern Greek €€
(Kalogera 16; dishes €14-21) A small but selective menu of Mykonian favourites keeps this cosy place popular. The mainly meat and poultry dishes can be preceded by salad mixes that include apple and pear, yoghurt and a balsamic vinegar sauce. A tasty choice is the tenderloin with feta, green peppers and lemon juice.

LA CASA   Greek €
(Matogianni 8; mains €9.90-18.90) The classic La Casa has a strong Greek basis with Italian, Arabic and Lebanese influences.

Starters of smoked cheeses with mushrooms and inventive salads – including a Mykonian special with *louza* (local smoked ham), local prosciutto, cheeses and rocket – lead on to mains such as pork fillet with mustard, *pleurotus* (mushrooms and tarragon).

Drinking & Entertainment

Hora's Little Venice quarter is not exactly the Grand Canal, but it does offer the Mediterranean at your feet as well as rosy sunsets, windmill views, glowing candles and a swath of colourful bars.

A top spot is Galleraki, which turns out superb cocktails. Nearby, it's the sunset view at Verandah Café, while La Scarpa lets you lean back from the sea on its cosy cushions. Further north, Katerina's **Bar** (Agion Anargyron) has a cool balcony and eases you into the evening's action with relaxing sounds.

Deeper into town, the relentlessly stylish **Aroma** (Enoplon Dynameon; ⏰breakfast-late) sits on a strategic

Little Venice, Hora (p207)

corner, providing the evening catwalk view. Further down Enoplon Dynameon is Astra, where the decor is modernist Mykonos at its best, and where some of Athens' top DJs feed the ambience with rock, funk, house, and drum and base. Just across from Astra, cocktail-cool Aigli has another useful terrace for people watching.

Head inland from Agios Nikolaos church, midway along the waterfront, to Agios Vlassos for Bubbles Bar, an out-of-the-ordinary champagne bar with a fine selection of top labels and other drinks and a quirky annexe full of Leonidas Belgian chocolates. They do tapas as well.

For big action into the dawn, **Space** (Laka;www.spacemykonos.com) is the place. The night builds superbly through a mix of techno, house and progressive, and the bar-top dancing fires up the late-night action. **Remezzo** (Polikandrioti) is run by the Space team but features lounge and dance for a more relaxing

scene. Entry is around €20 to both clubs.

Shopping

Style and art venues jostle for attention throughout Hora's streets and outstanding brands include authentic Lacoste, Dolce & Gabbana, Naf Naf, Diesel and Body Shop. Clothes hanging apart, there are some stand-out galleries worth seeking out.

SCALA SHOP GALLERY   Arts & Crafts
(www.scalagallery.gr; Matogianni 48) Scala is one of the more stylish galleries of Mykonos. It stages changing displays of fine art and also sells contemporary jewellery and ceramics.

ART STUDIO GALLERY   Arts & Crafts
(✆ 22890 22796; www.artstudiogallery.gr; Agiou Saranta 22) A fascinating gallery exhibiting the works of a number of accomplished Greek painters and sculptors including

Left: Mykonos (p206); Below: Fishing boat docked in Mykonos (p206)
(LEFT) DENNIS JOHNSON/LONELY PLANET IMAGES ©; (BELOW) DAN HERRICK/LONELY PLANET IMAGES ©

he gallery's founder, Mag-
alini Sakellaridi.

ℹ Information

elia Travel (☎ 22890 22322; travel@delia.
·; Akti Kambani) Halfway along the inner
aterfront. Sells ferry tickets and tickets for
elos. **Mykonos Accommodation Centre**
☎ 22890 23408; www.mykonos
ccommodation.com; 1st fl, Enoplon Dynameon
) Well organised and very helpful for a range
information.

ea & Sky (☎ 22890 22853; Akti Kambani)
formation and ferry tickets.

Around Mykonos

 Activities

IVE ADVENTURES   Diving
☎ 22890 26539; www.diveadventures.gr;
aradise Beach) Offers a full range of diving
ourses with multilingual instructors. Two

introductory dives cost €130; snorkelling
costs €45.

PLANET WINDSAILING   Windsurfing
(☎ 22890 72345; www.pezi-huber.com) On a
great location at Kalafatis Beach, Planet
Windsailing has one-hour or one-day
windsurfing for €30 or €70, respectively,
or a two-hour beginner's course for two
people for €70.

KALAFATI DIVE CENTER   Diving
(☎ 22000 71677; www.mykonos-diving.com)
Located at Kalafatis Beach, this dive
centre offers the full range of diving
courses. A single boat dive with tank
and weights costs €50, or a dive with all
equipment costs €60. A 'discover scuba
diving' session is €68. A snorkelling trip
with equipment is €20. There's a 10%
discount for prepaid bookings. Check
the website or email for details.

JOHN HENSHALL/ALAMY

Don't Miss Beaches

Mykonos has a good number of beaches and most have golden sand in attractive locations. They're not so big that you'll escape from the crowds, especially from June onwards.

You need to be a party person for the likes of Paradise and Super Paradise. It can all get very claustrophobic, but it's heaven for the gregarious. Most beaches have a varied clientele, and attitudes to toplessness and nudity also vary, but what's accepted at each beach is obvious when you get there.

An excellent guide to island beaches and their specific or mixed clientele can be found on the beaches link of www.mykonos-accommodation.com.

The nearest beaches to Hora (Mykonos), which are also the island's least glamorous beaches, are **Malaliamos**; the tiny and crowded **Tourlos**, 2km to the north of town; and **Agios Stefanos** (4km; pictured above). About 3.5km south of Hora is the packed and noisy **Ornos**, from where you can hop onto boats for other beaches. Just west is **Agios Ioannis**. The sizeable package-holiday resort of **Platys Gialos** is 4km from Hora on the southwest coast. All of the above beaches are family orientated.

Platys Gialos is the caïque jumping-off point for the glitzier beaches to the east, such as **Paradise** and **Super Paradise**.

North-coast beaches can be exposed to the *meltemi* (dry northerly wind), but **Panormos** and **Agios Sostis** are fairly sheltered and becoming more popular.

 Eating

CHRISTOS Seafood €
(Agios Ioannis Beach; mains €6-18) Fisherman, chef and sculptor Christos runs his beachside eatery with unassuming style. It's right on the 'Shirley Valentine' shoreline, but Christos really is authentic Mykonos, where the best fish and seafood, not least unbeatable *astakos* (crawfish or spiny lobster), is prepared with skill.

ASOS TRATTORIA Taverna €

Paraga Beach; mains €9-19) Central to Paraga Beach, this popular taverna does terrific ~sh, chicken, pork and veal dishes and a ~reat mix of vegie options.

 Entertainment

AVO PARADISO Club

www.cavoparadiso.gr) When dawn gleams ~st over the horizon, hard-core bar-~oppers move from Hora (Mykonos) to ~avo Paradiso, the megaclub that's been ~lasting at Paradise Beach since 1993 ~nd has featured top international DJs ~ver since, including house legends David ~orales and Louie Vega.

DELOS ΔΗΛΟΣ

~he Cyclades fulfil their collective name ~yklos by encircling the sacred island of ~elos (☏ 22890 22259; museum & sites adult/ ~ncession €5/3; ◷ 8.30am-3pm Tue-Sun), but ~ykonos clutches the island jealously to ~s heart. Delos has no permanent popula-~on and is a soothing contrast to the ~elentless liveliness of modern Mykonos, ~lthough in high summer you share it all ~ith fellow visitors. The island is one of ~he most important archaeological sites ~ Greece and the most important in the ~yclades. It lies a few kilometres off the ~est coast of Mykonos.

Delos still hides its secrets and every ~ow and then fresh discoveries are made. ~ recent years a gold workshop was ~ncovered alongside the Street of the ~ons.

History

~elos won early acclaim as the mythical ~rthplace of the twins Apollo and Artemis ~nd was first inhabited in the 3rd mil-~nnium BC. From the 8th century BC it ~ecame a shrine to Apollo, and the oldest ~mples on the island date from this era. ~he dominant Athenians had full control ~ Delos – and thus the Aegean – by the ~th century BC.

Delos reached the height of its power in Hellenistic times, becoming one of the three most important religious centres in Greece and a flourishing centre of commerce.

The Romans made Delos a free port in 167 BC. This brought even greater prosperity, due largely to a lucrative slave market that sold up to 10,000 people a day. During the following century, as ancient religions lost relevance and trade routes shifted, Delos began a long, painful decline.

ℹ Getting There & Away

Boats for Delos (return €17, 30 minutes) leave Hora (Mykonos) around six times a day from about 9am in high season with the last outward boat about 12.50pm. Departure and return times are posted on the ticket kiosk at the entrance to the Old Port at the south end of the harbour. There are fewer boats outside July and August. There are no boats on Monday when the site is closed. Boats return from the island between 11am and 3pm. When buying tickets, establish which boat is available for your return, especially later in the day. In Hora (Mykonos), **Delia Travel** (☏ 22890 22322; travel@delia.gr; Akti Kambani) and the **Mykonos Accommodation Centre** (☏ 22890 23408; www.mykonos-accommodation.com; 1st fl, Enoplon Dynameon 10) sell tickets. You pay an entrance fee of €3 at a kiosk on the island.

The Mykonos Accommodation Centre organises guided tours to Delos at 10am every day except Monday between May and September (adult/child €38/30, three hours). Overnight stays on Delos are forbidden and boat schedules allow a maximum of about six or seven hours there. Bring water and food. Wear a hat and sensible shoes.

ΝΑΧΟΣ ΝΑΞΟΣ

POP 12,089

Naxos is the largest of the Cyclades and has the mountains to prove it. It offers the best of both worlds, a classic island expe-rience balanced by an occasional sense of being pleasantly landlocked in the deep heart of the mountains.

Naxos was a cultural centre of classical Greece and of Byzantium, while Venetian and Frankish influences have also left their mark. It is more fertile than most of the other islands and produces olives, grapes, figs, citrus fruit, corn and potatoes. **Mt Zeus** (1004m; also known as Mt Zas) is the Cyclades' highest peak and is the central focus of the island's interior, where you find such enchanting villages as Halki and Apiranthos. There are numerous sandy beaches and the island is a great place to explore on foot along the many surviving paths between villages, churches and other sights. There are walking guides and maps available from local bookshops.

Getting There & Away

There is a daily flight to and from Athens (€71, 45 minutes).

Getting Around

TO/FROM THE AIRPORT

The airport is 3km south of Hora. There is no shuttle bus. A taxi costs €10 to €15 depending on luggage amounts, the time of day, and if booked.

BUS

Buses leave from the end of the ferry quay in Hora; timetables are posted outside the bus information office (☑ 22850 22291; www. naxosdestinations.com), diagonally left and across the road from the bus stop. You have to buy tickets from the office or from the machine outside.

CAR & MOTORCYCLE

Rental Center (☑ 22850 23395; Plateia Evripeou) is a good bet.

Hora (Naxos) ΧΩΡΑ (ΝΑΞΟΣ)
POP 6727

Busy, colourful Hora, on the west coast of Naxos, is the island's port and capital. It's a large town, divided into two historic neighbourhoods of the Venetian era: Bourgos, where the Greeks lived, and the hill-top Kastro, where the Roman Catholics lived. The town has spread well beyond the harbour area.

Sights

To see the **Bourgos** area, head into the winding backstreets behind the northern end of Paralia. The most alluring part of Hora is the residential **Kastro**. Marco Sanudo made the town the capital of his duchy in 1207, and several Venetian mansions survive. Take a stroll around the Kastro during siesta to experience its hushed, timeless atmosphere.

FREE **MITROPOLIS MUSEUM** Museum
(☑ 22850 24151; Kondyli; ⏰ 8.30am-3pm Tue-Sun) A short distance behind the northern end of the waterfront are several churches and chapels, and the Mitropolis Museum. The museum features fragments of a Mycenaean city of the 13th to 11th centuries BC that was abandoned because of the threat of flooding by the sea. It's a haunting place where glass panels underfoot reveal ancient foundations and large areas of excavated buildings.

DELLA ROCCA-BAROZZI VENETIAN MUSEUM Museum
(☑ 22850 22387; guided tours adult/student €5/3; ⏰ 10am-3pm & 6.30pm-late mid-May–Oct) This museum, a handsome old tower house of the 13th century, is within the Kastro ramparts (by the northwest gate). There are changing art exhibitions in the vaults. Tours are multilingual. The museum also runs tours (adult/student €15/12) of the Kastro at 11am Tuesday to Sunday; tours last just over two hours. Evening concerts and other events are staged in the grounds of the museum (see p220).

Activities

FLISVOS SPORT CLUB Windsurfing
(☑ 22850 24308; www.flisvos-sportclub. com; Agios Georgios) This club is very well organised and has a range of windsurfing options, starting with a beginner's course of six hours for €150, or a four-hour Hobie Cat sailing course for €95. The club also organises walking trips in the mountains for €29, shorter walking tours

AMANA IMAGES INC./ALAMY ©

Don't Miss Ancient Delos

The following is an outline of some significant archaeological remains on the site. For further details, a guidebook from the ticket office is advisable, or take a guided tour.

The rock-encrusted **Mt Kythnos** (113m) rises elegantly to the southeast of the harbour. It's worth the steep climb, even in the heat; on clear days there are terrific views of the surrounding islands from its summit.

The path to Mt Kythnos is reached by walking through the **Theatre Quarter**, where Delos' wealthiest inhabitants once built their houses. These houses surrounded peristyle courtyards, with colourful mosaics (a status symbol) being the most striking feature of each house.

The **theatre** dates from 300 BC and had a large **cistern**, the remains of which can be seen. It supplied much of the town with water. The houses of the wealthy had their own cisterns – essential, as Delos was almost as parched and barren then as it is today.

Descending from Mt Kythnos, explore the **Sanctuaries of the Foreign Gods**. Here, at the **Shrine to the Samothracian Great Gods**, the Kabeiroi (the twins Dardanos and Aeton) were worshipped. At the **Sanctuary of the Syrian Gods** there are the remains of a theatre where an audience watched ritual orgies. There is also the **Shrine to the Egyptian Gods**, where Egyptian deities including Serapis and Isis were worshipped.

The **Sanctuary of Apollo**, to the northeast of the harbour, is the site of the much-photographed **Terrace of the Lions**. These proud beasts, carved from marble, were offerings from the people of Naxos, presented to Delos in the 7th century BC to guard the sacred area. To the northeast is the **Sacred Lake** (dry since it was drained in 1925 to prevent malarial mosquitoes breeding) where, according to legend, Leto gave birth to Apollo and Artemis.

Boat Services from Naxos

DESTINATION	DURATION	FARE	FREQUENCY
Kos	9hr 50min	€24.50	2 weekly
Mykonos	2hr 25min	€12	1 weekly
Mykonos*	45min	€26.50	2 daily
Piraeus	4¾hr	€31	4-5 daily
Piraeus*	3¾hr	€48	4 daily
Rafina*	3hr	€52.50	1 daily
Santorini (Thira)	2hr	€16.50	5 daily
Santorini (Thira)*	1hr 35min	€37	2-3 daily

*High-speed services

of Naxos town for €15, and hires out mountain bikes at a per-week rate of €60. These prices are for guests at the club's adjacent **Hotelnaxos Beach1** (☎22850 22935;www.naxosbeach1.com). Non-residents pay 10% more. There's a surf shop and beach cafe.

NAXOS HORSE RIDING　Horseriding (☎6948809142; www.naxoshorseriding.com) Organises daily horse rides (10am to 1pm and 5pm to 8pm) inland and on beaches (€50 per person). You can book a ride up until 6pm the day before and can arrange pick-up and return to and from the stables. Beginners, young children and advanced riders are catered for.

 Tours

There are frequent excursion boats to Delos and Mykonos (adult/child €45/23) and Santorini, including a bus tour (adult/ child €55/30). Book through travel agents (see p220).

 **Sleeping**

HOTEL GROTTA　Hotel €€ (☎22850 22215; www.hotelgrotta.gr; Grotta; s/d incl breakfast €70/85; P ✲ @ 🤶) Located on high ground overlooking the Kastro and main town, this fine modern hotel has comfortable and immaculate rooms, great sea views from the front, spacious public areas and a jacuzzi. It's made even better by the cheerful, attentive atmosphere.

HOTEL GLAROS　Boutique Hotel €€ (☎22850 23101; www.hotelglaros.com; Agios Georgios Beach; d €95-100, ste €110-115; ✲ @ 🤶) This well-run and immaculate hotel has been upgraded recently and retains its decor and fittings, which reflec the colours of sea and sky. Service is efficient and thoughtful and the beach is only a few steps away. There's a jacuzzi t back up the beach experience. Breakfast is €8. The owners also have attractive studios nearby (€65 to €100).

NAXIAN COLLECTION　Luxury Hotel €€€ (☎22850 24300; www.naxiancollection.com; Stelida; ste €350-420, villas €640; P ✲ 🤶 ✈) In a beautiful hill-top location near Agios Prokopios beach, these luxurious villas and suites with their subtle and elegant Cycladean style merge with the environ- ment in every way. The Naxian Collection is also developing into an arts hotel with displayed work by leading Aegean artists in the public areas. There are individual villas and suites with private or shared

...mming pools depending on the ac-
...mmodation.

DESPINA'S ROOMS Rooms €

(22850 22356; www.despinarooms.gr;
...astro; s/d/tr/q €40/50/60/70; ❄) These
...ecent rooms are tucked away in the
...astro and some have sea views. Rooms
...n the roof terrace are popular despite
...heir small size. There's a communal
...itchen.

 Eating

MELTEMI Taverna €

...Agiou Arseniou; mains €7.50-14) The top
...ishes at this family-run taverna are
...amb flavoured with fresh lemon juice
...nd oregano and *kaloyeros* (eggplant
...tuffed with slices of veal and Naxian
...ruyère). Yum! The restaurant also of-
...ers three-course fixed menus for €10
...o €12.50, all served with courtesy and
...ood humour on a leafy terrace that
...nakes up for an otherwise dull street
...cene. The family's own wine, olive oil
...nd ouzo are all delicious.

...istant view of Hora, Naxos (p216)

MEZE 2 Seafood €

(22850 26401; Paralia; mains €6-14) The
emphasis at this hugely popular place
right in the middle of the Paralia is on fish,
and even the local fishermen eat here.
Superb seafood is prepared with flair and
commitment and served in a lively atmosphere that is never less than sociable.

ANNA'S GARDEN CAFÉ Bistro €

(Paparrigopoulou; dishes €5-10) This appealing
place is part of Anna's Organic Shop and
is 100% organic. Breakfasts are €3.50 to
€8.50 and there's a dish of the day for
lunch including both vegetarian and
vegan, encompassing a range of international options. Soft drinks, beer and
wine are available, and Anna also supplies
picnic baskets ordered a day in advance.

O APOSTOLIS Greek €

(Old Market; mains €5.50-17) Right at the
heart of the labyrinthine Old Market area
of Bourgos, Apostolis serves up rewarding
dishes such as mussels in garlic butter
and parsley, and *bekri mezes,* a popular Cretan dish of casseroled beef. The
kleftiko, lamb wrapped in filo pastry with
sautéed vegetables and feta cheese, is
particularly good.

If You Like...
Peace & Quiet

If you like the quiet corners of **Naxos** (p215) we think you'd like these other peaceful and less-visited islands in the Cyclades:

1 **ANDROS**
Satisfyingly remote in places, **Andros** (www.greeka.com/cyclades/andros) is a mix of bare mountains, green valleys and out-of-the-way beaches. Neoclassical mansions and Venetian tower houses contrast with the rough unpainted stonework of farm buildings and patterned dovecotes. A network of footpaths is also maintained, and the island has a fascinating archaeological and cultural heritage.

2 **AMORGOS**
This lovely island rises from the sea in a long dragon's back of craggy mountains. There's plenty of scope for beaching, but **Amorgos** (www.amorgos.net) is much more about archaeology and the outdoor world – there's great walking, scuba diving and a burgeoning rock-climbing scene for experienced climbers.

3 **SIFNOS**
As you approach by sea, **Sifnos** (www.travel-to-sifnos.com) seems a barren place of heavy hills until the port of Kamares appears, as if by magic. Beyond the port and between the flanking slopes of rugged mountains lies an abundant landscape of terraced olive groves, almond trees, juniper and aromatic herbs. Plenty of unspoilt paths link the island villages, and the island has a tradition of pottery making, basket weaving and cooking.

Drinking & Entertainment

LA VIGNE   Wine Bar
For a cooler take on Naxian nightlife, head for this cheerful wine bar just behind Plateia Mandilara. It's run by two French ex-pats who know more than a thing or two about fine wines and good conversation. Mezedhes-style dishes (€3.60 to €6) such as fish croquettes with yoghurt and lemon sauce and sweets such as *tarte tatin,* add to the pleasure.

BOSSA NOVA   Bar
In a terrific location by the water's edge at the southern end of the harbour, Bossa Nova is where Hora's young set hang out for coffee, drinks, breakfast, sandwiches and snacks, and a happy hour for drinks from 2pm to 9pm.

DELLA ROCCA-BAROZZI VENETIAN MUSEUM   Classical Music
(☎22850 22387; Kastro; events admission €15-20; ⊗8pm Apr-Oct) Special evening cultural events are held at the museum, and comprise traditional music and dance concerts, and classical and contemporary music recitals. Prices depend on seat position.

Information

Naxos Tours and Zas Travel both sell ferry tickets and organise accommodation, tours and rental cars.
Naxos Tours (☎22850 22095; www.naxostours.net; Paralia)
Zas Travel (☎22850 23330; zas-travel@nax.forthnet.gr; Paralia)

Around Naxos
South of Hora

Conveniently located just south of the town's waterfront is **Agios Georgios**, Naxos' town beach. It's backed by hotels and tavernas at the town end and can get very crowded, but it runs for some way to the south and its shallow waters mean the beach is safe for youngsters.

The next beach south of Agios Georgios is **Agios Prokopios**, which lies in a sheltered bay to the south of the headland of Cape Mougkri. It merges with **Agia Anna**, a stretch of shining white sand, quite narrow but long enough to feel uncrowded towards its southern end. Development is fairly solid at Prokopios and the northern end of Agia Anna.

Sandy beaches continue down as far as **Pyrgaki** and include **Plaka**, **Kastraki** and **Alyko**.

One of the best of the southern beaches is **Mikri Vigla**, where golden granite slabs and boulders divide the beach into two.

A great 'away from it all' sleeping option is **Oasis Studios** (☎ 22850 75494; www.oasisnaxos.gr; d/tr/apt €90/105/120; ⓟ ❄ @ ☲) at Mikri Vigla, 20km south of Hora. It is close to the beach and has lovely big rooms with kitchens and a swimming pool.

South of Mikri Vigla, at Kastraki, is one of the best restaurants on the island – **Axiotissa** (☎ 22850 75107), noted for its sourcing of organic food and for its traditional dishes with added Anatolian flair.

Tragaea Τραγαία

The Tragaea region is a vast plain of olive groves and unspoilt villages, couched beneath the central mountains with **Mt Zeus** (1004m; also known as Mt Zas) dominating overall.

Filoti, on the slopes of Mt Zeus, is the region's largest village. From Filoti, you can reach the **Cave of Zeus**, a large, natural cavern at the foot of a cliff on the slopes of Mt Zeus. There's a junction signposted Aria Spring and Zas Cave, about 800m south of Filoti. From the road-end parking, follow the walled path past the **Aria Spring**, a fountain and picnic area, and on to a very rough track uphill to reach the cave. The path leads on from here steeply to the summit of Zas. From beyond the fountain area, it's a stiff hike of several kilometres and it's essential to have stout walking footwear, water and sunscreen, and to have some hill-climbing experience.

Halki ΑΛΚΕΙΟ

One of Naxos' finest experiences is a visit to the historic village of Halki, which lies at the heart of the Tragaea, about 20 minutes' drive from Hora. Halki is a vivid reflection of historic Naxos and is full of the handsome facades of old villas and tower houses, legacy of a rich past as the one-time centre of Naxian commerce.

Paths and lanes radiate from Halki through peaceful olive groves and flower-filled meadows. The atmospheric 11th-century **Church of St Giorgios Diasorites** lies a short distance to the north of the village. It contains some splendid frescoes.

Since the late 19th century, Halki has had strong connections with the production of *kitron*, a unique liqueur. The citron (*Citrus medica*) was introduced to the Mediterranean area in about 300 BC and thrived on Naxos for centuries. The fruit is barely edible in its raw state, but its rind is very flavoursome when preserved in syrup as a *ghlika kutalyu* (spoon sweet). *Kitroraki, a raki*, can be distilled

Filoti village at the foot of Mt Zeus
NICHOLAS PITT/ALAMY ©

from grape skins and citron leaves, and by the late 19th century the preserved fruit and a sweet version of *kitroraki*, known as *kitron*, were being exported in large amounts from Naxos.

The **Vallindras Distillery** (☎22850 31220; ⏱10am-11pm Jul-Aug, 10am-6pm May-Jun & Sep-Oct) in Halki's main square, distils *kitron* the old-fashioned way. There are free tours of the old distillery's atmospheric rooms, which still contain ancient jars and copper stills. *Kitron* tastings round off the trip and a selection of the distillery's products are on sale.

SANTORINI (THIRA)
ΣΑΝΤΟΡΙΝΗ (ΘΗΡΑ)
POP 12,440

Santorini rocks in more ways than one. Few will be unmoved by the scale of the island's 16 or so kilometres of multicoloured cliffs, which soar up over 300m from a sea-drowned caldera, the vast crater left by one of the biggest volcanic eruptions in history. Lesser islands curl around the fragmented western edge of the caldera, but it is the main island of Thira that will take your breath away with its snow drift of white Cycladic houses lining the cliff tops and, in places, spilling like icy cornices down the terraced rock.

Thira is geared to a conspicuous tourism that is underpinned by enthralling archaeology, fine dining, major wineries, front-row sunsets and a vibrant nightlife. There are even multicoloured beaches of volcanic sand. You'll share the experience for most of the year with crowds of fellow holidaymakers and day visitors from huge cruise ships, but the island somehow manages to cope with it all.

❶ Getting There & Away

There are several flights a day to and from Athens (€113, 45 minutes). There are also a good number of ferries each day to and from Piraeus and to and from many of Santorini's neighbouring islands.

❶ Getting Around

TO/FROM THE AIRPORT

There are frequent bus connections in summer between Fira's bus station and the airport, located southwest of Monolithos Beach. A taxi to the airport costs €12.

Boat Services from Santorini (Thira)

DESTINATION	DURATION	FARE	FREQUENCY
Iraklio	4½hr	€51.50	1-2 daily
Kos	5hr	€30	2 weekly
Mykonos*	2½hr	€50	2-3 daily
Naxos	2hr	€16.50	5 daily
Naxos*	1½hr	€37	2-3 daily
Nisyros	8hr	€30	2-3 weekly
Piraeus	9hr	€33.50	4-5 daily
Piraeus*	5¼hr	€58-61.50	3 daily
Rafina*	4¾hr	€58-62	1 daily
Rhodes	13½hr	€30	1-2 daily
Sitia (Crete)	7hr 25min	€25	2 weekly

*High-speed services

Detour:
Panagia Drosiani Παναγία Δροσιανή

The **Panagia Drosiani** (⊗10am-7pm May–mid-Oct), just below Moni, 2.5km north of Halki, is one of the oldest and most revered churches in Greece. It has a warren of cavelike chapels, and several of the frescoes date back to the 7th century. Donations are appreciated.

US

summer buses leave Fira every half-hour for Oia 1.60), Monolithos (€1.60), Kamari (€1.60) and rissa (€2.20).

ABLE CAR

cable car (☎22860 22977; M Nomikou) hums noothly between Fira and the small port below, nown as Fira Skala); every 20 minutes 6.30am to pm June to August); from where volcanic island uises leave. One-way cable-car tickets cost €4/2 r adult/child and luggage is €2. Less frequent rvices operate outside the peak season.

AR & MOTORCYCLE

car is the best way to explore the island ring high season, when buses are intolerably ercrowded and you're lucky to get on one at all. e very patient and cautious when driving – e narrow roads, especially in Fira, can be a ghtmare. Note that Oia has no petrol station, the arest being just outside Fira.

Two very good local hire outfits are **Damigos** ent a Car (☎22860 22048, 6979968192) d, for scooters, **Zerbakis** (☎22860 33329, 944531992).

AXI

ra's taxi stand (☎22860 23951/2555) is Dekigala just round the corner from the bus ation.

Fira ΦΗΡΑ
OP 2291

antorini's main town of Fira is a vibrant, ustling place, its caldera edge layered ith hotels, cave apartments, infinity ools and swish restaurants, all backed y a warren of narrow streets full of shops nd even more bars and restaurants. multitude of fellow admirers cannot diminish the impact of Fira's stupendous landscape. Views over the multicoloured cliffs are breathtaking, and at night the caldera edge is a frozen cascade of lights that eclipses the displays of the gold shops in the streets behind.

◉ Sights & Activities

ARCHAEOLOGICAL MUSEUM   Museum
(☎22860 22217; M Nomikou; adult/student €3/2; ⊗8.30am-3pm Tue-Sun) This museum, near the cable-car station, houses finds from Akrotiri and Ancient Thira, some Cycladic figurines, and Hellenistic and Roman sculptures.

MUSEUM OF PREHISTORIC THERA   Museum
(☎22860 23217; Mitropoleos; admission €3; ⊗8.30am-8pm Tue-Sun Apr-Sep, 8.30am-3pm Tue-Sun Oct-Mar) Near the bus station, this museum houses extraordinary finds that were excavated from Akrotiri. Most impressive is the glowing gold ibex figurine, measuring around 10cm in length and dating from the 17th century BC.

MEGARO GYZI MUSEUM   Museum
(☎22860 23077; Agiou Ioannou; adult/student €3.50/2; ⊗10.30am-1.30pm & 5-8pm Mon-Sat, 10.30am-4.30pm Sun May-Oct) The Megaro Gyzi has local memorabilia including fascinating photographs of Fira before and immediately after the 1956 earthquake.

FOLKLORE MUSEUM OF SANTORINI   Museum
(☎22860 22792; adult/child €3/free; ⊗10am-2pm & 6-8pm Apr-Oct) Located about 600m along the east-side road from Fira to

223

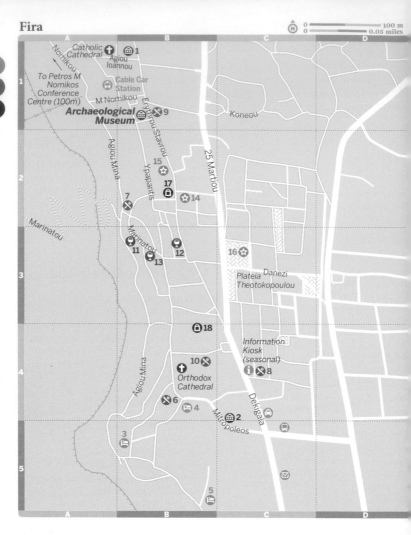

Vourvoulos, this museum houses an intriguing collection that casts light on Santorini's traditions and history.

Tours

Tour companies operate various trips to and fro across the caldera. Options include a tour to the volcanic island of **Nea Kameni** (€15), to the volcano and hot springs (including swimming) of **Palia Kameni** (€20), full-day boat tours to the volcanic islets, **Thirasia** and **Oia** (€28), a **sunset boat tour** (€35) and a bus tour including **wine tasting** (€25). Book at travel agencies.

The *Thalassa,* an exact copy of an 18th-century schooner, scoots around the caldera every afternoon on a **sunset buffet dinner tour** (€50, from May to October), stopping for sightseeing on Nea Kameni and for ouzo on Thirasia. Most travel agencies sell tickets.

Santorini's lauded wines are its crisp, clear, dry whites, such as the delectable

Fira

syrtiko (Greek white wine), and the amber-coloured, unfortified dessert wine *vinsanto*. Most local vineyards hold tastings and tours. A worthwhile visit is to **Santo Wines** (☎22860 22596; www.santowines.gr; Pyrgos) where you can sample a range of wines and browse a shop full of choice vintages as well as local products including fava beans, tomatoes, capers and preserves.

 **Sleeping**

LOIZOS APARTMENTS   Hotel €€
(☎22860 24046; www.loizos.gr; s/tr/apt 75/110/140, d €85-95; P ❄ @ 🖥 🏊) One of the best places in Fira, Loizos is located in a quiet cul-de-sac, yet has the advantage of vehicular access and is only minutes from the centre of town and the caldera edge. Rooms range from standard to deluxe and all are well equipped, clean and comfortable. Those in the front upper floor have a panoramic view towards Kamari and the sea. Breakfast is €9.

AROMA SUITES   Hotel €€
(☎22860 24112; www.aromasuites.gr; Agiou Mina; s €120, d €140-160; ❄ 🖥) Overlooking the caldera at the quieter southern end of Fira, and more accessible than similar places, this boutique hotel has charming service to match its overall ambi-

ence. Stylish, modern facilities enhance traditional caldera interiors, such as in the honeymoon suite: a classic Fira cave chamber, complete with jacuzzi.

HOTEL ATLANTIS   Hotel €€€
(☎22860 22232; www.atlantishotel.gr; Mitropoleos; s €175, d €205-315. incl breakfast; P ❄ 🏊) The Atlantis is a handsome old building that overlooks the widest section of the caldera-edge promenade. It's full of cool, relaxing lounges and terraces, and the bright and airy bedrooms are quiet and very well equipped. Front rooms have caldera views. The price range indicates views and window or balcony options.

KARTERADOS CAVELAND HOSTEL   Hostel €€
(☎22860 22122; www.cave-land.com; Karterados; dm incl breakfast €15-21; d without/with bathroom incl breakfast €50/70, apt incl breakfast €120; P ❄ 🖥 🏊) This new facility, opened in 2011, is based in a fascinating old winery complex in Karterados about a kilometre from central Fira. It was once a local tennis club and the courts are playable for guests. Accommodation is in the old wine caves, all of them with creative and colourful decor and good facilities. The surrounding garden and public areas are peaceful and relaxing. There are yoga classes on offer for €7 to €35.

Eating

KOUKOUMAVLOS Modern Greek €€
(☎22860 23807; mains €28-36) Discreet in location and outstanding for cuisine, the terrace of this fine restaurant has good views, while the interior has retained the vaulted style of its original Fira mansion. An uncrowded menu offers such certainties as lobster and monkfish terrine or fillet of beef on a base of Santorinian fava beans perfumed with summer truffle, feta and marjoram ice cream. The wine list matches it all with style. Look for the wooden doorway down to the right of the Hotel Atlantis.

OUZERI Mezedhes €
(Fabrika Shopping Centre; dishes €6.50-15) Fish dishes are especially good at this central *mezedhopoleio* and include mussel *saganaki* in tomato and feta sauce and a seafood platter of mixed fish. Meat dishes include *youvetsi* (veal in tomato sauce with pasta) and pork fillet in a mustard sauce. Vegetarians can enjoy *dakos* (Cretan rusks) salads and a variety of nonmeat starters.

LITHOS Greek €
(Agiou Mina; mains €7-19.50) Amid a swath of eateries on the caldera edge, Lithos stands out for its well-prepared dishes and attentive service. Choose from persuasive starters such as fava beans with cheese and cherry tomatoes. Salads are crisp and fresh and mains cover poultry, meat, fish and shellfish dishes.

MAMA'S HOUSE Greek €
(mains €7-18) Down steps just before the main square is this 'institution' famed for its mega breakfasts (€6 to €8.50) and for its hearty Greek dinner favourites all enjoyed in fresh, bright surroundings and with a pleasant terrace.

NAOUSSA Modern Greek €
(☎22860 24869; mains €7-28) The cheerful enthusiasm of the chef at this long-established Fira restaurant is reflected in the good food. Fish dishes, such as the fresh sea bass, are especially well sourced and prepared; the meat and vegetarian options likewise.

 **Drinking**

Drinks prices can be cranked up in Fira, even for beer, never mind the stellar cocktail prices. You're often paying for the view, so don't glaze over too early.

KIRA THIRA Bar
(Erythrou Stavrou) The oldest bar in Fira and one of the best. Smooth jazz, ethnic sounds and occasional live music fill out the background beneath the barrel roof. It lies between two streets and there are entrances from both sides. Locals always enter by a certain entrance, but they're not telling.

TROPICAL Bar
(Marinatou) Nicely perched just before the caldera edge, Tropical draws a vibrant crowd with its seductive mix of rock, soul and occasional jazz, plus unbeatable balcony views.

FRANCO'S BAR Cocktail Bar
(Marinatou) Check your cuffs for this deeply stylish and ultimate sunset venue below the caldera edge. Music means classical only. Drinks of all brands, especially the expensive cocktails, match the sheer elegance and impeccable musical taste.

Entertainment

After midnight Erythrou Stavrou fires up the clubbing caldera of Fira.

ENIGMA Club
(Erythrou Stavrou) A Fira top spot with three bars and a big dance space, this is the catwalk clientele's favourite spot amid cool decor and full-on sounds from house to mainstream hits.

KOO CLUB Club
(Erythrou Stavrou) Several bars with variable moods rise through the levels here. Sounds are soft house, trance and Greek hits, and you're never alone.

ITHORA Club

off Danezi) Fira's rock venue 'underneath
the arches', where you can bliss out to big
sounds.

 Shopping

Fira's jewellery and gold shops are
legion. The merchandise gleams and
sparkles, though prices may dull the
gleam in your eye.

EW ART Clothing

(Erythrou Stavrou & Fabrika Shopping Centre)
Forget the standard painted-on T-shirts.
If you want quality to take back home,
the subtle colours and motifs of designer
Werner Hampel's tees have real style.

EONI ATELIER Arts & Crafts

(Firostefani) For art lovers, the studio and
gallery of the internationally acclaimed
artist Leoni Schmiedel is a worthwhile
visit. Here, the artist creates her nuanced and multilayered collages that are
inspired by Santorini's geology, natural
elements and intense colours. The studio
is reached by heading north past the

windmill in Firostefani and then by following signs to the left.

ⓘ Information

Aegean Pearl (☏ 22860 22170; www.aptravel.
gr; Danezi) A helpful agency that sells all travel
tickets and can help with accommodation, car
hire and excursions.

Pelican Tours & Travel (☏ 22860 22220; fax
22860 22570; Plateia Theotokopoulou) Sells
ferry tickets and can book accommodation and
excursions.

Oia Οία
POP 962

A cliff edge walkway and road ramble
north from Fira through a series of linked
settlements to the lovely village of Oia
(ee-ah), known locally as Pano Meria, on
the northern tip of the island. The village
reflects the renaissance of Santorini
after the devastating earthquake of 1956.
Restoration work and upmarket tourism
have transformed Oia into one of the
loveliest villages in the Cyclades. Built on
a steep slope of the caldera, many of its
dwellings nestle in niches hewn into the
volcanic rock.

Cycladic Cuisine at its Finest

Santorini's internationally acclaimed restaurant, **Selene** (☏ 22860 22249 www.
selene.gr; dishes €14-31), once based in Fira, has moved to the lovely hill-top village
of Pyrgos to the very heart of Santorinian farming and culinary culture. Selene's
handsome new premises incorporates restaurant, cafe and wine bar, and stands
above the Drosos-Chrysos Rural and Folklore Museum, a fitting juxtaposition.
Selene's visionary proprietor, Giorgos Hatziyannakis, his chef, Konstantina
Faklari, and their staff continue to fly the flag for creative cuisine based on
Cycladic produce and unique local ingredients such as Santorini's small
tomatoes and fava beans. In keeping with the Selene ethos creative changes are
always being made to the menu, but signature dishes such as the green salad
accented with strawberries and *xinomyzithra* cheese in a basil crust, or mains
such as lamb with wild greens and lemon foam, give some idea of the quality
and creativity. The cafe and wine bar menu is every bit as inventive – think
fava-bean tart with egg and tomatoes – but less expensive. A cellar of the finest
wines, especially Santorinian vintages, enhances the experience, and Giorgos
Hatziyannakis continues to run his popular cooking courses and other culinary
activities at Pyrgos.

From the bus terminal, head left and uphill to reach the rather stark central square and the main street, Nikolaou Nomikou, which skirts the caldera.

 Sights & Activities

AMMOUDI Port

This tiny port with good tavernas and colourful fishing boats, lies 300 steps below Oia at the base of blood-red cliffs. It can also be reached by road. In summer, boats and tours go from Ammoudi to Thirasia daily; check with travel agencies in Fira (p227) for departure times.

 Sleeping

CHELIDONIA TRADITIONAL VILLAS Apartments €€€

(✆22860 71287; www.chelidonia.com; Nikolaou Nomikou; studios & apartments €180-210; ✳@) Traditional cliffside dwellings that have been in the owner's family for generations offer a grand mix of old and new at Chelidonia. Buried beneath the rubble of the 1956 earthquake, the rooms have been lovingly restored. Modern facilities are nicely balanced by the occasional fine piece of traditional furniture and each unit has a kitchenette. Some places are reached by several flights of steps.

PERIVOLAS Luxury Hotel €€€

(✆22860 71308; www.perivolas.gr; ste €620-1600; ✳@🖥🏊) Ultimate caldera-edge accommodation at over-the-edge prices. This is one of Greece's most renowned hotels, however, and features beautiful rooms with vaulted ceilings, individual terraces and kitchenettes. Breakfast, of rare quality, is included. There's a wellness studio, a bar and restaurant, and an infinity pool.

OIA YOUTH HOSTEL Hostel €

(✆22860 71465; www.santorinihostel.gr; dm incl breakfast €18; 🕐May–mid-Oct; @) One o

Left: View of Oia (p227) from the sea
Below: Ammoudi
(LEFT) KUTTIG · TRAVEL/ALAMY ©; (BELOW) APROTTVIEW PORTFOLIO/ISTOCKPHOTO ©

DISCOVER SANTORINI, MYKONOS & THE CYCLADES OIA

e best-run hostels you'll
ope to find. There's a small
ar and a lovely rooftop terrace
th great views. To find the hostel, keep
raight on from the bus terminus for
bout 100m.

 Eating

.OO Modearn European €€
ikolaou Nomikou; dishes €13-35) A slow-
od ethos and enthusiasm for the
nest Mediterrancan cuisine makes this
ne-time sea captain's mansion a top
noico. Sca bass with an aromatic spell
quinoa, artichoke and fennel purée
ets the standard for a creative menu.
ne cellar has the best of Santorini and
reek wines.

KALA Modern Greek €
ikolaou Nomikou; dishes €8.50-14) Watch
e pass up and down to Ammoudi from
e high ground of Skala's lovely terrace.
ubtle international touches enhance

the traditional Greek dishes here, such
as octopus in Vinzanto wine, and chicken
fillet with cream and pistachios. The
mezedhes are special. Try the cheese pies
with added onion and pine nuts.

KATINA Seafood €
(Ammoudi; dishes €4.50-14) A stand-out fish
taverna right on the water's edge at Ammoudi, Katina has built a strong reputation over the years without sacrificing its
family atmosphere and cheerful service.
Fish are by the kilo, so can be quite pricey.
You choose what you want from the display. There's a choice of vegetarian and
meat dishes, too.

ℹ Information

NSTravel (☎22860 71199; www.nst
-santorinitravel.com) In the bus terminal
square; sells ferry tickets and can arrange
accommodation and car hire.

229

GAIL MOONEY/CORB

Don't Miss Ancient Thira

First settled in the 9th century BC, Ancient Thira consists of Hellenistic, Roman and Byzantine ruins and is an atmospheric and rewarding site to visit. Ruins include temples, houses with mosaics, an *agora* (market), a theatre and a gymnasium. There are splendid views from the site. From March to October **Ancient Thira Tours** (☎22860 32474; Kamari) runs a bus every hour from 9am until 2pm, except on Monday, from Kamari to the site. If driving, take the surfaced but narrow, winding road from Kamari for just over 1km.

THINGS YOU NEED TO KNOW
admission €4; ⏱8am-2.30pm Tue-Sun

Around Santorini

The island slopes gently down to sea level on its eastern and southern sides and you'll find dark-coloured beaches of volcanic sand at popular resorts such as Kamari and Perissa. Inland lie charming villages such as Vourvoulos, to the north of Fira, and Pyrgos and Megalohori to its south.

 Sights

ANCIENT AKROTIRI   Ancient Site
(☎22860 81366) Excavations at Akrotiri, the Minoan outpost that was buried dur-

ing the catastrophic eruption of c 1613 BC, began in 1967 and have uncovered an ancient city beneath the volcanic ash. Buildings, some three storeys high, survive. Outstanding finds are the stunning frescoes and ceramics, many of which are now on display at Fira's Archaeological Museum (p223) and the Museum of Prehistoric Thera (p223).

At the time of writing the site was closed for remedial work. See the 'archaeological sites' section of www.culture.gr and check thoroughly on arriv to Santorini before making a bus or taxi journey to the site.

rt Space Gallery

(📞 22860 32774; Exo Gonia) This unmissable gallery is just outside Kamari. It is located n **Argyros Canava**, one of the oldest vineries on the island. The atmospheric ld wine caverns are hung with superb rtworks, while sculptures transform ost corners and niches. The collection s curated by the owner and features ome of Greece's finest modern artists. Winemaking is still in the owner's blood, nd part of the complex is given over to roducing some stellar vintages. A tasting f *vinsanto* greatly enhances the whole xperience.

Beaches

At times, Santorini's black-sand beaches become so hot that a sun lounge or mat is essential. The best beaches are on the east and south coasts.

One of the main beaches is the long stretch at **Perissa**, a popular destination in summer. **Perivolos** and **Agios Georgios**, further south, are more relaxed. **Red Beach**, near Ancient Akrotiri, has high red cliffs and smooth, hand-sized pebbles submerged under clear water. **Vlyhada**, also on the south coast, is a pleasant venue.

Crete

Crete is the culmination of the Greek experience. Nature has been prolific here, creating a dramatic quilt of big-shouldered mountains, stunning beaches and undulating hillsides blanketed in olive groves, vineyards, wildflowers and herbs. There are deep, chiselled gorges, including Europe's longest, the Samaria Gorge, and palm tree–lined beaches that conjure up the Caribbean.

Crete's natural beauty is equalled only by the richness of a history that spans millennia. The Palace of Knossos is only the most famous of many vestiges of the mysterious Minoan civilisation. Venetian fortresses, Turkish mosques and Byzantine churches, meanwhile, bring history alive all over the island, but nowhere more so than in charismatic Hania and Rethymno. Ultimately, though, it's the people – not stones – that create the most vivid memories. Crete's hospitable and spirited locals uphold their unique culture and customs, and time-honoured traditions remain a dynamic part of the island's soul.

Agios Nikolaos (p270)

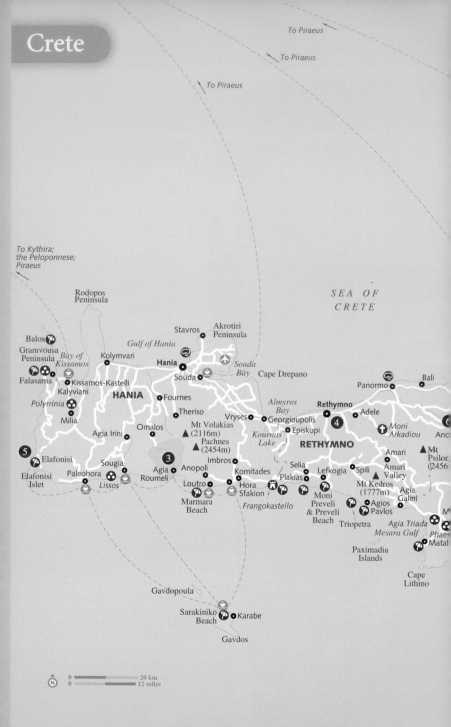

Crete

To Piraeus

To Piraeus

To Piraeus

To Kythira;
the Peloponnese;
Piraeus

Rodopos
Peninsula

*SEA OF
CRETE*

Balos
Gramvousa
Peninsula
Falasarna
Kalyviani
Polyrrinia
Milia

*Bay of
Kissamos*
Kolymvari
Kissamos-Kastelli
HANIA
Fournes
Theriso

Gulf of Hania
Stavros
Hania
Souda

Akrotiri
Peninsula

*Souda
Bay*
Cape Drepano

Panormo
Bali

Agia Irini
Omalos
3
Agia
Roumeli

Mt Volakias
▲ (2116m)
▲ Pachnes
(2454m)
Imbros

Anopoli
Loutro

Vryses
Georgioupolis
Episkopi

*Almyros
Bay*
*Kournas
Lake*

Rethymno
Adele
4

*Moni
Arkadiou*
Anc

5
Elafonisi
Elafonisì
Islet
Paleohora
Lissos
Sougia

Komitades
Hora
Sfakion
Marmara
Beach
Frangokastello

Selia
Plakias
Lefkogia
Spili

RETHYMNO

Amari
Amari
Valley
▲ Mt
Psilor
(2456

Moni
Preveli
& Preveli
Beach
Agios
Pavlos
Triopetra

Mt Kedros
(1777m)
Agia
Galini

Gavdopoula

Sarakiniko
Beach
Karabe

Gavdos

Agia Triada
Mesara Gulf
Phaes
Matal

Paximadia
Islands

Cape
Lithino

M

N
0 ————— 20 km
0 ————— 12 miles

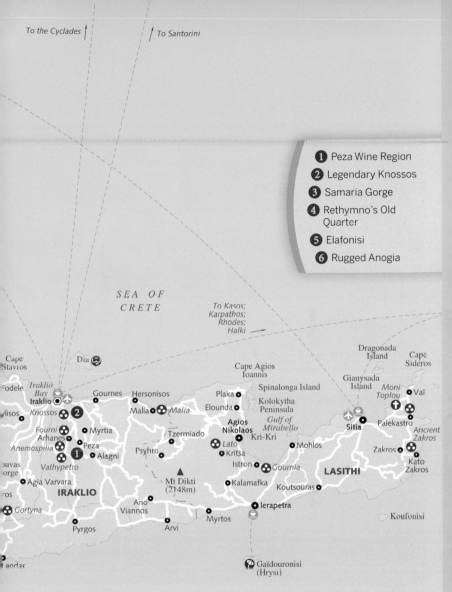

To the Cyclades

To Santorini

① Peza Wine Region
② Legendary Knossos
③ Samaria Gorge
④ Rethymno's Old Quarter
⑤ Elafonisi
⑥ Rugged Anogia

SEA OF CRETE

To Kasos;
Karpathos;
Rhodes;
Halki

Dragonada Island
Cape Sideros

Cape Stavros

Dia

Gianysada Island
Moni Toplou
Vaï

Fodele

Iraklio Bay
Iraklio
Knossos ②
Gournes
Hersonisos
Plaka
Spinalonga Island
Elounda
Kolokytha Peninsula

Malia ● Malia
Agios Nikolaos
Gulf of Mirabello
Sitia
Palekastro
Ancient Zakros

ylisos

Fourni
Arhanes
Myrtia
Tzermiado
Lato
Kri-Kri
Mohlos
Zakros
Kato Zakros

Anemospilia
Peza ①
Alagni
Psyhro
Kritsa
Istron
Gournia

Vathypetro
Istron
LASITHI

uvas
orge

Agia Varvara
Mt Dikti (2148m)
Kalamafka
Koutsouras

ros

Gortyna
IRAKLIO
Ano Viannos
Myrtos
Ierapetra
Koufonisi

Pyrgos
Arvi

endas

Gaïdouronisi (Hrysi)

LIBYAN SEA

Crete's Highlights

①

Peza Wine Region

Crete is known for its unique regional cuisine coupled with satisfying and often exceptional local wines. The majority of the island's grapes are grown in Peza, a fertile plain with abundant sunlight, sea breezes and excellent soil. The result is unique-tasting wine that opens yet another window into Cretan culture.

Need to Know
BEST TIME TO VISIT
Summer –the vineyards are full of fruit, and mid-August to mid-September for harvesting **BEST WINE TO TAKE HOME** Vin de pays

Peza Don't Miss List

BY EVELYNNE BAKINTA, PEZA UNION OF LOCAL PRODUCERS

1 LOCAL RED

Kotsifali and *mantilari* are two local grape varieties that balance one another in a popular Cretan red wine. A glass of this offers you the opportunity to taste red wine the way we have been producing it in our region for generations. The youthful, vivid purple colour, the intense aroma and the full flavour define the unique force of this wine.

2 LOCAL WHITE

Vilana is known for its abundance, *thrapsathiri* for its delicacy and *malvazia* for its nobility. These three grape varieties complement one another in this much-loved Cretan white wine. The youthful shades, the subtlety and finesse in its aromas, and the full taste make it a favourite with locals.

3 WINE TOUR

Head to Peza Union's **exhibition space** (☏28107 41945-7; www.pezaunion.gr; Kalloni Heraklion; ⌚9am-5pm Mon-Sat), located at an old wine-bottling factory 15km south of Iraklio. Watch a movie about wine-making in the area and see exhibits of early equipment. Then proceed to the wine-tasting area to linger over various wines, traditional mezedhes and locally produced olive oil. Then shop for your favourite bottle at the onsite market. Peza Union represents many of the region's vineyards.

4 A GLASS WITH DINNER

My favourite Cretan meal and wine combination is roasted lamb with honey and sage, accompanied by a glass of *kotsifali*, *mantilari* and *syrah*. This wine combines the local red varieties with the international Syrah grape, cultivated on Cretan slopes, adding a cosmopolitan character to this wine.

5 WINE FESTIVAL

During the summer, the municipality of Nikos Kazantzakis organises a three-day wine festival called Oenopolitia. This takes place in various villages in the Peza region and includes wine-tasting, concerts, painting exhibitions and group visits to local museums. For dates and details, visit www.dimos -nikoskazantzakis.gr (in Greek only).

Legendary Knossos

The Minoan Palace of Knossos (p251) has been imaginatively reconstructed and gives you
window back in time. Colourful columns, vibrant frescoes and intriguing advancements, su
as light wells and drainage systems, make this 3500-year-old palace all the more impressi
Look out for the Throne Room, Griffin Fresco, Grand Staircase, Dolphin Fresco and one of t
earliest flushable water closets.

③ Samaria Gorge

Pack your hiking boots. Touted as Europe
longest gorge – and certainly one of
the most gorgeous – it's worth putting
up with the crowds to walk through
Samaria Gorge (p268). You'll follow th
river amidst wildflowers, cliffs of up to
500m and, if you're lucky, the shy *kri-k*
Crete's beloved wild goat. Cross wood
bridges, wade through rivers and finish
up with a refreshing dip in the sea.

IMAGE BROKER ©

Rethymno's Old Quarter

4

Be charmed by the Venetian old town of Rethymno (p254). Its maze of narrow streets, which are lined with graceful houses and ornate monuments, lead down to a lively harbour. Take in the stunning Rimondi Fountain and the remnants of the town's defensive walls before losing yourself in the 16th-century fortress. When you surface from the old quarter, there's a beach right in town where you can plant yourself in the sand.

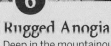

5

Elafonisi

With soft white-and-pink sand between your toes and warm turquoise water lapping at the shore, Elafonisi (p269) feels like the tropics. Tiny coves and islets and dolphins jumping offshore complete the picture. Wander along the lengthy, wide stretch of sand or plonk yourself down under a colourful umbrella. You won't have the place to yourself, but some things are worth sharing.

6

Rugged Anogia

Deep in the mountainous hinterland, the tiny village of Anogia (p250) is perched next to Mt Psiloritis and has cultivated a rebellious spirit for centuries. Here you'll find an undiluted Cretan character, evident in the old school machismo, moustaches, traditionally dressed locals, handmade rugs and stirring local music. Sit in the main square and soak it all up.

Crete's Best...

Beaches

○ **Golden Beach** (p271) Simply a long, long stretch of sand.

○ **Preveli Beach** (p268) Sandy with palm-fringed riverbanks.

○ **Gavdos Island** (p268) Europe's most southerly point with a string of unspoilt beaches.

○ **Falasarna** (p268) Soft coves and spectacular sunsets.

○ **Frangokastello** (p268) Wide, white sand; ideal for kids.

Cultural Experiences

○ **Nikos Kazantzakis Museum** (p248) Learn about Crete's most famous writer in his ancestral village.

○ **Iraklio Archaeological Museum** (p246) Superb Minoan collection.

○ **Byzantine & Post Byzantine Collection of Hania** (p261) Glittering collection in a restored fortress.

○ **Phaestos** (p254) Unreconstructed ruins of a mysterious Minoan palace-city.

○ **Anogia** (p258) Village life and undiluted Cretan character.

View-filled Hotels

○ **Lato Hotel** (p247) Boutique lodgings, panoramic harbour views.

○ **Casa Delfino** (p265) Plush rooms and sunset views from the rooftop terrace.

○ **Du Lac Hotel** (p271) Lakeside look-out over the pretty lagoon.

○ **Kronos Hotel** (p247) Sea views at budget prices.

○ **Splanzia Hotel** (p265) Views of a flower-filled courtyard and rare Turkish well.

Need to Know

Local Cuisine

• **Portes** (p266) Gourmet Cretan cooking with international flourishes.

• **Avli** (p257) Farm-fresh fare beautifully presented.

• **Agreco Farm** (p255) Traditionally produced food served at a 17th century–style estate.

• **Chrysofillis** (p271) Fresh mussels and barley pasta with prawns plus water views.

ADVANCE PLANNING

○ **Two months before** Book your accommodation.

○ **One month before** Check online for upcoming events and reserve tickets.

RESOURCES

○ **Interkriti** (www.interkriti.org) Island life, maps, city and town guides, and links for accommodation bookings.

○ **Top 100 Crete Travel Sites** (www.infocrete.com) Links to Crete's top 100 travel sites, including accommodation and car rentals.

○ **Explore Crete** (www.explorecrete.com) Links, listings, facts, beach guides and activities.

GETTING AROUND

○ **Air** Direct flights from most major cities and islands in Greece.

○ **Bus** Buses link the major northern towns. Less frequent services between the north coast and southern towns, via inland mountain villages.

○ **Ferry** Direct ferry connections with the mainland and Santorini. Regular boats connect beaches along the south coast.

○ **Car** If you're wanting to get out and explore (especially the countless beaches and mountain villages), it's best to have your own wheels.

BE FOREWARNED

○ **Flights** It's often cheaper to fly directly from Europe to Crete than via Athens.

○ **Beaches** Those along the south coast can get sandblasted by strong winds.

fresco at the Iraklio Archaeological Museum (p246); **Above:** Falasarna (p268)

Crete Itineraries

As Greece's largest island, Crete can easily fill your itinerary all on its own. With magical old towns, some of the country's finest beaches, outdoor activities and truly impressive sights, Crete is a culturally rewarding destination that is sure to fulfil your expectations of island life.

SEA OF CRETE

Hania
①
Rethymno ①   Moni Arkadiou
              ②   ③ Anogia
③   ②   Crete
Elafonisi   Samaria Gorge
                    ④
              Preveli Beach   ⑤ Phaestos

LIBYAN SEA

---

3 DAYS

HANIA TO ELAFONISI
The Wild West

Spend a day in **(1) Hania**, Crete's most evocative city. An atmospheric jumble of Venetian and Turkish architecture, set alongside a magnificent harbour, it's an excellent place to explore. Stay in one of the mansions now restored into a boutique hotel, and take in the worthwhile museums and galleries and shop for local handicrafts. Walk the seawall to the restored lighthouse and dine in seaside restaurants dishing up excellent local cuisine. Visit the nearby Milia Mountain Retreat for an impressive seasonal menu at the taverna and even a peaceful stay in a restored farmhouse. From Hania, take a day trip to the **(2) Samaria Gorge**, Europe's largest gorge, boasting stunning scenery, carpets of wildflowers and a chance to see the *kri-kri*, Crete's shy wild goats. It's impossible not to be awed as you hike along the river flowing between soaring, vertical walls. After a day spent hiking through the gorge with the crowds, head to **(3) Elafonisi**. The shallow, turquoise water, tiny islets, coves and tropical setting make it Crete's top beach and a wonderful place to dig your toes into the sand.

RETHYMNO TO PHAESTOS
Mixed Bag

5 DAYS

Base yourself in beautiful **(1) Rethymno**. Get settled in characterful accommodation, dine on Cretan-style food and join in the nightlife, which is lively year-round due to the city's energetic student population. Explore the old town, including the impressive fortress, and look out for the beautiful Rimondi Fountain. Enjoy a walking tour to take in the surrounding scenery or join a dive school to explore under the sea. Rethymno is excellently located for day trips. Visit **(2) Moni Arkadiou**, a striking 16th-century Venetian baroque church with a dramatic past. Next, head into the mountains to the village of **(3) Anogia**

to experience strong Cretan character. Travel south to sandy **(4) Preveli Beach**, nicknamed Palm Beach for the palm-lined riverbanks that offer freshwater pools for swimming. Backed by rugged cliffs and overlooked by an impressive monastery, it's one of Crete's most photogenic beaches. From there, head east to **(5) Phaestos**, the ruins of a mysterious Minoan city set in an awe-inspiring location between mountains and a wide plain.

Phaestos (p254)
JOHN ELK III/LONELY PLANET IMAGES ©

243

Discover Crete

Milia Mountain Retreat (p266)
RAWDON WYATT/ALAMY ©

ⓘ Getting There & Away

AIR

Most travellers arrive in Crete by air, usually with a change in Athens. Iraklio's **Nikos Kazantzakis Airport** (www.heraklion-airport.info) is Crete's busiest airport, although **Hania** (www.chania-airport.com) is convenient for travellers heading to western Crete.

Between May and October, European low-cost carriers and charter airlines operate direct flights to Crete, mostly from UK and German airports. Aegean Airlines has year-round direct flights to Crete from London, Milan, Paris and Rome; coming from another destination requires connecting in Athens. Olympic Air serves Crete from Athens and Thessaloniki

To reach Crete by air from other Greek islands usually requires changing in Athens, except for flights operated by Crete-based airline **Sky Express** (www.skyexpress.gr)

BOAT

Crete is well served by ferry with at least one daily departure from Piraeus (near Athens) to Iraklio and Hania year-round and three or four per day in summer. Ferry companies operating from Crete are **Anek Lines** (www.anek.gr), **Hellenic Seaways** (www.hellenicseaways.gr), **Lane Lines** (www.lane.gr), **Minoan Lines** (www.minoan.gr) and **Sea Jets** (www.seajets.gr).

For current routes and timetables, consult the ferry company's website or go to www.gtp.gr, www.openseas.gr, www.ferries.gr or www.greekferries.gr.

ⓘ Getting Around

Buses are the only form of public transport in Crete, but a fairly extensive network makes it relatively easy to travel around the island. For schedules and prices, go to www.bus-service-crete-ktel.com.

Boat Services from Crete

ROUTE	FERRY COMPANY	DURATION	FARE	FREQUENCY
Iraklio-Mykonos	Hellenic Seaways	4¾hr	€77	1 daily
Iraklio-Piraeus	Minoan, Anek	6½-9½hr	€28-36	1-2 daily
Iraklio-Rhodes	Anek	12½hr	€29	1 weekly
Iraklio-Santorini (Thira)	Anek	4¼hr	€15	2 weekly
Iraklio-Santorini (Thira)	Sea Jets, Hellenic Seaways	2hr	€48.50-51.50	1 daily per company
Hania-Piraeus	Anek	8½hr	€35	1-2 daily

There's hourly service along the main northern coastal road and less frequent buses to the inland villages and towns on the south coast. Buses also go to major tourist attractions, including Knossos, Phaestos, Moni Arkadiou, Moni Prevell, Omalos (for the Samaria Gorge) and Hora Stakion. For details, see individual destinations.

Taxis are widely available except in remote villages. Large towns have taxi stands that post a list of prices, otherwise you pay what's on the meter. If a taxi has no meter, settle on a price before driving off.

Iraklio ΗΡΑΚΛΕΙΟ
POP 137,390

Crete's capital city, Iraklio (ee-*rah*-klee-oh, also called Heraklion), is Greece's fifth-largest city and the island's economic and administrative hub. It's a somewhat hectic place, roaring with motorbikes throttling in unison at traffic lights and airplanes thrusting off into the sky over a long waterfront lined with the remnants of Venetian arsenals, fortresses and shrines.

Though not pretty in a conventional way, Iraklio can grow on you if you take the time to explore its nuances and wander its backstreets. A revitalised waterfront invites strolling and the newly pedestrianised historic centre is punctuated by bustling squares rimmed by buildings from the time when Columbus set sail.

 Sights

HISTORICAL MUSEUM OF CRETE
Museum

(28102 83219; www.historical-museum.gr; Sofokli Venizelou; adult/concession €5/3; 9am-5pm Mon-Sat) Exhibits at this highly engaging museum hopscotch from the Byzantine to the Venetian and Turkish periods, culminating in WWII. There's excellent English labels and multimedia and listening stations throughout.

NATURAL HISTORY MUSEUM
Museum

(28102 82740; www.nhmc.uoc.gr; Sofokli Venizelou; adult/concession €6/4; 9am-4pm Mon-Fri, 10am-4pm Sat & Sun Jun-Sep; shorter hr Oct-May) In a cleverly recycled power station, this museum delivers the predictable introduction to regional fauna and flora but also gets creative kudos for its hands-on Discovery Centre, living zoo and earthquake simulator. The star exhibit, though, is the life-size representation of the elephant-like *Deinotherium gigantum*, the world's third-largest land mammal known to have existed, standing 5m tall.

NEIL SETCHFIELD/LONELY PLANET IMAGE

Don't Miss **Iraklio Archaeological Museum**

This outstanding museum is one of the largest and most important in Greece. There are artefacts spanning 5500 years from neolithic to Roman times, but it's rightly most famous for its extensive Minoan collection. A visit here will greatly enhance your understanding and appreciation of Crete's history and culture. Don't skip it.

The main museum building has been closed for restoration since 2006 with no firm reopening date available at the time of writing. In the meantime, the key exhibits are beautifully displayed in an annex entered from Hatzidakis St. The treasure trove includes pottery, jewellery, figurines and sarcophagi, plus some famous frescoes. The most exciting finds come from the sites of Knossos, Phaestos, Zakros, Malia and Agia Triada.

The superlative Knossos frescoes include the **Procession fresco**, the **Griffin fresco** (from the Throne Room), the **Dolphin fresco** (from the Queen's Room) and the amazing **Bull-leaping fresco**, which depicts a seemingly double-jointed acrobat somersaulting on the back of a charging bull.

Also from Knossos are **Linear A and B tablets** (the latter have been translated as household or business accounts), an ivory statue of a **bull leaper** and some exquisite **gold seals**.

THINGS YOU NEED TO KNOW

📞 28102 79000; http://odysseus.culture.gr; Xanthoudidou 2; adult/concession €4/2, incl Knossos €10/5; ⏱ 8.30am-3pm Nov-Mar, extended hr Apr-Oct, call for details

---

KOULES FORTRESS   Fortress (adult/concession €2/1; ⏱ 8.30am-7pm Tue-Sun May-Oct, to 3pm Nov-Apr) Iraklio's main landmark, this squat and square 16th-century fortress at the end of the Old Harbour jetty was called Rocca al Mare under the Venetians. It stopped the Turks for 21 years and later became a Turkish prison for Cretan rebels. The 26 restored rooms sometimes host art exhibits and performances.

FREE MUNICIPAL ART GALLERY   Art Gallery
(28103 99228; 25 Avgoustou; 9am-1.30pm & 6-9pm Mon-Fri; 9am-1pm Sat) The triple-aisled 13th-century Agios Markos Basilica was reconstructed many times and turned into a mosque by the Turks. Today, it's an elaborate backdrop for art by Maria Fiorakis, Lefteris Kanakakis, Thomas Fanorakis and other Cretan creatives.

CHURCH OF AGIOS TITOS   Church
(Plateia Agiou Titou) This majestic church has Byzantine origins in AD 961; it was subsequently converted to a Catholic church by the Venetians and turned into a mosque by the Ottomans. It has been an Orthodox Church since 1925. Since 1966, it has once again sheltered the much prized skull relic of St Titus, returned here after being spirited to Venice for safe-keeping during the Turkish occupation.

MUSEUM OF RELIGIOUS ART   Museum
(28102 88825; Moni Odigitrias) The former Church of Agia Ekaterini houses this superb collection of Cretan icons, including six by El Greco–mentor Mihail Damaskinos.

 Sleeping

LATO HOTEL   Boutique Hotel €€
(28102 28103; www.lato.gr; Epimenidou 15; d incl breakfast €90-120; P ❄ @ 🛜) Iraklio goes Hollywood – with all the sass but sans attitude – at this mod boutique hotel near the Old Harbour. Rooms here are dressed in warm reds and sport rich woods, custom furniture, pillow-top mattresses and a kettle for making coffee or tea.

KRONOS HOTEL   Hotel €
(28102 82240; www.kronoshotel.gr; Sofokli Venizelou 2; s/d €44/50; ❄ @ 🛜) After a thorough makeover this waterfront hotel has pole-vaulted to the top of the budget hotel category. Rooms have double-glazed windows as well as balconies, a

Iraklio Wine Country

About 70% of wine produced in Crete comes from the Iraklio Wine Country, which starts just south of Knossos and is headquartered in Peza. Almost two dozen wineries are embedded in a harmonious landscape of shapely hills, sunbaked slopes and lush valleys. Winemakers cultivate many indigenous Cretan grape varietals, such as *kotsifali*, *mandilari* and *malvasia*; quite a few now offer tours, wine museums and wine tastings. Pick up the free *Wine Roads of Heraklion* map at the Iraklio tourist office or at any of the estates, including the following:

Arhanes Coop (28107 53208; 9am-5pm Mon-Fri) Wine has been produced in Arhanes since Minoan times.

Boutari (28107 31617; www.boutari.gr; 9am-5pm Mon-Fri year-round, 10am-6pm Sat & Sun summer) This sleek and modern operation is in Skalani, about 8km from Iraklio.

Lyrarakis (28102 84614; www.lyrarakis.gr; 10am-1pm, call to confirm) In Alagni, 6km south of Peza, this winery has won international awards and is famous for reviving two nearly extinct white Cretan wine varietals.

Minos-Miliarikis (28107 41213; www.minoswines.gr; 9am-4pm Mon-Fri, 10am-3pm Sat) Right on the Peza main street, Minos was the first winery to bottle its product in Crete in 1952.

phone, a tiny TV and a fridge. Doubles with sea views cost €58. Breakfast is €6.

CAPSIS ASTORIA
Hotel €€

(28103 43080; www.capsishotel.gr; Plateia Eleftherias; s/d incl breakfast €108/140; P ✳ @ 🛜 ≋) The hulking exterior does not impress but past the front door the Capsis is a class act all the way to the rooftop pool. Rooms have been spiffed up and now sport soothing neutral tones, ultracomfy mattresses and historic black-and-white photographs. Fabulous breakfast buffet.

GDM MEGARON
Hotel €€€

(28103 05300; www.gdmmegaron.gr; Doukos Beaufort 9; s/d incl breakfast from €140/168; ✳ @ 🛜 ≋) This towering harbour-front hulk is a distinctive designer abode with comfortable beds, jacuzzis in the VIP suites, and plasma-screen TVs and a fax in every room. Unwinding by the glass-sided pool and drinking in the sweeping views from the rooftop restaurant and bar are both pleasing diversions.

 Eating

BRILLANT/HERB'S GARDEN
Cretan €

(28102 28103; www.brillantrestaurant.gr; Epimenidou 15; mains €10-23; 🛜) The avant-garde decor at Brillant, the Lato Hotel's hip culinary outpost, might just almost distract you from the creatively composed, feistily flavoured Cretan cuisine. Orange-marinated chicken cooked with

vine-leaf juice, walnuts and tomato is a typical palate tantaliser. From May to October, the restaurant renames itself Herb's Garden and moves to the hotel's rooftop for al fresco dining with harbour views.

PRASSEIN ALOGA
Mediterranean €

(28102 83429; cnr Handakos & Kydonias 21; mains €7-23) This rustic neighbourhood favourite has an ever-changing menu of sharp and innovative Mediterranean cuisine. Expect heaping salads, pasta loaded with shrimp and mussels, and dishes based on Ancient Greek recipes. At press time, there were plans to move into bigger digs by 2012.

KOUZINA TIS POPIS
International €

(Smyrnis 19; mains €7-11) With its big wooden tables, fireplace and photographs, this place feels as warm and welcoming as a friend's kitchen. The menu draws influences from Greek, Arabic and Mediterranean cuisines and may include smoked mackerel fillet, mustard chicken or zucchini-stuffed pastry rolls.

ISTIOPLOIKOS
Fish €

(Port; mains €6-14) Watching the bobbing boats on a balmy evening is a special treat at this port restaurant affiliated with the local yacht club. Whatever is caught that day ends up on the plates, expertly cooked to order over a lusty wood fire. The meatless lachanodomadhes (stuffed cabbage) are a highly recommended side dish.

Literary Village

Myrtia, some 15km southeast of Iraklio, is the ancestral village of *Zorba the Greek* author Nikos Kazantzakis and home to the excellent **Nikos Kazantzakis Museum** (28107 41689; www.kazantzakis-museum.gr; adult/child €3/1; 🕑9am-5pm Mar-Oct, 10am-3pm Sun Nov-Feb). In a modern building overlooking the *kafeneio* (coffee house)–flanked central plaza, the aesthetically lit presentation zeroes in on the life, philosophy and accomplishments of Crete's most famous writer. Watch a short documentary, then nose around personal effects, movie posters, letters, photographs and other paraphernalia. Rooms upstairs present an overview of Kazantzakis' most famous works including, of course, *Zorba the Greek*.

CAMI MOUDAVARIS/ALAMY ©

Don't Miss Iraklio Summer Festival

From July to mid-September Iraklio celebrates the summer with top-notch dance, music, theatre and cinema performances held primarily at the Nikos Kazantzakis Open-Air Theatre and the Manos Hatzidakis Open-Air Theatre. With close to 200 performances, it encompasses everything from flamenco to comedy and draws performers and spectators from around the globe. Previous years have seen the Bolshoi Ballet and Vienna Opera take the stage, as well as plenty of Greek performers from Crete and further afield.

THINGS YOU NEED TO KNOW

✏ 6979 395 287; www.nowheraklion.com/festival

RAKLIO MARKET Market €

)dos 1866) This busy, narrow market has verything you need to put together a deliious picnic. Stock up on fruit and vegetales, creamy cheeses, local honey, succu- ent olives, fresh breads and whatever else rabs your fancy. There are also plenty of ther stalls selling pungent herbs, leather oods, hats, jewellery and souvenirs.

🍷 Drinking

he see-and-be-seen scene sprawls in versized sofas along Korai, Perdikari nd Milátou (sometimes called the Koraï

quarter) and around El Greco Park. West of here, Handakos, Agiostefaniton and Psaromiligkon have more alternative-flavoured hang-outs.

FIX Cafe, Bar

(Perdikari 4) If the trendy cafes along this pedestrian strip don't do it for you, grab a table in this down-to-earth joint that's sought out by an older crowd of chatty conversationalists.

MAYO LOUNGE & HAREM ORIENTAL CLUB Lounge Bar

(Milátou) This high-octane hot spot has dramatic design and is a good place to

249

sample the buzz. Sink into comfy wicker sofas on terraced platforms lidded by a wooden roof that's held up by giant funnel-shaped lamps or heed the call of the kasbah upstairs where there's an overstuffed cushion with your name on it in one of the sultry tented nooks.

VENETO Cafe, Bar
(Epimenidou 9) This lofty space with exposed wooden rafters and clubby leather chairs has panoramic windows overlooking the Venetian harbour and is a good spot for coffee, cocktails or a light meal.

UTOPIA Cafe
(Handakos 51) This hushed old-style cafe has the best hot chocolate in town (also a decadent chocolate fondue), although the prices are utopian indeed.

 # Entertainment

BIG FISH Club
(cnr Sofokli Venizelou & Makariou 17; ☉from 10pm) At this fun-for-all party pen in an old stone building on the waterfront, local and international spinmeisters feed the young and flirty with high-energy dance music.

PRIVILEGE Club
(Doukos Beaufort 7; ☉from 10pm) This massive, mainstream club lures up to 1000

revellers with a high-octane mix of dance rock, electro and Greek sounds.

ℹ Information

Tourist Office (☎28102 46299; Xanthoulidou 1; ☉8.30am-8.30pm Apr-Oct, 8.30am-3pm Nov-Mar) Staffed by university interns with various depths of knowledge and enthusiasm. Meagre selection of brochures and maps.

ℹ Getting There & Away

Air

Nikos Kazantzakis International Airport (☎2810 228401; www.heraklion-airport.info) Crete's biggest airport is about 5km east of the city centre and has a bank, an ATM, a duty-free shop and a cafe-bar.

Boat

The ferry port is 500m to the east of the old port. In season, boats to Piraeus leave several times daily and there's also weekly service to Karpathos, Kasos, Milos, Rhodes and Santorini (Thira). Daily ferries head for Mykonos, Paros and Santorini.

Bus

Iraklio has two major bus stations. Bus Station A, near the waterfront east of Koules Fortress, serves eastern and western Crete (including Knossos). Local buses also stop here. For details, see www.bus-service-crete-ktel.com.

ℹ Getting Around

To/from the Airport

The airport is just off the E75 motorway. Bus No 1 connects it with the city centre every 10 minutes between 6.15am and 10.45pm (€1.10). Buses stop on the far side of the car park outside the terminal building. In town, buses terminate at Plateia Eleftherias. A taxi into town costs around €10.

Car & Motorcycle

Iraklio's streets are narrow and chaotic, so it's best to leave your car in one of the car parks dotted round the city centre. Rates range from €3 to €5 per day.

All the international car-rental companies have branches at the airport. Local outlets line

Bus Services from Iraklio

DESTINATION	DURATION	FARE	FREQUENCY
Agios Nikolaos	1½hr	€7.10	hourly
Hania	3hr	€10.50	up to 17 daily
Knossos	20min	€1.50	3 hourly
Rethymno	1½hr	€7.60	up to 17 daily
Sitia	3¼hr	€14.70	4 daily

Detour:
Cretaquarium

The massive **Cretaquarium** (☎28103 37788; www.cretaquarium.gr; adult/child & senior €8/6; ☺9.30am-9pm May-Sep, to 5pm Oct-Apr; 📶) at Gournes, 15km east of Iraklio, is a vast high-tech indoor sea on the grounds of a former US Air Force base. Inhabited by some 2500 Mediterranean and tropical aquatic critters, this huge aquarium will likely bring smiles to even the most Playstation-jaded youngster. Interactive multimedia help explain the mysteries of this underwater world.

Half-hourly buses (€1.70, 30 minutes) from Iraklio's Bus Station A can drop you on the main road; from there it's a 10-minute walk.

he northern end of 25 Avgoustou and include the ollowing:

Motor Club (☎28102 22408; www.motorclub. r; Plateia Anglon 18)

un Rise (☎28102 21609; www.sunrise-cars bikes.gr; 25 Avgoustou 46)

Taxi

here are small taxi stands all over town, but the main ones are at Bus Station A and on Plateia eftherias. To order one by phone, dial ☎28102 0 102/146/168.

Knossos Κνωσσός

Crete's must-see historical attraction is he Minoan **Palace of Knossos** (☎28102 1940; adult/concession €6/3; ☺8am-30pm Apr-Oct, 8am-3pm Nov-Mar), he capital of Minoan Crete and only 5km south of Iraklio. To beat the crowds and avoid he heat, get there before 0am and budget at least wo hours. Guided tours in English, €10) last bout 90 minutes and eave from the kiosk ast the ticket booth.

The ruins of Knossos vere unearthed in 900 by the British rchaeologist Sir Arthur Evans (1851–1941). Evans vas so enthralled by his discovery that he spent 35 years and £250,000 of his own money excavating and reconstructing sections of the palace. Evans' reconstruction methods continue to be controversial, with many archaeologists believing that he sacrificed accuracy to his overly vivid imagination. For the casual visitor, though, the reconstructions help tremendously in visualising what the palace might have looked like in its heyday.

Knossos
ANDREY KUDINOV/SHUTTERSTOCK ©

Palace of Knossos

The Highlights in Two Hours

The Palace of Knossos is Crete's busiest tourist attraction, and for good reason. A spin around the partially reconstructed complex delivers an eye-opening peek into the remarkably sophisticated society of the Minoans, who dominated southern Europe some 4000 years ago.

From the ticket booth, follow the marked trail to the **North Entrance** ❶ where the Charging Bull fresco gives you a first taste of Minoan artistry. Continue to the Central Court and join the queue waiting to glimpse the mystical **Throne Room** ❷, which probably hosted religious rituals. Turn right as you exit and follow the stairs up to the so-called Piano Nobile, where replicas of the palace's most famous artworks conveniently cluster in the **Fresco Room** ❸. Walk the length of the Piano Nobile, pausing to look at the clay storage vessels in the West Magazines, to a staircase descending to the **South Portico** ❹, beautifully decorated with the Cup Bearer fresco. Make your way back to the Central Court and head to the palace's eastern wing to admire the architecture of the **Grand Staircase** ❺ that led to the royal family's private quarters. For a closer look at some rooms, walk to the south end of the courtyard, stopping for a peek at the **Prince of the Lilies fresco** ❻, and head down to the lower floor. A highlight here is the **Queen's Megaron** ❼ (bedroom), playfully adorned with a fresco of frolicking dolphins. Stay on the lower level and make your way to the **Giant Pithoi** ❽, huge clay jars used for storage.

South Portico
Fine frescoes, most famously the Cup Bearer, embellish this palace entrance anchored by a massive open staircase leading to the Piano Nobile. The Horns of Consecration recreated nearby once topped the entire south facade.

Fresco Room
Take in sweeping views of the palace grounds from the west wing's upper floor, the Piano Nobile, before studying copies of the palace's most famous art works in its Fresco Room.

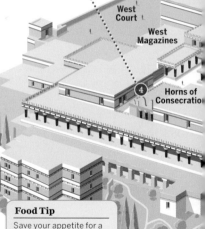

West Court

West Magazines

❹

Horns of Consecration

Food Tip
Save your appetite for a meal in the nearby Iraklio Wine Country, amid sunbaked slopes and lush valleys. Just south of Knossos.

Prince of the Lilies Fresco
One of Knossos' most beloved frescoes was controversially cobbled together from various fragments and shows a young man adorned in lilies and peacock feathers.

Planning

Throne Room

Evans imagined the mythical King Minos himself
holding court seated on the alabaster throne of
this beautifully proportioned room. However,
the lustral basin and griffin frescoes suggest a
religious purpose, possibly under a priestess.

North Entrance

Bulls held a special status in Minoan society as
evidenced by the famous relief fresco of a charging beast gracing the columned west bastion of
the north palace, which harboured workshops
and storage rooms.

Grand Staircase

The royal apartments
in the eastern wing
were accessed via this
monumental staircase
sporting four flights
of gypsum steps
supported by columns.
The lower two flights are
original. It's closed to
the public.

Piano Nobile

Central Court

Royal Apartments

Queen's Megaron

The queen's bedroom
is among the prettiest
in the residential
eastern wing thanks
to the playful
Dolphin Fresco. The
adjacent bathroom
(with clay tub) and
toilet are evidence of a
sophisticated drainage
system.

Giant Pithoi

These massive clay jars are rare remnants from
the Old Palace period and were used to store wine,
oil and grain. The jars were transported by slinging
ropes through a series of handles.

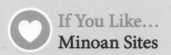

If You Like…
Minoan Sites

If you like exploring the ruins of **Knossos** (p251), we think you'll enjoy encountering these other impressive Minoan sites:

1 PHAESTOS
(☏28920 42315; adult/student €4/2, incl Agia Triada €6/3; ☺8am-7.30pm Jun-Oct, 8am-5pm Nov-Apr) Only 63km from Iraklio, this was the second-most-important Minoan palace-city, enjoying the most awe-inspiring location, with panoramic views of the Mesara Plain and Mt Ida. There's an air of mystery about the desolate, unreconstructed ruins that's not found at Knossos.

2 MALIA
(☏28970 31597; admission adult/under 18 €4/ free; ☺8.30am-3pm Tue-Sun) Smaller than Knossos, this ancient palace complex was built on a flat, fertile plain. Look for the Kernos Stone, a disc with 34 holes around its edge that archaeologists still can't explain, and the Loggia, used for religious ceremonies.

3 AGIA TRIADA
(☏28920 91564; admission adult/student €3/1.50, incl Phaestos €6/3); ☺10am-4.30pm summer, 8.30am-3pm winter) This was possibly a royal summer villa, judging by the opulence of the objects discovered here. North of the palace, the *stoa* (long, colonnaded building) of an erstwhile settlement has been unearthed.

4 GORTYNA
(☏28920 31144; admission adult/under 18 €4/ free; ☺8am-7.30pm, to 5pm winter) This vast and intriguing site was inhabited from Minoan to Christian times, and became capital of Rome's Cyrenaica province. The massive stone tablets inscribed with the wide-ranging Laws of Gortyna (5th century BC) comprise Gortyna's most significant exhibit.

5 ZAKROS PALACE
(☏28430 26897; Kato Zakros; admission €3; ☺8am-7.30pm Jul-Oct, 8.30am-3pm Nov-Jun) Once a major Minoan port, this palace comprised royal apartments, storerooms and workshops on a low plain near the shore. Rising water levels have since submerged parts of the palace. While the ruins are sparse, the wildness and remoteness of the setting make it attractive.

Evans' reconstruction brings to life the palace's most significant parts, including the columns that are painted deep brown-red with gold-trimmed black capitals and taper gracefully at the bottom. Vibrant frescoes add dramatic flourishes. The advanced drainage system and a clever floorplan that kept rooms cool in summer and warm in winter are further evidence of Minoan advanced living standards.

❶ Getting There & Away

With parking at a premium in summer, it's best to visit Knossos by taking bus No 2 from Iraklio's Bus Station A (€1.50, every 20 minutes). If you do drive, there's no shortage of signs directing you to the site.

Rethymno ΡΕΘΥΜΝΟ
POP 28,850

Basking between the commanding bastions of its 15th-century fortress and the glittering azure waters of the Med, Rethymno (*reth*-im-no) is one of Crete's most delightful towns. Its Venetian-Ottoman quarter is a lyrical maze of lanes draped in floral canopies and punctuated by graceful wood-balconied houses and ornate monuments; minarets add an exotic flourish. Crete's third-largest town has lively nightlife, some excellent restaurants and even a decent beach right in town. The busier beaches, with their requisite resorts, stretch almost without interruption all the way to Panormo, some 22km east.

 Sights

VENETIAN FORTRESS   Fortress
(Paleokastro Hill; adult/senior/family €4/3/10; ☺8am-8pm Jun-Oct, 10am-5pm Nov-May) Lording it over the Old Quarter is Rethymno's 16th-century fortress built in reaction to multiple pirate raids and the mounting threat from the Turks. Although its massive walls once sheltered numerous buildings, only a church and a mosque survive. Nevertheless, there are

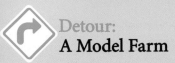

Detour:
A Model Farm

Embedded in the rolling hills near the village of Adele, about 13km east of Rethymno, **Agreco Farm** (☏ 28310 72129, 6947275814; www.agreco.gr; tour & lunch or dinner €30; ⏲ 11am-10pm Tue-Sat May-Oct) is a replica of a 17th-century estate and a showcase of centuries-old organic and eco-friendly farming practices. The brainchild of the Daskalantonakis family, owners of the Grecotel hotel chain, it uses mostly traditional machinery, including a donkey-driven olive press, a flour watermill, a wine press and a giant vat for grape crushing.

Farm tours start at 6pm and culminate in a 30-course Cretan feast in the taverna, which was named Best Organic Restaurant by *Vanity Fair* in 2009. If you're more the hands-on type, swing by on Sunday at 11am when visitors are invited to participate in **traditional agricultural activities**. Depending on the time of year, you could find yourself shearing a sheep, milking a goat, making cheese or smashing grapes (see the website for the schedule). This is followed by a buffet-style **Harvest Festival Lunch**. Reservations are essential for the farm tour and the Sunday experience.

If you're just stopping by during the day, you can enjoy snacks and drinks at the **kafeneio** and stock up on farm-grown products at the shop. Do call ahead, though, to make sure it's open.

many ruins to explore and great views from the ramparts. Enter via the eastern gate.

ARCHAEOLOGICAL MUSEUM Museum
(adult/concession €3/2; ⏲ 8.30am-3pm Tue-Sun) Near the fortress entrance in the old Turkish prison, this small museum displays excavated regional treasures from neolithic to Roman times, including bronze tools, Minoan pottery, Mycenaean figurines, Roman oil lamps and a 1st-century-AD sculpture of Aphrodite.

OLD QUARTER Neighbourhood
Pride of place among Rethymno's many Venetian vestiges goes to the **Rimondi Fountain** (cnr Paleologou & Petihaki Sq), with its spouting lion heads and Corinthian capitals, and the nearby **Loggia**, which was once a meeting house for nobility and is now a gift shop. South of here, the **Porta Guora** (Great Gate; cnr Ethnikis Antistaseos & Dimakopoulou) is the only remnant of the Venetian defensive wall.

Among the few remaining Ottoman structures, the most important is the triple-domed **Neratzes Mosque**

(Vernardou), which was converted from a Franciscan church in 1657 and is now used as a music conservatory and concert venue.

On the same street, the five-room **Historical & Folk Art Museum** (Vernardou 26-28; adult/student €4/2; ⏲ 9.30am-2.30pm Mon-Sat), in a lovely Venetian mansion, documents traditional rural life with displays of clothing, baskets, weavings and farming tools.

 **Activities**

DOLPHIN CRUISES Boat Trips
(☏ 28310 57666; Venetian Harbour; www.dolphin-cruises.com; cruises €15-35) Dolphin runs boat trips to pirate caves, day cruises to Bali and fishing trips.

HAPPY WALKER Hiking
(☏ 28310 52920; www.happywalker.com; Tombazi 56; walks from €30; ⏲ 5-8.30pm daily, closed Sat & Sun Jul & Aug) Happy Walker runs tours through gorges, along ancient shepherd trails and to traditional villages in the lush hinterland.

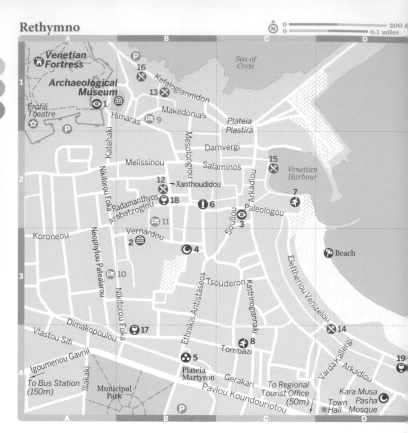

 **Sleeping**

HOTEL VENETO   Boutique Hotel **€€**
(✆ 28310 56634; www.veneto.gr; Epimenidou
4; studio/ste €125/145; ❄ ☎) This charmer
personifies everything Rethymno has
to offer: history, beauty, art and great
food. Soak up the vibe in 10 rooms that
mix polished wood floors and ceilings
with such mod cons as satellite TV and
kitchenettes. Note the stunning pebble
mosaic in the foyer. Optional breakfast
is €8.

**AVLI LOUNGE
APARTMENTS**   Boutique Hotel **€€€**
(✆ 28310 58250; www.avli.gr; Xanthoudidou 22,
cnr Radamanthyos; r incl breakfast €189-263;
❄ ☎) Luxury is taken very seriously
at this discrete retreat where you'll be
ensconced in warmly furnished studios
sporting stone walls, beamed ceilings and
jacuzzi tubs. Retire to plush beds after a
first-rate dinner in Avli's romantic courtyard garden restaurant.

ATELIER   Pension **€**
(✆ 28310 24440; http://frosso-bora.com;
Himaras 25; d €45-55; ❄ ☎) With their
exposed stone walls and Venetian
architectural features, these four rooms
attached to a pottery workshop near the
fortress are our top budget pick. Both
are run by the local ceramic artist Frosso
Bora.

CASA DEI DELFINI   Pension **€€**
(✆ 28310 55120, 6937254857; www.rethymno
holidays.gr; Nikiforou Foka 66-68; studios €60-
65; ❄ ☎) The four rooms in this elegant
guesthouse orbit a small courtyard

Rethymno

with a dolphin mosaic. Each has unique features, such as a *hammam* (Turkish bath) in the bathroom or a bed tucked into an arched stone alcove. All have kitchenettes.

 Eating

AVLI Cretan €€
(☎ 28310 58250; www.avli.com; Xanthoudidou 2, cnr Radamanthyos; mains €13.50-30). This Venetian garden villa serves modern Cretan food with a side of romance. Farm-fresh fare steers the menu that may include lamb with wild mountain greens in lemon sauce or goat with honey and thyme, all punctiliously prepared and beautifully presented.

EN PLO Greek €€
(Kefalogiannidon 28; mezedhes €5.50-9) Our favourite waterfront taverna, En Plo kicks Greek and Cretan comfort food up a notch or two. Mountain greens get a tangy twist with tamarind dressing, plump *bacalao* (salt cod) is paired with a feisty garlic sauce, and the feta *saganaki* (fried cheese) snuggles up to caramelised figs. Sit in the arty interior or snag a table next to the waves.

TAVERNA KNOSSOS Greek €
(www.knosos-rethymno.com; Old Venetian Harbour; mains €6-12; set menu for 2 €30) Most tout-fronted tavernas in the Venetian harbour focus more on the ambience than on the quality of the food. Owned by the Stavroulaki family for half a century, Knossos is a happy exception. The fish is outstanding and the service swift and gracious.

THALASSOGRAFIA Greek €
(☎ 28310 52569; Kefalogiannidon 33; mains €6.50-13.50) This casual alfresco cafe has a breathtaking cliffside setting with enviable views of the fortress and the sea. The grilled sardines are excellent, as are the stuffed mushrooms, all best washed down with the organic local Brink's beer.

 Drinking

ALI VAFI'S GARDEN Cafe, Bar
(Tzane Bouniali 65a) Choice pieces by the ceramic-artist owners decorate the stone-vaulted front room of this watering hole, but in summer there are few locations more enchanting than the garden behind their on-site pottery workshop.

LIVING ROOM Lounge Bar
(www.living.com.gr; Eleftheriou Venizelou 5) The sleekest and slickest bar on the waterfront strip wows with its eclectic decor (big mirrors, velvet chairs, stylish lamps) and is always abuzz with Rethymno's young and restless.

FUSION ENOTECA Wine Bar
(Xanthoudidou 22, cnr Radamanthyos) Owned by the same team as the Avli Restaurant,

Bus Services from Rethymno

DESTINATION	DURATION	FARE	FREQUENCY
Hania	1hr	€6.20	hourly
Hora Sfakion	2hr	€7.30	1 daily
Iraklio	1½hr	€7.60	hourly
Moni Arkadiou	40min	€2.80	up to 3 daily
Omalos (Samaria Gorge)	1¾hr	€15	3 daily
Preveli	1¼hr	€4.50	2 daily

this handsome wine shop-cum-bar is chock-full with over 450 hand-selected labels. If you feel like stronger stuff, hop across the street to the affiliated Raki Baraki bar, which often has live music.

ⓘ Information

Regional tourist office (☎ 28310 25571; www. rethymnon.gr; Dimokratias 1; ⊙ 8am-2.30pm Mon-Fri)

ⓘ Getting There & Away

Buses leave from the terminal at Igoumenou Gavriil, about 600m west of the Porta Guora.

ⓘ Getting Around

Auto Motor Sports (☎ 28310 24858; www. automotosport.com.gr; Sofoklis Venizelou 48) rents cars and motorbikes.

Anogia ΑΝΩΓΕΙΑ

POP 2125

Perched aside **Mt Psiloritis**, 37km southwest of Iraklio, Anogia is known for its rebellious spirit and determination to express its undiluted Cretan character. Its famous 2000-guest weddings involve the entire village. It's also famous for its stirring music and has spawned many of Crete's best known musicians.

During WWII, Anogia was a centre of resistance and suffered heavily for it. The Nazis burned down the town and massacred all the men in retaliation for their role in sheltering Allied troops and aiding in the kidnapping of a Nazi general.

Hence, most of the buildings you see today are actually of relatively recent vintage, yet Anogia seems to desperately cling to time-honoured traditions. Black-shirted moustachioed men lounge in the *kafeneia*, baggy pants tucked into black boots, while elderly women hunch over their canes, aggressively flogging woven blankets and embroidered textiles displayed in their shops.

 Eating

TA SKALOMATA   Cretan €
(☎ 28340 31316; mains €4-9) In the up-per village, Skalomata has provided sustenance to locals and travellers for about 40 years, with great grilled meats (the roast lamb is especially good), homemade wine and bread, and such tasty meatless options as zucchini with cheese and eggplant.

ⓘ Getting There & Away

There are up to three buses daily from Iraklio (€3.80, one hour) and two buses Monday to Friday from Rethymno (€5.50, 1¼ hours).

Moni Preveli Μονη Πρεβελη

The historic **Moni Preveli** (☎ 28320 31246; www.preveli.org; admission €2.50; ⊙ 8am-7pm mid-Mar–May, 9am-1.30pm & 3.30-7.30pm Jun-Oct) stands in splendid isolation high above the Libyan sea. Like most Cretan monasteries, it was a centre of anti-Ottoman resistance and was burned by the Turks during the 1866 onslaught.

In summer, there are two daily buses from Rethymno (€4.50, 1¼ hour) and one from Plakias (€2.30, 30 minutes).

JOHN ELK III/LONELY PLANET IMAGES ©

Don't Miss Moni Arkadiou ΜΟΝΗ ΑΡΚΑΔΙΟΥ

The 16th-century **Moni Arkadiou**, some 23km southeast of Rethymno, has deep significance for Cretans. It's a stark and potent symbol of human resistance and considered a spark plug in the struggle towards freedom from Turkish occupation.

In November 1866, massive Ottoman forces arrived to crush island-wide revolts. Hundreds of Cretan men, women and children fled their villages to find shelter at Arkadiou. However, far from being a safe haven, the monastery was soon besieged by 2000 Turkish soldiers. Rather than surrender, the Cretans set light to stored gunpowder kegs, killing everyone, Turks included. One small girl miraculously survived and lived to a ripe old age in a village nearby. A bust of this woman and another of the abbot who lit the gunpowder are outside the monastery not far from the old windmill, which is now a macabre **ossuary** with skulls and bones of the 1866 victims neatly arranged in a glass cabinet.

Arkadiou's most impressive building is its Venetian **church** (1587), which has a striking Renaissance facade marked by eight slender Corinthian columns and topped by an ornate triple-belled tower. There's a small museum left of here and the old wine cellar where the gunpowder was stored at the end of the left wing.

There are three buses (two on weekends) from Rethymno to the monastery (€2.80, 40 minutes).

THINGS YOU NEED TO KNOW

Arkadi Monastery; ☎28310 83136; www.arkadimonastery.gr; admission €2.50; ⊙9am-8pm Jun-Sep, shorter hr rest of year

Preveli Beach
Παραλια Πρεβελη

Right below Moni Preveli, Preveli Beach (aka Palm Beach) is one of Crete's most celebrated strands. The setting is truly stunning. The beach sits at the mouth of the Kourtaliotiko Gorge, from where the river Megalopotamos slices across it before emptying into the Libyan sea. The palm-lined riverbanks have freshwater pools good for a dip, while rugged cliffs begin where the sand ends.

A steep path leads down to the beach (10 minutes) from a car park 1km before Moni Preveli.

Hania XANIA
POP 53,838

Hania (hahn-*yah*; also spelt Chania) is Crete's most evocative city, with its pretty Venetian quarter, criss-crossed by narrow lanes, culminating at a magnificent harbour. Remnants of Venetian and Turkish architecture abound, with old townhouses now transformed into atmospheric restaurants and boutique hotels.

Although all this beauty means the Old Town is deluged with tourists in summer, it's still a great place to unwind. Excellent local handicrafts mean there's good shopping, too. The Venetian harbour is a good place for a stroll and pockmarked with galleries and museums.

 Sights

ARCHAEOLOGICAL MUSEUM Museum
(Halidon 30; admission €2, incl Byzantine collection €3; ☾8.30am-3pm Tue-Sun) This museum's collection of finds from western Crete spans from the neolithic to the Roman era and includes statues, vases, jewellery, floor mosaics and some stunning painted sarcophagi from a late Minoan cemetery. It occupies the impressive 16th-century Venetian Church of San Francisco; outside, a Turkish fountain

Left: Preveli beach; **Below:** Hania
(LEFT) DUODUO/SHUTTERSTOCK ©; (BELOW) JOHN ELK III/LONELY PLANET IMAGES ©

ttests to its former incar-
ation as a mosque.

NAVAL MUSEUM   Museum
(Akti Koundourioti; admission €3; ⊙9am-7pm
Mon-Fri, shorter hr Sat & Sun) A former Turkish
prison is the backdrop for this interesting
collection of model ships from the Bronze
Age as well as naval instruments, paintings, photographs and memorabilia from
the Battle of Crete.

VENETIAN
FORTIFICATIONS   Fortifications
Part of a defensive system begun in
1538 by Michele Sanmichele, who also
designed Iraklio's defences, Hania's
massive fortifications remain impressive. Best preserved is the western
wall, running from the **Firkas Fortress**
to the **Siavo Bastion**. Entrance to the
fortress is via the gates next to the Naval
Museum. The bastion offers good views
of the Old Town.

BYZANTINE & POST BYZANTINE
COLLECTION OF HANIA   Museum
(Theotokopoulou; admission €2, incl Archaeological Museum €3; ⊙8.30am-3pm Tue-Sun)
In the fortress' restored Church of San
Salvatore, this is a small but fascinating
collection of artefacts, icons, jewellery
and coins, including a fine mosaic floor
and a prized icon of St George slaying the
dragon.

CRETAN HOUSE
FOLKLORE MUSEUM   Museum
(Halidon 46; admission €2; ⊙9.30am-3pm &
6-9pm) This interesting museum contains
traditional crafts and implements, including weavings with traditional designs.

ELEFTHERIOS VENIZELOS
RESIDENCE & MUSEUM   Museum
(☎28210 56008; Plateia Helena Venizelou;
admission €2; ⊙10.30am-1.30pm daily & 6-8pm
Mon-Fri) Some 1.5km east of the old town
in the Halepa neighbourhood, this building

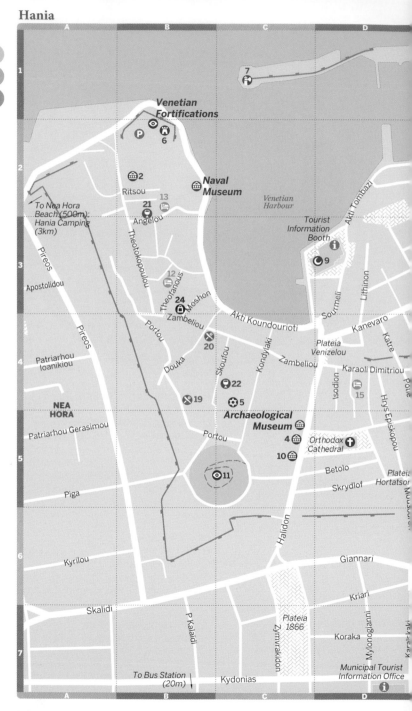

Venetian
Fortifications

P ⊙ 🏛 6

🏛 2
Ritsou
21 🏛 13
Angelou

Naval
Museum 🏛

Venetian
Harbour

Tourist
Information
Booth ℹ

Akti Tombazi

To Nea Hora
Beach (500m);
Hania Camping
(3km)

Pireos

Apostolidou

Theotokopoulou

12 🏛

24 🔒
Moshon
Zambeliou

Akti Koundourioti

🌓 9
Lithinon

Sourmeli

Pireos

Patriarhou
Ioanikiou

Portou

Douka

20 ❌
Shoufou

Kondylaki

22 ☕

Zambeliou

Plateia
Venizelou

Karaoli Dimitriou

15 🏛

Kanevaro

Katre

Poule

NEA
HORA

Patriarhou Gerasimou

Portou

19 ❌   5 ❄

Archaeological
Museum 🏛

4 🏛   Orthodox ✝
Cathedral

10 🏛

Isodion

Hrys Episkopou

Piga

11 ⊙

Betolo

Skrydlof

Plateia
Hortatson

Mousouron

Kyrilou

Giannari

Kriari

Skalidi

P Kalaidi

Plateia
1866

Zymvrakidon

Halidon

Koraka

Mylonogianni

Karaoskaki

To Bus Station
(20m)

Kydonias

Municipal Tourist
Information Office
ℹ

Sea of Crete

3 Plateia Katehaki

Agiou Markou

Arholeon

Arholeon

Venetian Shipyards (Neoria)

Kalergon

Kallistou

Sifaka

Sifaka

Gavaladon

Sarpaki

SPLANTZIA

Mihali Dalani

Tsouderon

Plateia Markopoulou

Agora

1

Ikarou

17

16

23

Epimenidou

Akti Miaouli

Kyprou

26

Vourdouba

Plateia 1821 **8**

Daskalogianni

18

Kallistou

Melidoniou

Minos

14

25

NikiforouEpiskopou

Nikiforou Foka

El Venizelou

To Hotel Doma (500m);
Eleftherios Venizelos
Residence & Museum (1.1km);

Stadium

Tzanakaki

Plastira

Apokoronou

Voloudakidon

Sfakion

Boniali

Andrea Papandreou

Trikoupi

Public Garden

To Thalassino
Ageri (250m)

0   200 m
0   0.1 miles

Hania

preserves the great statesman's home in splendid fashion, with original furnishings, maps and other memorabilia. Guided tours are available. Hours are reduced in winter.

AGORA   Market
The central bastion of the city wall was demolished to make way for this magnificent municipal covered market that's worth a visit even if you don't want to shop. If you do, it's a good source for take-home purchases such as spices, honey, olive oils and wines.

Other Attractions

The restored Venetian **lighthouse** at the entrance to the harbour is a 1.5km walk around the sea wall. On the inner harbour's eastern side, the prominent **Mosque of Kioutsouk Hasan** (also called Mosque of Janissaries) holds regular art exhibitions. The well-restored Venetian **Great Arsenal** houses the **Centre for Mediterranean Architecture**, which hosts regular events and exhibitions. Similarly, Hania's **Municipal Art Gallery** (www.pinakothiki-chania.gr; Halidon 98; admission €2, free Wed; ⏰10am-2pm & 7-10pm Mon-Fri,

10am-2pm Sat) hosts exhibitions of modern Greek art.

The restored **Etz Hayyim Synagogue** (Parodos Kondylaki; www.etz-hayyim-hania.org; ⏰10am-8pm Tue-Fri, 5-8pm Sun, 10am-3pm & 5-8pm Mon) has a moving memorial to the Jews of Hania who were annihilated by the Nazis.

 **Activities**

Those looking for free information on all outdoor sports, including serious climbing in the Lefka Ori, mountain refuges and the E4 trail, should first visit the Hania branch of EOS, the **Greek Mountaineering Association** (☎28210 44647; www.eoshanion.gr; Tzanakaki 90; ⏰8.30am-10pm). EOS also runs regular weekend excursions.

 **Sleeping**

HOTEL DOMA   Boutique Hotel €€
(☎28210 51772; www.hotel-doma.gr; Venizelos 124; s/d/tr/ste incl buffet breakfast €65/90/120/150; ⏰Apr-Oct; ❄️🛜) One

ould imagine Hercule Poirot peering down the curving stairway at the Doma, a quiet, century-old classic overlooking the sea in the Halepa district. Decorated with period furnishings, this former consulate attracts couples, writers and solitude-seekers. Rooms are classy and well-kept, and the flowering back garden is relaxing. Days start with tasty, all-natural breakfasts.

SPLANZIA HOTEL Boutique Hotel €€
(☏28210 45313; www.splanzia.com; Daskalogianni 20; d incl buffet breakfast €100; ❄ @) This smart designer hotel in an Ottoman building in the Splantzia quarter has eight stylish rooms, some decorated with four-poster timber beds and drapery. The back rooms overlook a lovely courtyard with cheerful bougainvillea and one of Hania's few remaining Turkish wells.

CASA DELFINO Boutique Hotel €€€
(☏28210 87400; www.casadelfino.com; Theofanous 7; ste & apt incl buffet breakfast €180-340; ❄ 🛜) This elegant 17th-century mansion is the most luxurious hotel in the Venetian quarter. The 24 individually decorated suites all have Italian marble baths, but those in the 'standard' cat-

egory don't have balconies. For maximum pampering, treat yourself to a massage in the Turkish-inspired spa. Breakfast is in the splendid pebble-mosaic courtyard, and there are great sunset views from the rooftop terrace.

PORTO DE COLOMBO Boutique Hotel €€
(☏28210 70945; www.portodelcolombo.gr; Theofanous & Moshon; d/ste incl breakfast €85/110; ❄) The former French embassy and office of Eleftherios Venizelos, this 600-year-old Venetian townhouse is now a charming boutique hotel with 10 lovely, well-appointed rooms; the top suites have fine harbour views.

PENSION THERESA Pension €
(☏28210 92798; www.pensiontheresa. gr; Angelou 2; r €40-50; ❄) Part of the Venetian fortifications, this creaky old house with a steep (and narrow!) spiral staircase and antique furniture delivers atmosphere aplenty. Some rooms have a view, but there's always the stunning vista from the rooftop terrace with a communal kitchen. Rooms are clean but fairly snug, though still a good bet for the price.

Hania (p260)

GARETH MCCORMACK/LONELY PLANET IMAGES ©

Milia Mountain Retreat

One of Crete's ecotourism trailblazers, the isolated **Milia Mountain Retreat** (28220 46774; www.milia.gr; d incl breakfast €75-85) was inspired by a back-to-nature philosophy. Sixteen abandoned stone farmhouses were restored into eco-cottages with only solar energy for basic needs (leave the laptop and hairdryer at home), antique beds and rustic furnishings.

Milia is one of the most atmospheric and peaceful places to stay on the island, but it is also worth a visit just to dine at the superb taverna, which has a frequently changing seasonal menu depending on what is available from the organic produce cultivated on its farm, including its own oil, wine, milk and cheese and free-range chickens, goats and sheep. Try the *boureki*, the stuffed rabbit with *myzithra* (sheep's milk cheese) or yoghurt, or pork with lemon leaves baked slowly overnight. There is local wine and *raki* (Cretan fire water) but no Coke or anything processed.

To get there, follow the road from Hania towards Elafonisi as far as the village of Topolia, turn right towards Tsourouniana, then left after 500m. After 8km turn right to Milia and follow a 2km-long graded dirt road to the retreat.

VRANAS STUDIOS — Studios €
(28210 58618; www.vranas.gr; Agion Deka 10; studio €40-70; ❄) On a lively pedestrian street in the heart of the Old Town, this place has spacious, immaculately maintained studios with kitchenettes. All units have polished wooden floors, balconies, TVs and telephones, and there's an internet cafe next door.

Eating

PORTES — Cretan €
(Portou 48; mains €6-9) Many locals agree that this is the best place in town for creative Cretan cooking with an international flourish. Menu stars include marinated *gavros* (little fish), wild snails and stuffed fish baked in paper, but you can't go wrong ordering whatever's on the specials board.

THALASSINO AGERI — Seafood €€€
(Vivilaki 35; fish per kg €55; ⏰dinner) It can be tricky to find, but this fish taverna in a tiny port among the ruins of Hania's old tanneries is one of Crete's top eateries. The setting is superb, the fish fresh and the mezedhes mouth-watering. Top picks include tender octopus in wine vinegar, calamari and the fisherman's salad. Follow Venizelou around the shore, turning left at Noel St as soon as you veer away from the coast.

KOUZINA E.P.E. — Greek €
(Daskalogianni 25; mayirefta €3-7; ⏰noon-8pm) This cheery, bright lunch spot in Splantzia is a local favourite away from the crowds, serving nourishing *mayirefta* (prepared dishes) and grilled meats. The playful name means 'Limited Liability Restaurant,' but there's no reason for concern – everything is great, from the sardines to the *pastitsio* (layers of buttery macaroni and seasoned mince lamb).

TAMAM — Greek €
(Zambeliou 49; mains €6-10) In a former *hammam*, Tamam offers Greek fare with an Ottoman flourish. There are plenty of superb vegetarian specialities (try the spicy avocado dip on potato) along with such Turkish-inspired dishes as the *tas kebab* (veal with spices and yoghurt) and the *beyendi* chicken with creamy aubergine purée.

APOSTOLIS I & II — Seafood €€
(Akti Enoseos; fish per kg from €40) In the quieter eastern harbour, this is a well-

respected place for fresh fish and Cretan dishes served in two buildings. Apostolis II is more popular as the owner reigns there, but the other one has the same menu at marginally cheaper prices. A seafood platter for two, including salad, is €30.

 # Drinking & Entertainment

SYNAGOGI Bar
(Skoufou 15) In a roofless Venetian building and former synagogue, this popular lounge is great for relaxing beneath the stone arches.

FAGOTTO Live Music
(Angelou 16; ☉7pm-2am Jul-May) This Hania institution in a Venetian building offers smooth jazz, soft rock and blues in a setting brimming with jazz paraphernalia, including a saxophone beer tap. It doesn't get busy until after 10pm.

TA DUO LUX Bar
(Sarpidona 8; ☉10am-late) Further along the harbour, this arty cafe-bar remains a perennial favourite among wrinkle-free alternative types and is popular day and night. Nearby Bororo and Hippopotamos are also popular hang-outs.

 # Shopping

EXANTAS ART SPACE Souvenirs
(cnr Zambeliou & Moschon; ☉10am-2pm & 6-11pm) This classy store has great old photos, lithographs and engravings, handmade gifts, Cretan music as well as a good range of travel, coffee table and art books.

GIORGOS PATERAKIS Shoes
(Episkopou Nikiforou 13) In a tiny shop in Splantzia, Giorgos is Hania's last maker of authentic Cretan leather boots. Local men typically don these knee-high creations at weddings, traditional dances and other special occasions, though shepherds too like their sturdy, waterproof nature.

MIDEN AGAN Food & Drink
(www.midenaganshop.gr; Daskalogianni 70) Unique 'house' wine and liquors, along with over 800 Greek wines, are sold at this foodie haven, which also stocks such local gourmet delights as olive oil, honey and a homemade line of spoon sweets (try the white pumpkin).

 # Information

For pretrip research, try www.chania.gr or www.chania-guide.gr.
Municipal Tourist Office (☎28210 36155; tourism@chania.gr; Kydonias 29; ☉8am-2.30pm) At the town hall. There's also an info booth behind the mosque in the Venetian harbour that's usually staffed between noon and 2pm.

Getting There & Away

Air
Hania's airport is 14km east of town on the Akrotiri Peninsula.

Boat
Hania's main port is at Souda, 7km southeast of town and site of a NATO base. At time of writing, the only ferry service was to Piraeus. There are buses to Hania (€1.65) as well as taxis (€9).

Bus
Hania's bus station is on Kydonias, two blocks southwest of Plateia 1866, from where the Venetian harbour is a short walk north up Halidon.

Bus Services from Hania

DESTINATION	DURATION	FARE	FREQUENCY
Elafonisi	2½hr	€11	1 daily
Hora Sfakion	1hr 40min	€7.60	3 daily
Iraklio	2¾hr	€13.80	half-hourly
Omalos (for Samaria Gorge)	1hr	€6.90	3 daily
Rethymno	1hr	€6.20	half-hourly

If You Like...
Cretan Beaches

If you like the sun-drenched sand of **Elafonisi** (p269), we think you'll like kicking back on these lovely Cretan beaches:

1 FALASARNA
Some 16km west of Kissamos, this long sandy beach is one of Crete's finest, comprising several coves separated by rocky spits. Falasarna's end-of-the-world feel is accentuated by spectacular sunsets, when pink hues are reflected from the sand's fine coral.

2 FRANGOKASTELLO
Lying just below a magnificent 14th-century fortress, this wide, packed white-sand beach, 15km east of Hora Sfakion, is one of Crete's best. The shallow warm water makes it ideal for kids. Be warned: when the wind's up, flying sand will chase you off quickly.

3 VAÏ
Europe's only 'natural' palm-forest beach has inviting white sand. A mere 24km east of Sitia, it gets packed in summer, though you can access a more secluded beach by clambering over a rocky outcrop behind the taverna.

4 GAVDOS ISLAND
Europe's most southerly point, 45km south of Hora Sfakion, is blissful and boasts several unspoilt beaches – some accessible only by boat. It attracts campers, nudists and free spirits seeking to peace out on balmy beaches under the stars.

ℹ Getting Around

To/From the Airport
From Hania bus station, there are at least three buses per day to the airport (€2.30, 20 mins); check the schedule locally. A taxi to or from the airport costs €20 (plus €2 per bag).

Bus
Buses for the western beaches leave from the main bus station on Plateia 1866. Local buses also congregate around Plateia Markopoulou and offer quick service to such suburbs as Halepa. Buy tickets (€1.10) from the coin-operated machine at the bus stop.

Car
Most of the Old Town is pedestrianised. The best place to park is in the free lot near the Firkas Fortress (turn right off Skalidi at the sign to the big supermarket car park on Pireos and follow the road down to the waterfront).

Car hire agencies include the following:
- Europrent (📞 28210 27810; Halidon 87)
- Tellus Travel (📞 28210 91500; www.tellustravel.gr; Halidon 108)

Samaria Gorge
ΦΑΡΑΓΓΙ ΤΗΣ ΣΑΜΑΡΙΑΣ

Although you'll have company (over 1000 people per day in summer), hiking the **Samaria Gorge** (📞 28210 67179; admission €5; 🕐 6am-3pm May–mid-Oct) makes for a memorable experience. Check climatic conditions in advance as many aspiring hikers have been disappointed when park officials close the gorge on exceptionally hot days.

At 16km, the Samaria (sah-mah-rih-ah) Gorge is reputedly Europe's longest. It begins just below the Omalos Plateau, carved out by the river that flows between the peaks of Avlimanakou (1858m) and Volakias (2115m) mountains. Samaria's width varies from 150m to 3m and its vertical walls soar up to 500m. Wildflowers bloom in April and May.

Samaria also shelters endangered species like Crete's beloved *kri-kri*, a shy and seldom-seen wild goat. To save it from extinction, the gorge became a national park in 1962.

Hiking the Gorge

An early start (before 8am) helps to avoid the worst of the crowds, but during July and August even the early bus from Hania to the trailhead can be packed. Overnighting in Omalos and getting an early lift from there allows you to get your toe on the line for the starting gun. There's nowhere to spend the night in the gorge so time your trek to finish by the time the gates close (3pm). Wear good hiking boots, and take sunscreen, sunglasses, a hat and a water bottle (springs with good water exist, though not the main stream). Be aware that falling rocks can be a hazard and people have been injured; in 2006 there were even two fatal incidents.

The hike from **Xyloskalo** (the name of the steep stone path that enters the gorge) to Agia Roumeli on the south coast takes from about four hours for the sprinters to six hours for the strollers. Early in the season it's sometimes necessary to wade through the stream.

Later, as the flow drops, the streambed rocks become stepping stones.

ℹ Getting There & Away

There are excursions to Samaria Gorge from every sizable town and resort in Crete, but you can get there easily enough from Hania by bus (via Omalos) and hike down the gorge to Agia Roumeli, catch a boat to Sougia and from there the bus back to Hania. There are also ferries to other south-coast towns, including Hora Sfakion, Loutro and Paleohora, in case you're tempted to linger a day or two.

Elafonisi ΕΛΑΦΟΝΗΣΙ

It's easy to understand why people enthuse so much about Elafonisi. At the southern extremity of Crete's west coast, the beach is long, wide and separated from the Elafonisi Islet by about 50m of knee-deep water. The clear, shallow turquoise water and fine white sand create a tropical paradise. There are a few snack bars on the beach and umbrella and lounge-chair rentals. The islet is marked by low dunes and a string of semi-secluded coves that attract a

Elafonisi

WOJCIECH JASKOWSKI/SHUTTERSTOCK ©

sprinkling of naturists. Unfortunately this idyllic scene can be spoilt by the busloads of day trippers who descend in summer.

ⓘ Getting There & Away

There is one boat daily from Paleohora to Elafonisi (€8, one hour) from mid-May through September. There is also one bus daily from Hania (€11, 2½ hours) and Kissamos-Kastelli (€7, 1¼ hours), which return in the afternoon. Neither option leaves much time to relax on both beaches, so driving is ideal.

Agios Nikolaos
ΑΓΙΟΣ ΝΙΚΟΛΑΟΣ
POP 11,286

Lasithi's capital, Agios Nikolaos (ah-yee-os nih-ko-laos) stands on the shores of the beautiful Mirabello Bay. It seems less Cretan in character than any of the other island towns, partly because of its resort-style flair and largely modern architecture. However, there's also a very strong local character to Agios Nikolaos that makes it a charming and friendly place to visit and hang out at.

Agios Nikolaos

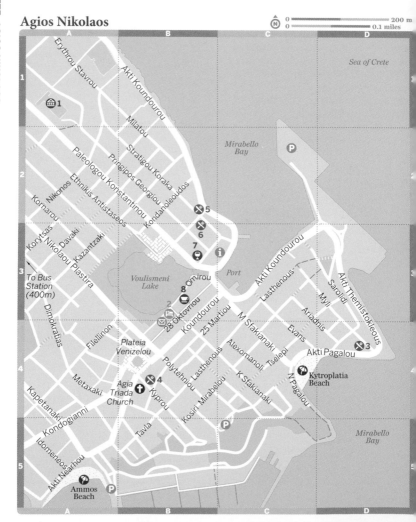

The town's harbour is linked by a narrow channel to the circular Voulismeni Lake. The main harbour-front road crosses the channel by a bridge and the pedestrianised lakeside is lined with cafes and restaurants. By day there's a cheerful buzz around the harbour and by night a decidedly chic ambience descends on the cafes and bars, where stylish young Greeks strut the harbour-side catwalk and holidaymakers pour into town from the neighbouring resorts.

Sights

ARCHAEOLOGICAL MUSEUM Museum
(☏ 28410 24943; Paleologou Konstantinou 74; admission €4; ☉8.30am-3pm Tue-Sun; 🛜)
Crete's most significant Minoan collection (after the Iraklio Archaeological Museum) includes clay coffins, ceramic musical instruments and gold from Mohlos as well as many other treasures from ancient times.

Activities

Within town, **Ammos Beach** and **Kytroplatia Beach** are small and crowded, though convenient for a quick dip. **Almyros Beach** (1km south) is also busy but much longer, with better sand. It can be accessed by taxi (€6) or foot along a coastal path.

Agios Nikolaos

Further south towards Sitia, **Golden Beach** (Voulisma Beach) and **Istron Bay** boast long stretches of sand.

Sleeping

VILLA OLGA Apartments €€
(☏ 28410 25913; www.villa-olga.gr; apt €80-95; ❄🛜🏊) These delightful self-catering apartments which sleep anywhere from two to six people are midway between Agios Nikolaos and Elounda. They have terrific jaw-dropping views across the Gulf of Mirabello from their rising terraces surrounded by lovely gardens. Units are well equipped and have traditional furniture and scattered artefacts. The attached bathrooms are modern and clean. There's a small swimming pool and Olga, the owner, is charming and helpful.

**MINOS BEACH
ART HOTEL** Boutique Hotel €€€
(☏ 28410 22345; www.bluegr.com; r incl breakfast from €200; P❄🛜🏊) This extremely classy resort is located in a superb location just out of town. It is a veritable art gallery, with sculptures from leading Greek and foreign artists adorning the grounds right down to the beach. The low-rise design and cool style maintain the hotel's position as one of the island's finest. Expect rooms with swish decor. There's also an on-site spa and whole host of dining outlets.

DU LAC HOTEL Hotel €€
(☏ 28410 22711; www.dulachotel.gr; 28 Oktovriou 17; s/d/studio €40/60/80; ❄) This central hotel has fine views over Voulismeni Lake from its decent rooms and spacious, fully-fitted-out studios. Both have stylish contemporary furnishings and nice bathrooms.

Eating

CHRYSOFILLIS Mezedhes €
(☏ 28410 22705; Akti Pagalou; mezedhes €4-8)
Well-priced food make this *mezedhopoleio* a classic small-plate place, with several varieties of ouzo as well as Greek wines to enhance the mood. Specials include cheese pies, fresh mussels and saffron chicken. Reserve.

PELAGOS
Seafood €€

(☎28410 25737; Stratigou Koraka 11; mains €9-28) Top-rated Pelagos is housed in a restored neoclassical building with a garden terrace and is especially noted for its fish and seafood. The menu also features meat and pasta dishes with Cretan flair. Reserve.

ITANOS
Cretan €

(Kyprou 1; mains €5-10) Report to this friendly local restaurant for terrific Cretan home-style cooking with a selection of several trays of fresh *mayirefta* (casseroles and oven-baked dishes) daily. Psst: owner Yiannis also makes his own pastry for delicious leek pies. Vegetarian? Don't fear. You'll have plenty of options to choose from.

MARE & MONTE
Mediterranean €€

(☎28410 83373; Akti Koundourou; www. maremonte-restaurant.com; mains €9-22) There's a subtle Italian influence on Cretan cuisine at this stylish seafront restaurant. A range of Greek, Italian and fish appetisers leads on to fine dishes such as grilled chicken with feta, olives and fennel or sea bass with lemon-and-thyme sauce.

 **Drinking**

ALEXANDROS ROOF GARDEN
Cocktail Bar

(cnr Kondylaki & Paleologou Konstantinou; ⏱noon-late) Enjoy classic musical sounds amidst hanging plants, shrubs and really funky decor.

PERIPOU CAFE
Cafe

(28 Otkovriou 13; @ ☎) This charming period piece has the added bonus of incorporating a bookstore and book exchange. The most coveted tables are on the narrow balcony overlooking the lake.

 Information

Municipal Tourist Office (☎28410 22357; www.agiosnikolaos.gr; ⏱8am-9.30pm Apr-Nov)

Left: Fortress on Spinalonga Island; **Below:** Sitia

(LEFT) ROLF RICHARDSON/ALAMY ©; (BELOW) NEIL SETCHFIELD/LONELY PLANET IMAGES ©

Opposite the north side of the bridge. Staff here can change money and assist with accommodation.

ℹ Getting There & Away

The bus station is at Plateia Venizelou just under km northwest of Voulismeni Lake.

ℹ Getting Around

Manolis Dikeo (☎28410 24940; 25 Martiou 12) as a huge range of scooters, motorcycles and quad bikes. Prices begin at €20 a day for a scooter nd €12 for a mountain bike.

Spinalonga Island
Νήσος Σπιναλόγκας

Spinalonga Island lies in a pretty setting off the northern tip of the Kolokytha Peninsula. Its massive **fortress** (admission €3; ⊙10am-6pm) was built in 1579 to protect Elounda Bay and the Gulf of Mirabello. With the explosion of interest n Spinalonga in the wake of the Virginia Hislop's bestselling novel *To Nisi* and the

Greek TV series spin-off, you're unlikely to feel lonely on the island. In fact, there is even a reconstructed section of a street from the period featured in the novel.

Ferries to Spinalonga depart half-hourly from Elounda (€10) and Plaka (€5), giving you an hour to see the sights (though you can stay longer and return on a different boat). From Agios Nikolaos, various companies run basic tours and day-trip excursions (from €20).

Sitia ΣΗΤΕΙΑ
POP 9257

Sitia (si-*tee*-ah) is an attractive seaside town with a big open harbour backed by a wide promenade lined with tavernas and cafes. It's a friendly place where tourism is fairly low key and where agriculture and commerce are the mainstays. A sandy beach skirts a wide bay to the east

Bus Services from Sitia

DESTINATION	DURATION	FARE	FREQUENCY
Agios Nikolaos	1½hr	€7.60	7 daily
Iraklio	3hr	€14.70	7 daily
Vaï	30min	€3.60	4 daily

of town. Sitia attracts French and Greek tourists, but even at the height of the high season the town retains its relaxed atmosphere.

Sitia is a good transit point for ferries to the Dodecanese islands. Plateia Iroon Polytehniou is Sitia's main square. It's recognisable by its palm trees and statue of a dying soldier.

 ## Sights

ARCHAEOLOGICAL MUSEUM
Museum

(☏28430 23917; Piskokefalou; admission €2; ⏱8.30am-3pm Tue-Sun) This showcase of archaeological finds from the area has objects spanning the arc from neolithic to Roman times, with an emphasis on Minoan civilisation. One of the key items is the Palekastro Kouros – a figure painstakingly pieced together from fragments made of hippopotamus tusks and adorned with gold. Finds from the palace at Zakros include a wine press, a bronze saw and cult objects scorched by the conflagration that destroyed the palace. Among the most valuable objects are the Linear A tablets, which reflect the palace's administrative function.

FREE VENETIAN FORT
Fort

(⏱8.30am-3pm) This towering structure, locally called *kazarma* (from the Venetian 'casa di arma'), was a garrison under the Venetians. These are the only remains of the fortifications that once protected the town. The site is now used as an open-air venue.

 ## Sleeping

HOTEL ARHONTIKO
Guesthouse €

(☏28430 28172; Kondylaki 16; s/d/studio €27/32/34; ❄) A quiet location uphill from the port enhances the charm of this guesthouse, situated in a neoclassical building. There's great period style and everything, from the entrance hall to the shared bathrooms, is spotlessly maintained.

SITIA BAY HOTEL
Apartments €€

(☏28430 24800 www.sitiabay.com; Paraliaki Leoforos 8; apt/ste from €115; P ❄ 🛜 🏊) This modern hotel delivers personal and friendly service of the highest order. Most of the comfortable and tasteful one- and two-room apartments have sea views and there's a pool, a hydrospa, a mini-gym and a sauna. Breakfast is €6.

 ## Eating

BALCONY
Fusion €€

(☏28430 25084; www.balcony-restaurant.com; Foundalidou 19; mains €12-19) Sitia's culinary pinnacle occupies the first floor of this neoclassical building, where owner-chef Tonya Karandinou infuses Cretan cuisine with Mexican and Asian influences (think grilled squid with a pistachio- and basil-based sauce). Fine Greek wines complement it all.

SERGIANI
Greek €

(Karamanli 38; mains €6.50-8.50) On the quiet southern end of the waterfront, this traditional place uses well-sourced local

Bus Services from Agios Nikolaos

DESTINATION	DURATION	FARE	FREQUENCY
Iraklio	1½hr	€7.10	half-hourly
Sitia	1½hr	€7.60	7 daily

ngredients and wood-burning cooking methods. The local fish is very good.

DINODEION   Greek €

(El Venizelou 157; mains €5-8) Kitted out with old-fashioned decor, this local place sits quietly alongside more glitzy cafes on the main waterfront. There's a good range of mezedhes, such as snails in vinegar sauce, and meat and fish standards.

 Information

ourist office (28430 28300; Karamanli; 9.30am-2.30pm & 5-8.30pm Mon-Fri, 9.30am-.30pm Sat) On the promenade.

 Getting There & Away

Air

Sitia's airport has an expanded international-size runway but at the time of writing there were still no international flights

Boat

Ferries dock 500m north of Plateia Agnostou and serve Karpathos, Kassos, Milos and Piraeus.

Bus

The bus station is at the eastern end of Karamanli, behind the bay. The buses to Vaï and Kato Zakros only run from May to October.

Rhodes & the Dodecanese

When the Greek gods were doling out sandy coves, blankets of wildflowers and lofty views, the Dodecanese seem to have received more than their fair share. Add to this a rich culture heavily influenced by Italian rule, azure waters lapping at their shores, and a wealth of natural and historical sites, and it's not surprising that the Dodecanese beckon to so many.

Strung out along the coast of western Turkey and far from the country's capital, Athens, the Dodecanese maintain a certain air of separateness. In this region, Christianity took root in Greece and the influences of consecutive invasions led by the Egyptians, Crusaders, Ottoman Turks and Italians are still seen in the islands' interesting architecture and regional cuisine. If you are a hiker, botanist, beachcomber, kitesurfer, archaeologist, historian or just someone longing for a lounge in the sun on a quiet beach, the Dodecanese won't disappoint.

Main beach on Rhodes (p295)
HOLGER LEUE/LONELY PLANET IMAGES ©

Donkeys on Lindos (p300)
IML IMAGE GROUP LTD/ALAMY©

Rhodes & the Dodecanese

0 — 40 km
0 — 20 miles

Özdere
Pamucak
Selçuk
Ephesus
AYDIN
Kuşadası
Samos
Vathy
Söke
Bayarasî
Dilek
Peninsula
Doyanbey

Agios
Georgios
Agathonisi
Arki
Arki
Marathi
Lipsi
Lipsi Village
Farmakonisi
Mandalya
Gulf
TURKEY

7 2
Patmos
Skala

AEGEAN
SEA

Leros
Agia Marina
Lakki
Kalymnos
Telendos
Pserimos
Bodrum
Kerme Gulf
Pothia
Pserimos
Mastihari
Zia
Kos Town
Marmaris
Kos
3 Kardamena
Kefalos
Datça
Mesa Vathy
Mandraki
5
Nisyros
Gialos
Symi 6
To Kastellorizo
(Megisti) (130km)
(See inset below)

0 — 16 km
0 — 10 miles

Skala
Astypalea

To Kalymnos
(72km)

o Piraeus
78km)
Astypalea
Tilos
Livadia
Rhodes Town
Rhodes
Old Town 1

Alimia
Skala Kamirou
Rhodes
Emborios
Halki
Laerma
Monolithos
Lindos
KARPATHIAN
SEA
4

Astypalea (72km)
e inset below);
eus (250km)

1 Rhodes Old Town
2 Spiritual Patmos
3 Beach-Bumming on Kos
4 Charming Lindos
5 Steaming Nisyros
6 Colourful Gialos
7 Patmos' Hora

Kattavia
Cape Prasonísi

Saria
Diafani
Olympos
Karpathos

Kastellorizo (Megisti)
TURKEY
Kaş

To Rhodes
(130km)
Kastellorizo
Village
Kastellorizo
(Megisti)

0 — 16 km
0 — 10 miles

Pigadia
Ammoöpi
Fry
Kasos

MEDITERRANEAN SEA

Rhodes & the Dodecanese's Highlights

1
Rhodes Old Town

Wandering the winding alleyways of Rhodes' medieval Old Town, you feel you have found your way into one of history's secret places. At dusk the light reflects beautifully off the stone architecture and you feel the centuries drop away around you. Above: Palace of the Grand Masters; Top Right: Museum of the Decorative Arts; Bottom Right: Old Town

Need to Know

NEIGHBOURHOOD? The Knights' Quarter REFUELING Traditional fare in Nireas BEST TIME OF DAY Dusk light creates honey-coloured buildings For more see p293

Rhodes Old Town Don't Miss List

BY VASILEIOS PERIKLIS SIRIMIS,
PROFESSIONAL BYZANTINE ICON PAINTER

1 EXPLORING THE OLD TOWN

Enclosed within impressive stone walls, a wander through the Old Town will awe you. Alleyways twist and turn, leading deeper into the labyrinth. Medieval mansions stand next to Byzantine chapels that lead on to Turkish baths and turreted palaces. Stone buttresses arch overhead as narrow passageways open on to leafy squares. The museums in the Old Town are also excellent.

2 PALACE OF THE GRAND MASTERS

This magnificent, lofty 14th-century fortress (p293) is as lavish on the inside as it is mighty on the outside. Of the 158 rooms, two dozen are open to explore. Be sure to take in the stunning Byzantine museum inside, with its high-quality icons, wall paintings and sculptures from churches throughout the Dodecanese.

3 ST MARY'S CHURCH

Located near St Mary's Gate, visit this tiny **church (Avenue of the Knights, Rhodes Old Town)** near mass time to see a steady stream of devout Orthodox Catholics, plumes of incense and exquisite decor. You'll come across countless chapels and churches in the Old Town; if the door is open, take a look inside. You are sure to be impressed.

4 STROLLING THE WALL & MOAT

From the Palace of the Grand Masters, wander along the top of the 12m-thick stone wall (p294), built to defend this ancient medieval city. Take in views before you that have been shared for centuries. Running along the outside of the Old Town, the lush Moat Walkway (p294) is a wide pedestrian path leading through trees and fields, offering a quiet escape with fantastic views of the imposing wall.

5 MUSEUM OF THE DECORATIVE ARTS

Those who enjoy art will relish in this overflowing museum (p293), with its simple exhibits displaying tiles, pottery, embroidered clothing, carving and musical instruments from the region. Housed in a square near St Paul's Gate, the ground outside the museum is covered in stunning *hohlakia* (black-and-white pebble mosaic).

Spiritual Patmos

There's something unique about Patmos. As St John's home-in-exile, it has been drawing religious pilgrims for centuries. But it's not just about the spiritual. Perhaps it's the light across the island at dusk, or the feeling of remoteness along the coast. Maybe it's the enchanting old town or the monks that dart between elaborate monasteries. Whatever it is, it's magnetic. Below: Skala (p315)

Need to Know

ETIQUETTE Cover shoulders and legs at holy sites **PHOTOGRAPHY** None inside churches or monasteries **BEST TIME TO VISIT** Easter so book ahead **For more see p314**

2

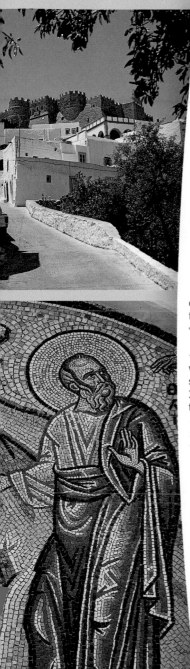

Patmos Don't Miss List

BY ARCHMANDRITE ANTIPAS, ABBOT OF PATMOS

1 CAVE OF THE APOCALYPSE

The most important spiritual site in Patmos is the sacred Cave of the Apocalypse (p314), which is the most holy place in Europe and the world's second Jerusalem. This is where John wrote the sacred Book of Revelation. Look for fissures on the ceiling which are believed to be where God's voice issued from.

2 MONASTERY OF ST JOHN THE THEOLOGIAN

Set like a fortress on the hill, this monastery (p318; pictured top and bottom left) was established in 1088 and is at its most impressive during a service. The power and beauty of the singing is incredibly moving. Members of the congregation listen in the courtyard, taking turns to enter the ornate and intimate church for a short while.

3 HOLY MONASTERY OF ZOODOHOS PIGI

Founded in the early 1600s, this convent (p318) is very atmospheric. Inside, flickering candles illuminate stunning frescoes. The convent is home to approximately 15 nuns and is especially worth visiting on Good Friday for the late-night candle-lit mass. At midnight, the candles are extinguished and the chapel is plunged into darkness, signifying Christ's crucifixion.

4 HERMITAGE HOLY SANCTUARY TEMPLE OF ST NEKTARIOS, LOUKAKIA

In pretty Sapsila Bay on the east coast of Patmos, this small **chapel** (Sapsila, southeastern Patmos) looks out at the tiny island of Pilafi. This chapel is built to commemorate the hermits that lived in the caves on Pilafi in the 1600s and who worshiped in its churches, of which there remain foundations. It is believed that when visiting the chapel, one can hear the voice of a hermit chanting.

5 HERMITAGE HOLY SANCTUARY TEMPLE OF VIRGIN MARIA, KOUMANA

At the northern tip of Skala's harbour, at the top of Mt Koumana, lies this **sanctuary** (Koumana, Skala) founded in the 1700s. For years, the church's dome was surrounded by a wall to protect it from the northern winds, pirates and invaders. The wall was recently removed to reveal amazing, well-preserved frescoes.

Beach Bumming on Kos

On the calm southern side of Kos rests the vast Kefalos Bay (p316), home to 12km of incredible, wide, sandy beaches. Nestled between green hills and warm turquoise water, these seven idyllic beaches offer everything from water sports and parties to tranquil patches of paradise.

3

④ Charming Lindos

With an old-world charm that draws the crowds, Lindos (p300) is a dazzling wh village. Its warren of narrow lanes are pedestrianised and lined with impressive 17th-century houses, tiny shops and cafes. Perched on a clifftop betwe the town and the sea, the spectacular Acropolis is the cherry on the cake. It looks down over the town's small, san bays.

IMAGESTATE MEDIA PARTNERS LIMITED - IMPACT PHOTOS/ALAMY ©

Steaming Nisyros

Early in the morning, you may find yourself standing alone in the centre of Nisyros' volcano (p309), surrounded only by the hissing, bubbling and steaming of the fumaroles, and the red, green and orange rocks scattered on the craters' edges. Hike between the five craters in this otherwordly landscape before heading back over the top of the caldera and down the phenomenally fertile slopes to the sea.

Colourful Gialos

ymi's harbourside town of Gialos (p303) idyllic. Colourful buildings, bobbing shing boats, wharfside cafes and plenty f fresh seafood sum up island life at its est. Wander through the backstreets en clamber up the hill to the old town r even more atmosphere and phenom- al views.

Patmos' Hora

Patmos' hilltop Hora (p318) is a delight. Wander along cobblestone alleyways between ancient buildings where life continues unabated. Visit the incense-infused monasteries with their glittering gold icons and impressive frescoes. Sample traditional home cooking, rub shoulders with artists and monks, and then follow the age-old Byzantine stone path back to the seaside.

ZACH HOLMES/ALAMY ©

Rhodes & the Dodecanese's Best…

Beaches

○ **St Paul's Bay** (p301) Warm, turquoise water in a sheltered bay.

○ **Kritika Beach** (p311) Long, sandy, easily accessible and polka-dotted with umbrellas.

○ **Exotic Beach** (p316) An undeveloped quiet stretch of sand.

○ **Kambos Beach** (p319) Swim, kayak or relax in a quiet bay.

○ **Psili Ammos Beach** (p319) Sandy, shaded, idyllic and remote.

Atmospheric Hotels

○ **Melenos** (p301) Pure luxury in a 17th century–style captain's house.

○ **Hotel Anastasia** (p296) Budget beds in an Italian mansion.

○ **Kalderimi Apartments** (p317) Secluded, traditional retreat with swish extras.

○ **Kos Aktis Hotel** (p312) Swish rooms on the edge of the sea.

Inspiring Architecture

○ **Captains' houses** (p301, p305) Impressive stone structures from the 17th-century.

○ **Kahal Shalom Synagogue** (p294) Greece' oldest synagogue.

○ **Palace of the Grand Masters** (p293) Huge and magnificent.

○ **Asklipieion** (p314) Ruins of a legendary religious sanctuary.

Cultural Experiences

Cafe Chantant (p299)
ive, traditional folk music.

Hammam Turkish Baths
(294) Baths in an Ottoman
lic.

Kalithea Thermi (p298)
atch *hohlakia* floors being
eated in this restored
alian spa.

Castle of the Knights
309) Site of Hippocrates'
er formances in an amazing
etting.

**Holy Monastery of
podohos Pigi** (p318)
andle-lit Mass on Good
iday.

Mosaic floor in the Palace of Grand Masters
(p293); **Above:** St Paul's Bay (p301)
(LEFT) HOLGER LEUE/LONELY PLANET IMAGES ©;
(ABOVE) JAN WLODARCZYK/ALAMY ©

Need to Know

ADVANCE PLANNING

o **Two months before** Book your accommodation.

o **One month before** Check online for upcoming events (especially in Rhodes Town) and buy tickets. Double-check ferry schedules.

RESOURCES

o **Rhodes Guide** (www.rhodesguide.com) What's on, where to stay and where to hang out in Rhodes.

o **Municipality of Rhodes** (www.rodos.gr) Upcoming events, links and background to Rhodes.

o **Dodecanese Tourism** (www.ando.gr/eot) Official Dodecanese tourist info with ferry schedules, opening hours and events.

o **Dodecanese Accommodation** (www.blueislands.gr) Family-friendly accommodation listings.

o **Nisyros Tourism** (www.nisyros.gr) Sights, history and environment of Nisyros.

o **Kos Tourism** (www.travel-to-kos.com) A guide to Kos.

o **Patmos Island** (www.patmos-island.com) Local info and listings for Patmos.

o **Patmos Tourism Guide** (www.patmosweb.gr) Listings and images of Patmos.

GETTING AROUND

o **Bus** Regular routes on Rhodes and Kos, with less-frequent routes on Nisyros and Patmos.

o **Ferry** Hydrofoils zip between the Dodecanese almost daily in summer, with overnight ferries to Piraeus.

o **Car** The best way to explore the islands is with your own wheels.

o **Bicycle** A popular way to get around the flat terrain on Kos.

BE FOREWARNED

o **Easter** If you're hoping to visit Patmos for Easter, book well in advance.

o **Ferries** Windy weather can affect hydrofoil schedules. Don't schedule ferries and homebound flights too close together.

287

Rhodes & the Dodecanese Itineraries

With good ferry connections, this area is ideal for island hopping. Rhodes packs a huge amount into its varied landscape. If you have more than a week, combine itineraries to experience all that the islands offer.

3 DAYS

RHODES TOWN TO GLYSTRA BEACH

Exploring Rhodes

Overflowing with opportunities to experience the diversity of island life, Rhodes has more than enough to keep you busy for a few days. Base yourself in **(1) Rhodes Town** and spend a day exploring within the walls of the Old Town. Check out the impressive museums, lose yourself in the cobbled alleyways and finish off the evening listening to live, local music in the atmospheric Cafe Chantant. On day two, rent a car and head out along the south coast, stopping at the beautifully restored **(2) Kalithea Thermi** with its amazing *hohlakia* (black-and-white pebble mosaic floors), stopping off for a swim at the nearby, sandy **(3) Stegna Beach**. On your final day, visit **(4) Lindos** and climb to the impressive Acropolis. Wander through the pedestrianised, white-washed village and dine at the famous Captain's House. Finish the day with a sunset view at the stunning, sheltered **(5) St Paul's Bay** on the edge of Lindos.

Top Left: *Hohlakia* at Kalithea Thermi (p298); **Top Right:** Kos Town (p308)

(TOP LEFT) HUBERT STADLER/CORBIS ©;
(TOP RIGHT) INGOLF POMPE 4/ALAMY/LONELY PLANET IMAGES ©

5
DAYS

OS TOWN TO PATMOS

Coastal Culture

egin your adventure on Kos island, basing yourself in **(1) Kos Town**. Spend the day taking
the ancient ruins within the town and at nearby Asklipieion. In the evening, sample one
the city's fantastic restaurants and then wander along the atmospheric harbour to see
e Castle of the Knights in lights. The next day, hop on the bus to the soft, endless sand of
) **Kefalos Bay**. Take a day trip to **(3) Nisyros** to visit the other-worldly landscape of the
lcano, have lunch in Emborios and visit the Volcanological Museum in Nikea. On day tour,
p on a fast ferry to **(4) Patmos**. Walk up the Byzantine footpath from the coastal town
Skala to the atmospheric Hora, visiting the Monastery of the Apocalypse where St John
rote the Book of Revelation. On your last day, hop on a bus for nearby Kambos Beach
ere you can swim, kayak or just soak up the sun.

Discover Rhodes & the Dodecanese

At a Glance

○ **Rhodes** (p290) Medieval Old Town, picturesque village of Lindos, beaches, monasteries and ruins.

○ **Symi** (p303) Picture-perfect harbour, small-village feel and fascinating monastery.

○ **Nisyros** (p309) Volcanic island with bubbling craters.

○ **Kos** (p308) Lively Kos Town; long, sandy beaches; and the striking ruins of Asklipieion.

○ **Patmos** (p314) Where St John wrote the Book of Revelation.

Ladiko Beach (p298)
KATJA KREDER/IMAGE BROKER ©

RHODES POΔOΣ

The largest of the Dodecanese Islands, Rhodes (ro-dos) is abundant in beaches, fertile wooded valleys, vivid culture and ancient history. Whether you seek the buzz of nightlife and beaches, diving in crystal-clear water or a culture-vulture journey through past civilizations, it's all here. The atmospheric Old Town of Rhodes is a maze of cobbled streets spiriting you back to the days of the Byzantine Empire and beyond. Further south is the picture-perfect town of Lindos, a weave-world of sugarcube houses spilling down to a turquoise bay. Family friendly, Rhodes is the perfect base for day trips to neighbouring islands.

ℹ Getting There & Away

AIR

Olympic Air (☎22410 24571; Ierou Lohou 9) has flights across Greece and the Dodecanese while **Aegean Airlines** (☎22410 98345; Diagoras airport) offers flights to Athens, most of Europe and to the U.S.

BOAT

Rhodes is the main port in the Dodecanese and offers a complex timetable of departures to Piraeus, Thessaloniki and many stops in between. **Dodekanisos Seaways** (☎22410 70590; Afstralias 3) runs daily catamarans up and down the Dodecanese. Tickets are available from the kiosk at the dock. The EOT (Greek National Tourist Organisation) in Rhodes Town can provide you with current schedules.

There is a daily catamaran from Rhodes' Commercial Harbour to Marmaris, Turkey (50 minutes), departing at 8am and 4.30pm from June to September. Tickets cost €30 one way plus €11 Turkish port tax. Same-day return

The Colossus of Rhodes

One of the Seven Wonders of the Ancient World, the bronze statue of Helios was apparently so vast that high-masted *triremes* (warships) were able to pass into the harbour through his legs. Built in 292 BC it took 12 years to build, stood 33m high and fell a few decades later when an earthquake struck in 226 BC. For almost a millennium it lay in ruins until it was broken into pieces and sold by invading Arabs to a Syrian Jew in 654 AD, then allegedly transported abroad on the back of 900 camels.

ckets are only €9 more. Book online at rhodes. armarisinfo.com or contact Triton Holidays. For formation on domestic routes, see p295.

❶ Getting Around

O/FROM THE AIRPORT

he Diagoras airport is 16km southwest of Rhodes wn, near Paradisi. Buses depart regularly etween the airport and Rhodes Town's Eastern us Terminal from 6.30am to 11.15pm (€2.20, 5 minutes). On Sunday, buses stop running at ound 11.45am.

CYCLE

range of bicycles is available for hire at **Bicycle** entre (☎22410 28315; Griva 39; per day €5).

OAT

ere are excursion boats to Symi (€25 return) ily in summer, leaving Mandraki Harbour at 9am d returning at 6pm.

US

hodes Town has two island bus terminals located block away from one another. Each services lf of the island. There is regular transport cross the island all week, with fewer services on aturday and only a few on Sunday. You can pick schedules from the kiosks at either terminal from the EOT office. Unlimited travel tickets are ailable for one/two/three days (€10/15/25).

AR & MOTORCYCLE

op around and bargain because the mpetition is fierce. Agencies will usually deliver e car to you. You can also book through Triton olidays.

Rent A Moto Thomas (☎22410 30806) Offers the best prices for scooters.

Drive Rent A Car (☎22410 68243/81011; www. driverentacar.gr; airport)

Etos Car Rental (☎22410 22511; www.etos.gr)

Orion Rent A Car (☎22410 22137)

TAXI

Rhodes Town's main taxi rank is east of Plateia Rimini. There are two zones on the island for taxi meters: Zone One is Rhodes Town and Zone Two (slightly pricier) is everywhere else. Rates are double between midnight and 5am.

Taxis prefer to use set-fare rates which are posted at the rank. Sample fares are as follows: airport €22, Lindos €55. Ring a taxi on ☎22410 6800, 22410 27666 or 22410 64712 in Rhodes Town and on ☎22410 69600 outside the city.

Rhodes Town
POP 56,130

The fortified Old Town bursts at its seams with medieval atmosphere, and losing yourself in its maze of alleyways and crumbling buildings is half the fun. Give your magpie tendencies free rein in the jewellery shops and leather boutiques, between letting your nose follow inviting aromas to hidden restaurants. Like the cocktail of yachties, families on holiday and cruise-ship passengers who come here, the architecture is equally cosmopolitan, with Roman ruins rubbing shoulders with Byzantine mosques and medieval castles.

The New Town, to the north, boasts upscale shops and waterfront bars servicing the package crowd, while in the

Rhodes Old Town

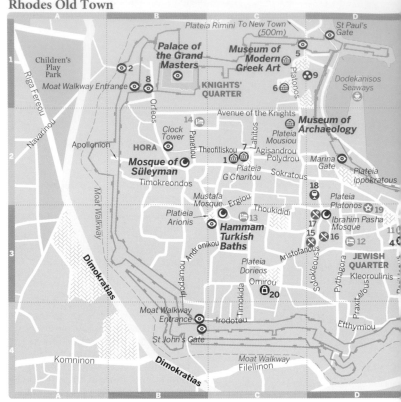

Rhodes Old Town

Inside you'll find maps and carvings. The main exhibition is now at the **New Art Gallery** (Plateia G Charitou) with an impressive collection of painting, engraving and sculpture from some of Greece's most popular 20th-century artists, including Gaitis Giannis, Vasiliou Spiros and Katraki Vaso. For the museum's temporary exhibits, head to the **Centre of Modern Art** (179 Sokratous St). All three galleries keep the same hours and one ticket gains you entrance to all three.

Across the pebbled street from the Museum of Modern Greek Art, take in the remains of the 3rd-century-BC **Temple of Aphrodite**, one of the few ancient ruins in the Old Town.

Continuing down Platonos, the **Museum of the Decorative Arts** (Plateia Argyrokastrou; admission €2; ⊙8.30am-2.40pm Tue-Sun) houses an eclectic array of artefacts from around the Dodecanese. It's chock-a-block with instruments, pottery, carvings, clothing and spinning wheels and gives a colourful view into the past. Captions are sparse; pick up explanatory notes at the door.

In the atmospheric 15th-century knights' hospital down the road is the **Museum of Archaeology** (Plateia Mousiou; admission €3; ⊙8am-4pm Tue-Sun). Its biggest draw is the exquisite *Aphrodite Bathing*, a 1st-century-BC marble statue that was recovered from the local seabed.

Wander up the **Avenue of the Knights** (Ippoton), once home to the knights themselves. To this day the street exudes a noble, forbidding aura. Its lofty buildings stretch in a 600m-long unbroken honey-coloured wall, its flat facade punctuated by huge doorways and arched windows.

On the right is the truly magnificent 14th-century **Palace of the Grand Masters** (Ippoton; admission €6; ⊙8.30am-3pm Tue-Sun), which was severely damaged by the Turkish siege and then destroyed by an explosion in the mid-1800s. The Italians rebuilt the palace following old plans for the exterior but introducing a grandiose, lavish interior. It was intended as a holiday home for

ackstreets are hidden bistros and boho ars worth seeking out. It's also where ou'll find the city's best beach.

The Commercial Harbour (Kolona) lies o the east of the Old Town. Excursion oats, small ferries, hydrofoils and private achts use Mandraki Harbour, further orth.

◉ Sights

hodes Old Town

NIGHTS' QUARTER   Neighbourhood
egin your tour of the Knights' Quarter at **iberty Gate**, crossing the small bridge to the Old Town. In a medieval build- g is the original site of the **Museum of lodern Greek Art** (www.mgamuseum/gr; 2 ateia Symis; 3 sites €3; ⊙8am-2pm Tue-Sat).

Mussolini and King Emmanuel III but is open as a museum. Only 24 of the 158 rooms can be visited; inside you'll find antique furnishing, sculptures, frescoes and mosaic floors.

From the palace, walk through **D'Amboise Gate**, the most atmospheric of the gates, which takes you across the moat. When the palace is open, you can also gain access to the walkway along the top of the wall from here, affording great views into the Old Town and across to the sea. Another option is to follow the peaceful **Moat Walkway**, which you can access next to **St Anthony's Gate**. It's a green oasis with lush lawns cushioned between trees and the old walls.

HORA   Neighbourhood

Bearing traces of its Ottoman past is the Hora. During Turkish times, churches were converted to mosques and many more Muslim houses of worship were built from scratch, although most are now dilapidated. The most important is the colourful, pink-domed **Mosque of Süleyman**, at the top of Sokratous. Built in 1522 to commemorate the Otto-

man victory against the knights, it was renovated in 1808. For a bird's-eye view follow the footpath along the side of the neighbouring (and now defunct) clock tower.

Continuing through the winding pedestrian streets will bring you to the municipal **Hammam Turkish Baths** (Plateia Arionis; admission €5; ⏱10am-5pm Mon-Fri, 8am-5pm Sat). They are open to the public, with separate male and female baths. Warm yourself on the marble stones or opt for a massage. Lockers are available.

JEWISH QUARTER   Neighbourhood

Built in 1577, **Kahal Shalom Synagogue** (Polydorou 5) is Greece's oldest synagogue and the only one surviving on Rhodes. The Jewish quarter once had six synagogues and, in the 1920s, a population of 4000. Have a look in at the **Jewish Synagogue Museum** (☎22410 22364; www. rhodesjewishmuseum.org; Dosiadou; ⏱10am-3pm Sun-Fri, closed winter) in the old women's prayer rooms around the corner. Exhibits include lots of early-20th-century photos, intricately decorated documents and displays about the 1673 Jews deported

Temple of Aphrodite (p293), Rhodes Old Town

FRANK FITZPATRICK/ALAMY

Boat Services From Rhodes

DESTINATION	PORT	DURATION	FARE	FREQUENCY
Kos	Commercial Harbour	3hr	€20	daily
Kos*	Commercial Harbour	2½hr	€30	daily
Nisyros	Commercial Harbour	4½hr	€13	3 weekly
Nisyros*	Commercial Harbour	2¾hr	€28	2 weekly
Patmos	Commercial Harbour	6hr	€32	3 weekly
Patmos*	Commercial Harbour	5hr	€46	5 weekly
Piraeus	Commercial Harbour	13hr	€59	daily
Symi	Mandraki	2hr	€9	daily
Symi*	Commercial Harbour	50min	€16	daily
Thessaloniki	Commercial Harbour	21hr	€65	weekly

*High-speed services

om Rhodes to Auschwitz in 1944. Only
ol survived.

Rhodes New Town

he **Acropolis of Rhodes**, southwest
f the Old Town on Monte Smith, was
ie site of the ancient Hellenistic city of
hodes. The restored 2nd-century-AD
ee-lined **stadium** once staged com-
etitions in preparation for the Olympic
ames. This unenclosed site can be
eached on city bus 5.

The town **beach**, beginning north of
landraki Harbour, stretches around the
land's northernmost point and down
ie west side of the New Town. The best
oots tend to be on the east side, where
iere's usually calmer water and more
and and facilities.

 Sleeping

During the summer, finding an affordable
bed in the Old Town is possible *if* you book
ahead. In winter, most budget places
close. For more atmosphere, definitely
stay in the Old Town.

**MARCO POLO
MANSION**　　　Boutique Hotel €€
(22410 25562; www.marcopolomansion.gr;
Agiou Fanouriou 40-42; d incl breakfast from €90-
180) With its melange of Italian, medieval,
Turkish and Greek influences, Marco Polo
is enchanting. Step through the mint-
green cave of the restaurant to a collection of stained-glass, sumptuous rooms
spiriting you to the 15th century when the
house was owned by an Ottoman official.
The generous hosts have recreated this
period with a wealth of antique furniture,

295

heavy drapes, four-poster beds and ochre rugs. Perfection.

NIKOS & TAKIS
HOTEL
Boutique Hotel €€€

(22410 70773; www.nikostakishotel.com; Panetiou 29; d from €150; P ❄ @ 🛜) From its perch on the hill, this charming boutique number has a gorgeous sun terrace choking in banana plants. Inside it's all Moorish arches, exposed-stone walls and individually decorated rooms. Check out the Moroccan-themed Marokino, with its marble tub, ornately tiled floor and authentic slippers.

HOTEL VIA VIA
Boutique Hotel €€

(22410 77027; www.hotel-via-via.com; Lisipou 2; d €70-80, tr €90; 🕐 year-round; ❄ @) 'Quirky boutique' might describe these beautifully finished cherry and mushroom–coloured rooms with high ceilings, refined bedspreads and tasteful furniture. The roof garden is Moorish with urns, comfy chairs and amazing sea views.

HOTEL CAVA D'ORO
Pension €€

(22410 36980; www.cavadoro.com; Kisthiniou 15; s/d/tr incl breakfast €65/85/120; P ❄ 🛜) This former storage building of the Knights of St John has an 800-year-old pedigree and plenty of appeal with a cool cafe, sunny terrace and very appealing stone-walled rooms with high-beamed ceilings. There's also a private section of the ancient wall that you can walk on if you stay here.

HOTEL SPOT
Pension €€

(22410 34737; www.spot hotelrhodes.gr; Perikleous 21; s/d/tr incl breakfast €50/90/110; ❄ @ 🛜) Atmospheric, upscale guesthouse with exposed-stone walls, refined furnishings and pleasant management. Outside there's a mellow courtyard to read in, a second-hand library and a very inviting breakfast area.

HOTEL ANASTASIA
Pension €

(22410 28007; www.anastasia-hotel.com; 28 Oktovriou 46; s/d/tr €46/54/74; ❄ 🛜) This homely Italian mansion has large

Left: Acropolis of Lindos (p300); **Below:** Avenue of the Knights (p293)

rooms with cool tiled floors, ⌐mon-hued walls, traditional ⌐rnishings and a house-proud ⌐spect throughout. Some rooms enjoy ⌐alconies. There's also an inviting outdoor ⌐ar in the lush garden.

 Eating

IREAS Taverna €
⌐ofokleous 45-47; mains €8-16) Quintes-⌐ntially Greek, bougainvillea-teeming ⌐ireas has lemon walled stone alcoves lit ⌐y candlelight and a sun-dappled terrace ⌐utside. Plenty of seafood on the menu, ⌐icluding calamari with batter that melts ⌐n your tongue. Look out too for the ⌐bster pasta and steamed mussels with ⌐arlic and white wine. Refined dining.

O MEGISTON Taverna €
⌐opokelous; mains €10-15; year-round) Fea-⌐uring alfresco dining facing an imposing ⌐inaret, this magically earthy taverna is ⌐nemorable. Heavy on seafood – the octo-pus is mouth-watering – it also dishes up tasty steak, pasta and pizza.

ROMIOS RESTAURANT Taverna €
(22410 25549; Sofokleous; mains €14) In the arbour of an enormous fig tree in a garden packed with gnarled wood sculptures, Romios occupies a romantic spot. Its menu is classically Rhodian, encompassing zucchini fried rolls, stuffed grilled squid and octopus with orange. The chef's veal is particularly tasty.

TO MELTEMI Taverna €
(Cnr Plateia Koundourioti & Rodou; mains €10-15) North of Mandraki Harbour, Meltemi's widescreen sea views are worth the walk alone. This bustling taverna with walls peppered in nautical miscellany is a real find for its trad cuisine ranging from homemade *moussaka* to grilled veal steak, and shrimp *saganaki* (stuffed with tomato and feta cheese) to octopus. The calamari portions could be a little bigger.

297

HUBERT STADLER/CORB

Don't Miss Kalithea Thermi

Restored to its former glory, **Kalithea Thermi** was originally an Italian-built spa, 9km from Rhodes Town. With grand buildings, colonnades, and countless archways delivering stunnin sea views, it's worth a wander. Exhibitions inside show the many films made here (including scenes from *Zorba the Greek* and *Escape to Athena* with Roger Moore). You'll also find a cafe and a small sandy beach good for swimming. The yet-to-be-completed, vast expanses of *hohlakia* (black-and-white pebble mosaic floors) have taken 14 years of work so far.

    Ladiko Beach, touted locally as 'Anthony Quinn Beach', is in fact two back-to-back coves with a pebbly beach on the north side and volcanic rock platforms on the south. The swimming is good, though the water is noticeably colder.

THINGS YOU NEED TO KNOW

☎22410 65691; Kallithea; www.kallitheasprings.gr; admission €2.50; ☺8am-8pm April-Oct, 8am-5pm Nov-Mar

---

KOYKOS   Greek €

(Mandilana 20-26; mains €3-8) Piping bouzouki music through its cavernous nooks and stone and wood interior, this locals' favourite makes for a perfect ret-sina pit stop accompanied by one of their celebrated homemade pies. There's also a range of sandwiches, tasty salads and seafood dishes plus a bakery that makes some heavenly take-away sweets.

Drinking & Entertainment

Take your pick between urban chic, chillsome bars and shadowy nautical dens that look as if they've been spewed up from the days of the pirates. The Old Town heaves with choices. The majority of nightlife happens around Platonos and Ippokratous squares.

AFE CHANTANT — Live Music

imokratou 3; ☺midnight-early) Locals sit at
ng wooden tables here, listening to live
aditional music while drinking ouzo or
eer. It's dark inside and you won't find
nacks or nibbles, but the atmosphere
palpable and the band is lively. It's an
xperience you won't soon forget.

PENADI Bar

vripidou 13-15) Step into a Moorish
mbience of colourful lounging cushions
trewn beneath exquisite chandeliers.
nd let's not forget the funky music,
nezedhes, cocktails and friendly service.
very Tuesday and Wednesday night
nere's live bouzouki music between
)pm and 2am.

ETHEXI CAFE Bar

8 Oktovriou, cnr Griva) This jazz-infused,
etro cafe has an eclectic interior of
earn catchers, antique furniture
nd vintage typewriters – it feels like
omeone's front room, but for the light
treaming through the bar's wide range of
hiskies. There's a lively sun terrace out
ont which has partial shade. It attracts a
iendly, young crowd.

HRISTO'S GARDEN Bar

rlva; ☺10pm-late) From the moment you
ep into the shadowy cool of its grotto-
ke bar and out into its whitewashed,
ebble mosaic courtyard abloom with
owers, a visit to Christo's is a flight into
anquillity. Come dark the fairy lights
vinkle. Perfect for a romantic drink.

ASA LA FEMME Bar €

nr 25 Martiou & Amerikis, ☺1pm-8am) This
uper slick lounge bar magnetizes Rhodl-
n fashionistas to its stylish flame of
hite walls, alfresco terrace, wood floors
nd occasional live sets from celebrated
zz musicians. Get your glad rags on – de
gueur white.

🔒 Shopping

YZANTINE ICONOGRAPHY Craft

♪22410 74127; Kisthiniou 42) With a year's
aiting list, it's easy to see why these

exquisite icons generate so much excite-
ment around the globe. Visit artisan
Basilios Per Sirimis in his cramped studio,
the walls shimmering with gold and the
air thick with resin and paint. Paintings go
for €210 to €2000.

ANTIQUE GALLERY Craft

(Omirou 45) This hole-in-the-wall down
a narrow street is an Aladdin's cave of
Byzantine-style mosaic glass lanterns.
Best visited by night for full visual impact,
the shop glows like an Arabian dream.

🛈 Information

Internet Resources

www.rhodesguide.com What's on, where to
stay and where to hang out in Rhodes.

www.rodos.gr Upcoming events, links and
background for Rhodes.

Travel Agencies

Skevos' Travel Agency (♪22410 22461; skeos@
rho.forthnet.gr; 111 Amerikis) Books flights and
boat tickets throughout Greece.

Triton Holidays (♪22410 21690; www.
tritondmc.gr; Plastira 9, Mandraki) Helpful
staff book air and sea travel, hire cars, book
accommodation and plan tours throughout the
Dodecanese. They also sell tickets to Turkey.

🛈 Getting Around

Local buses leave from the urban bus stop on
Mandraki Harbour and charge a flat €1. Bus
11 does a circuit around the coast, up past the
aquarium and on to the Acropolis. Hopping on for
a loop is a good way to get your bearings.

Eastern Rhodes

The majority of Rhodes' sandy beaches
are along its east coast, which is home to
its summer resorts filled with package-
holidaymakers and endless strips of
tourist bars.

The beaches of **Kolymbia** and
Tsambika are sandy but get crowded in
summer. Further up the road is a turn-off
to sandy, idyllic **Stegna Beach.**

Lindos Λίνδοσ

POP 1090

Ancient Lindos, with its sugarcube houses tumbling into the turquoise sea, is a revelation. Founded by the Dorians around 2000 BC – thanks to its excellent harbour and vantage point – it's overlaid with a conglomeration of Byzantine, Frankish and Turkish remains. Above the warren of narrow streets threaded with jewellery and clothing stalls, Greek busts and evil eyes, towers the magnificent Acropolis, flanked by silvery pine trees. Not surprisingly, Lindos is popular with tourists, but beyond the beaches are rocky recesses to bathe in, and take a step away from the pedestriansed thoroughfares and you soon find yourself in whitewashed tranquillity.

Look out for the 17th-century naval captains' houses with their carved relief facades, intricately painted wooden ceilings and raised beds.

Sights & Activities

ACROPOLIS OF LINDOS

Ancient Site

(admission €6; ⊙8.30am-2.40pm Tue-Sun Sep-May, until 6pm Tue-Sun Jun-Aug) An alluring mix of Byzantine architecture on the outside and insulating 2nd-century-BC Doric architecture on the inside, this beautifully preserved Acropolis is well worth the climb up the 116m-high rock it's perched on. The Acropolis is particularly atmospheric thanks to its partial reconstruction allowing you a glimpse of its former greatness. Look out for the 20-columned **Hellenistic stoa** (200 BC) and the Byzantine **Church of Agios Ioannis**, with its ancient frescoes, to the right of this. The wide stairway behind the stoa leads to a 5th-century-BC propylaeum, beyond which is the 4th-century **Temple to Athena**, the site's most important ancient ruin. Athena was worshipped at Lindos as early as the 10th century BC; this temple has replaced earlier ones on the site.

Donkey rides to the Acropolis cost €5 one way, but to get here on your own steam, head straight into the village from the main square, turn left at the church and follow the signs. The last stretch is a strenuous 10-minute climb. There's no shade at the top so pack a hat and some water.

BEACHES

Main Beach, to the east of the Acropolis, is sandy with shallow water, making it a perfect swimming spot for kids. You can follow a path north to the western tip of the bay to the smaller taverna-fringed **Pallas Beach**, beyond which are some rocks you can bathe on if it gets too crowded. Avoid swimming near the jetty as it's home to black stinging

St Paul's Bay

nemones. A ten-minute walk from town, on the western side of the Acropolis, is the sheltered **St Paul's Bay**. It's quiet and the turquoise water will make your heart ache.

 ## Sleeping

Accommodation in Lindos is expensive and usually reserved so be sure to call ahead.

MELENOS　　　　Boutique Hotel €€€
✆ 22440 32222; www.melenoslindos.com; te incl breakfast €310-400; ❉ @ 📶) As if drawn from the pages of *Hip Hotels*, his stunning boutique hotel reminds of an Arabian Dream, with its Moorish accented interior, hanging forest of glass bauble lights and lantern-strung restaurant. Overlooking the bay, with unbroken views of the Acropolis above, by night it's enchanting. Treat yourself to a menu of fresh garden salads and tenderloin steaks, before retiring to your suite with its traditional raised-platform bed and heavy Ottoman influences. It took 15 years to complete; once you've sampled Melenos' treasures, you'll see why.

ANASTASIA STUDIO　　Apartments €
✆ 22440 31751; www.lindos-studios.gr; d/ r €55/60; P ❉) On the eastern side of town, these six split-level apartments based around a geranium-filled courtyard are family-oriented with private verandas and plenty of space in the studios themselves. Each has a well-equipped kitchen and separate bedroom; there's a minimarket across the road.

 ## Eating & Drinking

CAPTAIN'S HOUSE　　Cafe, Bar €
(snacks €3-6) Descend to the left from the Acropolis and your tired feet will bring you to this 16th-century sea captain's residence. Its crest relief facade is flanked by a cosy bar piping soft music into the wood-and-stone interior. It sells snacks, juice, coffee, ice cream and smoothies.

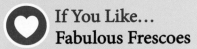

If You Like...
Fabulous Frescoes

If you were spellbound by the intricacy of the Byzantine frescoes in Rhode Town's **Palace of the Grand Masters** (p293), it's worth renting a car to seek out Byzantine art at these other locations:

1　CHURCH OF AGIA PANAGIA
It's impossible not to be awed by the abundance of vibrant frescoes covering the walls of the 14th-century **Church of Agia Panagia** (Plateia Elftherias, Lindos). Look up at the vaulted ceiling and dome for work by the famous Gregorious of Symi, completed in 1779.

2　CHURCH OF KIMISIS THEOTOKOU
The tiny 11th-century **Church of Kimisis Theotokou** (main square, Asklipleio Village) is Rhodes' oldest Christian church that's still in use. Inside are extraordinary 15th-century Byzantine frescoes in great condition.

3　MONI THARRI
Set in the hilly, green countryside outside Lardoes, the peaceful, atmospheric 9th-century **Moni Tharri** (entrance by donation; Lardos) was Rhodes' first monastery. The monks welcome you into the church to appreciate the well-preserved 13th-century frescoes that cover every square of the chapel's interior.

4　MONI TSAMBIKAS
Follow 300 steps up to **Moni Tsambikas** (eastern Rhodes), a place of pilgrimage for women hoping to conceive. This tiny 10th-century chapel has stunning frescoes and a magnificent 360-degree view of the island's green interior to out across the brilliantly blue Mediterranean.

KALYPSO　　　　　Taverna €
(mains €10-12) Admire the sea captain's facade as you tuck into sea bream, swordfish and calamaris that would even bring a smile to Poseidon. Plenty of children's options and vegie dishes too. Take the second right off the main drag to find it.

MARE MARE   Cafe, Bar **€**

(mains €9) The only chic option on Pallas Bay, the decor is white and the tunes chillsome. Best enjoyed late afternoon over a cool Mythos and plate of calamari. Most of the menu is seafood based.

. . . .

ⓘ Getting Around

The village is totally pedestrianised. All vehicular traffic terminates on the central square of Plateia Eleftherias, from where the main drag, Acropolis, begins. The donkey terminus for rides up to the Acropolis itself is a little way along here.

Western Rhodes & the Interior

Western Rhodes is redolent with the scent of pine, its fertile hillsides green and silver with shimmering forests and lush valleys. More exposed than the east side, it's also windier – a boon for kite- and windsurfers – so the sea tends to be rough and the beaches mostly pebbled. If you're cycling or have a scooter or a car, the east–west roads that cross the interior have great scenery and are worth exploring.

Ancient Ialysos Αρχαία Ιαλυσόσ

The Doric city of **Ialysos** (adult €3; ⏱8.30am-3pm Tue-Sun) was built on Filerimos Hill and has attracted successive invaders throughout the centuries. Over time, it became a hotchpotch of Doric, Byzantine and medieval remains. As you enter, stairs lead to the ancient remains of a 3rd-century-BC temple and the restored 14th-century **Chapel of Agios Georgios** and **Monastery of Our Lady**. All that's left of the temple are the foundations, but the chapel is a peaceful retreat.

Take the path left from the entrance to a 12th-century **chapel** (looking like a bunker) filled with frescoes.

Outside the entrance you'll find a small kiosk, a whole lot of peacocks and a popular tree-lined path with the **Stations of the Cross**. There are also ruins of a **Byzantine church** below the car park. Ialysos is 10km from Rhodes, with buses running every half hour.

Ancient Kamiros

Detour:
Ancient Kamiros To Monolithos Αρχαία Κάμειροσ Προσ Μονόλιθο

About 15km south of ancient Kamiros, before the town of Skala, is a turning for Kritinia. This will lead you to the ruined 16th-century **Kritinia Castle** with awe-inspiring views along the coast and across to Halki. It's a magical setting where you expect to come across Romeo or Rapunzel.

From Skala Kamirou the road winds uphill to **Siana**, a picturesque village below Mt Akramytis (825m), famed for its honey and *souma* – a spirit made from seasonal fruit. The village of Monolithos, 5km beyond Siana, has the spectacularly sited 15th-century **Castle of Monolithos** perched on a sheer 240m-high rock and reached via a dirt track. To enter, climb through the hole in the wall. Continuing along this track, bear right at the fork for **Moni Agiou Georgiou**, or left for the very pleasant shingled **Fourni Beach**.

Ancient Kamiros Αρχαία Κάμειρο

The extensive **ruins** of the Doric city of Kamiros stand on a hillside above the west coast, 34km south of Rhodes Town. The ancient city, known for its figs, oil and wine, reached the height of its powers in the 7th century BC. By the 4th century BC it had been superseded by Rhodes. Most of the city was destroyed by earthquakes in 226 and 142 BC, leaving only a discernable layout. Ruins include a **Doric temple**, with one column still standing, **Hellenistic houses**, a **Temple to Athena** and a 3rd-century **great stoa**. It's best visited in the afternoon when there are few people to break the spell cast on your imagination.

SYMI ΣΥΜΗ
POP 2610

Symi (see-me) summons superlatives more than most, and lays claim to water so clear in places the boats look as if they're floating in mid air; in other's it's so turquoise it looks as if it's been airbrushed. Gialos (the capital and port) must surely have one of the prettiest harbours in the whole of the Dodecanese (thanks to the colonisation of the Italians) with its neoclassical facades, tempting waterfront cafes and tavernas. Above

it rising steeply up the mountainside is the town of Horio, to which it is connected by the Kali Strata, a steep cobbled stairway winding through sea captains' houses and crumbling remains. Venture inland and you'll find a surprisingly green interior with great trekking opportunities, a sprinkling of scattered beaches and an enormous monastery that is one of the few religious sites that warrants its own ferry connection.

ℹ Getting There & Away

There are catamarans, excursion boats and ANES (☏22460 71444; www.anek.gr) run regular boats between Symi and Rhodes (€15). The Symi-based *Symi I* and *Symi II* usually go via Panormitis.

ℹ Getting Around

Several excursion boats do trips from Gialos Harbour to Moni Taxiarhou Mihail Panormiti (€25). Check the boards for the best-value tickets.

Gialos ΓΙΑΛΟΣ
pop 2200

With its colourful neoclassical harbour punctuated by its basilica and clock tower, this stylish little village is much sought after by day trippers and Hollywood A-listers. The turquoise water teems with quicksilver fish and there's a

DISCOVER RHODES & THE DODECANESE

palpable sense of chic here, be it the traditional sea captains' houses (some of which have been revived as atmospheric guesthouses) or the sheer calibre of the restaurants. Given its former history as a sponge-diving island it's no surprise Gialos is dotted with shops hawking sponges, soaps and pumice stones. Wander its charming backstreets by redolent bakeries and decent seafood restaurants and you'll be instantly charmed by the place.

Settled as an antidote to marauding pirates, **Horio** winds itself up the sheer hillside through a warren of crumbling and gloriously restored villas. There's a couple of inviting tavernas at the summit to savour your Herculean climb up the 500 steps. Perched at the top of Horio is the **Knights of St John Kastro**. The *kastro* (castle) incorporates blocks from the ancient acropolis and the **Church of Megali Panagia** is within its walls. You can reach the castle through the maze of Horio's cobbled pedestrian streets or along a road that runs southeast of Gialos.

 Eating

NIKOLAS PATISSERIE   Bakery €
(sweets €1-4) This treasure trove of cakes, pies, cookies and culinary delights in opposition to your waistline is also a great spot for baklava. Don't miss the homemade profiteroles and organic ice cream.

MANOS FISH RESTAURANT   Seafood €
(mains €8-10) Allegedly the best seafood restaurant in the Dodecanese, this cosy haunt has tanks adance with lobsters, as well as anchors and nets festooned from its rafters. This is the place to sample gourmand dishes from stingray to lobster and king prawns to sea-urchin salad. Popular with the glitterati, the owner, Manos, is full of noise and Greek charm.

Moni Taxiarhou Mihail Panormiti Μονή Ταξιάρχου Μιχαήλ Πανορμίτη

A winding sealed road leads south across the island through scented pine forests, before dipping in spectacular zigzag fashion to the large, protected Panormitis Bay. This is the site of Symi's biggest attraction – the large **Moni Taxiarhou Mihail Panormiti** (Monastery of Archangel Michael of Panormitis; admission free; ☉dawn-sunset). The large monastery complex occupies most of the foreshore of the bay.

A monastery was first built here in the 5th or 6th century AD, however the present building dates from the 18th century. The principal church contains an intricately carved wooden iconostasis, frescoes and an icon of St Michael that supposedly appeared miraculously where the

Gialos (p303)

GEORGE TSAFOS/LONELY PLANET IMAGES ©

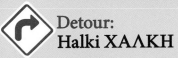

Detour:
Halki ΧΑΛΚΗ

Arriving in Halki (population 310) from the bustle of Rhodes is like stepping into a game of 'freeze frame'. Then, in the neoclassical harbour, you sense movement – an old fisherman shelling prawns under a fig tree, the shadow of an Orthodox priest flitting down a narrow alley... All the limited action of this former sponge-diving island is based around the harbour, with earthy tavernas pecking through mounds of yellow nets to the turquoise sea beyond. Many come to reside in sea captain's houses, adding to the scattering of yachties who are drawn to Halki's pretty harbour. For the most part the island is rocky, but there's some temptingly quiet beaches to escape to. In between sunning yourself, keep your eyes peeled – there are 14 types of butterflies, over 40 kinds of birds, fields of oregano and marjoram, countless bee boxes and around 6000 goats! Visit in spring to see the island blanketed in wildflowers.

Owned by the town hall, **Hiona Art Hotel** (☎ 22460 45208; www.hionaart.gr; d €120) is a former sponge factory that has recently emerged from its cocoon to become an appealing hotel with 20 refined rooms. Each boasts chic furniture and decked private balconies, and there's a palatial marbled lobby and contemporary restaurant. A few yards away on the old loading pier are steps leading into the sea for swimming.

Two local ferries, the *Nissos Halki* and *Nikos Express*, run daily between Halki and Skala Kamirou on Rhodes (€10, 30 minutes).

monastery now stands. St Michael is the patron saint of Symi and protector of sailors. When pilgrims and worshippers ask the saint for a favour, it's tradition to leave an offering; you'll see piles of these, plus prayers in bottles, that have been dropped off boats and found their own way into the harbour.

The large monastery complex comprises a **Byzantine museum** and a **folkloric museum**, a bakery with excellent bread and apple pies and a basic restaurant-cafe to the north side. A taxi here from Gialos costs €45. Dress modestly to enter the monastery. The monastery is a magnet for day trippers, who commonly arrive at around 10.30am on excursion boats; it's a good idea to visit early or after they have left.

NISYROS ΝΙΣΥΡΟΣ
POP 950

Given that most people are pulled into the magnetic flux of nearby Kos, you'll feel as if you have this magical place to yourself – bad for the islanders of Nisyros (*ni*-see-ross), but very nice for you. And what magic – whitewashed streets, pebble-mosaic squares and blankets of wildflowers that cover much of the island. And don't forget the unearthly 'Stefanos' caldera, which gives rise to the island's fertility, drawing botanists and gardeners from around the world to see its unique flora. Legend has it that during the battle between the gods and Titans, Poseidon ripped a chunk off Kos and used it to trap the giant Polivotis in the bowels of the earth. Today's volcano is his angered voice. The beaches here are black and volcanic with a few exceptions, so this is less of a place to come and flop in the sun and more an island for exploring dazzling hilltop villages, hiking a little and sampling the local produce. Keep an eye out for *koukouzina*, a drink produced from grapes and figs.

COLINSPICS/ALAMY

ℹ Information

Diakomihalis (📞22420 31015; diakomihalis@kos.forthnet.gr; Mandraki) Ferry tickets and car hire.

Enetikon Travel (📞 22420 31180; agiosnis@otenet.gr) Run by the excellent Michelle, Enetikon dispenses free advice, sells tickets and owns the small tourist boat that goes to Kos every morning (€12). It also rusn bus trips to the crater (€8, leaves 10.30am). Located 100m from the quay towards Mandraki.

ℹ Getting There & Away

BOAT

Nisyros is linked by regular ferries to Rhodes, Kos and Piraeus. The *Dodekanisos Pride* catamaran has connections to neighbouring Dodecanese islands. The small local ferry *Agios Konstantinos* links Mandraki with Kardamena on Kos (€8, two hours, daily), while the larger *Panagia Spyliani* links Nisyros with Kos Town (€11, daily). Check with the harbour office or Enetikon Travel for up-to-date schedules.

ℹ Getting Around

In summer, bus companies run up to 10 excursion buses daily between 9.30am and 3pm (€8 return)

that give you about 40 minutes at the volcano. In addition, three daily buses travel to Nikea (free) via Pali. The bus stop is located at Mandraki's port. For a cab call Irini on 📞22420 31474. A taxi from Mandraki to the volcano costs €20 return, to Nikea €11 and to Pali €10. For cars, try **Diakomihalis** (📞22420 31015, 6977735229) in town.

Nikea & Emborios
Νίκαια & Εμπορειόσ

Nikea, like some geometrical sugarcube miracle, clings to the rim of the caldera with widescreen views of the depression below. At the edge of town is the **Volcanological Museum** (🕙11am-3pm May-Sep) detailing the history of the volcano and its effects on the island. The steep path down to the volcano begins from Plateia Nikolaou Hartofyli. It takes about 40 minutes to walk it one way.

Emborio, just a few kilometres away is equally pretty with whitewashed streets punctuated by crimson bougainvillea and yawning cats. It too sits on the caldera's edge. **Ampia Taverna** (📞22420 31377; Emborios; mains €3-12), located behind the church, has tasteful burgundy and mustard–coloured walls. Its menu excels with souvalkia, octopus, meatballs and stuffed peppers. Emborios' only gourmet draw, the smells from the kitchen should be bottled; eat upstairs for Olympian drama – with views fit for the gods.

KOS ΚΩΣ

POP 17,890

With a landscape veering from barren rock to hidden green valleys and alpine climbs carpeted in Aleppo pine, Kos (koss) is full of surprises. Aside from its beaches and deserted coves lapped by peacock-blue sea, there are sights for history lovers, including Hippocrates' superbly preserved sanatorium and the Byzantine wonder of Kos Town's centrepiece fortress. The package-tour crowd are stowed in Kardamena, and but for a few pockets of hedonism, the island still feels particularly Greek.

❶ Getting There & Away

AIR

Olympic Air has two daily flights to Athens (€85; 55 minutes) and three weekly to Rhodes (€59, 20 minutes). Buy tickets from Kos Travel (☎ 22420

22359; kostravel@otenet.gr; Akti Koundourioti, Kos Town) on the harbour.

BOAT

INTERNATIONAL In summer, daily excursion boats leave at 8.30am from Kos Town to Bodrum in Turkey (return €20, one hour), and return at 4pm.

DOMESTIC Kos is well connected to Piraeus and all the islands in the Dodecanese, as well as to the Cyclades and Thessaloniki. Services are offered by three ferry companies: Blue Star Ferries (☎ 22420 28914), Anek Lines (☎ 22420 28545) and the ANE Kalymnou (☎ 22420 29900). Catamarans are run by Dodekanisos Seaways at the interisland ferry quay. For tickets, visit helpful Fanos Travel & Shipping (☎ 22420 20035; www.kostravel.gr; 11 Akti Kountourioti, Kos Town) on the harbour.

❶ Getting Around

TO/FROM THE AIRPORT

The airport (☎ 22420 51229) is 24km southwest of Kos Town. An Aegean Airlines bus (€4) ferries passengers from Kos Town, leaving the airline's office two hours before the Athens flights depart. Kefalos-bound buses also stop at the big

Turkish Delights

From many of the Greek islands, Turkey looms large on the horizon. At times it appears so close, it seems you could reach out and touch it. From many islands you can hop on a day trip to get a glimpse into this rich culture next door. Here are a few of the options:

o **Rhodes to Marmaris** This tourist hotspot has a bustling harbour and bazaar, a buzzing nightlife and is the yachty capital of Turkey. Not far away is an unspoilt, azure coastline backed by pine-covered mountains.

o **Samos to Kusadasi** One of Turkey's most popular ports for day trippers, you need to dig beyond the tourist hype; explore the Old Quarter and visit the remarkable nearby site of Ancient Ephesus.

o **Symi to Datca** With small sandy beaches and a pretty harbour, Datca is a family-friendly destination. With no sights, it's a good place to just kick back and absorb Turkish culture.

o **Kos to Bodrum** It may be a big resort town with an influx of tourists, but it's also got lots of charm, stylish restaurants and a gorgeous modern marina. The Museum of Underwater Archaeology is worth a visit.

DISCOVER RHODES & THE DODECANESE KOS TOWN

roundabout near the airport entrance. A taxi from the airport to Kos Town costs around €30.

BOAT

From Kos Town lining the southern arm of Akti Koundourioti, there are half a dozen boats that make excursions around Kos and to other islands. Return fares to Kalymnos, Pserimos and Platy are €30, including lunch. The boats vary in age and appeal but keep an eye out for the bonniest babe in the bay, **Eva** (☏694369300; Akti Koundourioti, Kos Town) a 110-year-old caïque with a finely crafted crow's nest and gunwhales. There's also a daily excursion boat from Mastihari to Kalymnos (€7).

BUS

Bus station (☏22420 22292; Kleopatras 7, Kos Town) Buses regularly serve all parts of the island, as well as the all-important beaches on the south side of Kos. A bus to the beaches will cost around €2 to €4.50.

CAR, MOTORCYCLE & BICYCLE

There are numerous car, motorcycle and moped-hire outlets; always ask at your hotel as many have special deals with hire companies. Cycling is very popular in Kos and you'll be tripping over bicycles for hire; prices range from €5 per day for a boneshaker to €10 for a half-decent mountain bike. In Kos Town try **George's Bikes** (☏22420 24157; Spetson 48; cycle/scooter per day €4/15) for decent bikes at reasonable prices.

Kos Town
pop 14,750

Scattered with ruins from the Hellenistic, Roman and Byzantine periods, this handsome and stylish town is a mix of the original old town – what remains of it after the 1933 earthquake, with its gauntlet of boutiques and closely-knit tavernas – and modern streets and parks bursting with palms and bougainvillea. And while there's a smattering of the lobster-red fish-and-chips crowd, the town retains its dignity with a sedate pace and friendly locals. The harbour is especially pretty with the Castle of the Knights picturesquely perched at its centre, and like some coastal Amsterdam, everybody here gets about on bikes.

What's left of Kos' old town is centred around the pedestrianised Apellou Ifestou.

 Sights & Activities

ARCHAEOLOGICAL MUSEUM   Museum
(Plateia Eleftherias; admission €3; ⏰8am-2.30pm Tue-Sun) Cool and calm, the Archaeological Museum is a pleasant place to take in local sculptures from the Hellenistic to late Roman eras. The most renowned statue is that of Hippocrates.

Boat Services From Kos

DESTINATION	PORT	DURATION	FARE	FREQUENCY
Nisyros	Kos Town	1hr 20min	€8	2 weekly
Nisyros*	Kos Town	45min	€16	2 weekly
Patmos	Kos Town	4hr	€17	3 weekly
Patmos*	Kos Town	2½hr	€29	6 weekly
Piraeus	Kos Town	10hr	€53	1 daily
Rhodes	Kos Town	3hr	€19	1 daily
Rhodes*	Kos Town	2½hr	€30	1 daily
Symi*	Kos Town	1½hr	€22	5 weekly

*high-speed services

IML IMAGE GROUP LTD/ALAMY ©

Don't Miss The Volcano Το Ηφαίστειο

Nisyros sits on a volcanic fault line. The island originally culminated in a mountain of 850m, but the centre collapsed 30,000 to 40,000 years ago after three violent eruptions. Their legacy are the white-and-orange pumice stones that can still be seen on the northern, eastern and southern flanks of the island, and the large lava flow that covers the whole southwest, around Nikea village.

Another violent eruption occurred in 1422 on the western side of the caldera depression (called Lakki); this, like all other eruptions since, emitted steam, gases and mud, but no lava. The islanders call the volcano Polyvotis after the eponymous Titan who was imprisoned under the rock of Nisyros. The hapless Polyvotis from that day forth has been groaning and sighing while trying to escape.

Descending into the **caldera** (admission €2.50; ⏰9am-8pm) is other-worldly. Cows graze near the craters amid sci-fi-set rocks. A path descends into the largest of the five craters, **Stefanos**, where you can examine the multicoloured fumaroles, listen to their hissing and smell the sulphurous vapours. The surface is soft and hot, making sturdy footwear essential. Don't stray too far out as the ground is unstable and can collapse. Also be careful not to step into a fumarole as the gases are 100°C and corrosive. Another unsignposted but more obvious track leads to **Polyvotis**, which is smaller and wilder looking but doesn't allow access to the caldera itself. The fumaroles are around the edge here so be very careful.

You can reach the volcano by bus, car or along a 3km-long trail from Nikia. Get there before 11am and you may have the place to yourself.

CASTLE OF THE KNIGHTS Castle
(Leoforos Finikon; admission €4; ⏰8am-2.30pm Tue-Sun) You can now reach the once impregnable Castle of the Knights by crossing a bridge over Finikon from Plateia Platanou. The castle, which had massive outer walls and an inner keep, was built in the 14th century and separated from the town by a moat (now Finikon). Damaged by an earthquake in 1495 and restored in

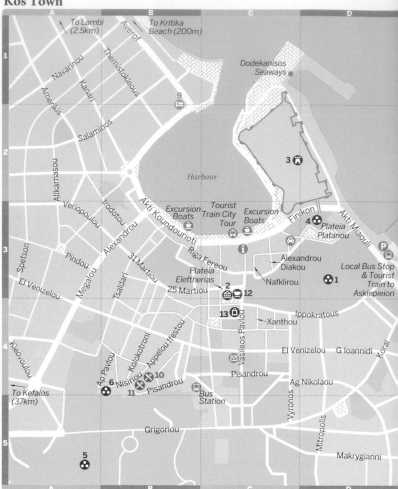

the 16th century, it was the knights' most stalwart defence against the encroaching Ottomans.

ARCHAEOLOGICAL SITES
Ancient Site

The **ancient agora** (admission free; ⏰8am-2pm) is an open site south of the castle. A massive 3rd-century-BC stoa, with some reconstructed columns, stands on its western side. On the north side are the ruins of a **Shrine of Aphrodite**, a **Temple of** **Hercules** and a 5th-century BC **Christian basilica**.

North of the agora is the lovely cobblestone Plateia Platanou, where you can sit in a cafe while paying respects to the once magnificent **Hippocrates Plane Tree**, under which Hippocrates is said to have taught his pupils. Beneath it is an old sarcophagus converted by the Turks into a fountain.

On the other side of town is the **western excavation site**. Two wooden shelters at the back of the site protect

N
N

0   200 m
0   0.1 miles

Kos Town

Beaches

On the east side of town, **Kos Town Beach** has a thin strip of sand and deep water for swimming. It tends to be dominated by the restaurants and hotels along this stretch. West of town, **Kritika Beach** is a long sandy stretch that's polka-dotted with umbrellas in the summer. It gets crowded but is within easy walking distance from the town centre.

 Sleeping

HOTEL AFENDOULIS Pension €
(☎ 22420 25321; www.afendoulishotel.com; Evripilou 1; s/d €30/50; ⊙ Mar-Nov; ❋ @ 🔊)
There's a sense of home away from home at this popular pension dripping with flowers and old-school hospitality. The simple whitewashed rooms with their balconies and pleasant decor are nice, but it's the family who run Afendoulis who make the experience. Breakfast in the communal cafe is lovely with homemade marmalade and jams and the owner, Alexis, will probably sit you down and run through the

the 3rd-century BC **mosaics of the House of Europa**. The best preserved mosaic depicts Europa's abduction by Zeus in the guise of a bull. On the opposite side of Grigoriou is the impressive 2nd-century AD **odeion**. It was initially a venue for the senate and musical competitions and was restored during the Italian occupation when it was discovered, filled with sculptures (many now in the Archaeological Museum).

If You Like...
Outdoor Activities

If you like hiking through the lush terrain of **Nisyros** (p309) or renting a bike on **Kos** (p308), we think you'd like these other Dodecanese activities:

1 CAPE PRASONISI
At the southern end of Rhodes, a 10km road snakes across windswept terrain to this remote and gorgeous sandy point. If you're into windsurfing, this is the place. The resort caters entirely to surfers and outside of the summer season it's totally shut.

2 TILOS
Basking in relative obscurity, tiny Tilos island is popular with migratory birds and avid birdwatchers. Rare species such as the Eleonora's falcon, the Mediterranean shag, and the Bonelli's eagle nest here and the island is home to countless rare orchids and mammals such as sea turtles and the Mediterranean monk seal. Watch for them as you strike out on the island's countless walking trails.

3 KALYMNOS
This island's spectacular limestone walls attract legions of climbers looking for seriously challenging extreme sport. There are over 20 documented climbs awaiting the adventurous, pulling in visitors from March onwards.

4 KARPATHOS
With some of the clearest water for snorkelling in the whole of the Aegean, consider Ammoöpi on Karpathos. Wind- and kitesurfers head for the broad **Afiartis Bay** in droves to enjoy world-class conditions. It's also home to the annual international kitesurfing competition (www.speedworldcup.com).

5 PETALOUDES
Better known as the **Valley of the Butterflies** (adult €3; ⊙8.30am-4.30pm), this is a popular sight on Rhodes. Visit in June, July or August when these colourful creatures mature, and you'll quickly see why. Come out of season and you'll miss the winged critters but you'll have the gorgeous forest path, rustic footbridges, streams and pools to yourself.

best things to see. Tellingly, most visitors are repeat customers.

HOTEL SONIA   Pension €
(☏22420 28798; www.hotelsonia.gr; Irodotou 9; s/d/tr €35/50/85; ❄ 🛜) On a peaceful street opposite the Roman Baths and within view of the harbour, this refurbished pension has sparkling rooms with parquet floors, flat-screen TVs, fridges, chic bathrooms and an extra bed if you need it.

KOSTA PALACE   Hotel €€
(☏22420 22855; www.kosta-palace.com; cnr Akti Kountourioti & Averof; d €60-80; ⊙year-round; ❄ @ 🏊) Easily spotted on the harbour's northern side, this imposing giant has 160 rooms elegantly finished with baths, cable TV and private balconies. The main draw is the rooftop swimming pool and kid's pool. Clean and functional but lacks character.

KOS AKTIS HOTEL   Hotel €€€
(☏22420 47200; www.kosaktis.gr; Vasileos Georgiou 7; s/d from €148/188; ❄ @ 🛜 🏊) With its decked outside bar, this sleek modern hotel is a great place for sundowners. There's a gym and a swimming pool. Rooms are contemporary with flat-screen TVs, glass balconies, tubs, darkwood furnishings and great views to nearby Turkey over the water.

Eating

ELIA   Mediterranean €
(Appelou Ifestou 27; mains €6.50) A visit to Elia is an education, even if it's your kids that give it to you as they spot the mythological gods and heroes painted in the rafters. In a rustic-cum-refined atmosphere of stone walls and wood floors, the eclectic menu alchemizes dishes like drunken pork (in wine), stuffed meatballs and our favourite, *lamb kapamas* – lamb and tomato with cinnamon. The aftertaste is so sweet you'll be heading back for more. Magical.

KAPILIO RESTAURANT Taverna €

(Plateia Diagora; mains €8-14) Extend your gastronomic horizons with an adventure to this welcoming taverna in a quiet part of the old town. The excellent 'Greek plate' allows you to sample a feast of *mousaka*, dolmadhes, spit-roasted lamb and Zakynthian rabbit in wine sauce. When you get full – which you will as the portions are generous – get your metabolism moving with a sip of *Tsipouro* (digestif). Other specialities include *moury* (roast lamb stuffed with rice, liver and kidneys).

Drinking & Entertainment

On weekends locals congregate at Plateia Eleftherias (Freedom Sq) to drink coffee and gossip in the many cafes. Kos' nightlife, geared for partying tourists, is centred a block south of the harbour, along Diakou. There's also a plethora of similar bars along the waterfront on Kritika Beach. If you're looking for clubs, they pass in and out of favour so just follow the crowds.

AENAOS Cafe

(Plateia Eleftherias; sweets €3.50) Next to the mosque, this lovely cafe with wrought-iron chairs and shade is a pleasant stop for an iced coffee or espresso (and maybe a brownie or slice of cheese cake) before heading to the nearby Archaeological Museum. The staff are delightful and you'll end up talking politics or mythology.

Shopping

Dimoiki Dorag (Plateia Eleftherias) is a bijou bazaar where you can buy anything from herbs, fresh cherries, olive oil and indigenous honey to mythological curios and Kalymnian sponges.

Information

Internet Resources
www.travel-to-kos.com Comprehensive guide to most of Kos' attractions.

Travel Agencies
Fanos Travel & Shipping (☎22420 20035; www.kostravel.gr; 11 Akti Koundourioti, Kos Town) Runs the hydrofoil service to Bodrum, sells boat tickets, rents cars, and offers yachting services.

Getting Around

Bus
Urban buses depart from Akti Miaouli and have two ticket prices: Zone A (€1.20) and Zone B (€1.60). Tickets from vending machines are slightly cheaper than those bought on board. You'll find one in front of the Blue Star Ferries office on the harbour. For schedules, check the local bus office.

Ancient Agora, Kos (p310)
ISLANDSPICS/ALAMY ©

Taxi

Taxis congregate at a stand on the south side of the port.

Tourist Train

In summer, a good way to get your bearings is to hop on the city's Tourist Train city tour (€4, 20 minutes), which runs from 10am to 2pm and 6pm to 10pm, starting from the bus station on Akti Kountouriotou. You can also take a train to the Asklipieion and back (€4), departing on the hour from 10am to 5pm Tuesday to Sunday, from the bus stop on Akti Miaouli.

Around Kos
Asklipieion Ασκληπιείον

The island's most important ancient site is the **Asklipieion** (Platani; adult/student €4/3; ⏰8am-7.30pm Tue-Sun), built on a pine-covered hill 3km southwest of Kos Town, with lovely views of the town and Turkey. The Asklipieion consisted of a religious sanctuary devoted to Asclepius (the god of healing), a healing centre and a school of medicine, where training followed the teachings of Hippocrates, the daddy of modern medicine. Until AD 554, when an earthquake destroyed the sanatorium, people came from far and wide for treatment.

The ruins occupy three levels. The **propylaea** (approach to the main gate), Roman-era public **baths** and remains of guest rooms are on the 1st level. On the 2nd level is a 4th-century-BC **altar of Kyparissios Apollo**. West of this is the **first Temple of Asclepius**, built in the 4th century BC. To the east is the 1st-century-BC **Temple to Apollo**. On the 3rd level are the remains of the once magnificent 2nd-century-BC **Temple of Asclepius**.

The hourly bus 3 and the Kos Town Tourist Train go to the site. It's also a pleasant cycle or walk.

ΡΑΤΜΟΣ ΠΑΤΜΟΣ
POP 3040

Unusual to say the least, Patmos has a distinctly spiritual presence. It drew an exiled St John here and delivered to him the apocalyptic visions that formed the Bible's book of Revelation. Contemporary visitors have a rosier time thanks to its abundance of wild beaches, remote tavernas and the stylish pull of Skala, its pretty harbour town. But perhaps the real ace is the magical mountaintop village of Hora, drawing hordes of Orthodox and Western Christians who make their pilgrimage to see the cave of St John. July through September Skala is buzzing with a cosmo cast of Italians, Athenians and other Europeans as well as the odd wall-eyed rock star. Greener than any of its neighbours, with gas-blue coves and rolling hills, leaving Patmos is always a wrench.

St John the Divine & the Apocalypse

Patmos' Hora is home to the Cave of the Apocalypse where St John the Divine was allegedly visited by God and instructed to write the Book of Revelation. He is often believed to be John the Apostle of Jesus or John the Evangelist, though many would dispute this due to his exile in AD 95 by the Roman Emperor Domitian. The Book of Revelation describes the end of the world – involving the final rebellion by Satan at Armageddon, God's final defeat of Satan and the restoration of peace to the world. Due to its heavy, dark symbolism some critics have suggested that it was the work of a deranged man. Whatever you choose to believe, it's worth visiting the cave where it all supposedly took place. Who knows – you may even have a bit of a revelation yourself.

Getting There & Away

Patmos is connected with Piraeus, Rhodes and a number of islands in between through mainline services with Blue Star Ferries and Anek Lines. Boat tickets are sold by Apollon Travel in Skala.

Getting Around

BOAT

Excursion boats go to Psili Ammos Beach from Skala, departing around 10am and returning about 4pm.

BUS

From Skala, there are eight return buses daily to Hora and four to Grikos and Kambos. Fares are a standard €1.

CAR & MOTORCYCLE

There are several car- and motorcycle-hire outlets in Skala. Competition is fierce, so shop around. Some have headquarters in the pedestrian street behind Skala's main harbour, including Moto Rent Faros (22470 29330), Avis (22470 33025) and Theo & Girogio (22470 32066).

TAXI

You can catch a taxi (22470 31225) from Skala's taxi rank opposite the police station.

Skala ΣΚΑΛΑ

After spending time on a secluded isle you'll find arriving at this busy little harbour is nothing short of exhilarating. From the chapel on the huge tree-clad boulders to the amphitheatrical tumble of houses down to the bay, it's magical. The whitewashed town is chic with plenty of jewellery shops, tasty cafes and stylish bars threaded through its maze of streets. There's also plenty of decent midrange accommodation.

Sights & Activities

Skala has a couple of religious sites, including the place where St John first baptised the locals in AD 96, just north of the beach. To find out more and to see

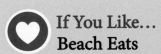

If You Like…
Beach Eats

If you like lazing on **Kambos Beach** (p319) and digging into excellent nosh at **George's Place** (p319), we think you'd like to dig your toes into the sand and your fork into the meals at these other Patmos beaches:

1 CAFE VAGIA
Vagia's quiet beach lies under the protected lee of the north arm of the island. Overlooking the beach is **Cafe Vagia** (22470 31658; mains €3-5; 9am-7pm) with its amazing vegie pies, hearty omelettes and local desserts, all served in a lush garden. It's especially popular with families.

2 LIVADI TOU GERANOU TAVERNA
Also in the north is picturesque, shaded Livadi Geranou Beach, with a small church-crowned island opposite. The road here is narrow and slightly treacherous but stunning. For lunch, stop at the cute **Livadi Geranou Taverna** (22470 32046; mains €3-5) overlooking the sea from a shaded garden.

3 BENETOS
The tiny settlement of Sapsila, just south of Skala, has a small beach offering peace and quiet. Dine at **Benetos** (22470 33089; mains €7-14; dinner Tue-Sun), just up the road. It's a working boutique farmhouse specialising in Mediterranean fusion dishes with an occasional Japanese kick.

4 KTIMA PETRA
Also in the south, Grikos is a relaxed, low-key resort with a long, sandy beach and warm shallow water. The bay is lined with tavernas and popular with yachties. At the southern end of the bay is **Ktima Petra** (22470 33207; mains €4-7), serving organic, home-grown produce. The stuffed wood-oven-baked goat melts in your mouth and the organic cheese and vegetables are scrumptious.

religious objects from across the island, visit the **Orthodox Culture & Information Centre** (9am-1pm Thu-Tue & 6-9pm Mon, Tue, Thu & Fri) in the harbourside church. If you feel like a workout, climb up to the remains of an ancient **acropolis** on the hillside to the west of town.

LOOK DIE BILDAGENTUR DER FOTOGRAFEN GMBH/ALAMY

Don't Miss Kefalos Bay Κέφαλοσ

Near Kos Town and southwest from Mastihari is the huge Kefalos Bay, fringed by a 12km stretch of incredible sand. Don't be put off by the tacky tourist shops, restaurants and hotels behind on the main road, these divine beaches are idyllic, backed by green hills and lapped by warm water. Each is clearly signposted from the main road. The most popular is **Paradise Beach** (pictured above), while the most undeveloped is **Exotic Beach**. **Banana Beach** (also known as Langada Beach) is a good compromise.

Agios Stefanos Beach, at the far western end, is reached along a short turn-off from the main road and worth a visit to see the island of **Agios Stefanos**. Within swimming distance, this tiny island is home to the ruins of two 5th-century basilicas and to another lovely, sandy beach.

The southern peninsula has the island's most rugged scenery. Rewardingly miles away from resort land, **Agios Theologos Beach** is backed by meadow bluffs carpeted in olive groves. You'll find the water here unusually clear and the waves invigoratingly large. Wander along until you find your own little nook to bask in. Above the beach the seasonal **Restaurant Agios Theologos** (mains €7-15) enjoys the best sunsets in Kos. The menu includes homemade feta, olives, bread and goat. The mezes dish is fantastic, the *taramasalata* and zucchini balls bursting with flavour.

 Sleeping

PENSION MARIA PASCALIDIS Pension €
(☎ 22470 32152; s/d €20/30) Welcoming host Maria has cosy rooms in a fragrant citrus-tree garden, sharing a communal kitchen and a bathroom. Fresh pine furniture, white walls and a very peaceful vibe makes this a traveller's favourite. It's on the road leading to Hora.

CAPTAIN'S HOUSE Hotel €€
(☎ 22470 31793; www.captains-house.gr; s/d incl breakfast €60/90) Rooms in this quirky

harfside hotel are tasteful with balco-
ies overlooking the nearby sea, dark
wooden furniture, fridges, flat-screen TVs
nd a lovely swimming pool out back.

ELFINI HOTEL Hotel €€
☏22470 32060; www.delfini-patmos.gr; s/d
65/70; ❄) Portside Delfini has bags
f appeal with a great cafe specialis-
ng in tasty homemade cakes – try the
mon pie. The rooms themselves are
imple with tiled floors, tangerine-hued
edspreads and harbour views. There's a
hilled reading area with sofas out back.
onsiderable discounts in the off-season.

ALDERIMI
PARTMENTS Boutique Hotel €€
☏22470 33008; www.kalderimi.com; apt incl
reakfast from €110; ❄) At the foot of the
ath up to the monastery and secluded
y trees, these gorgeous apartments have
raditional design with wooden beams
nd stone walls, along with lots of swish
xtras. A full kitchen, shaded balcony
nd lots of privacy make them a perfect
etreat for longer-term stays.

 Eating

MELTEMI Cafe €
full breakfast €5; ⊙9am-late; @) Start your
norning off right with breakfast on the
earby beach. Later in the day, come here
or milkshakes, quiche and coffee while
he waves lap at your toes.

TZIVAERI Seafood €
(mains €7; ⊙dinner) With its walls be-
shacked in shells, sponges and black-
and-white photos and the air thick with
bouzouki, this is a memorable stop for
calamari, shrimp, octopus and plenty
more seafood.

 Shopping

Koukoumavia (www.patmos-island.com/
koukoumavia) has funky handmade T-shirts,
bags, Kahloesque art, lamps and badges.
On the harbour, Selene is tastefully
crammed with jewellery, sculptures,
pottery, wood carvings and oil paintings
depicting traditional Greek life.

ⓘ Information

All transport arrives at the centre of the quay in
the middle of Skala. To the right the road leads to
a narrow, sandy beach, the yacht port and on to
the north of the island. To the left the road leads
to the south side of the island. From a roundabout
near the ferry terminal, a road heads inland and
up to Hora. The bus terminal and taxi rank are at
the quay and all main services are within 100m.

Apollon Travel (☏22470 31324; apollontravel@
stratas.gr) Ticketing for flights and ferries as
well as advice on accommodation.

www.patmos-island.com Lots of local listings
and info.

www.patmosweb.gr History, listings and
photos.

Boat Services From Patmos

DESTINATION	PORT	DURATION	FARE	FREQUENCY
Kos*	Skala	3hr	€29	6 weekly
Piraeus	Skala	7hr	€37	4 weekly
Rhodes	Skala	6hr	€32	3 weekly
Rhodes*	Skala	5hr	€46	6 weekly
Symi*	Skala	4hr	€44	5 weekly

*high-speed services

JON ARNOLD IMAGES LTD/ALAMY

Don't Miss Monastery of St John the Theologian

The immense **Monastery of St John the Theologian** crowns the island of Patmos. Attending a service here, with plumes of incense, religious chants and devoted worshippers, is unforgettable. To reach it, many people walk up the Byzantine path which starts from a signposted spot along the Skala–Hora road.

Some 200m along this path, a dirt trail to the left leads through pine trees to the **Monastery of the Apocalypse** (admission free, treasury €6; 🕙8am-1.30pm daily, plus 4-6pm Tue, Thu & Sun), built around the cave where St John received his revelation. It's strange to think that this benign grotto, now hung in gold candelabra, icons and votive candles, gave rise to such disturbing visions. You can see the rock that the saint used as a pillow and the triple fissure in the roof from where the voice of God issued. Grab a pew and try not to think of *The Omen!*

A five-minute walk west of St John's Monastery, the **Holy Monastery of Zoodohos Pigi** (admission free; 🕙8am-noon & 5-7pm Sun-Fri) is a women's convent with incredibly impressive frescoes. On Good Friday, a beautiful candle-lit ceremony takes place here.

THINGS YOU NEED TO KNOW

admission free; 🕙8am-1.30pm daily, plus 4-6pm Tue, Thu & Sun

Hora ΧΩΡΑ

Take an early-morning hike up to Hora and its centrepiece monastery of St John, and you cannot help but pick up its rarefied vibe. Revelation, that curiously frightening book, was written in a cave nearby and some of its Boschian spectres seem to scuttle invisibly behind you as

you wander the 17th-century maze of streets.

Just east of St John's Monastery, **Andreas Kalatzis** is a Byzantine icon artist who lives and works in a 1740s traditional home. Inside, you'll find an interesting mix of pottery, jewellery and paintings by local artists. Seek out

atmos Gallery for an eclectic range
f abstract and figurative paintings,
wellery and illuminated sculptures.
urprisingly reasonable, it's run by
keable artist, Andreas Kalatis.

Archontariki (☏ 22470 29368; www.
chontariki-patmos.gr; ste incl breakfast €220-
00) is a 400-year-old building with four
orgeous suites equipped with every
onvenience, traditional furnishings
nd plush touches. Relaxing under the
uit trees in the cool and quiet garden,
ou'll wonder why the hotel isn't named
aradise.

At the **Vangelis Taverna** (mains €6-10)
ou can dine in a private garden, taking
the spectacular view from under the
nade of a carob tree. On the menu
re fresh goat, mackerel cooked in oil,
olmadhes and many more traditional
shes.

North of Skala

ust north of Skala on the road to Kam-
os is the plush **Porto Scoutari Hotel**
☏ 22470 33123; www.portoscoutari.com; d incl
reakfast €80-180; P ❄ @ ☃) with its lobby
pilling with clocks and antiques. Backed
y a lavish swimming pool and nearby
pa centre, this elegant hotel has amazing
ea views and palatially sized rooms with
uge beds, cream sofas, four-poster beds
nd private terraces.

Further up the road is the inland
illage of Kambos, from where the road
escends to the relatively wide and
sandy **Kambos Beach**, perhaps the most
popular and easily accessible beach on
the island. Situated on an enclosed bay,
it's great for swimming and you can hire
kayaks and sun beds.

Super-chilled **George's Place** (snacks
€7) sits by the peacock-blue bay with a
shaded terrace to sip wine, munch a salad
or consider doing something active at the
nearby water-sports centre. Ask about
the full moon parties where they dish up
Thai fare.

South of Skala

Small, tree-filled valleys and picturesque
beaches fill the south of Patmos. Closest
to Skala is the tiny, peaceful settlement
of **Sapsila**. Set in a beautiful lemon grove
garden, **Mathios Studios** (☏ 22470 32583;
www.mathiosapartments.gr; d €40-65; ❄ @) is
chic and homely at the same time, with its
apartments 200m from the beach.

Dine at **Benetos** (Sapsila; mains €7-14;
🕑dinner Tue-Sun), just up the road. It's
a working boutique farmhouse and
specialises in Mediterranean fusion
dishes with an occasional Japanese
kick. Try zucchini blossoms stuffed with
mushrooms and cheese, or the herb-
crusted, pan-seared tuna.

Diakofti is the last settlement in the
south. From here you can follow a half-
hour walking track to the island's best spit
of sand; tree-shaded **Psili Ammos Beach**,
where there's a seasonal taverna. You can
also get here by excursion boat.

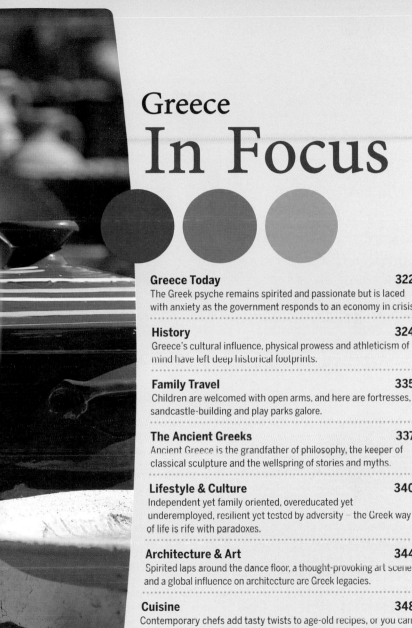

Greece
In Focus

Greek pottery at a market in Crete (p233)
PHOTOGRAPHER: FEFERONI|DREAMSTIME ©

Greece Today

Greek gentlemen enjoying an afternoon coffee

> *The drama is far from over, as the current leadership navigates between recovery and further recession*

belief systems
(% of population)

98

Greek Orthodox

1.3

Muslim

0.7

Other

if Greece were 100 people

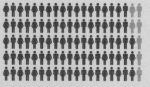

93 would be Greek
7 would be other

population per sq km

GREECE

USA

UK

= 30 people

Spirit of Rebellion

Personal freedom and democratic rights are sacrosanct to Greeks, and a residual mistrust of authority and disrespect of the state is integral to the national psyche. This spirited characteristic has recently been evident, with many Greeks resisting Prime Minister George Papandreou's economic reforms to help curb Greece's soaring national debt.

In June 2011, as the world watched to see whether Papandreou could achieve a majority vote in parliament for his austerity measures and the next EU/IMF bailout, the streets of Athens were red with riot. The vote went through and the rescue package for the ailing economy was put in motion. The drama is far from over though. On 10 November 2011, Papandreou stepped down in order to allow a provisional coalition government take the reigns. The next day, economist Lucas Papademos took on the role of Prime Minister and under his leadership the government is attempting to navigate between incremental recovery and further recession. Once the

Greek Orthodox Church after a number of scandalous stories – from sexual indecency to narcotics – emerged in recent times. However, the Church is still a key element of Greek life, even taking into account the drop off in the younger generation's footfalls to the local house of worship.

National Psyche

Greeks are passionate, loyal and fiery. Issues are debated with strong will in the local *kafeneio* (coffee house), and rather than living to work, Greek people work to live, with an emphasis on fun and shared company rather than slaving all hours in an office.

In 2011 the average Athenian saw their wage severely cut, some say as much as 15%, while living costs were soaring. All this with a rising rate of around 16% unemployment, with one in four public sector jobs planned to be shelled to cut the deficit. No surprise then that the Greek psyche has shifted from relaxed to anxious, 'A state,' one Athenian told us, 'That we're just not used to.'

Greeks pride themselves on their *filotimo* (dignity and sense of honour), and their *filoxenia* (hospitality). Despite their current fiscal problems, the average Greek will still lavish you with free drinks, fresh cake from their kitchen and the warmth they have always been famous for. Curious by nature, nothing is off limits for conversation, and you may find yourself quizzed as to why you haven't got children, why you're not married or how much you earn.

Greek society remains dominated by the family, and while many men may appear soaked with machismo, the matriarchal domestic model is still very much a commonplace, with women subtly pulling the strings in the background.

ANTHONY PIDGEON/LONELYPLANET IMAGES ©

President of the European Central Bank, Papademos' goal is to allow the EU bailout to proceed and to pave the way forward for elections in 2012

The Winds of Change

Greeks are steadily increasing their awareness of the issues regarding local environmental degradation – cue recycling and a cap on sprawling tourist developments.

Another hot potato of debate is immigration, with an influx of people from Afghanistan, Iraq, Africa and Albania flooding into the country, despite Greece having the lowest acceptance rate of any EU country for asylum requests. Not surprisingly these new arrivals disappear as 'illegals' into the fringes of Greek society.

The Church

Seismic faults have begun appearing in the once unblemished image of the

History

Palace of Knossos (p251)

TREVOR CREIGHTON/LONELYPLANET

Since its earliest days, the Greek landscape has been trudged across by countless invaders, occupiers and settlers. Experience the influence of the Ottomans in the north, the Italians in the Dodecanese and the Venetians in the Ionian Islands. Greece's past is very much a part of its current terrain, from ancient ruins scattered throughout the land to the origins of democracy which continue to be struggled for today.

Earliest Days

A Neanderthal skull found in a cave on the Halkidiki Peninsula of Macedonia in northern Greece shows that humans have been hanging out in Greece for at least 700,000 years. Around 6500 BC, folks from the Palaeolithic times left bones and tools scattered in the Pindos Mountains, while pastoral communities emerged during neolithic times (7000 to 3000 BC), mainly in the fertile region that is now Thessaly. Around 3000 BC,

7000–3000 BC

Early inhabitants live a simple agrarian life, growing crops and herding animals.

Indo-European migrants arrived with the know-how to process bronze, sparking the beginning of three remarkable civilisations: Cycladic, Minoan and Mycenaean.

Ancient Civilisations

Cycladic Civilisation

The Cycladic civilisation was a cluster of fishing and farming island communities with a sophisticated artistic temperament. The most striking legacy of this civilisation is the carving of statuettes from Parian marble – the famous Cycladic figurines. Cycladic sculptors are also renowned for their impressive, life-sized *kouroi* (marble statues), carved during the Archaic period.

Minoan Civilisation

Named after King Minos, the mythical ruler of Crete, the Minoans were Europe's first advanced civilisation. Around 2000 BC, splendidly decorated palace complexes like Knossos were built, marking a sharp break from village life. The Minoans were also great seafarers, exporting goods to Asia Minor (the west of present-day Turkey), Europe and North Africa, as well as to continental Greece.

Nobody really knows what happened to the Minoans. They may have succumbed to a massive tsunami and ash fallout from the volcanic eruption on Thira (Santorini) around 1500 BC. Or perhaps a second, powerful quake a century later decimated the society. Others blame their demise on invading Mycenaeans.

Mycenaean Civilisation

The Mycenaean civilisation reached its crescendo between 1500 and 1200 BC with mainland city-states like Corinth and Mycenae. The Mycenaeans created impressive palace frescoes and documented commerce in Linear B (a form of Greek language 500 years older than the Ionic Greek used by Homer). Their most extraordinary legacies are magnificent gold masks, refined jewellery and ornaments; check them out in the National Archaeological Museum in Athens.

Geometric & Archaic Ages

The Dorians were an ancient Hellenic people who were settled in the Peloponnese by the 8th century BC. In the 11th or 12th century BC these warrior-like people fanned out to occupy much of the mainland, seizing control of the Mycenaean kingdoms and enslaving the inhabitants. The following 400-year period is often referred to as

3000–1100 BC
Increased prosperity sees the birth of the Cycladic and Minoan – and later, the Mycenaean – civilisations.

1700–1550 BC
Santorini erupts with a cataclysmic explosion, one of the largest volcanic events in recorded history.

1200–800 BC
The Dorian tribes herald a 400-year 'dark age' in terms of international trade.

The Spartans

A dominant military power from 650 to 363 BC, the Peloponnese-based Spartans were held in mythic awe by their fellow Greeks for their ferocious and self-sacrificing martial supremacy, living (and very often dying) by the motto 'return with your shield or on it'.

Every male Spartiate began his military training almost from birth and was bound to military service until the age of 60. Poor recruits were weeded out early, with newborn babies who didn't pass muster being left on a mountaintop to die. The surviving children endured 13 years of training to foster supreme physical fitness and suffered institutionalised beating 'competitions' to toughen them up.

Greece's 'dark age; however the Dorians can be credited with bringing iron and developing a new style of pottery, decorated with striking geometric designs.

The Dorians were followed by the Archaic period (1000 to 800 BC) when Greek culture developed rapidly. Many of the advancements in literature, sculpture, theatre, architecture and intellectual endeavour began; this revival overlapped with the Classical age (the two eras are often classified as the Hellenic period). Advances included the Greek alphabetic script; the verses of Homer; the founding of the Olympic Games; and central sanctuaries such as Delphi. These common bonds gave Greeks a sense of national identity.

Democracy

During the Archaic Age, Athens was firmly in the hands of aristocrats when Solon was appointed *arhon* (chief magistrate) in 594 BC to soothe tensions between the haves and have-nots. He cancelled all debts and freed those who had become enslaved because of them. Solon went on to abolish inherited privileges and restructured political power, establishing four classes based on wealth. Although only the first two classes were eligible for office, all four could elect magistrates and vote on legislation. Solon's reforms have become regarded as a harbinger of the ideological democratic system found in most current Western legal traditions.

Classical Age

Greece's golden age (6th to 4th centuries BC) brought a boom in economic and political prosperity and cultural creativity. Literature and drama blossomed with innovations like dramatic tragedies and political satire. Athens reached its zenith and

800–700 BC

Homer composes Greece's earliest pieces of literary art, the 'Iliad' and the 'Odyssey' around this time.
Bust of Homer

700–500 BC

Having originated around 1000 BC in the Peloponnese, the Spartans dominate for around 200 years.

founded the Delian League in 477 BC, a naval alliance based on Delos to liberate the city-states still occupied by Persia. Many of the Aegean islands and Ionian city-states swore allegiance to Athens and made a mandatory annual contribution to the treasury of ships.

When Pericles became leader of Athens in 461 BC, he moved the treasury from Delos to the Acropolis and used the treasury's funds to construct new and grander temples on the Acropolis, such as the Parthenon and the Temple of Zeus at Ancient Olympia.

With the Aegean Sea safely under its wing, Athens began to look westwards, bringing it into conflict with the Sparta-dominated Peloponnesian League. A series of skirmishes subsequently led to the Peloponnesian Wars.

Hellenistic Age

In the century following the Peloponnesian Wars, the battle-weary city-states came under the rule of the Macedonian king Philip II. It was his young son though, Alexander the Great, who was determined to unite the Greeks and spread Greek language and culture throughout the wider empire. The Greeks now perceived themselves as part of a larger empire, and contemporary arts, drama, sculpture and philosophy reflected this growing awareness of a Greek identity.

Hellenism continued to prosper even under Roman rule and experienced an unprecedented period of peace for almost 300 years, known as the Pax Romana. The Romans had always venerated Greek art, literature and philosophy, and spread its unifying traditions throughout their empire.

The Romans were also the first to refer to the Hellenes as Greeks, derived from the word *graikos* – the name of a prehistoric tribe.

The Byzantine Empire & the Crusades

Roman rule began to crumble in AD 250 when the Goths invaded Greece, the first of a succession of invaders. In an attempt to save his empire, Roman Emperor Constantine I transferred the capital from Rome to Byzantium (present-day İstanbul) in AD 324. While Rome went into terminal decline, the Eastern capital began to grow in wealth and strength and Byzantine Greece managed to retain its stronghold over the region.

The Frankish Crusaders brought about the demise of the Byzantine Empire in their mission to liberate the Holy Land from the Muslims. Driven as much by greed as by religious zeal, they decided that Byzantium (renamed Constantinople) presented richer pickings than Jerusalem. Constantinople was sacked in 1204 and much of the Byzantine Empire was partitioned into fiefdoms. The Venetians, meanwhile, had also secured a foothold in Greece. Over the next few centuries they acquired all the key Greek ports and Crete, becoming the wealthiest traders in the Mediterranean.

479 BC
The Greeks smash the Persian army under Spartan leadership. The Persian Wars are finally over.

431–404 BC
Sparta becomes the main enemy of Athens, sparking the two Peloponnesian Wars.

334–323 BC
Alexander the Great sets out to conquer the known world.

The Best...
Ancient
Ruins

1 Acropolis (p67)

2 Ancient Delphi (p160)

3 Knossos (p251)

4 Delos (p217)

5 Ancient Olympia (p128)

Despite this sorry state of affairs, Byzantium was not yet dead. In 1259 the Byzantine emperor Michael VIII Palaeologos recaptured the Peloponnese and made the city of Mystras his headquarters. Many eminent Byzantine artists, architects, intellectuals and philosophers converged on the city for a final burst of Byzantine creativity.

Ottoman Rule

Constantinople was soon facing a much greater threat from the Muslim Ottomans in the East. When Constantinople fell under Turkish Ottoman rule in 1453, Greece became a battleground between the Turks and Venetians. Eventually, with the exception of the Ionian Islands (where the Venetians retained control), Greece became part of the Ottoman Empire.

Ottoman power reached its zenith under Sultan Süleyman the Magnificent, who ruled between 1520 and 1566. Although they captured Crete in 1669 after a 25-year campaign, the ineffectual sultans that followed in the late 16th and 17th centuries saw the empire go into steady decline.

Independence

The first Greek Independence party, the underground Filiki Eteria (Friendly Society), was founded in 1814. On 25 March 1821, the Greeks launched the War of Independence. Uprisings broke out almost simultaneously across most of Greece and the occupied islands. Within a year the Greeks had captured the fortresses of Monemvasia, Navarino (modern Pylos) and Nafplio in the Peloponnese, and Messolongi, Athens and Thebes. The Greeks proclaimed Independence on 13 January 1822 at Epidavros.

Regional differences over national governance escalated into civil war in 1824 and 1825, which the Ottomans took advantage of by recapturing most of the Peloponnese, as well as Messolongi and Athens, by 1827. The Western powers intervened and a combined Russian, French and British naval fleet sunk the Turkish-Egyptian fleet in the Battle of Navarino in October 1827. Fighting continued until 1829 when, with Russian troops at the gates of Constantinople, the sultan accepted Greek Independence with the Treaty of Adrianople. Independence was formally recognised in 1830.

86 BC–AD 224

Roman expansion inevitably includes Greek territory and ultimately overtakes the mainland.

394

Christianity is declared the official religion. All pagan worship of Greek and Roman gods is outlawed.

1453

Greece becomes a dominion of the Ottoman Turks.

The Modern Greek Nation

The Greeks, meanwhile, had been busy organising the independent state they had pro-claimed several years earlier. In April 1827 they elected Ioannis Kapodistrias, a Corfiot and former diplomat of Russian Tsar Alexander I, as the first president of the republic; and chose Natplio, in the Peloponnese, as the capital.

However, there was much dissension within Greek ranks. Kapodistrias was assassinated in 1831 after he had ordered the imprisonment of a Maniot chieftain. Amid the ensuing anarchy, Britain, France and Russia declared Greece a monarchy, placing a non-Greek, 17-year-old Bavarian Prince Otto on the throne in 1833. The new kingdom consisted of the Peloponnese, Sterea Ellada, the Cyclades and the Sporades.

After moving the capital to Athens in 1834, King Otto managed to alienate the independence veterans by giving the most prestigious official posts to his Bavarian court. In 1862, Otto was ousted in a bloodless coup and Britain eased a young Danish Prince William onto the throne, crowned King George I in 1863. His 50-year reign brought some stability to the country, beginning with a new constitution in 1864 that established the power of democratically elected representatives.

Painting depicting the 1827 Battle of Navarino, during the Greek War of Independence, Museum der Stadt Wien, Vienna
PHOTOGRAPHER: THE ART ARCHIVE/ALAMY ©

1460
Medieval Peloponnese falls to the Turks, leading to centuries of power struggles between the Turks and Venetians.

1684–87
The Venetians expel the Turks from the Peloponnese.

1822–29
Greek Independence is declared in 1822, but the fight against the Turks continues for seven years.

The Greek Royals

Danish by descent and English by residence, the Greek royal family fled Greece following a military coup in 1967 and the monarch was officially disposed of in 1974. While they no longer represent Greece, the family remains part of the extended Danish royal family and continue to use their titles.

After leaving Greece, the family requested compensation for assets seized by the Greek Government – namely three properties, including a palace on Corfu where Britain's Prince Phillip was born. Former King Constantine II took his case to the European Court of Human Rights and was awarded €12 million in 2002.

WWI & Smyrna

After an initial stance of neutrality, Greece was pressured into joining the Allies in WWI, with land in Asia Minor promised in return. Despite Greek troops serving with distinction, when the war ended in 1918, the promised land was not forthcoming.

In an attempt to get what he felt was rightfully Greece's, Prime Minister Eleftherios Venizelos led a diplomatic campaign into Smyrna (present-day İzmir in Turkey) in May 1919, under the guise of protecting the half a million Greeks living in the city. Believing he had a hold in Asia Minor, Venizelos ordered his troops to march ahead, and by September 1921 they'd advanced as far as Ankara. Turkish forces, commanded by Mustafa Kemal (later to become Atatürk), halted the offensive and recaptured Smyrna in 1922, when tens of thousands of its Greek inhabitants were killed.

The outcome of these hostilities was not at all what Venizelos had in mind. The Treaty of Lausanne in July 1923 gave Turkey eastern Thrace and the islands of Imvros and Tenedos, while Italy kept the Dodecanese (which it had temporarily acquired in 1912 and would hold until 1947). The treaty also called for a population exchange between Greece and Turkey to prevent future disputes. Almost 1.5 million Greeks left Turkey and almost 400,000 Turks left Greece. The exchange put a tremendous strain on the Greek economy and caused great bitterness and hardship for the individuals involved.

The Republic of 1924–35

The arrival of the Greek refugees from Turkey coincided with, and compounded, a period of political instability unprecedented even by Greek standards. After to-ing and fro-ing of the throne between various Danish descendents, George II found himself

1862–63

King Otto is deposed in a bloodless coup and the British return the Ionian Islands to Greece.

1863–64

The British engineer the ascension of Danish Prince William to the Greek throne.

PASCALE BEROUJON/LONELYPLANET IMAGES ©

on the throne in 1920 but was no match for the group of army officers who seized power. A republic was proclaimed in March 1924 amid a series of coups and counter-coups.

A measure of stability was attained with Prime Minister Venizelos' return to power in 1928, although progress was inhibited by the Great Depression and he was defeated at the polls in March 1933. The new government was preparing for the restoration of the monarchy when Venizelos and his supporters staged an unsuccessful coup in March 1935. Venizelos was exiled to Paris and in November 1935, King George I reassumed the throne and installed the right-wing General Ioannis Metaxas as prime minister. Nine months later, Metaxas assumed dictatorial powers with the king's consent.

WWII

Metaxas exiled or imprisoned opponents, banned trade unions and the recently established Kommounistiko Komma Elladas (KKE, the Greek Communist Party), imposed press censorship, and created a secret police force and fascist-style youth movement. But Metaxas is best known for his reply of *ohi* (no) to Mussolini's ultimatum to allow Italians passage through Greece at the beginning of WWII. When the British asked Metaxas if they could land troops in Greece, he gave the same reply, but then died suddenly in January 1941. The king replaced him with the more timid Alexandros Koryzis, who agreed to British forces landing in Greece. German troops invaded Greece on 6 April 1941 and vastly outnumbered the defending Allied troops, and the whole country was under Nazi occupation within a few weeks. The civilian population suffered appallingly during the occupation, many dying of starvation. The Nazis rounded up more than half the Jewish population and transported them to death camps.

Civil War

By late 1944 the royalists, republicans and communists were locked in a serious battle for control. The British-backed provisional government was in an untenable position; the left was threatening revolt, and the British were pushing to prevent the communists from further legitimising their hold over the administration. On 3 December 1944 the police fired on a communist demonstration in Plateia Syntagmatos (Syntagma Sq)

IN FOCUS HISTORY

The Best...
Ancient
Treasure
Troves

1 National Archaeological Museum, Athens (p78)

2 Acropolis Museum (p76)

3 Iraklio Archaeological Museum (p246)

4 Delphi Museum (p161)

1896
The staging of the first modern Olympic Games in Athens marks Greece's coming of age. Panathinaiko Stadium

1924–34
Greece is proclaimed a republic but the Great Depression affects stability.

1935
The monarchy is restored and dictatorial Prime Minister Metaxas governs.

in Athens, killing several people. The ensuing six weeks of fighting between the left and the right, known as the Dekemvriana (events of December), marked the first round of the Greek Civil War. The royalists won the March 1946 election and George II landed back on the throne.

In October the left-wing Democratic Army of Greece (DSE) was formed to resume the fight against the monarchy and its British supporters – they swiftly occupied a large swath of land along Greece's northern border. In 1947 the USA intervened and the civil war developed into a setting for the new Cold War theatre. Communism was declared illegal and the government introduced its notorious Certificate of Political Reliability, which declared that the document bearer was not a left-wing sympathiser; without this certificate Greeks could not vote and found it almost impossible to get work (the certificate remained valid until 1962).

The civil war left Greece politically frayed and economically shattered. More Greeks had been killed in three years of bitter civil war than in WWII, and a quarter of a million people were homeless. The sense of despair became the trigger for a mass exodus. Almost a million Greeks headed off in search of a better life elsewhere, primarily to countries such as Australia, Canada and the USA.

Former Prime Minister of Greece, Andreas Papandreou
PHOTOGRAPHER: LAMBI/ISTOCKPHOTO ©

1941–44
Germany invades and occupies Greece.

1944–49
The end of WWII sees Greece descend into civil war, pitching monarchists against communists.

1967–74
A right-wing military coup establishes a junta, imposing martial law and abolishing many civil rights.

Colonels, Monarchs & Democracy

Greece's political right staged a coup on 21 April 1967, establishing a military junta. The colonels declared martial law, banned political parties and trade unions, imposed censorship, and imprisoned, tortured and exiled thousands of dissidents.

On 17 November 1973 tanks stormed a building at the Athens Polytechnio (Technical University) to quell a student occupation calling for an uprising against the US-backed junta. While the number of casualties is still in dispute (more than 20 students were reportedly killed and hundreds injured), the act meant the death knell for the junta.

Shortly after, the junta dictatorship collapsed. Former Prime Minister Konstandinos Karamanlis was summoned from his exile in Paris to take office and his New Democracy (ND) party won a large majority at the November elections in 1974.

The 1980s & 1990s

When Greece became the 10th member of the EU in 1981, it was the smallest and poorest member. In October 1981, Andreas Papandreou's PASOK party was elected as Greece's first socialist government. PASOK ruled for almost two decades (except for 1990–93). PASOK promised ambitious social reform, and that they would close the US air bases and withdraw from NATO. US military presence was reduced, but unemployment was high and reforms in education and welfare were limited. Women's issues fared better: the dowry system was abolished, abortion legalised, and civil marriage and divorce were implemented.

Papandreou stepped down in 1996 and his departure produced a dramatic change of direction for PASOK, with the party abandoning Papandreou's left-leaning politics and electing experienced economist and lawyer Costas Simitis as the new prime minister (who won a comfortable majority at the October 1996 polls).

The 21st Century

The new millenium saw Greece join the eurozone in 2001, amid rumblings from existing members that Greece was not ready economically – its public borrowing was too high, as was its inflation level. Membership had already been denied them in 1999, and many Greeks were keen to ditch the drachma and nestle under the stable umbrella of the euro. In hindsight, many look back on that year, and bemoan the miscalibration of the drachma against the euro, claiming Greece's currency was undervalued, and that overnight, living became disproportionately more expensive. That said, billions of euros poured into large-scale infrastructure projects across Greece, including the redevelopment of Athens – spurred on largely by its hosting of the 2004 Olympic Games, which was a tremendous boost for the city. However, rising unemployment, ballooning public debt, slowing inflation and the squeezing of consumer credit took its toll. Public opinion soured further in 2007 when Prime Minister Kosta Karamanlis' government was widely criticised for its handling of the emergency response to severe

1974
The junta falls and Greece's parliamentary democracy is restored.

1981
Greece joins the EU and the economy grows smartly.

2004
Greece hosts the 28th Summer Olympic Games and wins the European football championship.

SINK or SWIM

In 2009 a lethal cocktail of high public spending and widespread tax evasion, combined with the credit crunch of global recession, threatened to cripple Greece's economy. In 2010 Greece's fellow eurozone countries agreed to a US$145 billion package (half of Greece's GDP) to get the country back on its feet, though with strict conditions – the ruling government, PASOK, still led by Georgios Papandreou, would have to impose austere measures of reform to reduce Greece's bloated deficit in order to receive these handouts. Huge cuts followed, including 10% off public workers' salaries, but it was too little too late and foreign creditors continued to demand ever higher interest rates for their loans. Greece was stuck between a real-life Scylla and Charybdis – to receive yet another bailout which was absolutely essential to stop them toppling the euro as a credible currency, they had to effect reforms that penalised the average Greek even further (pushing formerly nonpolitical citizens towards revolution). Some longed for a return to the drachma (the former currency); however, many believe that Greece would still be saddled with massive debt and a monetary system with absolutely no standing.

summer fires, which were responsible for widespread destruction throughout Greece. Nevertheless, snap elections held in September 2007 returned the conservatives to power, albeit with a diminished majority.

Over recent years, a series of massive general strikes and blockades highlighted mounting electoral discontent. Hundreds of thousands of people protested against proposed radical labour and pension reforms and privatisation plans that analysts claim would help curb public debt. The backlash against the government reached boiling point in December 2008, when urban rioting broke out across the country, led by youths outraged by the police shooting of a 15-year-old boy in Athens following an alleged exchange between police and a group of teenagers. Concern continues over political tangles in numerous ongoing investigations regarding corruption among state executives. This follows another controversy that involved land-swap deals between a monastery and the government, which some commentators believe to have gone heavily in the monastery's favour, at the expense of taxpayers. A general election held in October 2009, midway through Karamanlis' term, saw PASOK (under Georgios Papandreou) take back the reins in a landslide win against the conservatives.

2010
Greece is granted the biggest EU financial bailout in history. Austerity measures are met with civil protest.

2011
The economy continues to shrink with rising unemployment. A second EU and IMF bailout is granted.

MENELAOS MICH/DEMOTIX ©

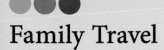

Family Travel

Children playing in Plateia Syntagmatos in Nafplio (p115)

IML IMAGE GROUP LTD/ALAMY ©

Greece is a safe and easy place to travel with children. Greek society welcomes children with open arms. Greeks will generally make a fuss over your children, who will find themselves on the receiving end of many small gifts and treats. Teaching your children a few words in Greek will ingratiate them further.

The Lowdown

Travelling is especially easy if you're staying at a resort hotel by the beach, where everything is set up for families with children. Elsewhere, it's rare to find cots and highchairs. The fast service in most restaurants is good news when it comes to feeding hungry kids. Ordering lots of small dishes to share gives kids the chance to try local cuisine, and omelettes, chips and spaghetti are omnipresent. Many hotels let small children stay for free and will squeeze an extra bed into the room.

A holiday in Greece can mean a lot of walking. If your kids aren't old enough to walk on their own for long, consider a sturdy carrying backpack; pushchairs are a struggle in towns and villages with slippery cobbles and high pavements.

Fresh milk is available in large towns and tourist areas, but harder to find on smaller islands. Formula is available almost

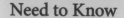

Need to Know

- o **Change facilities** Rare
- o **Cots** Only available in top-end hotels
- o **Health** Carry a first-aid kit and rehydration supplies
- o **Highchairs & kids' menus** Nearly unheard of
- o **Milk & formula** Fresh milk is available in large towns and tourist areas; formula available almost everywhere
- o **Nappies (diapers)** Everywhere
- o **Transport** Lots of discounts; bring your own car seat for car rentals

everywhere, as is condensed and heat-treated milk. Disposable nappies are also available everywhere.

Travel on ferries, buses and trains is free for children under four. They pay half-fare up to the age of 10 (ferries) or 12 (buses and trains). On domestic flights, you'll pay 10% of the adult fare to have a child under two sitting on your knee. Kids aged two to 12 pay half-fare. If you plan to rent a car, it's wise to bring your own car or booster seat as many of the smaller local agencies won't have these.

Matt Barrett's website (www.greektravel.com) has lots of useful tips for parents.

Family Fun

Most towns will have at least a small playground, while larger cities often have fantastic, modern play parks. You'll also find play-centred children's museums. Check out the Hellenic Children's Museum in Athens, where your kids can join Greek cooking and craft classes.

Most kids enjoy exploring at ancient sights; young imaginations go into overdrive when let loose somewhere like the 'labyrinth' at Knossos. Exploring Ancient Olympia in the Peloponnese or climbing to the top of the rock pinnacles of Meteora will thrill parents and kids alike.

Many of Greece's beaches are ideal for families, with warm, shallow water. Others have activities popular with older children and teenagers, such as snorkelling and kayaking. And then there's the endless stretches of sand for castle-building, digging and beachcombing.

The Ancient Greeks

Illustration of Hercules taking the Belt of Hippolyte

STEFANO BIANCHETTI/CORBIS ©

When the Roman Empire assimilated Greece it did so with considerable respect and idealism. They found themselves dazzled by a culture that was dripping with mythology and artistic and intellectual achievements. The Romans in many ways based themselves on the Ancient Greeks, absorbing their deities (and renaming them), literature, myths, philosophy, fine arts and architecture. So what made them so special?

Mythology

Ancient Greece revolved around a careful worship of 12 central gods and goddesses, all of which played a major role in the *mythos* (mythology). Each city-state had its own patron god or goddess, to be appeased and flattered, while on a personal level a farmer might make sacrifice to the goddess Demeter to bless his crops, or a fisherman to Poseidon to bring him fish and safe passage on the waves.

Some of the greatest stories of all time – and some say the wellspring of *story* itself – are to be found in the Greek myths. For many of us fantastical stories of Heracles and Odysseus linger in our imagination. Standing in the ancient ruins of an acropolis peering across to the watery horizon, it's not difficult to picture the Kraken (Poseidon's pet monster) rising from the Aegean, nor to imagine that fishing boat

you see heading into the sunset as Jason's *Argo* en route to Colchis for the Golden Fleece. Greek mythology is a rich, fantastical tapestry that stretches all the way from the mists of Mt Olympus down to the farthest reaches of Hades.

The Golden Age of Drama

In the 5th century BC Athens had a cultural renaissance that has never been equalled. Some historians also call this era the 'Age of Pericles', after the statesman and patron of the arts who dominated for some 40 years and fiercely encouraged free speech and free thought. Like Paris in the 1930s, Athens magnetised a hotbed of talent. Any artist or writer worth their salt left their hometown and travelled to the great city of wisdom to share their thoughts and hear the great minds of the day express themselves. The great dramatists like Aeschylus *(The Oresteia)*, Aristophanes, Euripides and Sophocles *(Oedipus Rex)* had transformed theatre from religious ritual to a compelling form of entertainment. They were to be found at the Theatre of Dionysos at the foot of the Acropolis, and their comedies and tragedies reveal a great deal about the psyche of the Ancient Greeks.

Across the country large open-air theatres were built on the sides of hills, with increasingly sophisticated backdrops and props, choruses and themes. The theatres were designed to maximise sound so even the people on the back row might hear the actors on stage. The dominant genres of theatre were tragedy and comedy. The first known actor was a man called Thespis from which we derive the word 'thespian'.

Philosophy

Late 5th- and early-4th-century BC philosophers Aristotle, Plato and Socrates introduced new trains of thought rooted not in myths but in rationality, as the new Greek mind focused on logic and reason. Athens' greatest, most noble citizen, Socrates (469–399 BC), was forced to drink hemlock for his disbelief in the old gods, but before he died he left behind a school of hypothetical reductionism that is still used today. Plato (427–347 BC), his star student, was responsible for documenting his teacher's thoughts, and without his work in books like the *Symposium*, they would have been lost to us. Considered an idealist, he wrote 'The Republic' as a warning to the city-state of Athens, that unless its people respected law, leadership and educated its youth sufficiently, it would be doomed. His student Aristotle (384–322 BC), at the end of the Golden Age, was the personal physician to Philip II, King of Macedon, and the tutor of

The Olympics

The Olympic tradition emerged around the 11th century BC as a paean to Zeus, in the form of contests, attended initially by notable men – and women – who assembled before the sanctuary priests and swore to uphold solemn oaths. By the 8th century BC attendance had grown from a wide confederacy of city-states, and the festival morphed into a male-only major event lasting five days at the site of Olympia. First prize might have been a simple laurel wreath, but it was the esteem of the people that most mattered, for Greek olympiads were as venerated as Roman gladiators. A ceremonial truce was enforced for the duration of the games. Crowds of spectators lined the tracks, where competitors vied for an honourable (and at times dishonourable) victory in athletics, chariot races, wrestling and boxing (back then there were no gloves but simple leather straps).

Alexander the Great. He focused his gifts on astronomy, physics, zoology, ethics and politics.

Sculpture

Classical sculpture began to gather pace in Greece in 6th century BC with the renderings of nudes in marble. Most statues were created to revere a particular god or goddess and many were robed in grandiose garments. Formerly the statues of the preceding Archaic period, known as *kouroi,* had focused on symmetry and form, but in the early 5th century BC, artists sought to create expression and animation. As temples demanded elaborate carvings, sculptors were called upon to create large reliefs upon them. During the 5th century BC the craft became yet more sophisticated, as sculptors were taught to successfully map a face and create a likeness of their subject in marble busts, catering to the vanity of politicians and rich men. Later still the Romans adopted this perfectionist school of sculpture and continued the tradition. Perhaps the most famous sculptor was Phidias, whose reliefs upon the Parthenon depicting the Greek and Persian Wars – now known as the Parthenon Marbles – are celebrated as among the finest from the Golden Age.

The Best...
Ancient
Theatres

1 Epidavros (p119)

2 Ancient Delphi (p160)

3 Odeon of Herodes Atticus (p72)

4 Theatre of Dionysos (p72)

5 Theatre of Dodoni (p190)

The Oracle of Delphi

Near the modern-day village of Delphi is the site of the Delphic oracle, the most important oracle in Ancient Greece. Its beginnings are shrouded in myth; some say Apollo, when looking for an earthly abode, found a home here but not before doing battle with the python who guarded the entrance to the centre of the earth. After he slew and threw it into the chasm it began to rot, producing noxious vapours. From this fissure came intoxicating fumes that the sibyl, or *pythia* (a clairvoyant crone, or seer), would sit above on a tripod, fall into a trance, and allow herself to be possessed by Apollo. While in this state the sibyl raved and her mumblings were interpreted by attendant priests. Citizens, politicians and kings – for a fee – consulted the sibyl on personal affairs and matters of state. City-states like Sparta and Athens made generous contributions to the oracle, as did nations like Persia, with some even establishing treasuries on the site. For more than six centuries, until it was destroyed by a Christian emperor, Delphi shaped the history of the world with its often eerily prescient prophecies (see p162).

Lifestyle & Culture

Folklore group dancing during Ash Monday celebrations

PORTOKALIS/SHUTTERSTC

Greece is both Mediterranean and Balkan and has long straddled East and West, so it's not surprising that Greeks have a very different character to the rest of Europe. The Greek way of life came under international scrutiny in the wake of Greece's 2011 debt crisis. There is no denying the crisis is not just political and economic, but social and even cultural. Nevertheless, Greeks remain undeniably passionate, fiercely independent and proud of their heritage.

The Greek Nature

Greeks have an undeniable zest for life, but aren't into making plans, with spontaneity a refreshing aspect of social life. Greeks are notoriously late; turning up to an appointment on time is often referred to as 'being English'.

Most Greeks are forthright and argumentative. They thrive on news, gossip and political debate and, while they will mercilessly malign their governments and society, they are defensive about external criticism and can be fervently nationalistic. Greeks have a work-to-live attitude and pride themselves on their capacity to enjoy life. They are social animals and enjoy a rich communal life. Greeks are unashamed about staring at strangers and blatantly discussing people round them. Few subjects are off limits, from your private life to how much money you earn.

In the major shift from a largely poor, agrarian existence to increasingly sophisticated urban dwellers, the current generation of Greeks is dealing with a massive generational and technological divide; multilingual children play games on their mobile phones while their illiterate grandfathers still get around on a mule.

Greeks have long enjoyed a reputation as loyal friends and generous hosts. They pride themselves on their *filotimo* (dignity and sense of honour), and their *filoxenia* (hospitality, welcome, shelter), which you will find in even the poorest household.

Social & Family Life

Greek society remains dominated by the family and kinship. They travel and socialise in packs, with family or their *parea* (companions). The vast majority of Greek businesses are small, often family-run, operations. Parents strive to provide homes for their children when they get married, with many families building apartments for each child above their own (thus the number of unfinished buildings you see).

Extended family plays an important role in daily life, with grandparents often looking after grandchildren while parents work or socialise. The trade-off is that children look after their elderly parents, rather than consign them to nursing homes, though foreign women are brought in to look after elderly parents in villages.

It's uncommon for Greek children to move out of home before they are married, unless they are going to university or to find work in another city. While this is changing among professionals and people are marrying later, low wages are also keeping young people at home.

Despite the machismo, it is very much a matriarchal society. Men love to give the impression that they rule the roost but, in reality, it's the women who often run the show both at home and in family businesses. Greek women (at least the older generation) are famously house-proud and take pride in their culinary skills. It's still relatively rare for men to be involved in housework or cooking, and boys are waited on hand and foot.

The New Greeks

In the 1990s, Greece changed from a nation of emigration to one of immigration. Greece is home to more than one million migrants (legal, illegal and of indeterminate status), the majority are economic migrants from Albania, the Balkans and Eastern Europe. Almost half have settled in Athens. Bulgarian women look after the elderly in remote villages, Polish kitchen-hands work on the islands, Albanians dominate the manual labour force, Chinese businesses have sprung up all over Greece and Pakistanis gather for weekend cricket matches in Athens car parks.

The Best...
Atmospheric
Churches

1 Moni Megalou Meteorou (p171)

2 Monastery of St John the Theologian (p318)

3 Moni Arkadiou (p259)

4 Church of Agii Theodori (p82)

5 Church of Agios Dimitrios (p174)

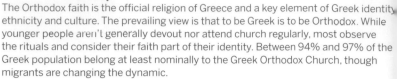

Faith & Identity

The Orthodox faith is the official religion of Greece and a key element of Greek identity, ethnicity and culture. The prevailing view is that to be Greek is to be Orthodox. While younger people aren't generally devout nor attend church regularly, most observe the rituals and consider their faith part of their identity. Between 94% and 97% of the Greek population belong at least nominally to the Greek Orthodox Church, though migrants are changing the dynamic.

Religious rituals are part of daily life. You will notice taxi drivers, motorcyclists and people on public transport making the sign of the cross when they pass a church; compliments to babies and adults are followed by the '*ftou ftou*' (spitting) gesture to ward off the evil eye. The Greek year is centred on saints' days and festivals of the church calendar. Name days (celebrating your namesake saint) are considered more important than birthdays. Most people are named after a saint, as are boats, suburbs and train stations.

With Greece's Muslim population estimated to be close to 500,000, many makeshift mosques operate in Athens. Greek Jews number about 5000. Greece also has more than 50,000 Catholics.

Music & Dance

For most people, Greek music and dance evokes images of spirited, high-kicking laps around the dance floor to the tune of the bouzouki (a musical instrument in the lute family), as seen at weddings, tourist hotels and Greek tavernas around the world.

Music was an integral part of ancient life and theatre, and Greece's regions today each have distinct musical styles, steeped in local traditions and history. Regional folk music is generally divided into *nisiotika* (the lighter, more upbeat music of the islands) and the more grounded *dimotika* (regional folk music) of the mainland. The music of Crete, a world-music genre in its own right, remains the most dynamic traditional form.

Contemporary Greek popular music merges elements of traditional *laïka* (urban popular music) with Western influences, but the music emerging from Greece today also includes local takes on folk rock, heavy metal, rap and electronic dance music.

Rembetika

Often referred to as the Greek 'blues', *rembetika* is one of the most enduring and internationally recognised forms of Greek music. With its underground roots, its themes cover heartache, hardship, drugs, crime and the grittier elements of urban life.

Markos Vamvakaris, acknowledged as the greatest *rembetis* (musician who plays *rembetika*), became popular with the first bouzouki group in the early 1930s, revolutionising the sound of popular Greek music.

Rembetika's anti-authoritarian themes made the genre popular among political exiles and left-wing activists during the junta years. Interest in genuine *rembetika* was revived in the late 1970s to early '80s – particularly among students and intellectuals – and it continues to be rediscovered by new generations of Greeks.

While few Greek performers have made it big internationally – 1970s genre-defying icons Nana Mouskouri and kaftan-wearing Demis Roussos remain the best known – here is a strong local music industry. Big names include veteran George Dalaras and Dionysis Savopoulos, dubbed the Dylan of Greece.

Acclaimed vocal artist Savina Yannatou and ethnic jazz fusion artists Kristi Stasinopoulou and Mode Plagal are making a mark on the world-music scene.

In the pop scene, Greece's answer to Madonna is Anna Vissi. Headline modern *laïka* performers include Yiannis Ploutarhos, Antonis Remos and Thanos Petrelis.

Dancing has been part of Greek social life since the dawn of Hellenism. Dance styles often reflect the climate of the region or disposition of the participants, and dance is a way of expressing sorrow and joy.

Contemporary dance in Greece is gaining prominence, with leading local dance groupes taking their place among the international line-up at the prestigious Kalamata International Dance Festival and the Athens International Dance Festival.

Musicians performing at a G

Architecture
& Art

Lion Gate at Ancient Mycenae (p114)

KARDMAR/SHUTTER

Get lost in Ancient Delphi or gaze up at the Parthenon and you'll quickly understand how Greece's architecture has inspired entire civilisations and spawned major architectural movements such as the Italian Renaissance. With four millenniums' worth of ruins, exploring Greece is like delving into a natural library of architectural ºference. Recently, Greeks have ºn their artistic talent to the ºs, creating modern pieces º gaining recognition on ºational scene.

Greek Architecture

Minoan Magnificence

Early Greek architecture begins from around 2000 BC with the Minoans, who were based in Crete but whose influence spread throughout the Aegean. Minoan architects constructed technologically advanced, labyrinthine palace complexes such as Knossos.

Several gigantic volcanic eruptions rocked the region in the mid-15th century BC, causing big chunks of palaces to fall to the ground. The Minoans resolutely rebuilt these crumbling palaces on an even grander scale, only to have more natural disasters wipe them out again.

Mycenaean Engineering

The Mycenaeans had a fierce reputation as spectacular structural engineers and expert builders of massive masonry. At their zenith, the Mycenaeans had constructed over 300 supersized citadels throughout mainland Greece and the Aegean. Usually built to a compact and orderly plan, the citadels' enclosing, fortified Cyclopean-stone walls were on average an unbreachable 3m (10ft) to 7m (25ft) thick. The famous Lion Gate at the citadel of Ancient Mycenae is the oldest monumental gate in Europe.

Classic Compositions

The Classical Age (5th to 4th centuries BC) is when most Greek architectural clichés converge, with the classical temple style underpinned by a refined knack for mathematics and aesthetics. Temples became characterised by the famous orders of columns, particularly the Doric, Ionic and Corinthian.

Doric columns feature austere cushion capitals, fluted shafts and no bases. The mother of all Doric structures is the 5th-century-BC Parthenon in Athen's Acropolis.

The Ionic order originates from Asia Minor and features a column base with several tiers, more flutes and ornamented necking. You'll find this on the Acropolis' Temple of Athena Nike and the Erechtheion.

Towards the tail end of the classical period, the Corinthian column was in limited vogue. Featuring a single or double row of ornate leafy scrolls, the order was adopted by the Romans and used only on Corinthian temples in Athens, such as the Temple of Olympian Zeus.

The Greek theatre design is also a hallmark of the classical period. The semicircle of steeply banked stone benches seated many thousands, but the perfect acoustics meant every spectator could hear every syllable uttered on the stage below. Visit Epidavros to test it out.

Hellenistic Citizens

In the twilight years of the Classical Age (from about the late 4th century BC), wealthy citizens lavishly remodelled their homes with painted stonework, columns, marble courtyards and striking mosaics. The best Hellenistic ancient home displays are the grand houses at Ancient Delos.

Byzantine Zeal

Church-building was particularly expressive during Byzantium (from around AD 700). The Byzantine church design has the perfect symbiotic relationship between structural form and function. The original Greek Byzantine model features a distinctive cross shape and spectacular devotional mosaics and frescoes. Symbolically, working down from the dome (which is always representative of Christ in heaven), images of the Virgin are shown in the apse, with the walls decorated with images of saints or apostles, representing the descent to earth (the nave). Visit Athens' Church of Agii Theodori.

Frankish Keeps & Venetian Strongholds

After the sack of Constantinople by the Crusaders in 1204, much of Greece became the fiefdoms of Western aristocrats. The Villehardouin family punctuated the Peloponnesian landscape with Frankish castles, such as Mystras. When the Veneti

The Best... Regional Originals

1 The Zagorohoria's slate mansions (p191)

2 Hamlet of Vathia (p129)

3 Volcanic-rock hewn village of Oia (p227)

4 Lindos' captains' houses (p300)

dropped by to seize a few coastal enclaves, they built the imposing 18th-century Pala-midi fortress at Nafplio and the rock-nest protecting the enchanting Byzantine village at Monemvasia.

Ottoman Offerings

Interestingly, remarkably few monuments are left after the four centuries of Otto-man Turkish rule (16th to 19th centuries) in Greece. Those that survive include the prominent pink-domed Mosque of Süleyman in Rhodes' Old Town; the walled quarter of Ioannina with its restored Fetiye Cami (Victory Mosque); and Athens' Turkish Baths. The streets of Thessaloniki showcase superb Turkish-designed homes with stained-glass windows, wooden overhangs on buttresses, decorated plasterwork and painted woodwork.

Neoclassical Splendour

Regarded by experts as the most beautiful neoclassical building worldwide, the 1885 Athens Academy reflects Greece's post-Independence yearnings for grand and geometric forms, and Hellenistic detail. Other neoclassical examples include the me-ticulously restored neoclassical mansion housing the Benaki Museum.

Greek Art

Traditional Art

Until the start of the 19th century, Byzantine religious painting was the primary art form. Byzantine church frescoes and icons were usually decorated with scenes from the life of Christ and figures of the saints; later centuries saw more detailed narratives such as scenes from the miracles of Christ. The Cretan School of icon painting, influ-enced by the Italian Renaissance and artists fleeing to Crete after the fall of Constanti-nople, combined technical brilliance and dramatic richness.

Contemporary Work

Modern Greek art per se started after Independence, when painting became more secular in nature. Artists focussed on portraits, nautical themes and representations

El Greco

Renaissance painter El Greco ('The Greek' in Spanish), née Dominikos Theotokopoulos, was born in Crete. He got his grounding in the tradition of late-Byzantine fresco painting during a time of great artistic activity on the island, following the arrival of painters fleeing Ottoman-held Constantinople.

In his early 20s, El Greco went to Venice but came into his own after moving to Spain in 1577, where his highly emotional style struck a chord with the Spanish. He lived in Toledo until his death in 1614. His fight for art and freedom was the subject of the €7 million biopic *El Greco* (2007).

El Greco's *Concert of Angels, The Burial of Christ* and *St Peter* can be seen in Athens at the National Art Gallery, two signed works hang in the Benaki Museum, while *View of Mt Sinai, The Monastery of St Catherine* and *Baptism of Christ* are in Iraklio's Historical Museum of Crete.

of the War of Independence. Major 19th-century painters included Nicholas Gyzis, a leading artist of the Munich School (where many Greek artists of the day went).

From the first decades of the 20th century, artists used their heritage and incorporated developments in modern art.

Significant artists of the '30s generation were cubist Nikos Hatzikyriakos-Ghikas and surrealist artist and poet Nikos Engonopoulos.

Other leading 20th-century artists include Alekos Fassianos, whose work fetches record prices for a living Greek artist. Yiannis Kounellis is a pioneer of the Arte Provera movement, while Giorgos Zongolopoulos is best known for his trademark umbrella sculptures.

Athens' National Art Gallery has the most extensive collections of Greek 20th-century art, along with the National Museum of Contemporary Art and the National Sculpture Gallery. The New Art Gallery in Rhodes Town also has an extensive collection of 20th-century Greek art.

Mosque of Süleyman (p294), Rhodes Old Town
PHOTOGRAPHER: PETER M. WILSON/ALAMY ©

Cuisine

Spanakopita (spinach pie)

ROBYNMACVIEW PORTFOLIO/ISTOCKP

Greece's culinary tradition incorporates mountain-village food, island cuisine and influences from various invaders and historical trading partners. Rustic Greek cooking reflects the bounty of the land and its diverse topography. Whether it's dining alfresco at a rickety table by the sea, enjoying modern Greek cuisine in stylish Athens or eating boiled goat in a mountain village, dining out in Greece is never just about what you eat, but the whole sensory experience.

The Basics

The essence of traditional Greek cuisine lies in its fresh, seasonal produce and generally simple, unfussy cooking that brings out the rich flavours of the Mediterranean. Olive oil is indeed the elixir of Greece, with extra-virgin oil produced in groves all over the country.

Vegetables, pulses and legumes – key elements of the healthy Mediterranean diet – feature prominently in Greek cooking, made tastier with plentiful use of olive oil and herbs. Meat was once reserved for special occasions but has become more prominent in the modern diet; lamb and pork dominate, though kid goat is also common. Fish has long been an essential ingredient, and is simply cooked. The ubiquitous Greek salad (*horiatiki,* translated as 'village salad') is the summer salad, and made with fresh tomatoes, cucumber, onions, feta and olives.